Jiny Lan and the Art of Subversion

Studies in German Literature, Linguistics, and Culture

Jiny Lan and the Art of Subversion

Chinese-German Culture and Politics through a Feminist Lens

Qinna Shen

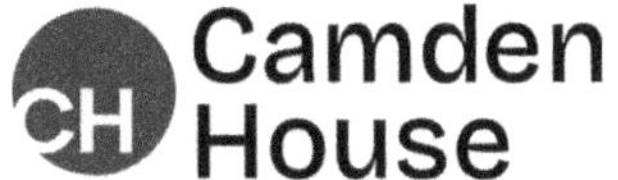

First published 2025
by Camden House

Camden House is an imprint of Boydell & Brewer Inc.
668 Mt. Hope Avenue, Rochester, NY 14620, USA
and of Boydell & Brewer Limited
PO Box 9, Woodbridge, Suffolk IP12 3DF, UK
www.boydellandbrewer.com

Our Authorized Representative for product safety in the EU is Easy Access System Europe - Mustamäe tee 50, 10621 Tallinn, Estonia, *gpsr.requests@easproject.com*

ISBN-13: 978-1-64014-222-0 hardback
ISBN 13: 978-1-64014-291-6 paperback

Library of Congress Cataloging-in-Publication Data
CIP data is available from the Library of Congress

Please be advised that this book contains graphic images that readers may find disturbing or shocking

Contents

Acknowledgments

WHILE WORKING ON an article on Chinese and East Asian reactions to the Syrian refugee crisis, I discovered online a Chinese-inflected portrait of Angela Merkel by Jiny Lan. My analysis of the painting drew the artist's attention. After learning more about her life and work, I realized that I had found the subject for a project that combines my research interests in visual culture and Asian German Studies. During the writing of this book, I have had numerous interactions with the artist, long and short, in person and via telecommunication. I thank Lan for her support of this project. She also facilitated a number of interviews: I was able to talk to Juan Xu, Uli Sigg, Michael Berger, Christian Lindner, Yuejun Qian, Irmtraud Mair, Tim Felgner, and her classmates and relatives. Her husband, Moritz Roidl, also helped with retrieving newspaper articles and high-resolution images.

I have presented aspects of this project at the 2021 Northeast Modern Languages Association conference, the 2021 International Conference of Europeanists, the 2022 and 2023 Summer Workshops organized by the Berlin Program for Advanced German and European Studies at the Free University in Berlin, and the eighth German-Asian Studientag at the Mori-Ôgai-Gedenkstätte of Humboldt University in Berlin in 2022, as well as at Asian German panels and seminars at the annual conferences of the German Studies Association. Professor Leslie Morris invited me to lecture on Lan's art at the University of Minnesota in 2022, and Lisa Zernicke invited me to speak at the Owls Fest at Bryn Mawr College in 2023. I am grateful for all the questions and suggestions I received at these events.

A number of colleagues – Mila Ganeva, Qingyang Freya Zhou, Zach Ramon Fitzpatrick, Martin Rosenstock, Nicole Thesz, Caroline Rupprecht, Séan Allan, and Randall Halle – have supported the project by either reading chapters or writing recommendation letters. Jim Walker, the editorial director at Camden House, Nick Bingham, the production manager for my project, and the staff members there have been an amazing team to work with. The two anonymous peer reviewers have been most generous in sharing their expertise, and their constructive feedback was instrumental in guiding me to improve the manuscript. Cynthia Col has created an impressive index with excellent entries and subentries that give a nice overview of the book.

I thank my home institution, Bryn Mawr College, especially Provost Timothy Harte and his office, for the faculty research grants and the one-year sabbatical which allowed me to make significant progress with the project. Our remarkable librarian Arleen Zimmerl has always been a great problem solver for me. I am blessed to work at Bryn Mawr with wonderful colleagues who have been inspiring conversation partners. Freelance editor Gene McGarry deserves a special heartfelt thanks here. He has been editing my English-language publications for years, and I can always count on him. My husband, Joachim Wintzer, who is a trained historian and political scientist, accompanied me on this autodidactic journey into the history of art and the work of a contemporary artist. I am blessed with his love, patience, humor, and steadfastness. I thank him for reading the manuscript and sharing his expertise. My two high-schoolers, Charles and Cindy, left their friends and familiar environment to attend the John F. Kennedy School in Berlin for a year during my sabbatical. They are the anchor and joy of my life.

Introduction

Message Painting: "I use my paintbrush to be heard!"

Jiny Lan, who was born in China in 1970 and moved to Germany in 1995, is a feminist conceptual artist whose politically engaged avant-garde art uniquely fuses Eastern and Western culture, as exemplified in "Buddhalisa," her idiosyncratic merger of the Buddha and the Mona Lisa. Tackling political topics makes Lan the artist she is. Her political awakening began with her ten-day participation in the 1989 student movement on Tiananmen Square. Once in Germany, she found a new "spiritual home" in the Chinese diasporic community, especially among the pro-democracy activists who left China after 1989. Her yearning for democracy, freedom, and the rule of law in China has intensified as the country sees increasing authoritarian tendencies under the current regime.

Recently, she achieved two major milestones in her career. On December 17, 2023, she was awarded the Löwe von Weilburg Prize by the Rosenhang Museum in Weilburg, Germany, for her installation project *Himmelsfragen* (*Tian wen*, Question Heaven, 2023), which uses ancient terra-cotta statues of Chinese warriors to reimagine China as a civil society.[1] A year later, on December 12, 2024, the City Council of Düsseldorf

1 The prize includes a monetary award of 60,000 euros. Volker Gerding, "'Freiheit' als zentraler Begriff ihrer Kunst: Wenn schon das Malen von 'Pu der Bär' gefährlich ist / Die chinesische Künstlerin Jiny Lan zu Gast im Rosenhang Museum," *Mittelhessen*, August 10, 2023; "Himmelsfragen: Im künstlerisch-demokratischen Dialog mit Jiny Lan im Rosenhang Museum Weilburg," September 27, 2023, <https://www.presseportal.de/pm/127810/5612551>; "Jiny Lan und ihre 'sprechende' Terrakotta-Armee im Weilburger Rosenhang Museum: Spektakuläre Kunstausstellung öffnet am 4.10.—Christian Lindner ist Gastredner," *Art28gallery*, September 28, 2023, <https://www.pressetext.com/news/jiny-lan-und-ihre-sprechende-terrakotta-armee-im-weilburger-rosenhang-museum.html>; "Rosenhang-Museum präsentiert Deutsch-chinesische Künstlerin Jiny Lan," *Evangelische Zeitung,* October 2, 2023, <https://evangelische-zeitung.de/rosenhang-museum-praesentiert-deutsch-chinesische-kuenstlerin-jiny-lan>; "Auszeichnung: Künstlerin Jiny Lan erhält hochdotierten Löwe von Weilburg Preis," *Monopol*, December 6, 2023, <https://www.monopol-magazin.de/kuenstlerin-jiny-lan-erhaelt-hochdotierten-loewe-von-weilburg-preis?amp>; "Kunstpreis

unanimously approved the establishment of the Jiny Lan Kunststiftung der Stadt Düsseldorf (Jiny Lan Art Foundation of the City Düsseldorf). It is the first German art foundation named after a Chinese artist and will support young artists and promote art education and public art exhibits.[2]

These two accomplishments are quite a vindication for an artist who came from a remote village in China. In Germany, she gradually attracted the critical attention of gallerists, art critics, and art collectors, while her works were frequently featured in exhibitions and art magazines. The late French philosopher Bruno Latour invited her to contribute a painting – *Rauchverbot* (The Smoking Ban, 2019) – to his edited volume *Critical Zones.*[3] Also in 2021, the German Bundestag purchased her painting *Doppelbelichtung* (Double Exposure, 2020, Fig. 7.4b), making her the first Chinese female artist to be represented in the German Parliament's art collection.[4] Uli Sigg, art collector and member of the International Council of the Museum of Modern Art (MoMA) and the International Advisory Council of the Tate Gallery, London, wrote: "The virtuoso painting technique of Jiny Lan is the link to her Chinese heritage – today she is an integral part of Western conceptual art, she is a virtuoso in this field with wit and cleverness. There is no limit to her provocations. I'm looking forward to her next performance, whose appeal is that certainly we have no idea what will happen."[5]

At the opening of the first International Art Expo on the Silk Road in Dunhuang, Professor Jeanine Meerapfel, president of the Berlin Academy

---

'Löwe von Weilberg' für Jiny Lan," *Kunstforum*, December 12, 2023, <https://www.kunstforum.de/nachrichten/kunstpreis-loewe-von-weilberg-fuer-jiny-lan/>.

2 "Errichtung der unselbständigen 'Jiny Lan Kunststiftung,'" Düsseldorf Ratsinfo, December 12, 2024, <https://www.duesseldorf.de/rat/buergerinfo> (enter the search word "Jiny Lan" in "Recherche"); Liu Ying 刘瑛, 首个!第一个以华人艺术家名字命名的基金会在德国成立 [First! The First Foundation Named after a Chinese Artist Is Established in Germany], 华商报 *Hua Shangbao—Chinesische Handelszeitung*, December 18, 2024, <https://mp.weixin.qq.com/s/jdZj3PCT3Shv3yKv_D-qPw>; "Künstlerin Jiny Lan gründet eigene Stiftung," *Monopol*, February 5, 2025. On February 20, 2025, the inauguration of the foundation was celebrated with political and cultural elites in Schloss Benrath in Düsseldorf; see "Treffpunkt: 'Rauchst du? Trinkst du? Nimmst du Drogen?'" *Welt*, March 2, 2025.

3 "Jiny Lan, *Rauchverbot* (2019)," *Critical Zones: The Science and Politics of Landing on Earth*, ed. Bruno Latour and Peter Weibel (Cambridge, MA: MIT Press, 2021), 431, fig. a.

4 "Ankäufe 2021 für die Artothek," Deutscher Bundestag, <https://www.bundestag.de/besuche/kunst/artothek/ankaeufe2021>.

5 Uli Sigg, cited in *Jiny Lan*, exhibition catalog (Essen: kunst-raum schulte-goltz+noelte, 2020).

of the Arts, was immediately drawn to Lan's painting *The Empty City Strategy* (*Kong cheng ji*, 2016, Fig. 8.2c). Meerapfel wrote:

> On our first visit to the exposition halls an unignorable figure popped up in front of me: her head almost clean shaven, dressed in a queer cap, strange shorts, boots, and an upended pink shopping bag, which had been converted into a blouse. She emanated great amiability and stretched out her hand, saying she was Jiny Lan. I took a look at the pictures in the exhibition and was first attracted by one that showed a big hand hovering above a landscape not otherwise specified. Was the hand fleeing or did it dominate the events below? Perhaps it would give us a warning? It was a puzzling, appealing picture which could not easily be interpreted. It was Jiny Lan's work.[6]

Puzzling, appealing, and resistant to interpretation, Lan's extensive oeuvre has not yet been systematically and holistically examined in any scholarly book. Interpreting and analyzing her artworks is challenging for both Western and non-Western viewers. The works contain private, often autobiographically informed, symbols and whimsical references. Lan also infuses her multilingual and multicultural background into her art, and its Chinese dimension poses a hermeneutic challenge even for Chinese speakers, let alone the Western viewers and critics who are her primary audience. Beyond the artist's explicit identification with the Fluxus and conceptual art movements, her paintings exhibit elements of New Figuration, Narrative Figuration, neo-expressionism, the Chinese avant-garde of the 1980s and 90s, and Political Pop. It is through the creative amalgamation of different styles that Lan's work comes to embody a true intersection of European and Asian cultures, i.e., a Eurasian culture.

The title of this book, *Jiny Lan and the Art of Subversion*, alludes to the political dimension of her art, as well as to her concept of *Versionierung* (versioning), the creation of a series of interrelated versions of images using a mixed-media repainting technique. Inspired by the Düsseldorf conceptual artist Hans-Peter Feldmann, Lan takes a picture of one of her chosen paintings and has the photo enlarged and printed onto a canvas, on which she then paints a subsequent version or "sub-version." The result resembles a giant family tree whose branches each constitute a *versioning* consisting of related paintings. She calls this painterly family tree "Jinyology," a homophone of "genealogy," or "Pictures Republic of Jiny," mimicking the People's Republic of China. Jinyology has its roots

6 Jeanine Meerapfel, "Jiny Lans poetisch-provokative Kunstwelt / Jiny Lan's Poetic-Provocative Art World," in *Jiny Lan: The World Is Sometimes Flat, Sometimes Round*, exhibition catalog (Berlin: Schultz Contemporary, 2018), German text on 3, English translation on 5.

in Lan's response to the patriarchal genealogical conventions that define how family trees are constructed in contemporary China.

This is the first book-length study to examine Lan's creation methods and formal characteristics, as well as themes and concepts. It uncovers subjective symbols, intertextual references, and implicit politics while exploring her dual cultural identity, which is crucial to her artistic inspiration. As a trained Germanist and cultural and visual studies scholar who is also of Chinese linguistic and cultural background, I approach Lan's artwork in the context of my interdisciplinary interests in visual and media studies, history, international relations, and Asian German Studies. I select a cross-section of Lan's works that invite a specific kind of literary, historical, sociopolitical, and transcultural interpretation. Lan has stated: "I use my paintbrush to be heard!"[7] Consequently, I focus on her thematically rich "message" paintings at the expense of artworks that are produced with a particular market in mind. As Lan explained, "people like to buy beautiful women," and so "I sell 'pretty women' to support my more political and controversial paintings." It is a curious position for a feminist artist to take, but Lan is acutely aware of the economics of art and the sexual politics that govern the art market and raise the value of paintings *of* women, even as artwork by men overall commands higher prices than paintings *by* women (chapter 5).

The book is divided into three parts. Part 1 (chapters 1–2) provides biographical and artistic contexts for Lan's work. Chapter 1, "From 'Bad Girl' to 'Bald Girl': Lan's Journey to the West," presents the first detailed account of her formative years. Her familial and personal stories encapsulate Chinese history during the twentieth century – from the fall of the Qing dynasty to the Japanese colonial period in Manchuria, the communist takeover of China, the Cultural Revolution, liberalization and westernization, and globalization. The chapter discusses her experiences in Beijing during the pro-democracy movement in 1989, the traumatic year of 1994–95 during which she was employed as an art editor at the *People's Daily* newspaper, her hasty departure for Germany in 1995, and the eventual launch of her artistic career as a "Bald Girl" in 2012. I delineate her trajectory from a "bad girl" to an idiosyncratic feminist artist. The biographical information will shed light on many of her highly personal artworks and provide essential context for understanding her artistic and political beliefs and creative methods.

Chapter 2, "From Maoist Posters and Narrative Figuration to Political Pop: Artistic Methods and Influences," traces influences, conscious or unconscious, from Cultural Revolution poster art to

7 Direct quotations of Lan's words are drawn from the numerous conversations we had since 2020. I have translated them from Chinese and edited them for legibility and succinctness.

post-Cultural Revolution avant-garde and Political Pop in China. Out of these traditions Lan cultivated her own artistic system, which she later termed "Jinyology." Though an admirable concept, Jinyology has its ideological limitations: it is not a dismantling of the idea of patriarchal succession but a regendering of it. The chapter uses her "Mao-imposter" and Tiananmen paintings to illustrate both artistic influences and her method of repainting sub-versions. Appropriating "ready-made" images, most prominently the face of Mao, is a method shared both by Chinese Political Pop artists and by Narrative Figuration artists such as the Icelandic pop artist Guðmundur Guðmundsson (better known as Erró). Contemporary Chinese artists have acknowledged a debt to the Narrative Figuration movement, which provides a helpful context for understanding Lan's art too.

Part 2 (chapters 3–5) focuses on Lan's exploration of feminist themes. Chapter 3, "The Bald Girls: Feminist Visual and Performance Art," analyzes the major performances, installations, and visual art projects Lan developed as a member of the Bald Girls, the first feminist art group in China. The chapter asks why such a feminist art group did not exist earlier in China and uses the discourse on socialism and feminism in the former German Democratic Republic (GDR) to show the challenges socialist patriarchy poses for feminist pursuits. Similar to Fluxus artists, the Bald Girls often accompany their exhibitions with performances and installations. Their projects condemn sexism, sex-selective abortion and infanticide, and sexual violence in patriarchal Chinese society. The chapter ends with the Bald Girls' tenth anniversary exhibition in 2022 and Lan's contribution, *Ping* (2022) – a portrait of "the chained woman," a victim of the one-child policy whose ironic fate was discovered long after China had abandoned the draconian rule. The case of the chained woman illuminates the change from the Bald Girls' slogan "the personal is political" to the Bald Girls 2.0's slogan "the political is personal," which replaced a call for female subjectivity with a call for political subjectivity.

In the Western context, Lan's feminist critique is primarily directed at the male-dominated art world, the realm in which she has the highest stakes. She has painted a series of portraits, titled *Meisterwerke* (Masterpieces, 2018–19), of the eight most important postwar German neo-expressionist artists: Joseph Beuys, Georg Baselitz, Markus Lüpertz, Jörg Immendorff, Anselm Kiefer, Sigmar Polke, Gerhard Richter, and A. R. Penck. Beuys has a special place in her artistic development. She worked for several years as the China project coordinator at the Museum Schloss Moyland, which houses the world's largest collection of Beuys's works, and has treated Beuys in a number of projects. Chapter 4, "*Selbstverfraulichung* with the 'Master's Tools': A Double-Edged Reception of Joseph Beuys," discusses Lan's both appropriative and critical reception of Beuys. It analyzes the Fluxus movement, Beuys's concept of social sculpture, and the first Beuys exhibition in China, which Lan helped curate. The chapter ends with a critical assessment of Lan's reception of Beuys and male artists in general, by pointing out the limitations of critiquing the masters with "the master's tools."

Chapter 5, "Contending with the 'Painter Princes' of Germany: Lan's *Masterpieces* (2018–19)," is dedicated to the other seven paintings in the series, where she pays homage to the "painter princes" while critically engaging with their legacies. More generally, Lan treats the postwar German artists, as well as other canonical male artists such as Leonardo da Vinci, Michelangelo, Titian, Tintoretto, Dalí, Maciunas, and Ai Weiwei, as rivals in her pursuit of artistic success. In *Jinyology – Silk Road* (2019, Fig. 8.1a), for example, she includes an image of the Italian Renaissance master Titian wearing Lan's own trademark outfit. Typical of her fusion method, she merges herself with Titian to express her aspiration to become a master herself. To challenge the masculine hierarchy of the German art world, she coined the word *Selbstverfraulichung* (a woman's self-glorification), a play on *verherrlichen*, which means to glorify or exalt. She replaced the root *-herr-* (meaning man or lord) with *-frau-* (meaning woman) in order to assert that it is proper for a woman to praise herself – even, or especially, an Asian woman, since modesty is her expected trait. The new coinage suggests that women (artists) have to exalt themselves instead of waiting for others to do so; this applies to Asian women artists in particular, due to their intersectional marginalization. The *Masterpieces* series constitutes Lan's feminist self-positioning in the German art world as a striving diasporic and minority artist.

Part 3 (chapters 6–8) is dedicated to Lan's political art, which is grounded in her personal experience of Chinese one-party rule and German democracy. Chapter 6, "Modernizing or Moldering: Criticism of Autocracies," takes its title from one of her paintings, *Hongkong wird modern* (Hong Kong Is Becoming Modern, 2020). The painting's title is ambiguous: the German adjective *modern*, with the stress on the second syllable, means "modern," but shifting the stress to the first syllable yields the verb *modern*, meaning "to rot or molder," alluding to the deleterious impact that autocracies have on their own societies and on vulnerable democracies like Hong Kong. This chapter examines paintings that criticize authoritarian regimes – mainly China, but also Russia, North Korea, and Iran.

As an émigré artist, Lan closely follows social and political developments in her country of origin. China's surveillance state, pseudo-democracy, one-child and zero-Covid policies, and suppression of the pro-democracy movement in Hong Kong all serve as subjects for her paintings. In addition to events in China, she has reacted to world events including the Russian invasion of Ukraine and the murder of Mahsa Amini in Iran. "Political art in a dictatorship is the opposite of political art in a democracy," noted Lan. "In a dictatorship, art is subordinate to politics and serves politics; in a democracy, art can intervene in politics, guide politics, or attack politics."[8] Her explicitly subversive art is a direct response to the impossibility of such art in her native country. According to Lan, "eighty percent of what I painted would not have been painted or exhibited in China; in fact, I would have faced personal consequences. That's why I indulge myself in expressing what I can to the fullest in Germany. I would not let this opportunity go to waste."

However, since these criticisms are articulated from a comfortable position in the democratic, liberal West, questions arise: where is the "subversion" located, and for whom is Lan "subversive"? Since she left China in 1995 before she was a full-fledged artist, most Chinese-language reports concerning her were published in newspapers based in Germany: *Ou Hua Dao Bao* (The Chinese-European Post) or *Hua Shang Bao – Chinesische Handelszeitung* (Chinese Trade Newspaper). The majority of her exhibitions take place in the West. In Western contexts, criticism of authoritarian regimes is standard. Western progressive politics, such as feminism and anti-authoritarianism, has been established as the liberal consumer norm. Therefore, her critique of China is literally deterritorialized and reaches only a diasporic Chinese audience.[9] But, alas, her critique of Chinese authoritarianism *has to be* deterritorialized, because, as shown repeatedly in the book, censorship in China is among the severest in the world.

Chapter 7, "Only Possible in a Democracy: Paintings of German Chancellors," turns to Lan's unique portraits of German chancellors: Gerhard Schröder, Angela Merkel, and Olaf Scholz. She met the ex-chancellor Schröder at a social event and her gallerist proposed that she paint him. Although her allegorical depiction of Schröder as Atlas holding up Tiananmen Gate was hardly presentable as an official portrait, this might have given her the initial inspiration to paint chancellors. The permanent loan of the paintings of Merkel, Schröder, and Scholz to the Free Democratic Party (FDP) chairman, Christian Lindner, gave her an entrée to the political sphere and increased her public visibility. As an immigrant from China, Lan is particularly interested in the democratization of the Federal Republic of Germany since 1945 and in comparing the political systems of her native and adopted countries. In the series of paintings *Ein Offener Prozess* (An Open Process, 2021–), she transforms the

8 Cf. Nora Partl, "Jiny Lan: The Right to Speak via Art: Feminist Art and Activism," *Expanded Art*, March 6, 2023, <https://www.expanded.art/articles/nora-partl-in-conversation-with-jiny-lan>.

9 In this book, the terms "deterritorialized" and "reterritorialized" are used primarily in a literal, geographic sense, as opposed to the broader sense they have acquired in critical theory.

winning candidate in a federal election into the defeated opponent, the could-have-been chancellor who lost the election. In this process, liminal portraits of the two emerge, mirroring a functioning democracy where candidates agree to honor election results.

Chapter 8, "Visualizing Sino-European Politics: Transcultural Art about the New Silk Road," groups works that demonstrate Lan's aesthetic and political engagement with China and the EU, using the Silk Road as a symbol for the historical and contemporary interconnections between China and Europe. As a minority artist in Germany, Lan is profoundly influenced by both Eastern and Western cultures and traditions. She frequently cites the visual canons of both East and West and fuses Eastern and Western geography, architecture, cultures, and people, reflecting her bicultural identity. In *Jinyology – Silk Road* (2019, Fig. 8.1a), she blends the Alps with the Yellow River Grand Canyon in Ningxia Province, China; the Silk Road functions as a stand-in for East-West exchange. In *Alternative Fiction* (2021), she superimposes an Eastern temple onto a Western church, visually coding Xi Jinping as Buddha and as an emperor presiding over his New Silk Road project. She appropriated the Qing-era tradition of paintings that depict ambassadors of the world's countries paying homage to China's ruler and created *Alternative Fiction* to criticize the Belt and Road Initiative (BRI) as a vanity project shaped by courtly dynamics.

The book uses an iconographical approach to analyze and interpret Lan's artworks as a way of introducing her concepts, beliefs, methodology, and technique. The art historian Lena Liepe differentiates iconography and iconology as follows: "According to customary usage within the discipline of art history, iconography deals with identifying and interpreting the direct or indirect meaning of the subject matter represented in a work of art, whereas iconology seeks to uncover the deeper or principal significance of a motif as a manifestation of the philosophical and metaphysical notions, worldviews, and persuasions of its time and place."[10] In this book, I take an iconographical approach to Lan's art. While I analyze her aesthetics, much space is devoted to the content of the paintings, performances, and installations that constitute her art of messaging. This emphasis leaves my analysis vulnerable to Susan Sontag's charge that contemporary interpretation stresses the content and meaning of an artwork at the expense of the sensuous experience of the work itself.[11] But Lan's

10 Lena Eva Liepe, "Introduction," in *The Locus of Meaning in Medieval Art: Iconography, Iconology, and Interpreting the Visual Imagery of the Middle Ages*, ed. Lena Eva Liepe (Kalamazoo, MI: Medieval Institute Publications, 2019), 1–10, here 16.

11 Susan Sontag, *"Against Interpretation" and Other Essays* (New York: Farrar, Straus and Giroux, 1966).

titling practice and her featuring of Chinese characters in numerous paintings indicate that she intends her paintings to be read as well as viewed. Her paintings do contain kitschy elements, including the Chinese almanac texts that are often used ornamentally or ironically to indicate that an artwork is "made in China" or "by a Chinese," but the communicative power of the paintings extends far beyond these elements. Thus, the book uses the Asian German Studies framework and presents Lan's paintings and performances with their sociohistorical and political contexts. It is precisely Lan's ability to embed politics in aesthetic forms and the communicative potential of her art of messaging that motivated an Asian German Studies scholar like me, who is not trained in art history, to write this book.

Some explanations of stylistic choices are in order. Lan titles her paintings in English, German, or Chinese, attesting to her penchant for wordplay in different languages. I usually refer to them by their English titles to facilitate reading. When Chinese personal names are used, the family name is listed first, following Chinese practice, unless the person has adapted their name according to Western conventions, as Jiny Lan has done. Pinyin transcriptions of Chinese text are italicized but the stresses are not indicated. An appendix of Chinese terms that correspond to pinyin or English phrases used in the text is provided. I welcome constructive criticism and own any mistakes that might have slipped into the manuscript.

Part One

Artistic Contexts and Concepts

1: From "Bad Girl" to "Bald Girl": Lan's Journey to the West

LAN WAS BORN in 1970, after the worst years of the Cultural Revolution. Although she is the daughter of two veteran communists, her parents trained her to have a mind of her own. They gave her a very girly name, but the experience of growing up in a patchwork family cultivated in her an ungirly, maverick, and rebellious spirit. Since early childhood, art has been an anchor in her life. During her teenage years, China underwent an exhilarating period of liberalization that culminated in the 1989 pro-democracy movement at Tiananmen Square in Beijing. Her ten-day participation in the student protests became a milestone experience that would leave many traces in her artwork. She returned to Beijing to work as an art editor at the *People's Daily* newspaper in 1994–95 – a traumatic year that led to her hasty departure for Germany in 1995. Her experiences in Beijing laid the foundation for her feminist and political art. It was not until 2012 that her artistic career began with the founding of the feminist art collective, the Bald Girls. At their first exhibition, also in Beijing, authorities unexpectedly censored three of her projects. Enraged, Lan and her collaborators shaved their heads in a spontaneous act of protest. This chapter delineates her trajectory from a wild "bad" girl to an idiosyncratic "Bald Girl" feminist artist. Lan's biography sheds light on many of her seemingly random and opaque yet highly personal and autobiographical works and helps us to better understand her artistic and political beliefs and creative methods.

Daughter of Communists in a Remote Village: Formative Years in Xiuyan, 1970–88

Jiny Lan's parents were born and raised in Xiuyan Manchu Autonomous County in Liaoning Province, near the North Korean border, in the region of China known as Manchuria. From 1932 to 1945, the region of Manchuria was administered by the Empire of Japan as the puppet state of Manchukuo. Her father, Lan Xuemin (1927–2018) attended a Japanese-run school in the city of Dandong in the early 1940s. He joined the Chinese Communist Party (CCP) in 1947, two years before the founding of the People's Republic of China (PRC) and later became a local cadre in Xiuyan. Lan's mother, Hu Jinrong (1936–2018), became

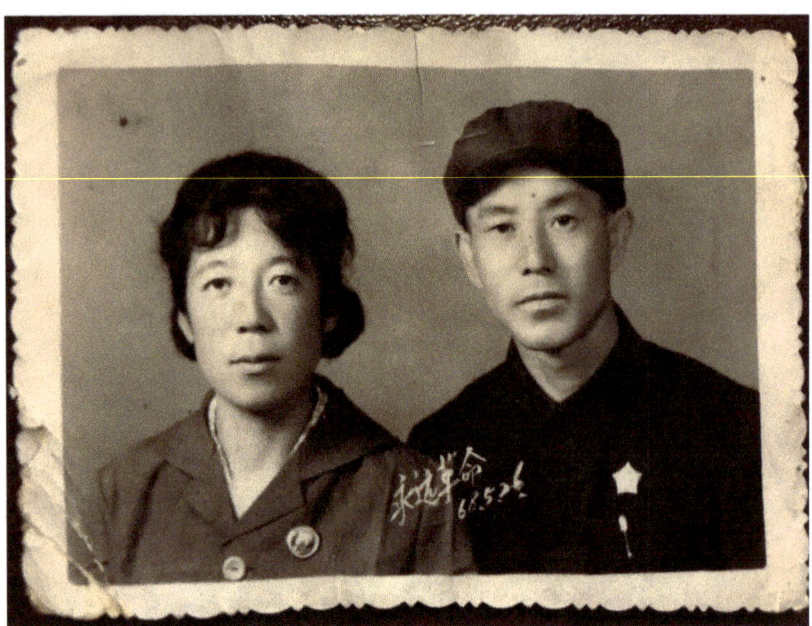

Fig. 1.1. Wedding photo of Lan's parents wearing Mao badges, dated May 26, 1968, with the inscription 永远革命 *yongyuan geming* (Eternal Revolution).

a candidate for the CCP in 1948, but due to her young age, she did not officially join until 1956. Hu did not bear any children in her first marriage and was kicked out of the house by her mother-in-law. After her divorce, Hu was introduced to Lan, who had lost his first wife to cancer and had three young daughters to take care of. They married in 1968, at the height of the Cultural Revolution (1966–76) (Fig. 1.1). Jiny Lan was born on May 3, 1970, and was given the personal name Jing 静, which means "quiet" or "still." Her mother doted on her, but since her father already had three daughters and was hoping for a son, she felt unwanted, especially after her little brother was born.

Growing up in a patchwork family was not easy. Lan's desire to be noticed developed at an early age. In kindergarten and primary school, she would deliberately make a scene to get attention by jumping out of the window during class or pointing out teachers' mistakes. Teachers regularly forced her to write self-criticism and read it out loud in front of the class. But Lan insisted on being a bad girl, earning the nickname Sun Wukong, known in the West as the Monkey King. This popular character from the classic Chinese novel *Journey to the West* wreaks havoc in heaven and displays an anti-authoritarian personality, and Lan took pride in the comparison. Later, she literally made her own journey to the West by going to Germany.[1] The monkey became her alter ego and source of energy, appearing in paintings such as *Königreich der Blumen und Früchte* (Kingdom of Flowers and Fruits, *Hua guo shan*, 2014).[2]

A story told by her mother helped her to develop a critical mind and question political movements and propaganda. Before the 7.3-magnitude Haicheng earthquake in Liaoning Province on February 4, 1975, several small earthquakes shook Lan's hometown. One of them interrupted a denunciation rally or "struggle session" (*pidou hui*), where "class enemies" were humiliated, beaten, and tortured. When the earth trembled, almost everyone ran outside immediately, but a "class enemy" who had been tortured at the rally picked up little Lan and carried her outside. When she heard the story from her mother years later, it made a deep impression on her: the "evil" man, a "capitalist roader" (Mao's term for someone who would lead China down the road to capitalism), was the only one who thought of her safety. In elementary school, Lan wrote an essay about the class enemy who rescued her, but her teacher criticized it for not being politically correct: How could she defend a class enemy?! But Lan realized that labeling people good or bad based on their supposed political identity was wrong. Later, in Germany, she created works such as *Ein-Personen-Chor* (One-Persons-Chorus, 2013, Fig. 2.4) and *Left, Right* (2014–18, Fig. 8.4b) that condemn the mass movements of the Cultural Revolution as a mass manipulation of minds.

Lan's teachers noticed her talent for drawing. Her family lived next door to a man who painted movie posters, and he gave her some early lessons. At the age of six, she began receiving formal drawing lessons from Liu Renjie. In 1968, during the height of the Cultural Revolution, Liu was sent from Dalian, a large port city in Liaoning, to Xiuyan to be reeducated by poor peasants as part of Mao's Down to the Countryside Movement. Liu started working as an art teacher at the Children's Cultural Palace in Xiuyan in 1971. Lan believes that the Down to the Countryside Movement wasted the education of hundreds of thousands of "sent-down" youths, but it gave her the opportunity to learn from a big-city artist.[3]

1 In 2009, she started blogging under the pen name Lan Liu'er 蓝六耳 on Wenxuecity, a popular overseas Chinese-language blog site. "Liu'er" signifies an imposter posing as Sun Wukong. As of December 19, 2024, the blog site has received 1,755,155 visits. <https://passport.wenxuecity.com/members/index.php?act=profile&cid=lanliuer>.

2 Martina Schürmann, "'Böses Mädchen' mit bunten Protestbildern," *Westdeutsche Allgemeine Zeitung* [=*WAZ*], February 11, 2015, <https://www.waz.de/staedte/essen/article10333174/boeses-maedchen-mit-bunten-protestbildern.html>.

3 "Liu Renjie," Chinesenewart, <https://www.chinesenewart.com/chinese-artists14/liurenjie.htm>. In 1987, Liu graduated with a master's degree from the Oil Painting Department at Lu Xun Academy of Fine Arts in Shenyang, where

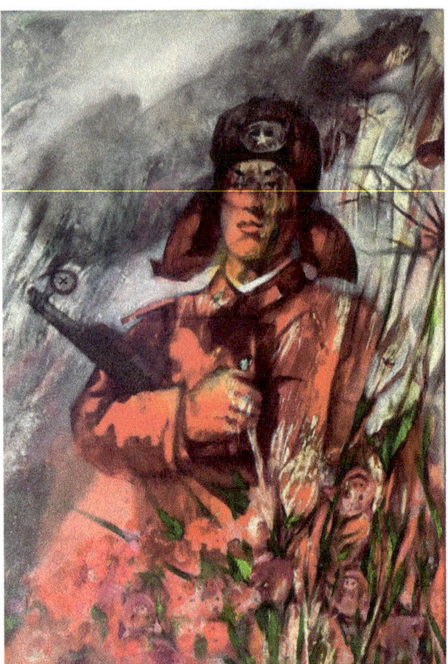

Fig. 1.2a. *Learning from Lei Feng's Good Example* (recreated in 2021, 100 × 70 cm).

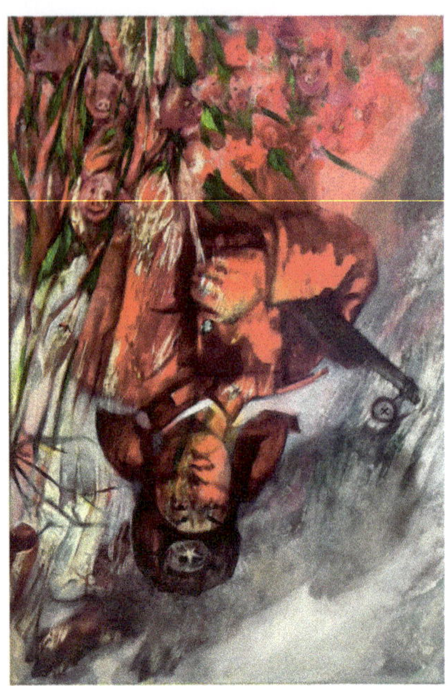

Fig. 1.2b. *Learning from Lei Feng's Good Example*, inverted view.

From a young age, Lan was already drawing serious portraits of communist heroes from photographs, including Marx, Engels, and Lenin. Drawing skills were especially valued in schools due to the high demand for "blackboard newspapers" (*heiban bao*) and propaganda posters. Drawing and painting made up for the scarcity of printing, especially color printing. Lan was frequently asked to draw on blackboards and to illustrate school bulletins, and although she was a difficult student, teachers had no choice but to put up with her lack of discipline. She drew many teacher-commissioned works. Posters of Lei Feng, celebrated in propaganda campaigns as a model soldier-citizen for his devotion to Mao and his selfless sacrifices, were popular requests. However, Lan's father was critical of the hagiography of Lei Feng. Under his influence, Lan subversively depicted Lei Feng as a pig in disguise, mocking propaganda images using her own art of camouflage. The original paintings have been lost,

he was a professor and chair of the department. He has received numerous honors, among them the silver medal in the tenth national art exhibition in China, held in 2004. In 2006, Lan exhibited her work at the same art show as Liu. The show *Phenomena and Situations since 1985: from "Polar Region" to "Tie Xi Qu"—Exhibition of Contemporary Art in Northeast China 1985–2006* took place in the Guangdong Art Museum.

but Lan repeated the steganographic joke in *Learning from Lei Feng's Good Example* (*Xuexi Leifeng hao bangyang*, 2021, Fig. 1.2a, b, image and inverse).

Every year on March 5, China celebrates "Learn from Lei Feng Day." Typical propaganda posters depict him as a soldier wearing a winter hat with earflaps and holding a rifle. Lan's poster shows him standing behind a spray of flowers; when viewed upside down, however, pink pig heads emerge from the red flowers, and the soldier's hat, adorned with a five-pointed Chinese star, turns into the head of a reclining pig whose snout is formed by the Communist symbol. Lan turned a propaganda poster of the Cultural Revolution into an anti-propaganda poster. She secretly shared her mischief with a few close friends. A teacher eventually got wind of the prank, but because of Lan's father's reputation as a Party cadre, the teacher did not punish her and simply told her parents to discipline her better. The Lei Feng paintings are an early example of her use of visual inversion to achieve a subversive goal. She used this technique, for instance, in her portraits of Gerhard Schröder, Angela Merkel, and Georg Baselitz.

Swollen Feet: College Years and the Tiananmen Square Protests, Jinzhou and Hangzhou, 1988–94

The rebellious spirit of early childhood never left Lan. She had dreamed of studying in Beijing, but she flunked the math section of the college entrance exam. Her family objected to her request to spend a year preparing to retake the exam, so in 1988 she began studying economics at Liaoning Commercial College in Jinzhou (now Bohai University). In May 1989, Lan and some classmates took a train to Beijing to participate in the student protests at Tiananmen Square (Fig. 1.3).[4] The pro-democracy protests, later known as the June Fourth Movement after the date on which the government forcefully intervened, started several weeks earlier on April 16, 1989, one day after Hu Yaobang died of a heart attack. Hu, the former general secretary of the CCP, had been forced to resign in 1986 for being too lenient toward pro-democracy student protests that year. Beijing students took to the streets to mourn his death and demand

4 I interviewed two of Lan's classmates who were in Beijing with her. She has also mentioned her participation at the Tiananmen protest in published interviews. See, for example, Schürmann, "'Böses Mädchen' mit bunten Protestbildern"; Simon Maurer, "Das Kombinationstier / Combination animals," in *Jiny Lan: The World is Sometimes Flat, Sometimes Round*, German text on 15–17, English translation 19–21; "Kunstpreis 'Löwe von Weilberg' für Jiny Lan," *Kunstforum*, December 12, 2023.

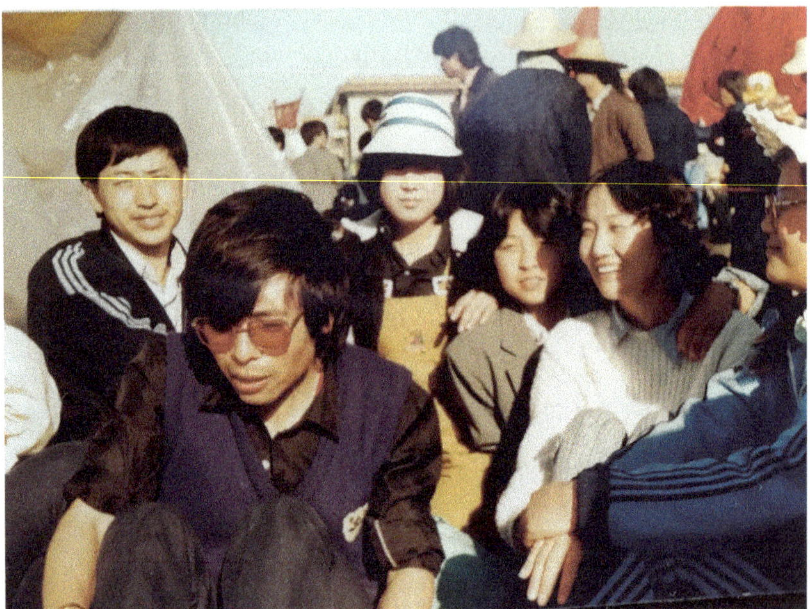

Fig. 1.3. Lan (in a cap) at Tiananmen Square in May 1989.

his rehabilitation. Criticizing the Party for rampant corruption, they called for freedom of the press and freedom of assembly.

When Lan and her classmates decided to go to Beijing, the pro-reform force in the government seemed to be gaining the upper hand. On May 13, two days before Mikhail Gorbachev arrived in Beijing for the Sino-Soviet summit, students started a hunger strike in Tiananmen Square to pressure the government to heed their demands. The hunger strike struck a chord with the population at large and forced the hardliners in the government to concede, albeit temporarily. On May 17 and 18, over one million people demonstrated in the center of Beijing. Workers, employees, entrepreneurs, intellectuals, and ordinary citizens joined the demonstrations, along with representatives of state-controlled organs such as the *People's Daily* and the China Central Television Station (CCTV), as well as members of the department of justice, the general logistics department of the People's Liberation Army (PLA), the public security forces, the propaganda department, and the foreign ministry.[5] Medical personnel

5 See Elizabeth J. Perry, "Casting a Chinese 'Democracy' Movement," in *Popular Protest & Political Culture in Modern China: Learning from 1989*, ed. Jeffrey N. Wasserstrom and Elizabeth J. Perry (Boulder, CO: Westview, 1994), 74–92, here 78; *June Four: A Chronicle of the Chinese Democratic Uprising*, trans. Jin Jiang and Qin Zhou (Fayetteville: University of Arkansas Press, 1989), 39–150; Frank Niming, "Learning How to Protest," in *The Chinese People's*

and ambulances were present to help the hunger strikers. CCP General Secretary Zhao Ziyang and his ally in the Politburo, Hu Qili, also encouraged media coverage of the student movement, and the *People's Daily* and other newspapers expressed much sympathy for the students.[6] It seemed that the tide was changing in favor of the student movement. Encouraged by their teachers, Lan and her college classmates demonstrated in Jinzhou and went to Beijing to join the protest at Tiananmen Square.

However, on May 19, the day Lan left for the capital, Premier Li Peng, a hardliner, imposed martial law on eight districts of Beijing. Lan arrived at Tiananmen Square the next morning, when martial law went into effect. She and her classmates were greeted with warm steamed buns at the train station by Beijing residents who shouted: "The Manchurian tigers have descended!" It was especially exhilarating for Beijing residents to see supporters coming from the northeast, a region that was politically and culturally more conservative than the provinces south of the capital. Sitting in front of the Monument to the People's Heroes at Tiananmen Square, student leaders Wang Dan, Chai Ling, and Wu'er Kaixi used megaphones to communicate with the protesters. They informed the demonstrators of the movements of army troops and warned that the government would "sacrifice the lives of twenty thousand students in exchange for twenty years of stability," Lan recalls. She witnessed an outpouring of public support for the students, including donations of food, blankets, and money. They slept on the lawn in front of Tiananmen or in buses parked on the square, and many romances blossomed. The so-called Four Gentlemen, including Liu Xiaobo, who won the Nobel Peace Prize in 2010, and the Taiwanese singer Hou Dejian, were active on the square.[7] Professors and celebrities came to show their support.

During a downpour in Beijing, Lan took shelter beneath a nearby underpass and her shoes got soaked. She continued to wear them day after day, even while sleeping. Eventually her feet became so swollen and infected that they stuck to her socks, and she could not remove her shoes. Meanwhile, the Chinese government was taking steps to curtail the student movement. The pro-reform head of the National People's Congress, Wan Li, was detained in Shanghai by Jiang Zemin and prevented from returning to Beijing after he visited North America. Zhao Ziyang, who was sympathetic to the students' demands and opposed the

Movement: Perspectives on Spring 1989, ed. Tony Saich (Armonk, NY: M. E. Sharpe, 1990), 83–105, here 95–101.

6 Seth Faison, "The Changing Role of the Media," in *Chinese People's Movement*, 145–63.

7 "Document of 1989: Four Gentleman's Hunger Strike Manifesto," June 2, 1989, <http://www.standoffattiananmen.com/2010/10/document-of-1989-four-gentlemans-hunger.html>.

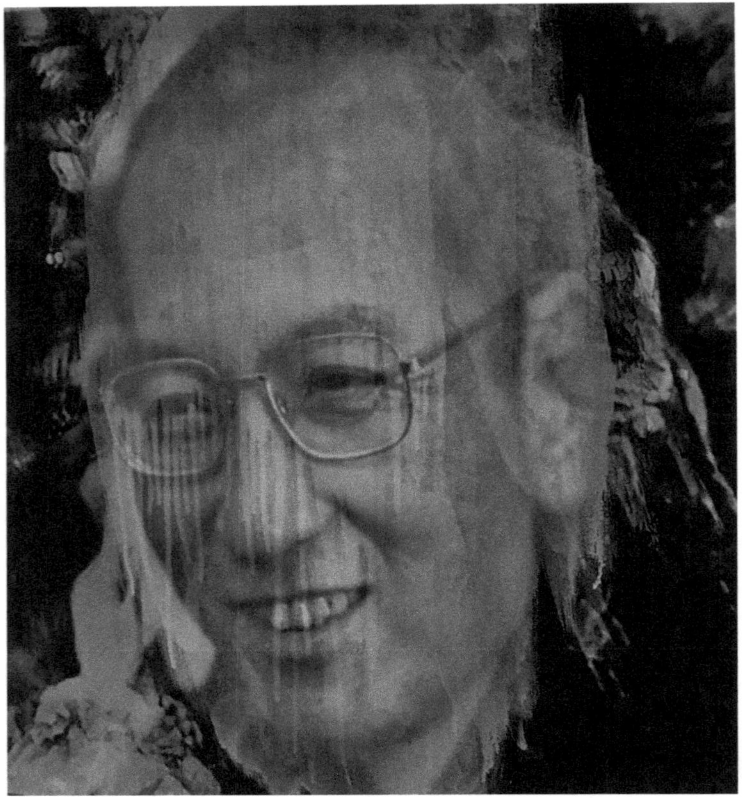

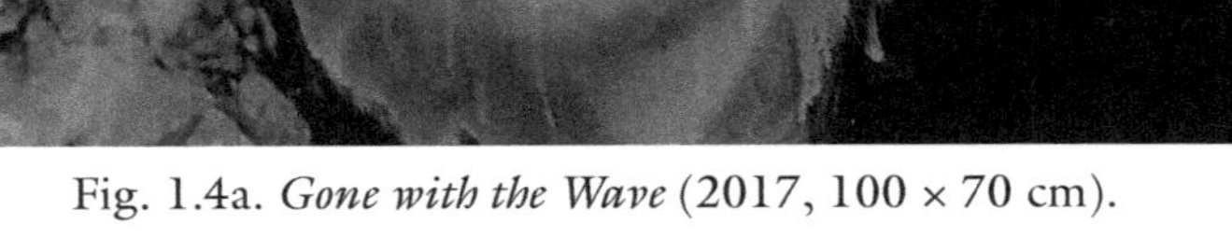

Fig. 1.4a. *Gone with the Wave* (2017, 100 × 70 cm).

Fig. 1.4b. *Gone with the Wave*, darkened image.

imposition of martial law, was placed under house arrest. By that time Lan could barely walk, and she left Beijing on May 31. Were it not for her swollen feet, she might have stayed until June 4, when government troops opened fire on the protestors. She later depicted rain and swollen feet in a number of her paintings out of gratitude for her misfortune, which may have saved her life.

The desire for democracy and freedom has stayed with her and is reflected in works such as her grayscale portrait of Liu Xiaobo, titled *Gone with the Wave* (*Sui bo liu shi*, 2017, Fig. 1.4a, b), which she painted after Liu died in prison in 2017. *Bo* in Liu's given name means wave, and his last name is a homophone of "flow" (流 *liu*). Lan took a photograph of the painting and then altered the canvas by darkening Liu's face. The resulting image shows a spectral, aged figure with barely distinguishable facial features. Lan uses this technique to indicate that the subject of a painting has passed away or fallen into oblivion. The Chinese buyer of this painting received the final darkened portrait (Fig. 1.4b) and a photo of an intermediary stage (Fig. 1.4a). Lan's portrait of Liu resembles Gerhard Richter's cycle *October 18, 1977* (1988), which comprises photo-realistic paintings related to the death of RAF (Red Army Faction) members in Stuttgart-Stammheim prison. *Gone with the Wave* showcases a few thematic and technical similarities between Lan and Richter: choosing subject matter of wide public interest, reproducing existing images, and blurring the image.

After receiving her undergraduate degree in economics in 1991, Lan studied at the China Academy of Art (CAA) in Hangzhou, Zhejiang Province, from 1991 to 1994.[8] The director of the academy was Professor Xiao Feng, who studied oil painting at the Repin Academy of Fine Arts in Leningrad from 1954 to 1960. He belonged to one of the delegations of Chinese artists who were trained in the Soviet Union before the Sino-Soviet split and came to occupy key administrative positions in Chinese art academies in the 1980s, when Sino-Soviet relations were on the mend.[9] He served as rector of the CAA for over a decade (1983–96) and increased its revenue by admitting self-funded students.[10] Beginning in the early 1980s, art education in China was liberalized and broadened to include Western art. As art historian Karen Smith writes: "Modernisation was the anthem of the age.... It was imperative to master one hundred

8 The CAA was founded as the Hangzhou National College of Art in 1929 and became the Zhejiang Academy of Fine Arts in 1958.

9 Lin Qi, "Works by Soviet-trained Chinese Artists Make Public Debut," *China Daily*, March 24, 2013; Julia Frances Andrews, *Painters and Politics in the People's Republic of China, 1949–1979* (Berkeley: University of California Press, 1994), 401–2.

10 Xiao Feng's daughter, Xiao Lu, later co-founded the Bald Girls.

and fifty years of Western cultural development from Modernism to Post-Modernism at the earliest moment possible, and apply the lessons learned to the local cultural conditions."[11] Nevertheless, Chinese academic training placed absolute emphasis on figurative realism and on technical skills.[12] But the models changed: busts of Marx and Lenin were replaced by plaster copies of classical Greek and Renaissance statues. These models often appear in Lan's later works; for example, she modeled her painting of the Austrian chancellor Sebastian Kurz on Michelangelo's David.[13]

Personal Trauma and Political Despair: Beijing, 1994–95

In 1994, Lan took an examination administered in Beijing by the *People's Daily*, the official newspaper of the CCP, and was hired as an art editor. She was one of only two out of about two hundred applicants to be offered a temporary contract, but she felt insecure because she came from a village in a nearby province and had no *guanxi* (personal relations) in Beijing. Her ambition to stand out made her a vulnerable prey in the Party's intricate world of money, power, and sex. Years later, she told the Berlin-based daily newspaper *Die Tageszeitung:* "After studying art, I worked for a year for the *People's Daily*, the 'mouthpiece of the Party.' I could write three books about that short time, two of which would be nightmare books."[14]

The nightmare had little to do with the editorial job itself, but with a princeling (*guan erdai*, a term referring to children of high-ranking Communist cadres) she met through professional connections. One day, she followed her superiors at the *People's Daily* to a social dinner that this man also attended. One of Lan's superiors noticed that the princeling was attracted to her and sent her on errands that brought them into closer contact. Lan quickly realized that the man, who was already married,

11 Karen Smith, *Nine Lives: The Birth of Avant-Garde Art in New China* (Zürich: Prestel, 2006), 20.

12 Smith, *Nine Lives*, 19.

13 "Künstlerin Jiny Lan malt 'Basti Kurz' vor Publikum," *Heute*, July 31, 2017, <https://www.heute.at/s/kunstlerin-jiny-lan-malt-basti-kurz-vor-publikum-52416116>; "Kurz und (k)nackig: 'Nackter Sebastian' sorgt für Aufsehen in Wien," *Kronenzeitung*, July 31, 2017; Günter Traxler, "Ein königlicher nackter Körper," *Der Standard*, August 5, 2017, <https://www.derstandard.at/story/2000062274928/ein-koeniglich-nackter-koerper>.

14 Max Florian Kühlem, "Tragödie oder Farce—neue Meisterwerke von Jiny Lan," in *Portfolio—Genealogies: Jiny Lan*, exhibition catalog (Venice: Biblioteca Nazionale Marciana, 2019), 80–1, reprinted in *Jiny Lan*, exhibition catalog (2020), 13. A large portion of this text appeared first in Kühlem's "Joseph Beuys hängt am rissigen Seil," *taz*, July 20/21, 2019, <https://taz.de/!5609356/>.

aimed to use her to beget a male heir. Due to the one-child policy, it was common for a married princeling to keep one or more mistresses (*er'nai*) to produce male heirs if his wife did not bear him a son. Around the fourth century BCE, Mencius, the chief successor of Confucius, wrote: "There are three things that make a man not filial, and not having an heir would make him the most unfilial" (*Bu xiao you san, wu hou wei da*). In traditional Confucian thought, which still dominates Chinese society, only a male can be an heir.

After discovering she was pregnant, Lan dreaded the prospect of living incognito and raising a child for a promiscuous man whose demand for loyalty would prevent her from loving and marrying another man. She feared that she would become a de facto prisoner of the princeling for the rest of her life. Although she had the option of going to a hospital for a legal and safe abortion, she was afraid that the princeling might intervene or retaliate if he learned of the procedure. In desperation, she risked her life to induce a miscarriage by jumping off a wall: she was willing to die rather than live the rest of her life like the princeling's other mistresses.[15]

This excruciating and mortifying experience later found artistic expression in many of her works. In *Midlife Hand* (2013, Fig. 1.5), a giant, grasping male hand stretches out, palm down, toward the spectator against a background of frothing splashes of white paint; a tiny, naked female figure with a slightly bulging belly stands precariously on the tip of its middle finger, as if on the edge of a cliff. Beneath the hand, an erect penis, partially obscured, arches across the foot of the painting. The woman seems determined to jump, leap, or fly to freedom. The disembodied hand implies the Chinese idiom *yishou zhetian*, literally to cover up the sky with one hand, and metaphorically to singlehandedly hide the truth from the masses. The hand and penis represent the patriarchal and chauvinistic forces in Chinese society that constrain women's lives.

After repeatedly jumping off the wall, Lan miscarried. To avoid infection, she secretly sought out a woman obstetrician from the Philippines in Beijing, rather than confiding in a Chinese doctor. The obstetrician's attestation of Lan's "natural miscarriage and possible infertility" enabled Lan to break off her relationship with the princeling without fear of retaliation. These events in Beijing constituted Lan's primal experience as a feminist artist. She has chosen to reveal the details of her traumatic past to clarify the autobiographical aspect of her feminist art and its subjective symbols.

The powerful "hand that covers up the sky" has a double meaning for Lan: the hand of a man and the hand of the state. She recalls another event that unsettled her during her time at the *People's Daily:* the Tian Mingjian incident in Beijing in 1994, also known as the Jianguomen Gate

15 Cf. Maurer, "Das Kombinationstier / Combination Animals."

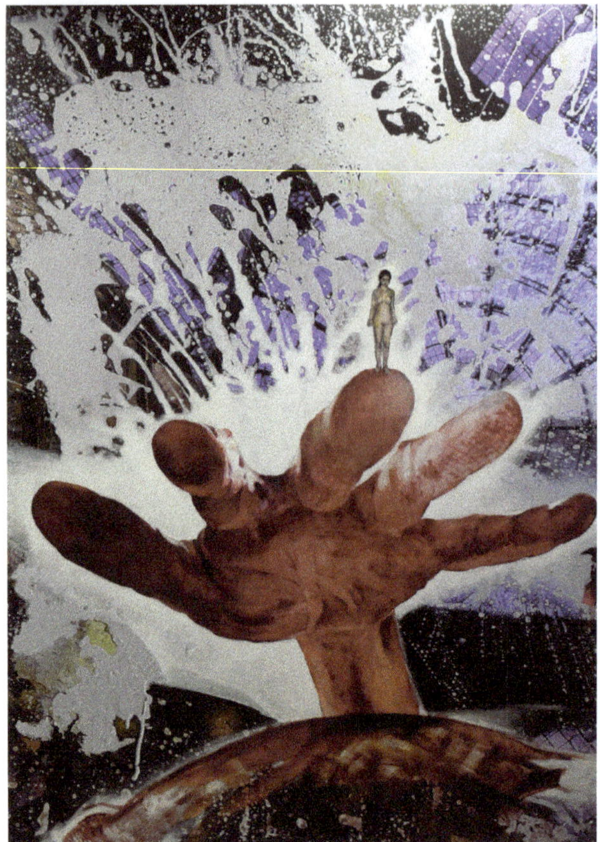

Fig. 1.5. *Midlife Hand* (2013, 200 × 140 cm).

mass shooting. This tragedy was not publicized in China, so most Chinese have never heard of it. For Lan, the incident demonstrated the bureaucratic cruelty inherent in the one-child policy. It was also an example of government censorship in China.

Thirty-year-old Tian Mingjian was a rising star in the military ranks: a promising first lieutenant and a skilled sharpshooter in the Twelfth Regiment of the Third Division of the Beijing Garrison, stationed in what is now the Tongzhou District. However, he was demoted for bribery and faced further disciplinary action for insubordination and for beating a soldier. As part of his disciplinary procedure, army inspectors read his personal letters and found out that his wife was about to give birth to a second child. The inspectors alerted the local birth control officials, who then forced his wife to have a late-term abortion. Both the mother and the unborn son died during the procedure. Seeing his life ruined, Tian took revenge on his superiors and the society at large.

On September 20, 1994, during morning roll call and training, Tian shot his superior officers and some fellow soldiers with an assault rifle and hijacked a jeep. The driver of the jeep, however, rammed the vehicle into the railing of the Jianguomen Bridge, which happened to be near the Diplomatic Residential Compound. Tian started shooting indiscriminately. Due to his superb marksmanship, he single-handedly battled against hundreds of police and military officers for an extended time. Before he was killed by a sharpshooter from his own military unit, he had claimed more than a dozen lives, including those of Iranian diplomat Yousef Mohammadi Pishknari and his nine-year-old son, and wounded dozens of civilians and law enforcement personnel.

The Chinese government shut down television satellite transmissions and barred journalists from covering the scene. But a Canadian news team had already broadcast the incident live because the shootout took place right next to their apartments. The mass shooting shocked the international community, but in China the news was covered up.[16] As a staff member of the *People's Daily*, Lan witnessed firsthand how the Chinese government banned coverage of the incident. She recalled receiving phone calls from Iranians protesting the suppression of the news and demanding an explanation. Because Lan spoke English, the Iranians asked her to convey their outrage. The government's heavy-handed interference with the press alarmed Lan and contributed to her decision to leave China. Recently, after the Chinese government completely reversed the one-child policy, the Tian Mingjian incident received renewed attention because Tian and his family were victims of the policy, something the Chinese government never admitted. Had it not been for the Canadian journalists who documented the event and the foreign nationals among the victims, Lan believes, the news of this mass shooting might never have reached the outside world.

16 1994 年北京建国门枪战视频: 田明建一人独战数百军警 [Video of the 1994 Beijing Jianguomen Gunfight: Tian Mingjian Fought Hundreds of Soldiers and Police Alone], Bowen Press, October 28, 2016, <https://bowenpress.com/news/bowen_141270.html>; "China Names Gunman in Shooting Spree," UPI Archives, September 21, 1994, <https://www.upi.com/Archives/1994/09/21/China-names-gunman-in-shooting-spree/2783780120000/>; Jeremiah Jenne, "25 Years Ago Today: The Tian Mingjian Incident," RadII China, February 27, 2020, <https://radii.co/article/25-years-ago-today-the-tian-mingjian-incident>; 悍匪田明建, 单手换子弹, 一人对抗6000名武警战士 [Tough Ruffian Tian Mingjian, Changing Bullets with One Hand, One Man against 6,000 Armed Police], May 28, 2022, <https://www.bilibili.com/video/BV1yS4y1z7hD/>.

The Artist Reborn: Apprentice and Journeywoman in Germany and Western Metropolises, 1995–2005

Having regained her independence, Lan decided to go abroad. At the *People's Daily*, she had developed contacts with foreign companies. She was able to secure an internship with a German business and left China as soon as she could. On February 20, 1995, at the age of twenty-four, she arrived in Germany, thus completing her journey to the West. A clerical error gave her a new personal identity when she noticed that the transliteration of her first name on her Chinese passport read "Jiny" instead of "Jing." Such a mistake was not unwelcome. In Germany, she had to cultivate a new self, and she started with a new name.[17] Due to her sudden decision to emigrate, Lan arrived with no knowledge of German. She remembers that on her first day in Cologne, she entered the wrong bathroom in a restaurant, reasoning that "Damen" contained the word "men" while "Herren" contained "her." This would not be the last linguistic misjudgment she made as she adjusted to a new life in a foreign land.

Lan needed practical help in dealing with German authorities. After settling in Bochum, she was assisted by Helmut Martin, a professor of Chinese language and literature at Ruhr University Bochum, and his wife, the writer Liao Tianqi. The process of overcoming language barriers sensitized her to German and English. In her later work as a professional artist, she played with words, coining terms such as Buddhalisa (from "Buddha" and "Mona Lisa"), Jinyology (from "genealogy"), and *Selbstverfraulichung* (from *verherrlichen*).

In 1996 she married a German national, but the marriage was short-lived.[18] Her husband's first birthday present to her was, to her great joy, an easel. Being married to a German meant that she was allowed to work and apply for German citizenship, but her work visa specifically limited her to "art-related employment." When she told her friends, they joked

17 The Chinese name on the passport contained the characters 蓝静, not 蓝镜 as she is known today. Both sets of characters are pronounced Lan Jing; her personal name on the passport means "quiet," but she preferred蓝镜, which literally means "blue mirror." She vaguely remembered a teacher telling a story from *Journey to the West* in which a blue mirror can reflect the truth and foretell the future.

18 Lan does not wish to disclose his identity but said he was a Marxist and a member of the Green Party. During an anniversary commemoration of the Tiananmen massacre, he read a protest statement in front of the Chinese embassy in Bonn and was henceforth blacklisted by the Chinese government. Xia Qingqing 夏青青 mentions Lan's first marriage in her essay 从蓝精灵到照妖镜 — 旅德女艺术家蓝镜 [From a Smurf to a Reveal-Goblin Mirror: The Chinese German Artist Lan Jing], Wenxuecity, September 25, 2019, <https://blog.wenxuecity.com/myblog/72140/201909/26428.html>.

that it was the German bureaucracy that forced her to become an artist. The restriction suited her well, and she started painting portraits at fairs (*Kirmessen*) and Christmas markets and on the street. Later, her practice of street portraiture led her to make the relationship between the artist and the public an important dimension of her performances.

Also in 1996, Lan was admitted to the advanced preparatory courses at the Studienkolleg of Dortmund University. From 1997 to 2002 she enrolled in courses in art, English, and Italian. She was so much more advanced than her fellow art students that a professor told the class not to worry because they did not have to draw as well as she did to graduate. One of her classmates, Irmtraud Mair, remembers that she took Professor Roland Tönne's experimental class on "The World Order" with Lan. For one assignment, the professor covered the entire floor of the large studio with cuttings from news magazines and other visual material. Students were asked to make a collage. When Mair saw Lan's collage, she was amazed: "Where did this young woman, a Chinese woman at that, get the inspiration for a work that, to my mind, exactly represents the situation of the world we live in?"[19] Praise from the professor and classmates motivated Lan to produce a pen-and-ink drawing based on the collage entitled *Die Weltordnung* (The World Order, 1997–98, Fig. 1.6).

The drawing features a nude male figure in midair, crouching with arms outstretched. One hand holds a rope and the other touches a globe-shaped cage containing a manacled prisoner. Below, seven men surround a table on which a body lies. Referring to the Old and the New Testament, Mair interprets the flying man as the archangel Lucifer, representing personal evil, as well as the Antichrist, standing for social evil:

> The collage shows a "Luciferian" person "riding" in the air with a triumphant gesture, and another person sitting trapped in a globe in a hopeless, conformist posture, a victim of social evil, of the Antichrist. Next to these extreme polarities, Jiny Lan has painted a group of helpless "specialists." They are bending over someone lying on a stretcher – a human being, or is it the planet itself? One of them turns to the viewer (the artist?) seeking advice.

A copy of the drawing hangs in Mair's house to this day. She also circulated a petition to obtain financial support for Lan after realizing that the latter was making a living by drawing portraits on the street: "The thought that Jiny would lose her inspiration by drawing routinely pained me."

19 I thank Irmtraud Mair for the interview on December 3, 2024, and the German text received on December 10, 2024, which is quoted in English translation in these passages.

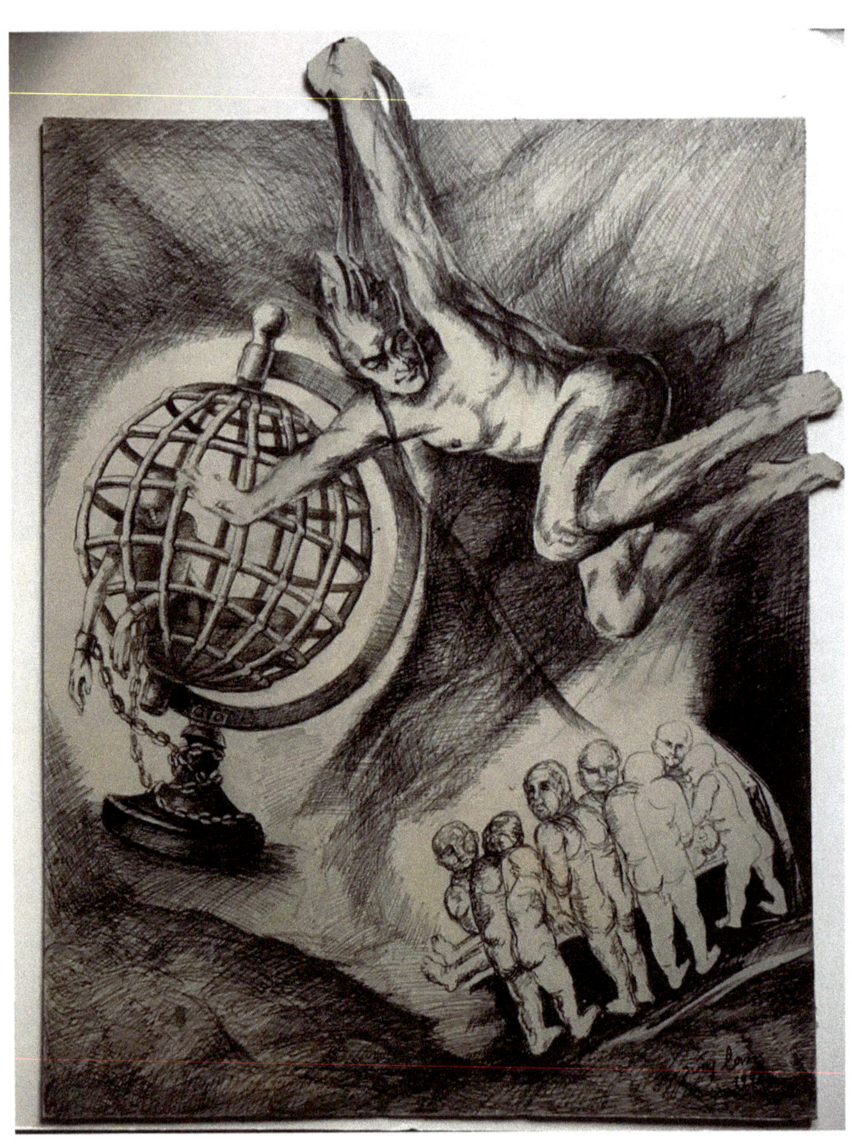

Fig. 1.6. *The World Order* (1997–98, 140 × 100 cm).

Lan met Moritz Roidl in the winter of 1998, when they both lived in the same student dormitory at Dortmund University. Roidl was studying computer science and wanted to minor in art. Lan gave him some instruction while he was putting together his portfolio for admission to art classes. In 1999 she became a naturalized German citizen. She did not wait long to visit London, New York, and other cities in Europe and North America, enjoying the ease of travel afforded by a German passport. Works from these years were later compiled into a series of impressionistic, improvisational paintings titled *Art of Nomad* (2002–5). In 2002–3, Roidl served a seven-month internship in computer science in New York. The couple lived in Borough Park, Brooklyn, one of the largest Orthodox Jewish communities outside of Israel. During this time, she painted in their apartment and in public.

In *18th Street* (2003), Lan painted several silhouetted figures walking along a subway platform, whom she revealed to be an Orthodox Jewish family (Fig. 1.7a). The image was created by applying bluish-white paint in varying thicknesses on a black field. *Smith 9th Street / 1* (2003, Fig. 1.7b) is a colorful painting that shows a range of New Yorkers waiting in the shade beneath an underpass on a sunny day. Some figures stand in the sunlight. A trestle and the upper floor of a building are visible in the background. *Smith 9th Street / 2* (2003, Fig. 1.7c), likewise comprised of ten panels, shows figures waiting on a train platform. One man stands alone at the center of the painting while other people are gathered along the wall. The image is rendered in various shades of blue.

In subway stations, Lan would place large rectangular sheets of paper on the floor and paint with diluted acrylic, which dries quickly. Back in her apartment, she would repaint with oil or a mixture of oil and acrylic. These sheets of paper were then assembled into large-format works. The realistic paintings capture everyday life in Western metropolises and are reminiscent of European modernist artworks. Her inclination to paint humans and enclosed spaces shows through in these early sketches. Positive feedback she received from spectators strengthened her confidence in her artistic abilities and her determination to pursue a career as a professional artist.

Lan and Roidl married in 2005 and settled down near Bochum. A year later in 2006, their first son, Gustav Roidl, was born. Lan was baptized into the Evangelical church at the same time as Gustav. Her paintings frequently feature church buildings as emblems of Western culture and religion. After the twins Nicola and Cornelius were born in 2010, she opened an adult drawing class at home, naming it Local Artists Network (LAN), and held group exhibitions.[20]

20 Gero Helm, "Ausstellung in der Bürgerhaus Galerie: Künstler des Local Artists Network zeigen ihre Werke," *WAZ*, January 21, 2011, <https://www.

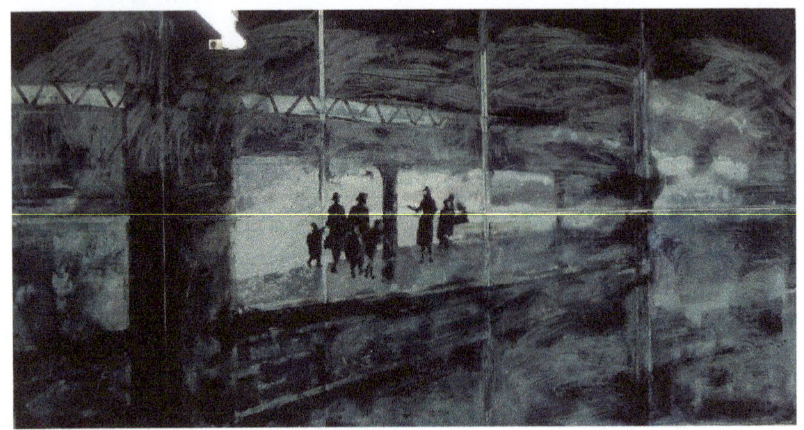

Fig. 1.7a. *18th Street* (2003, oil on cappa, 143 × 250 cm).

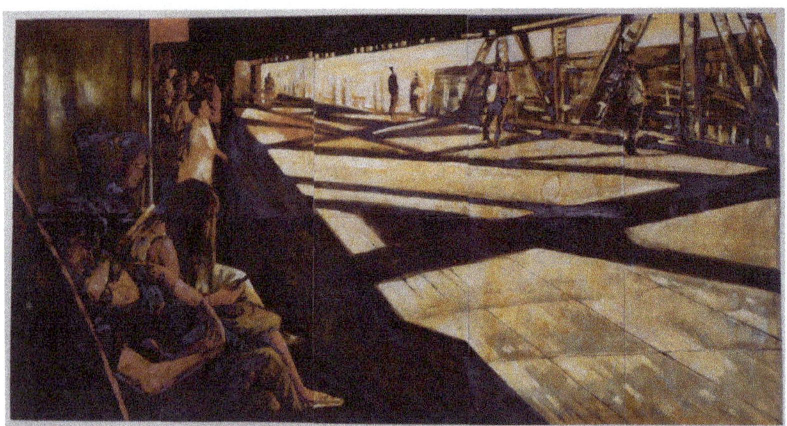

Fig. 1.7b. *Smith 9th Street / 1* (2003, oil on cappa, 143 × 250 cm).

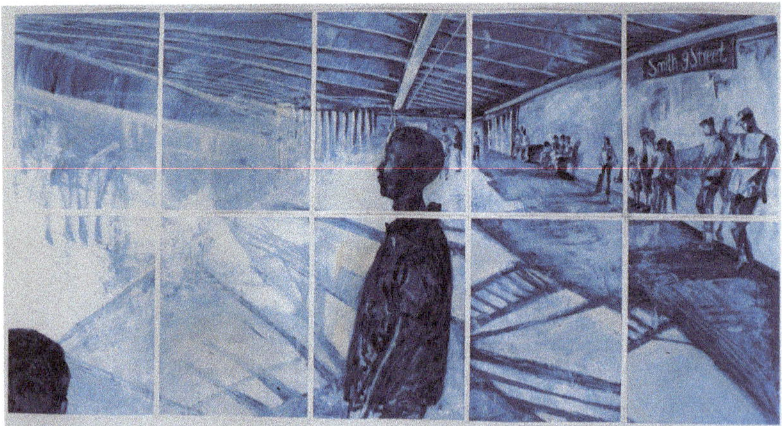

Fig. 1.7c. *Smith 9th Street / 2* (2003, oil on cappa, 143 × 250 cm).

The Founding of the Bald Girls (2012)

The overseas Chinese community first became aware of Lan through her often provocative and irksome blog posts.[21] A 2009 essay by Lan in the Chinese-language newspaper *Chinese-European Post* (*Ou hua dao bao*), under the pen name Lan Liu'er, caught Juan Xu's attention, and the editor-in-chief Yuejun Qian connected them.[22] Xu came to Germany in 1988 and was a secretary of the Chinese Students Association in Germany; Qian was the president and Yi'ne Zhang the first secretary. Qian and Zhang were prominent pro-democracy activists in the Chinese diaspora community in Germany. In 1989, Qian founded and served as editor-in-chief of the *Chinese European Post*, which operated until 2019. Zhang became a successful businessman and philanthropist who was the first Chinese member of the town council in Kaarst, North Rhine-Westphalia, and founder of the Yiyuan-Stiftung. It was in this network of overseas Chinese that Lan found community and support for her artistic aspirations.

Through the Gao brothers (Chinese avant-garde artists Gao Zhen and Gao Qiang[23]), Xu became acquainted with Li Xinmo, who also knew Xiao Lu.[24] The many performances of Li Xinmo could be classified as Shock Art (*chongji yishu* or *xiuke yishu*), which employs the body and

---

waz.de/staedte/castrop-rauxel/article4192138/ausstellung-in-der-buergerhaus-galerie.html>; Thomas Nitsche, "Ausstellung in Haus Herbede: Die Gruppe LAN (Local Artists Network) stellt aus," *WAZ*, January 23, 2014, <https://www.waz.de/staedte/witten/article8908015/austellung-in-haus-herbede.html>.

21 Lan's blogsite on wenxuecity.com: <https://passport.wenxuecity.com/members/index.php?act=profile&cid=lanliuer>.

22 Qian was an associate editor of *Rheinische Korrespondenz* (莱茵通信 *Laiyin tongxin*, 1987–2005) and president of the Chinese Students Association at Ruhr University Bochum (1988–89). When the student movement began in Beijing in 1989, he threw himself into organizing protests in Germany. On May 4, 1989, the seventieth anniversary of the May Fourth Movement, Qian announced the founding of the Chinese Students and Scholars Association in Germany. The association organized a large-scale protest in Bonn on June 4, 1989, which was attended by tens of thousands of people. In December 1989, Qian was elected president of the association.

23 See "Gao Brothers," Artnet, <https://www.artnet.com/artists/gao-brothers/>. When Gao Zhen returned from the United States to visit his hometown in 2024, he was arrested. See Yan Zhuang and Zixu Wang, "Gao Zhen, Artist Who Critiqued the Cultural Revolution, Is Detained in China," *New York Times*, September 2, 2024.

24 See Tong Yujie, "Li Xinmo: An Avant-Garde Critical Realist Artist in China," 秃头戈女: 三个女性主义艺术家展 [Bald Girls: Three Feminist Artists' Exhibit], ed. Yong Xian 庸现 (pen name of Juan Xu), catalog of the first Bald Girls exhibition (Tai Pei: 自由文化, 2012), 17–20. "Li Xinmo," in *Stepping Out!: Female Identities in Chinese Contemporary Art*, ed. Nils Ohlsen and Thorsten

blood to demonstrate the brutality women endure.[25] These women artists immediately hit it off and decided to launch the first Chinese feminist art collective, with Xu as the curator. By joining forces with Xiao and Li in China, the two Germany-based artists, Xu and Lan, reconnected with the contemporary art scene in China, which was strongly influenced by the '89 avant-garde art movement. Xiao Lu gained instant fame after firing two shots at her installation *Dialogue* (1989) at the *China/Avant-Garde* exhibition in Beijing's National Art Museum of China on February 5, 1989; the action was broadcast worldwide and retrospectively became "the first gunshots of Tiananmen."[26] Similarly, the *China/Avant-Garde* exhibition itself – curated by Gao Minglu, a Harvard-educated scholar of contemporary Chinese art and US-based art critic – was shut down twice and later came to be known as a small Tiananmen Square of the art world.[27]

The Bald Girls have declared that they aim to "fight against patriarchal chauvinism, demand equal human rights, and restore feminism to its rightful place" and to "remain independent of conventional gender definition."[28] The Bald Girls have had many benefactors, such as Yi'ne Zhang, who sponsored their first exhibition. Their activities were reported in the *Chinesische Handelszeitung* (*Hua shangbao*, Chinese Trade Newspaper), which was founded by the president of the Federation for a Democratic China, Xiu Haitao (1957–2021), who decided to stay in Germany after the Tiananmen massacre. Thus, the genesis of the Bald Girls was linked to Chinese pro-democracy activism in Germany.

Xu initially named the group 秃头歌女 *Tutou genü*, literally "The Bald Sopranos," because she was inspired by Eugène Ionesco's *La Cantatrice chauve* (The Bald Soprano, first produced in 1950). She intended to use the theater of the absurd to express the absurdities in Chinese society. Lan suggested to replace 歌 *ge* (singing) with its homophone 戈 *ge* (dagger), changing the collective's Chinese name to 秃头戈女 *Tutou genü*, literally "The Bald Swordswomen." The idea of using art as a weapon to attack social problems is effectively conveyed through the new word choice.[29]

Sadowsky (Berlin: Hatje Cantz, 2022), 98–101; for more information on Li Xinmo, see her website: <https://li-xinmo.com/>.

25 Monica Merlin, "Mapping Women Artists in Chinese Contemporary Art," in *Stepping Out!*, 20–6, here 24; "Li Xinmo," in *Stepping Out!*, 98–101.

26 Gao, *Total Modernity*, 166; Ariana Guo, "Introduction to the Beginning of Contemporary Chinese Art: 1979–1989," Hua Gallery, August 3, 2019; "Xiao Lu. *Dialogue*, 1989," Moma, <https://www.moma.org/audio/playlist/290/3759>.

27 See for example Gao, *Total Modernity*, 94–5, 154, 158, 161, 166.

28 Juan Xu, 秃头戈女: 序 [Bald Girls: Preface], in *Bald Girls: Three Feminist Artists' Exhibit*, 2–6, here 6.

29 My interview with Juan Xu on April 21, 2023, in Berlin; Belinda Grace Gardner, "Jinyology," *ARTMAPP* 28 (Winter 2021/22): 28–30.

Thanks to Xiao Lu's international reputation at that time, the Bald Girls were able to secure renowned international guests for their inaugural exhibition at the Iberia Center for Contemporary Art, located in Beijing's 798 art district. Tony Cragg, the director of the Düsseldorf Art Academy, and Gao Minglu, who curated the *China/Avant-Garde* exhibition in 1989 as well as the 1998 New York exhibition *Inside Out: New Chinese Art*, attended.[30] Their exhibition catalog also featured a short essay titled "Das chinesische Glasauge" (The Chinese Glass Eye) by the 2009 Nobel Prize in Literature laureate Herta Müller, who had campaigned for the human rights activist Liu Xiaobo to be awarded the Nobel Peace Prize.[31] Journalists, including one from the *New York Times*, also attended the event. However, before the show opened, authorities censored three of Lan's projects: *Artist* (2011), *Chinese Apple* (2012), and *Red Sun* (2012).

To protest the action of the secret police, Xiao Lu suggested that they add an impromptu performance to the opening: shaving each other's heads in front of visitors, literally transforming themselves into bald girls (Fig. 1.8).[32] This spontaneous performance echoed the happening art of the Fluxus movement. Becoming bald was a serendipitous result of censorship. Indeed, Chinese censors often inadvertently catalyzed their targets' rise to fame, and incurring censorship in China ironically became a litmus test for success. The *New York Times* began its report by describing the intervention of the police: "It almost wouldn't be a real Chinese art opening without security officials barging in and ordering paintings off the wall. By that yardstick alone, this Saturday opening of Bald Girls, a feminist art show in the 798 arts district of Beijing, was a tremendous success."[33]

30 Shuqin Cui, *Gendered Bodies: Toward a Women's Visual Art in Contemporary China* (Honolulu: University of Hawai'i Press, 2015), 3–4.

31 Herta Müller, "Das chinesische Glasauge," in *Bald Girls: Three Feminist Artists' Exhibit*, 140–5.

32 According to Lan, some audience members misread the English name "Bald Girls" as "Bad Girls." This was a welcome mistake, given the rebelliousness that being "bad" evokes. A series of feminist shows titled "Bad Girls" were staged in the US and the UK in the 1990s, celebrating "the multiplicity of feminisms." However, the "post-feminist Bad Girls" in the West resisted "offending proscriptive feminism," whereas the Chinese "Bad Girls" fought for basic existential and human rights for Chinese women—a difference that the Bald Girls later addressed in their project *Timelag*. See Maura Reilly, "'Bad Girls' to the Rescue: An Exhibition of Feminist Art from the 1990s Has Much to Teach Us Today," *ARTnews*, May 16, 2018, <https://www.artnews.com/art-news/news/bad-girls-rescue-exhibition-feminist-art-1990s-much-teach-us-today-10326/>.

33 Didi Kirsten Tatlow, "In Art, a Strong Voice for Chinese Women," *New York Times*, March 7, 2012, <https://www.nytimes.com/2012/03/08/world/asia/08iht-letter08.html>.

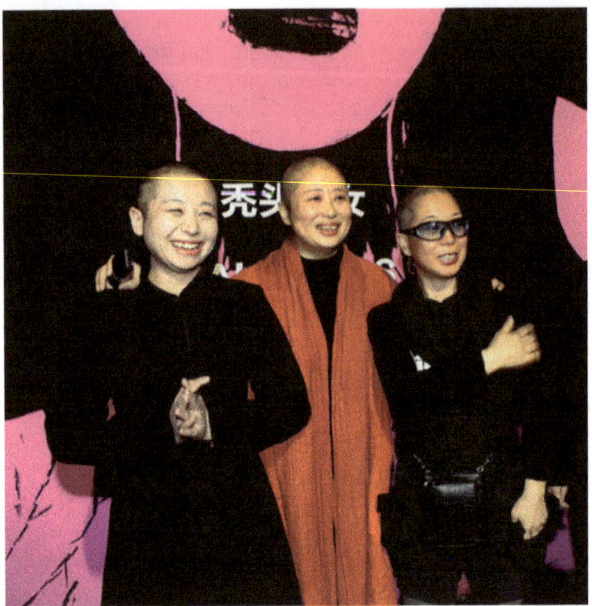

Fig. 1.8. Three Bald Girls from left to right: Li Xinmo, Xiao Lu, and Jiny Lan (photo: Juan Xu).

The collective head-shaving challenged what was considered the norm for women in China. As the *New York Times* put it, "going bald was a show of defiance against traditional Chinese standards of female beauty, which, importantly, include long, glossy hair."[34] But the shaved heads of the artists evoked the appearance of Buddhist nuns, who are self-reliant, renounce the company of men, and sacrifice themselves for the public good. This rebellious act jumpstarted Lan's career as a conceptual, visual artist who often opens her exhibitions with a performance project. Her closely cropped hair became an indispensable part of her image and a good PR move.

34 Tatlow, "In Art, a Strong Voice for Chinese Women."

2: From Maoist Posters to Political Pop: Artistic Methods and Influences

LAN RECEIVED HER secondary and college educations in the 1980s and early 1990s, as successive avant-garde movements stirred Chinese artists. As Minglu Gao points out, the Chinese avant-garde of the 1980s targeted "a totalized society with its tradition and ideology."[1] Gao traces the avant-garde movement in China back to the May Fourth New Cultural Movement of the 1920s, when the first group of Chinese artists who studied abroad brought back realism and modernism and incorporated them into their teaching and practice. But modernism was suppressed by both the Nationalist and the Communist governments from the 1920s to the 1970s.[2] In the first thirty years of the PRC, founded in 1949, Chinese art underwent a radical period of homogenization under the decree of Mao-style revolutionary realism, which adapted socialist realism to the Chinese context.[3] The making of nonpolitical art, either in its traditional Chinese form or in Western form, was banned.

The Cultural Revolution marked a new radicalization in Chinese political art. In 1967, Mao's wife, Jiang Qing – known in the West as Madame Mao – staged an art show called *The Exhibition of the Accomplishments of the Red Guard's Military Struggles.* The artworks displayed included pictures of Red Guards standing in solidarity with Africans and people of other Third World nations.[4] The so-called Red Guard art was essentially Maoist mass art, which Gao calls "red pop" (*hongse bopu*).[5] By

1 Minglu Gao, *Total Modernity and the Avant-Garde in Twentieth-Century Chinese Art* (Cambridge, MA: MIT Press, 2011) 138. See also Peter Bürger's canonical work on the subject, *Theory of the Avant-Garde* (Minneapolis: University of Minnesota Press, 1984).

2 Li Xianting, "The Stars: Explorers of Chinese Contemporary Art," in *Stars 79–80*, ed. Li Xianting and Rui Huang (Hong Kong: The Chinese University of Hong Kong Press, 2019), 20–5, here 20; Alex Burchmore, "The China/Avant-Garde exhibition and Xiao Lu: 30 Years On," *4A Papers* 6, <https://4a.com.au/articles/china-avant-garde-exhibition-xiao-lu-alex-burchmore>; Gao, *Total Modernity*, 33–42.

3 Li Xianting, "The Stars: The Flag-Bearers of Chinese Modern Art," trans. Philip Tinari (from the Chinese text entitled "星星" – 中国现代艺术的揭竿人, written in 1993), in *Stars 79–80*, 258–9; Smith, *Nine Lives*, 10.

4 Andrews, *Painters and Politics in the PRC*, 342.

5 Gao, *Total Modernity*, 42.

1979, when Deng Xiaoping opened China's door to the West, the art of Mainland China was strikingly different in content and form from both contemporary Western art and the art practiced in other Sinophone regions, such as Taiwan, Hong Kong, and Singapore.[6]

The art of the post-Cultural Revolution period, especially from 1976 to 1984, did not manifest a substantial change in iconography; it rejected the political content of Cultural Revolution art but inherited its two-dimensional, centralized, and front-facing aesthetic and stylistic form, which is frequently seen in Lan's portraiture.[7] According to Li Xianting, a Beijing art pundit and curator who is considered the "godfather of contemporary Chinese art,"[8] Chinese contemporary art began in 1979 with the Stars, the best-known avant-garde group, and their soon-to-be censored exhibitions.[9] The Stars called for political democratization and artistic freedom. They took Käthe Kollwitz and Pablo Picasso as their role models. Due to the political pressure they faced in China, many of these artists moved overseas. The avant-garde movement of 1985 – '85 Art New Wave (85 *yishu xinchao*) – looked to the Stars as "flag-bearers," and the work of their followers was well represented in the *China/Avant-Garde* exhibition organized by Minglu Gao in 1989 in Beijing (chapter 1). However, in the early 1990s, a new trend emerged among Chinese artists, which Li Xianting dubbed "Political Pop."[10] Although Lan matured as a visual artist later in Germany, this chapter traces influences on her work, conscious or unconscious, back to China's avant-garde tradition, specifically to Political Pop, which mutated from the 1989 avant-garde.

One of the Western art movements that anticipates Lan's work is New Figuration or Neofiguration (Nueva Figuración). New Figuration originated in the 1950s and 1960s in Spanish-speaking countries, particularly Argentina, Mexico, and Venezuela, where artists rejected abstract art, Informalism, and expressionism. Instead, they sought to bring art closer to everyday life, addressing social concerns such as political repression and poverty, and they used the human figure as a medium to express

6 Andrews, *Painters and Politics in the PRC*, 1–3.

7 Esp. Gao, *Total Modernity*, 33, 65; Andrews, *Painters and Politics in the PRC*, 315–16, 383–4; Wu Hung, *Remaking Beijing: Tiananmen Square and the Creation of a Political Space* (Chicago: University of Chicago Press, 2005), 78.

8 Wang Keping, "Memories of the Stars Exhibition," in *Stars 79–80*, ed Li and Huang, 160–75, here 175.

9 Li, "The Stars: Explorers of Chinese Contemporary Art," 24; see also Wu Hung, *Transience: Chinese Experimental Art at the End of the Twentieth Century* (Chicago: The David and Alfred Smart Museum of Art and University of Chicago Press, 2005), 17–18.

10 Gao, *Total Modernity*, 255; see also Wu, *Transience*, 20–2.

a sense of disillusionment.[11] A little later, a similar movement, Narrative Figuration, occurred in France in the 1960s and early 1970s. I will focus on Narrative Figuration, which emerged around the same time as Maoist art in China, as a precedent for Lan's work. One of the methodological similarities between Political Pop and Narrative Figuration is that artists employed pre-existing images as source materials. The two most important ready-made symbols of Communist China are Mao and Tiananmen, and Chinese experimental artists have frequently appropriated them.[12] I use Lan's "Mao-imposter" and Tiananmen paintings to illustrate her political subversion as well as her method of sub-version in an art system called Jinyology.

Red Sun, Black Moon (2012): "Mao-Imposters" and the Vagaries of Censorship

Before the opening of the Bald Girls' first exhibition, the secret police reviewed the paintings on display and ordered *Red Sun* (2012, Fig. 2.1b) to be taken off the wall. *Red Sun* was Lan's first pastiche of a famous propaganda poster, *Chairman Mao Is the Red Sun in the Hearts of the People of the World* (1967, Fig. 2.1a), which was used during the height of the Cultural Revolution.[13] Similar to the Maoist cult song "The East Is Red," the poster depicts Mao radiating light like the sun. Below him, a diverse crowd of people in various ethnic costumes marches forward on red earth, holding the Little Red Book high, with a sea of red flags fluttering behind them. The poster reflects Mao's theory of the Three Worlds, which called on the people of Asia, Africa, and Latin America to unite against American imperialism and Soviet revisionism. Designed to reinforce the personality cult, the poster asserts that Mao is the leader of the Third World and enjoys worldwide worship and deification.

In *Red Sun*, Lan imitated the composition of the poster but replaced Mao with his wife Jiang Qing. Not only was this a provocative choice in itself, but Lan's depiction of Jiang Qing, she reveals, was actually a self-portrait that enhanced her resemblance to Mao's wife, enacting a form of artistic self-inscription whereby Lan put herself in Mao's place. The

11 See Patrick Frank, *Painting in a State of Exception: New Figuration in Argentina, 1960–1965* (Gainesville: University of Florida Press, 2016); Donald B. Kuspit, "New German Painting: The Discovery of Expression," in *New Figuration: Contemporary Art from Germany; Work by Georg Baselitz*, exhibition catalog (Los Angeles: The Gallery, 1983), 1–10.

12 Wu, *Remaking Beijing*, 190.

13 "Chairman Mao Is the Red Sun in the Hearts of People of the World," Library Digital Collections, UC San Diego, <https://library.ucsd.edu/dc/object/bb9557574s>.

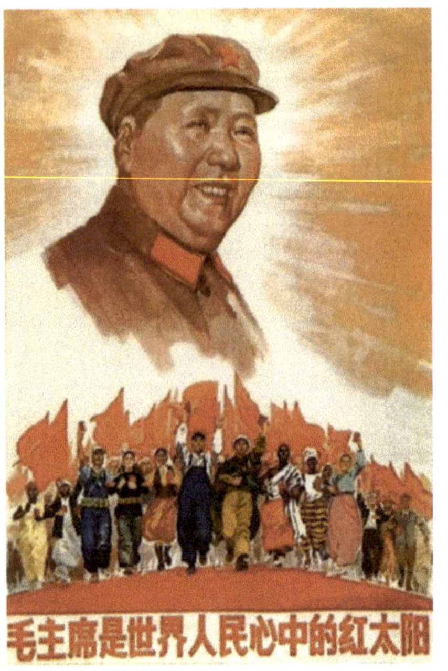

Fig. 2.1a. *Chairman Mao Is the Red Sun in the Hearts of the People of the World* (1967).

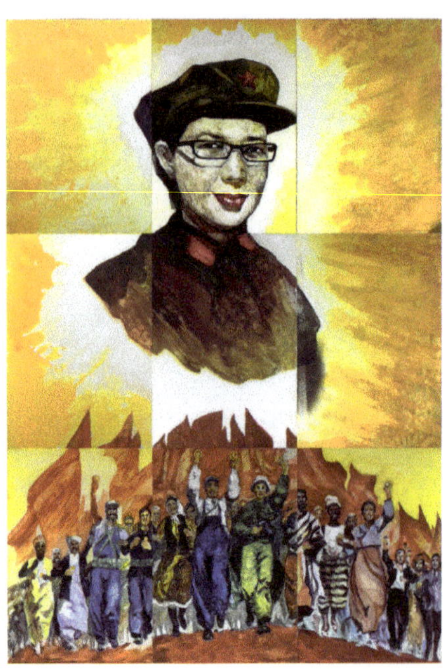

Fig. 2.1b. *Red Sun* (2012, 300 × 210 cm).

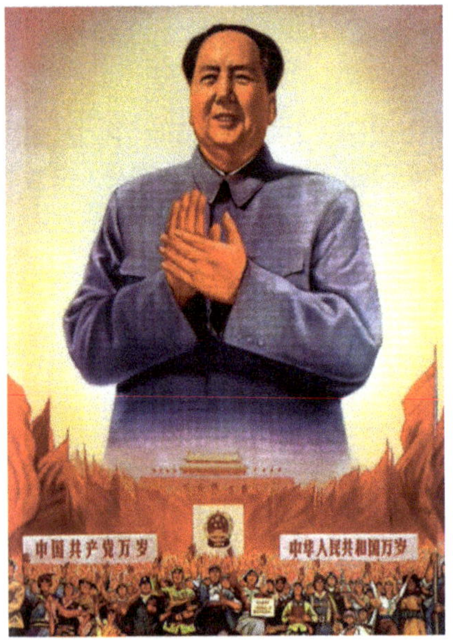

Fig. 2.2a. *Long Live the Great Leader Chairman Mao* (1975).

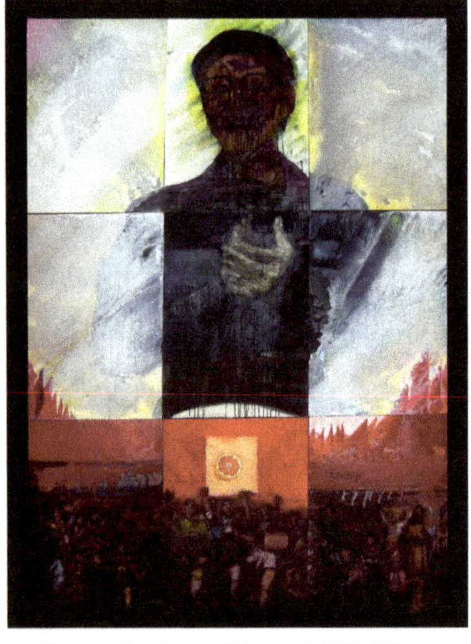

Fig. 2.2b. *Black Moon* (2012, 300 × 210 cm).

white mass around Jiang's head does not look like the rays of the sun, but rather clouds or splashing water, alluding to the proverb *hongyan huoshui* (rouged face, treacherous waters), a well-known Chinese idiom warning against *femmes fatales.* After Mao's death, Jiang was arrested as the lead member of the Gang of Four, a quartet of high-ranking CCP officials who were blamed for the Cultural Revolution in order to ensure that the official image of Mao remained unblemished. Lan wonders why many Chinese accept such propaganda and do not question it: "In Western society, such a theory that Jiang, not Mao himself, was responsible for the Cultural Revolution would have been scrutinized and subjected to intense and critical debate." But in China, the attack on Jiang drew strength from an attitude of suspicion toward politically powerful women that has deep cultural roots. Just as Yang Guifei, the consort of Emperor Xuanzong, was blamed for the decline of the Tang Dynasty, and Cixi, the concubine of Emperor Xianfeng who became the infamous Empress Dowager, was held responsible for the fall of the Qing Dynasty, Jiang was scapegoated for the Cultural Revolution, even though she defended herself by arguing that she was Mao's agent. As she notoriously said at her trial, "I was Chairman Mao's dog. Whoever he told me to bite, I bit." The sexism and misogyny behind the historiographical narrative condemning Jiang were absurd, but not widely challenged. Thus, though embedded in the tradition of Chinese agitprop art, *Red Sun* is a sarcastic and subversive subversion of the Maoist cult poster: Jiang, Mao's faithful dog, takes Mao's place, becoming the cult figure she was never allowed to be. The secret police probably recognized the woman as Jiang Qing, thought it audacious of Lan to replace Chairman Mao with a woman the Chinese were told to despise, and ordered the canvas to be taken down. Lan painted a white frame on the wall where the painting had been hung to draw attention to the police intervention.

The secret police censored *Red Sun* but allowed *Black Moon* (Fig. 2.2b) to be exhibited. The latter survived censorship only because the secret police failed to detect the subversive core of the painting. *Black Moon* uses as its source image another Maoist cult poster, *Long Live the Great Leader Chairman Mao / Warmly Celebrate the Opening of the Fourth National People's Congress* (1975, Fig. 2.2a), in which an enormous Mao clad in his eponymous suit towers over Tiananmen like a god while clapping his hands. In the foreground, a front-facing crowd is cheering Mao, waving copies of the Little Red Book and carrying banners and signs. Tiananmen is visible in the distance, above a cluster of red flags. In *Black Moon*, Lan has again replaced Mao's face with her own, as a stand-in for Jiang Qing, but this time she has obscured it with black paint. Jiang is metaphorically the moon, because the moon does not shine on its own but only reflects the sun. When Mao died and the sun set forever, Jiang, the moon, also remained dark, denigrated and demonized by Chinese historiography and propaganda. Here Lan is playing with the Chinese phrase *mo hei*, literally to blacken or black out something, figuratively to denigrate someone. She splashed black ink on Jiang's face, mimicking the smear campaign that shifted the blame for the Cultural Revolution from Mao to his wife, turning her into a monster while Mao remained a god.

According to Lan, publicly defacing a leader's portrait in Germany would be a simple form of happening art, but in China it could expose the offender to great danger. For example, the three young protesters who hurled pigment-filled eggs at Mao's portrait at the Tiananmen Gate on May 23, 1989 – Lu Decheng, Yu Dongyue, and Yu Zhijian – were arrested and sentenced to sixteen years, twenty years, and life imprisonment, respectively; after being released on parole, they fled to the United States and Canada.[14] On July 4, 2018, Dong Yaoqiong, known as the "Ink Girl," splashed ink on Xi Jinping's portrait in Shanghai. She was arrested by national security agents and forced into a psychiatric ward, and her father was later beaten to death in prison.[15]

In the original Mao poster, crowds in front of the Tiananmen Gate are carrying a huge sign of the national emblem as well as two giant banners that read "Long Live the Communist Party" and "Long Live the PRC." In Lan's *Black Moon*, however, Tiananmen, the symbol of Communist dictatorship in China, has been effaced. In place of the national emblem, Lan painted half of an orange. The two banners in the original poster have been covered with red paint, as if blood were dripping from those spots, and the joyous crowd of peasants, workers, and soldiers has been replaced by a murky depiction of a seemingly suffering crowd. The gloom and darkness are implicitly caused by the denigration of Jiang, leaving the peoples of the world benighted. Thus, *Black Moon* is no less subversive than *Red Sun*. A depiction of Jiang Qing as the red sun was presumed blasphemous and thus censored, but an image of Mao as a defaced "monster" was approved for public display. The secret police may have assumed that *Black Moon* was a defacement of Jiang, not Mao.

14 Liao Yiwu, "Interview with Yu Zhijian, One of the 'Three Hunan Hooligans' Who Defaced the Portrait of Mao Zedong Over Tiananmen Square in 1989," chinachange.org, June 1, 2017, <https://chinachange.org/2017/06/02/interview-with-yu-zhijian-one-of-the-three-hunan-hooligans-who-defaced-the-portrait-of-mao-zedong-over-tiananmen-square-in-1989-part-one/>.

15 Kassy Cho and William Yang, "This Woman Threw Ink on a Photo of China's President on a Livestream and Now She's Disappeared," *BuzzFeed*, July 6, 2018, <https://www.buzzfeednews.com/article/kassycho/chinese-woman-ink-xi-jinping-live-stream-disappeared>; Gao Feng, "Father of Woman Who Splashed Xi Jinping Poster with Ink Dies Suddenly in Jail," *rfa*, September 26, 2022, <https://www.rfa.org/english/news/china/ink-girl-father-09262022133150.html>.

The use of the colors red and black to label the two paintings immediately calls to mind Mao's color-coded political campaigns that divided people into good and bad, red and black, based on their class identity. The Five Red Categories (*hong wu lei*) refer to revolutionary soldiers, cadres, workers, poor peasants, and slightly wealthier peasants (*xia zhong nong*). The Five Black Categories (*hei wu lei*) refer to landlords, rich peasants, counterrevolutionaries, bad elements, and rightists. The Five Black Categories were later expanded to Nine Black Categories (*hei jiu lei*) by adding traitors, enemy agents, "capitalist roaders," and bourgeois intellectuals.[16] The stark color-coding evoked the tensions of Chinese political confrontations. Art historian Wu Hung noted that in the art of the Cultural Revolution, "in contrast to the glorified red of the Cultural Revolution, the color black stood for counter-revolution, degeneration, and evil," as in the term "black painting."[17] In 1966, at the start of the Cultural Revolution, Jiang Qing ordered the propaganda department to arrange "black painting" exhibitions in big cities such as Beijing, Shanghai, and Xi'an.[18] These exhibitions featured revisionist, counterrevolutionary, or apolitical, avant-garde art – including Western examples – as well as Chinese traditional ink paintings (*guohua*), and in their admonitory function they resembled the exhibition of "Degenerate Art" that the Nazis organized in Munich in 1937.[19]

Together, *Red Sun* and *Black Moon* formed the installation *Collective Efforts – Red Sun, Black Moon* (2012, Fig. 2.3); the photograph shows the installation before *Red Sun* was banned by the secret police. The origin of *Collective Efforts* lies in the performance project *Made in Germany, Quality of China* (*Deguo zhizao, zhongguo pinzhi*); the eight Chinese characters forming those words appeared above the two paintings in the exhibition at the Iberia Center.[20] Both *Red Sun* and *Black Moon* are composed of nine rectangular panels. Each panel was in fact painted by a different volunteer. For the project, Lan invited a group of eighteen German amateur artists to her studio, located in a former BMW factory in Düsseldorf, and assigned each person the task of painting one of the eighteen rectangular images she sketched. The collective of painters worked

16 Smith, *Nine Lives*, 8.

17 Wu Hung, *Contemporary Chinese Art: A History, 1970s–2000s* (London: Thames & Hudson, 2014), 23.

18 Gao, *Total Modernity*, 221. Wu Hung mentions such exhibitions organized in 1974: see Wu, *Contemporary Chinese Art*, 23.

19 See Andrews, *Painters and Politics in the PRC*, 321, as well as the sixth chapter on the Cultural Revolution, esp. 368–476 on "The Black Painting Exhibitions."

20 Lan wanted the title to suggest not only that the project had Chinese and German imprints, but also that communism could be "made in Germany" and take on "Chinese qualities."

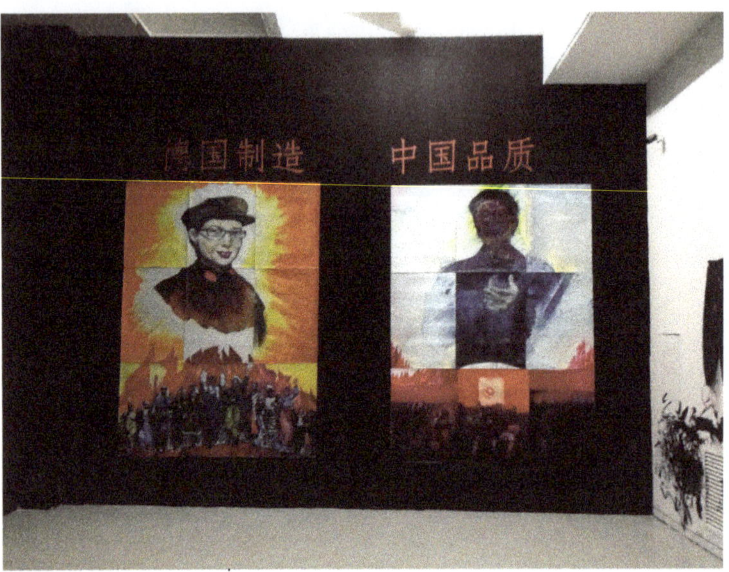

Fig. 2.3. Performance Installation, *Collective Efforts – Red Sun, Black Moon* (2012, 300 × 420 cm, photo: Juan Xu).

independently, unaware of the larger images to which the pieces belonged, but when Lan assembled the panels into two giant posters, the relationships between the pieces became clear. She put the finishing touches on the posters by adding her own face to each one, painting a radiant face in *Red Sun* and a blackened one in *Black Moon*. Thus, not only are *Red Sun* and *Black Moon* travesties of Mao's agitprop posters, but the collective effort through which she created them mimicked Mao's appeal to collectivism. Lan quipped: "I instructed the eighteen German amateur artists to paint; each resembled a cog in the revolutionary machine, and I took credit for the people's collective effort."

An Anti-Climactic Finale to *Red Sun: One-Persons-Chorus* (2013)

The story of *Red Sun* did not end in 2012 in Beijing; it ended where it started, in Germany. The following year, during the Shanghai Biennale (October 2012–March 2013), Lan reused *Red Sun* in the design of fifty-six large billboards she erected to advertise her exhibition *One-Persons-Chorus* (2013, February 15–22) at the Nordrhein-Westfalen (NRW) Forum in Düsseldorf. She placed the billboards throughout the city on highways, main streets, and alleyways (Fig. 2.4). The billboard features a color image of Lan as Madame Mao in uniform on a white background, emitting red rays, also a typical feature of Mao posters. The oxymoronic

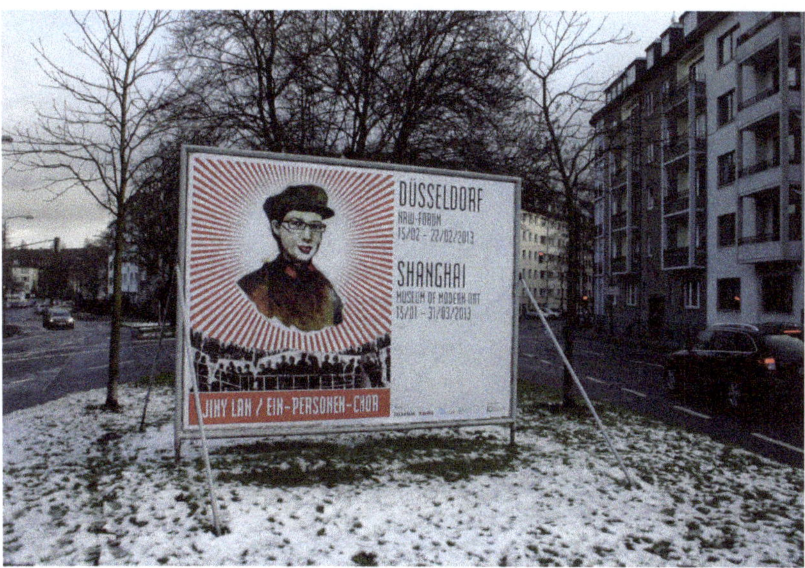

Fig. 2.4. *One-Persons-Chorus* Billboard (2013, photo: Kangping Piao).

title *One-Persons-Chorus* alludes to Mao. During his rule, what appeared to be a chorus was actually Mao's echo chamber. The billboard design captures the essence of both a (proletarian) dictatorship and a people's democratic republic. But unlike the ebullient people of the world portrayed in *Long Live the Great Leader Chairman Mao*, the rows of people depicted in black and white at the bottom of the billboard are devoid of emotion and unmoved by the frenzy of a personality cult. They appear to be standing behind a railing, perhaps on board a ship captained by "the Great Helmsman," one of Mao's epithets. With this installation project, Lan criticizes the political manipulation and mind control of the masses in China.

But this publicity stunt was a flop. While in China the secret police banned the public display of *Red Sun*, in Germany she could install her poster wherever she wanted. Yet people did not pay attention, nor did she receive any inquiries from the German media. Whether Germans recognized the portrait as Madame Mao was questionable. Even if they did, the idea that Mao was a dictator and Jiang Qing a scapegoat is neither novel nor subversive in the German context. People in the West are accustomed to seeing unorthodox, provocative, and exotic billboard advertisements. Art that carries a subversive charge in one society may appear banal once it has been deterritorialized.[21] Still, the German public's lack of interest sobered Lan: "Different cultures have different pain points [*Schmerzpunkte*]. The Cultural Revolution touches the wound of the Chinese, not of the Germans. However, if I added a dot under Jiang Qing's nose, it would immediately receive media attention in Germany. It shows how differently cultures tick."

Versioning and the Matriarchal Pedigree of Jinyology

A poster from 1967 featuring a beaming Mao, the "imposter" painting *Red Sun*, and the billboard *One-Persons-Chorus*: these images, each dependent on the one that preceded it, form a pictorial lineage. Lan's notion of a generational relationship between artworks started to crystallize in 2012, and she later summed it up in the neologism "Jinyology."[22] The origin of the concept can be traced back to her family visits to China. In 2004, the year before she married Roidl, the couple visited her family in her hometown. Relatives took out their family genealogy book (*zu pu*), but Lan could not find her own name or those of her sisters. In traditional Chinese societies, women were often recorded not in the family into which they were born, but only in their husband's family, after they married. Even then, while male family members retained their personal names in the genealogy book, married women were identified simply by their maiden family names – for example, "surname Wang" (*wang shi*) – written in small characters after their husband's full name. If a family had only daughters, the family lineage was considered broken.[23]

21 Although the billboard action did not attract the desired attention, this exhibition led to subsequent collaboration with Tim Felgner, the owner of the Digital Printshop Terminal A0 in Düsseldorf, which printed Lan's posters for the city fair. Their collaboration has continued to this day, as Mr. Felgner told me in a conversation on December 19, 2024.

22 This self-referential term was inspired by the title of the exhibition *Portfolio – Genealogies* that Lan participated in at the National Library of St. Mark in Venice in 2019. See Gardner, "Multidimensionale Um- und Neudeutungen von Jiny Lan: 'Jinyology.'"

23 Lee Meiyu, "The Jiapu Chronicles: What's in a Name?," biblioasia, National Library, Singapore, January 1, 2014, <https://biblioasia.nlb.gov.sg/vol-9/issue-4/jan-march-2014/jiapu-chinese-family-lineage>; "Women To Be Included in Confucius' Family Tree," July 26, 2006, Xinhua, <https://www.chinadaily.com.cn/china/2006-07/26/content_649722.htm>. This sexist practice continued until the one-child policy made it untenable, although more conservative regions such as Guangdong, Fujian, or rural areas still retain the custom. To cite a recent example: not until the fifteen-year-old professional diver, Quan Hongchan 全红婵, won an Olympic gold medal in Tokyo in 2021 did she enter her

The fact that Lan was not considered worthy of a place in her own family's genealogy disturbed her deeply. Then, in 2012, when her brother, the family's only male heir, had a daughter, a female relative sighed, "Too bad it is a girl! Now our family line is cut off." Hearing these words from a college-educated relative irritated Lan so much that she quarreled with her. Anger has often been the driving force behind Lan's artwork, and out of the quarrel the idea of using repainting to create a pedigree of artworks began to materialize: "I do not exist in the genealogy of my own family. So I create my own genealogy, of which I am the owner, the master, the creator."

The first generation of the matriarchal family of pictures was a painting based on an advertisement for the Galleria Vittorio Emanuele II in Milan, often called the world's oldest shopping mall. The advertisement features the mall's unique glass dome, as seen from inside the building. Lan photographed it and had the image printed on a canvas. She then repainted it in blue, green, and pink tints to create her first "man": Adam. Using the color invert function in a smartphone app, she created the first "woman": Eve. *Adam and Eve* (2012, Fig. 2.5a, b) consists of two reciprocal paintings in inverted colors. Departing from the long tradition of figural paintings of the biblical progenitors, Lan's *Adam and Eve* is geometric and abstract. Through the iterative process of photographing, printing, and repainting, Adam/Eve begat a second generation of seven paintings, which according to Lan correspond to God's seven days of creation, including the Sabbath. Each of these, in turn, produced its own offspring. The choice of the shopping mall in Milan as the primal scene is pregnant with meaning: A high-end shopping mall is a cathedral of commerce and consumption, yet the glass dome reveals the heavens and the universe, indicating spiritual pursuits. Thus, this architectural design signifies both the commercial and transcendental dimensions of art.

Lan has used this mixed-media production process to produce dozens of paintings belonging to multiple generations. The result resembles a giant family tree, and each branch constitutes a *versioning* consisting of related paintings, as seen in Figure 2.6. The parent paintings are at the center, and the daughters are laid out in rows radiating from the center. Several paintings have spawned new lines of descent, depicted on a smaller scale. "Versioning" is a term appropriated from the computer software industry. Lan's painterly versioning, however, does not emulate the evolutionary model of improvement at the heart of software development. Instead, versioning allows her to cannibalize her own paintings. Sometimes, the sub-version replicates the layout of the previous version;

Guangdong-based family's genealogy book; see 追认全红婵为全氏子孙 [Quan Hongchan recognized as a Quan descendent], *China Digital Times*, August 9, 2021, <https://chinadigitaltimes.net/chinese/669474.html>.

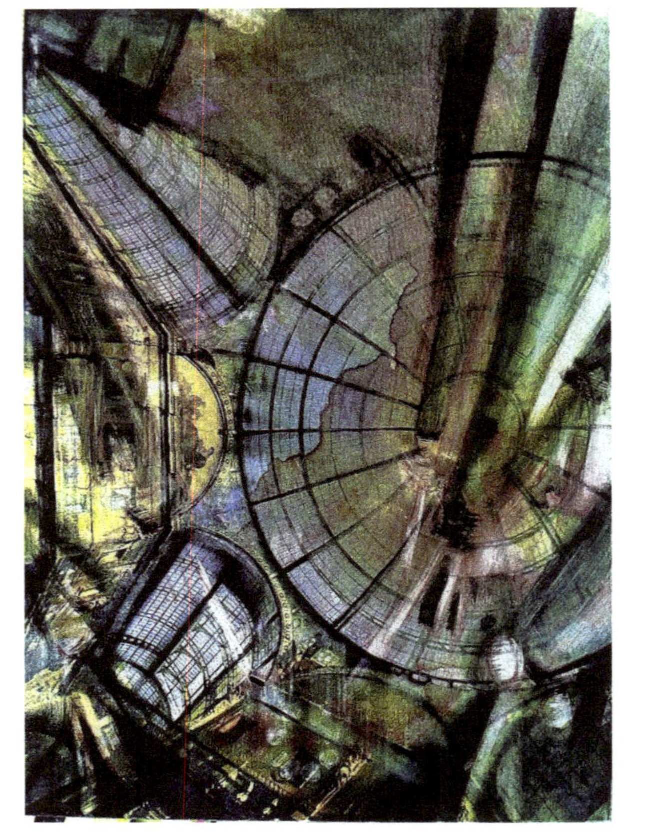

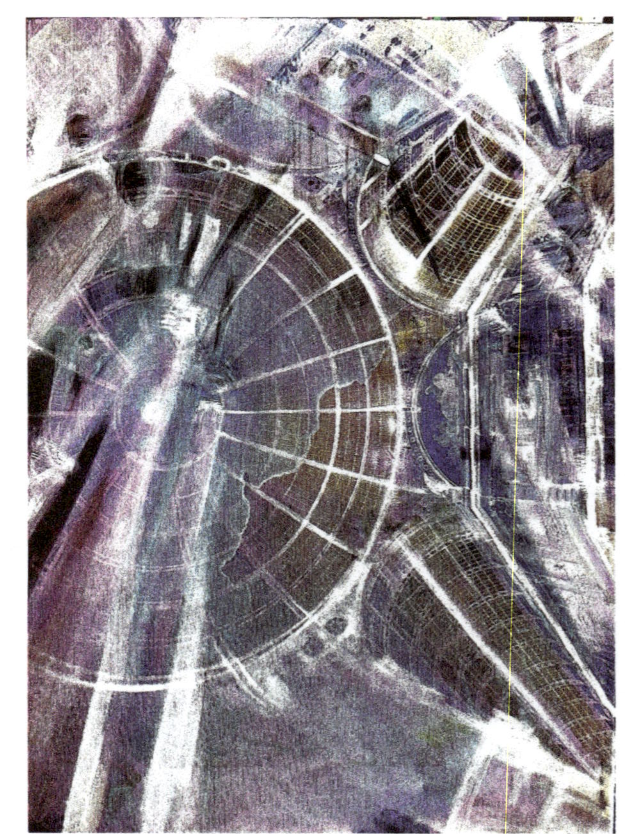

Fig. 2.5a, b. *Adam and Eve* (2012, 140 × 100 cm each).

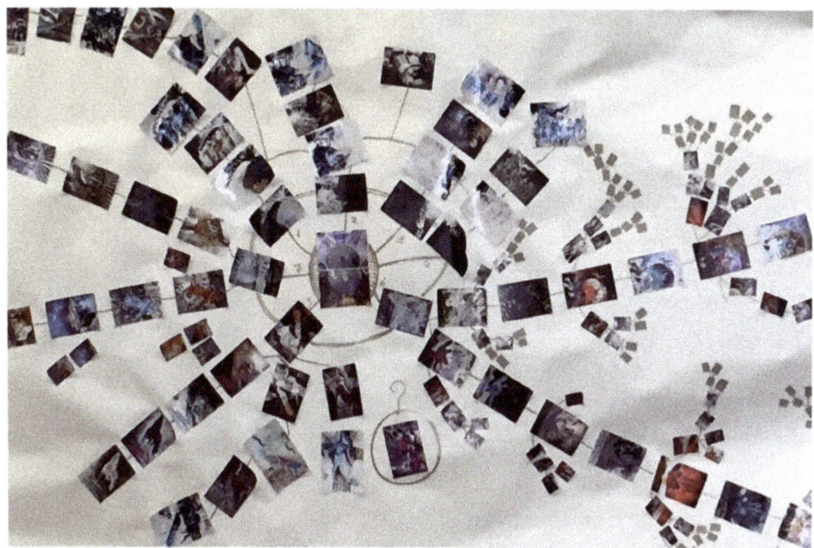

Fig. 2.6. Jinyology and versioning: a "matriarchal" family of pictures.

other times, there is little family resemblance between the two paintings. This serial production process resembles how human genes are transmitted and expressed from generation to generation. In this way, Lan creates a humanoid network of images in which she herself is the creator and matriarch. At some point, however, this repainting system became self-limiting. Thus, as an additional mechanism for growing her painterly heritage, she uses paint left over from one canvas to establish a new painting's lineage within Jinyology. Like adoption in human families, using leftover paint is a way to create a non-genetic kinship affiliation between paintings.

Her iterative method of multilayered, mutating versioning evokes the image of a palimpsest, a manuscript that has been partially erased and then reused to copy a different work. But each of Lan's sub-versions is transmitted separately: A daughter painting is printed on a new canvas, creating a duplicate for reworking. Then Lan paints over the parts she no longer needs while leaving other parts visible. A layer of varnish evens out the surface of the painting so that the old merges with the new, the intentional with the accidental. As the director of the Ludwig Museum in Koblenz, Beate Reifenscheid, wrote of Lan's paintings: "In the end, the viewers of her artwork cannot distinguish between photography, print, and painted sections. Images and paintings are inextricably merged."[24]

24 Beate Reifenscheid, "Pedigree of Life – About Jiny Lan's Epic Painting," translated by W. G. Müller, *Chinese-European Post*, November 12, 2017;

The director of Helmhaus Zürich, Simon Maurer, describes Lan's mixed-media artworks as "Kombinationstiere" (combined animals).[25]

Each sub-version is a subsequent, but not a subordinate painting. It is not less valuable than or inferior to its ancestor. On the contrary, she has added to second-generation paintings the label "Mehrwertbewegung" (MWB) or "value-added movement."[26] In the world of Jinyology, art is always in flux, capable of reproducing itself or spawning progeny. Each sub-version preserves some aspects of its predecessor and erases others. It is, therefore, reactive and derivative, but at the same time generative, since it also anticipates the next version; different versions can exist in dialogue with each other. Each sub-version is self-contained and independent, but, when seen in its generational sequence, it gains meaning from its relationship with its predecessor. Thus, the meaning of a painting is always deferred along the chain of sub-versions.

Tiananmen Paintings as Political Manifestos (2013–14)

The last of the seven siblings in the second generation is *Value-Added Movement 7A* (2013, Fig. 2.8a). Elements of the Milan shopping mall and its glass dome are visible in the background amid spatters of white paint. The concave shape of the glass roof creates spatial depth in the paintings. Defying structural realism, two small female figures, representing the artist herself and a friend, are seen walking with an umbrella and a poncho. What appear to be paint pour and drip-splash techniques are indebted to the Chinese painting techniques of "broken-ink" (*po mo*) and "splashing colors" (*po cai*), represented par excellence by Chang Dai-chien (or Zhang Daqian), who was inspired by Western abstract expressionism.[27] Instead of splashing colors and ink on rice paper, Lan mixes water-soluble paints, acrylics, oil-soluble oil paints, and water, plus liquid kitchen cleaner (Fig. 2.7). When these pigments and liquids are splashed and sprayed onto a canvas, the ingredients cause unexpected chemical interactions and leave unpredictable traces. Although individual components of the composition have realistic references, their construction as a whole creates a dreamlike and surreal atmosphere. The water motif is autobiographically grounded not only in the rain during the Tiananmen Square protest in 1989 but also in Lan's childhood. Her mother told her

---

the German text is printed in *Jiny Lan: The World Is Sometimes Flat, Sometimes Round*, 7–9, here 7.

25 Maurer, "Das Kombinationstier / Combined Animals."

26 She later gave up labeling paintings MWB due to practical difficulties.

27 "'Splashed-color' landscape – Zhang Daqian," The Met, <https://www.metmuseum.org/art/collection/search/49805>.

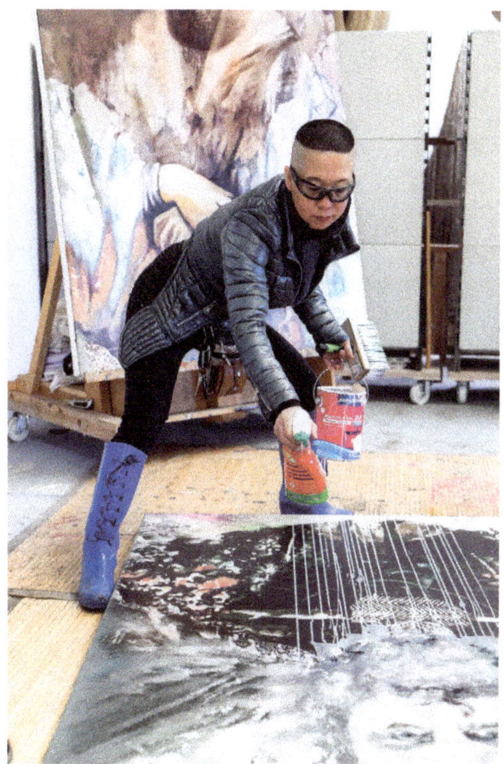

Fig. 2.7. Lan sprays liquid on her painting *Penck Solution* (=Fig 5.2b, 2019, photo: Sebastian Drüen).

about an incident that happened when she was a toddler: she fell into the water while tied to a stroller and nearly drowned. This partly explains her aquaphobia, but paradoxically she derives an indescribable pleasure from painting water, as if painting it had a therapeutic and redemptive function.

Value-Added Movement 7A begat numerous offspring. In the subversion *Feet of Heavenly Freedom* (2013, Fig. 2.8b), Lan makes a bold entrance by placing herself naked in the center of the painting, holding a helicopter that represents her desire to be flown to freedom. If she had remained in the clutches of the princeling, she would never have become the artist she wanted to be. The painting defies both spatial and temporal logic, depicting the artist herself twice, as a recumbent figure and as one of the women walking in the rain. Unlike classical reclining female nudes, who are typically posed lying sideways on a bed or divan, she lies at a revealing angle, legs crossed, in foreshortened perspective. Her two giant and blistered feet fill the center of the painting. In her pubic hair sits a naked man with his arms around his knees. The depiction of herself naked and floating captures the uncertainty and suspense of her life in Beijing before she emigrated.

While the location of *Feet of Heavenly Freedom* is only implied, the setting of its sub-version, *Place of Heavenly Freedom* (2013, Fig. 2.8c), is clear. For the first time, the Tiananmen Gate appears prominently in Lan's artwork, suggesting that this painting serves as a political manifesto. Tiananmen is depicted brightly in the center of this painting. Visitors walk toward the gate along a plaza in the rain. The naked, supine self-portrayal that filled the previous canvas is eclipsed by the Gate of Heavenly Peace, which now dominates the composition, leaving a disembodied foot in the foreground. The helicopter, however, is not faded in color like the rest of the self-image, indicating that the will to fly away remains as strong as before. The shining North Star, the beacon of hope and guidance, has been added in this sub-version. If *Feet of Heavenly Freedom* anticipates sexual freedom, *Place of Heavenly Freedom* expresses the desire for political freedom, individual and collective.

In the next versioning, *Prophezeiung* (Prophecy, 2014, Fig. 2.8d), only the disembodied foot remains visible on Tiananmen Square, and the rest of the self-portrayal has been covered by a translucent terrestrial globe and a cosmic backdrop, depicted in a purple tint. The striking placement of Tiananmen *within* a globe can be read in two ways. On the one hand, China desires to be incorporated on the world stage, particularly because of its forced isolation after the violence at Tiananmen in 1989. In the painting, the sky above Tiananmen is transformed into outer space and an upside-down astronaut, or taikonaut (from the word *taikong*, "outer space"), drifts by. By 2014, when the painting was made, China had launched its tenth manned spaceship, Shenzhou 9, with its first woman taikonaut, Liu Yang, on board in 2012; Shenzhou 10, carrying its second woman taikonaut, Wang Yaping, was launched in 2013. China had also launched three Chang-e spacecraft, named after the moon goddess Chang'e, into lunar orbit. To the right of the globe, fiber optic cables with Chinese labels represent high-speed internet and telecommunications technology. Chinese tech giants have rapidly built China into a country whose cutting-edge digital technologies challenge the United States.

On the other hand, with advances in telecommunications came the "Great Firewall" and digital censorship. Thus, the containment of Tiananmen within a sphere visualizes China's suffocating political atmosphere. The State Internet Information Office (SIIO), established in 2011 to regulate cyberspace security and internet content, keeps Chinese society in a bubble of censorship, making China one of the least free countries in the world.[28] The painting thus presents a jarring contrast between

28 In 2014, the SIIO was renamed the Cyberspace Administration of China (CAS). See Jamie P. Horsley, "Behind the Façade of China's Cyber

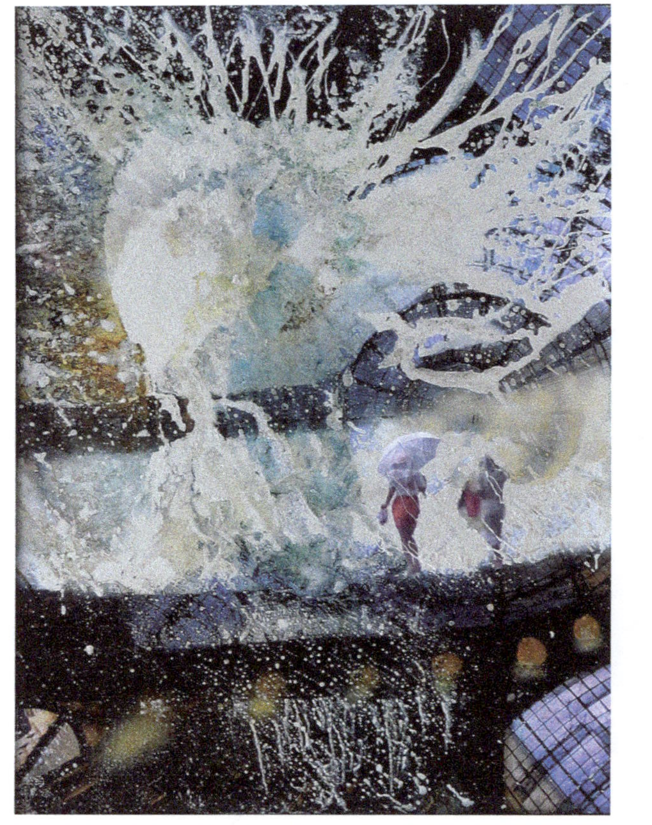

Fig. 2.8a. *Value-Added Movement 7A* (2013, 200 × 140 cm).

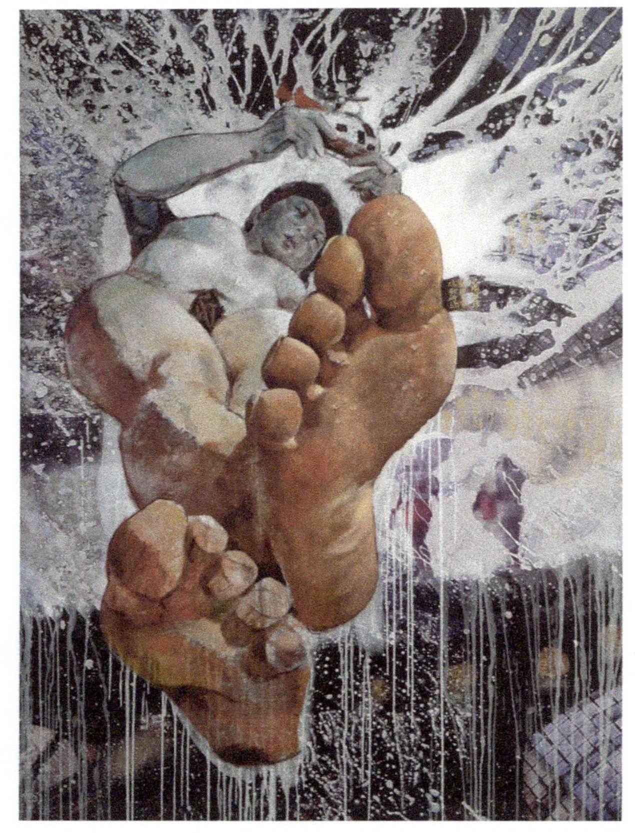

Fig. 2.8b. *Feet of Heavenly Freedom* (2013, 200 × 140 cm).

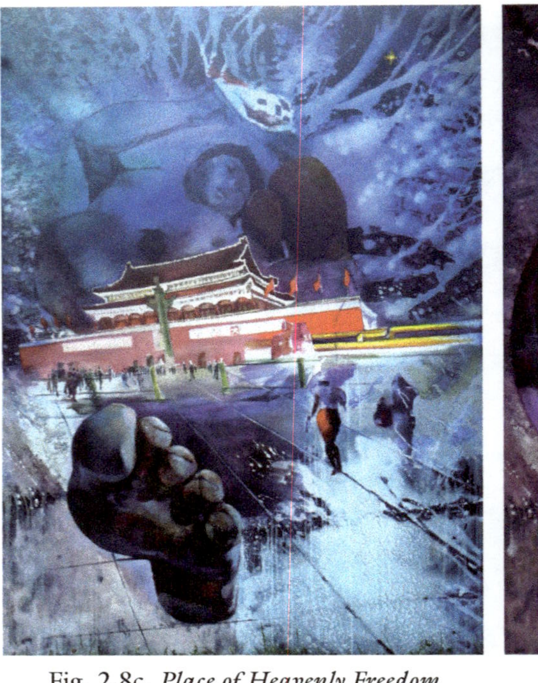

Fig. 2.8c. *Place of Heavenly Freedom* (2013, 200 × 140 cm).

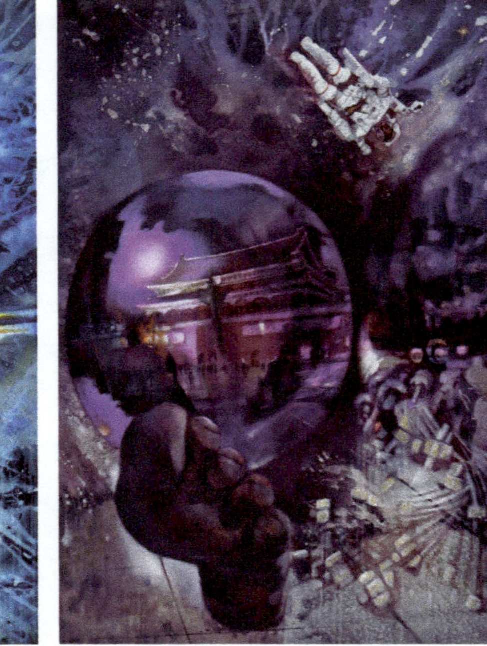

Fig. 2.8d. *Prophecy* (2014, 200 × 140 cm).

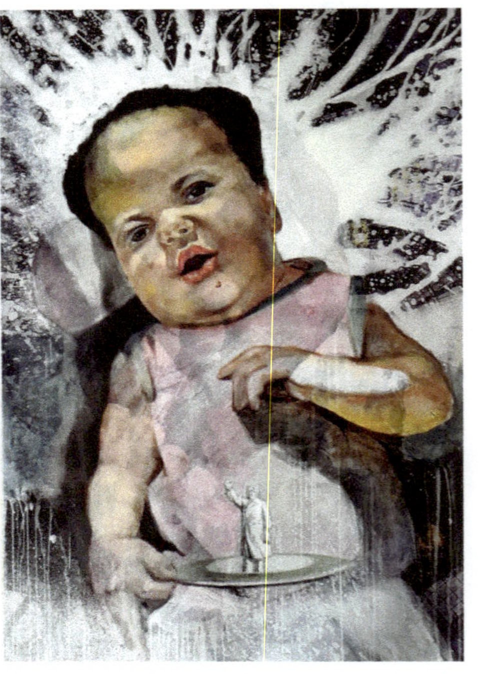

Fig. 2.8e. *Who Is the Ruler of This World?* (2017, 100 × 70 cm).

China's economic and technological ambitions on the world stage and its domestic political suppression. The transparent sphere also evokes the crystal ball of the Wicked Witch of the East in *The Wizard of Oz* (dir. Victor Fleming, 1939), which has the magical power to predict the future. What the sorceress Lan scries in the ball here is Tiananmen, a symbol of China's Communist rule and political illiberalism, making it a myopic and pessimistic prophecy, in fact a backward-looking prophecy. Yet the foot seems to be giving the boot to political and digital authoritarianism.

After Mao announced the founding of the PRC at Tiananmen, the Gate of Heavenly Peace, in 1949, it became a political symbol of Communist power in China.[29] Tiananmen has been a frequent motif in socialist realist and Maoist paintings, for example, Dong Xiwen's *The Founding Ceremony of the Nation* (original version in 1953) and Sun Zixi's *In Front of Tian'anmen* (1964). It is also a touchstone in post-Cultural Revolution art where avant-garde artists experiment with "counter images," in the words of the art historian Wu Hung, to "demystify this most sacred symbol of Communist China."[30] According to Wu, experimental artists "follow the basic strategy of political pop to invert Maoist symbolism while satirizing contemporary life."[31] Subversive artworks that attracted international attention to Chinese contemporary art include, to cite just a few, Yang Yiping's *The Square* (1987–88), Hung Liu's *Chinese Pietà* (1989), Wang Jinsong's *Taking a Picture in Front of Tiananmen* (1991), Zhao Bandi's *Listen to Me* (1992), Ai Weiwei's *June* (1994) and *Study of Perspective – Tiananmen* (1995), Song Dong's *Breathing* (1996), Wang Youshen's *News Paper: Tiananmen* (2001), and Yin Zhaoyang's *Tiananmen Square* (2004). This basic formula of countering official representations of Tiananmen is also reflected in Lan's work.

A 2017 descendant of *Prophecy* is *Who Is the Ruler of This World?* (2017, Fig. 2.8e), which depicts a giant infant boy in a pink garment holding a plate on which a miniature statue of Mao stands. The giant baby is recognizable as Mao from his facial features: a high forehead, receding hair, plump cheeks, and a mole on the chin.[32] The figurine on

---

Super-Regulator," DigiChina, Stanford University, August 8, 2022, <https://digichina.stanford.edu/work/behind-the-facade-of-chinas-cyber-super-regulator/>; Beina Xu and Elanor Albert, "Media Censorship in China," Council on Foreign Relations, February 17, 2017, <https://www.cfr.org/backgrounder/media-censorship-china>; "Freedom in the World," Freedom House, <https://freedomhouse.org/report/freedom-world>.

29 Wu, *Transience: Chinese Experimental Art*, 54–9; Wu, *Remaking Beijing*, especially 165–82.

30 Wu, *Transience: Chinese Experimental Art*, 54; Wu, *Remaking Beijing*, 183–324.

31 Wu, *Transience: Chinese Experimental Art*, 54.

32 Faye Yan Zhang, "Portraits of Mao," *The Harvard Advocate* 149, no. 3 (2014), <https://theharvardadvocate.com/content/portraits-of-mao>.

the plate is also unmistakably Mao. After an oversized statue of Mao waving his right arm was built at Tsinghua University in Beijing at the start of the Cultural Revolution, similar statues sprouted across the nation until Mao himself called a halt in 1970.[33]

The phrase "giant infant," referring to an adult whose psychological age remains that of a baby, became an internet buzzword after the publication of psychologist Wu Zhihong's *Nation of Giant Infants* (*Ju ying guo*, 2016). The bestseller was soon censored in China for likening the Chinese "national character" to that of a giant infant.[34] Wu was writing about familial and social issues, but Lan's painting leans toward a political and ideological application of the term. Her impetus was the firing of Bi Fujian, once a famous television celebrity employed by the state broadcaster, CCTV. After he insulted the memory of Mao at a private dinner party in 2015, calling him the "motherf---er who has ruined us all,"[35] he was swiftly taken off the air. His punishment sent a shock wave through society, warning that even private criticism of Mao was forbidden, and the fear of denunciation increased.

The title "Who Is the Ruler of This World?" was inspired by a line in Mao's own poem "Changsha": "I ask the huge greenblue earth, / Who is master of nature?" (*Wen cangmang dadi, shei zhu chenfu?*).[36] The Chinese text expresses far more ambitious aspirations than the English translation conveys. Writing in 1925, Mao was deliberating who should become the master of the vast land, meaning China, or even the world, as reflected in Lan's title. Mao masterfully transformed himself into a supreme leader in China and attracted worldwide admirers. Lan stated: "Mao's ghost is still haunting China. The biggest problem is that China has been afraid to confront Mao. But I am most angry that the international discourse is ambivalent about Mao. Mao has not been treated as an evil monster like Hitler or Stalin."

33 侯艺兵 Hou Yibing, 第一尊毛主席塑像是怎样诞生的 [How the First Statue of Chairman Mao Came About], *Sina*, December 7, 2003; 第一座毛主席像修建:引发各地争相修建热潮 [The First Statue of Chairman Mao Was Built: It Triggered a Rush to Build It Across the Country], *Phoenix*, December 31, 2009.

34 高雨莘 Gao Yuxin, "China's 'Giant Infants,'" *New York Times*, August 9, 2017, <https://cn.nytimes.com/opinion/20170809/china-millennials-tiger-mothers-giant-infants/zh-hant/dual/>.

35 "China TV Anchor Bi Fujian To Be Punished for Mao Insult," *BBC*, August 10, 2015; "Chinese TV Host To Be Punished for Insulting Chairman Mao," *CBS*, August 10, 2015.

36 Mao Zedong, "Changsha" [沁园春·长沙 *Qin Yuan Chun: Changsha*], in *The Poems of Mao Zedong*, trans. Willis Barnstone (Berkeley: University of California Press, 2008), 31.

Red Sun's Sub-Versions: *The Collar* (2017) and *Progressive Lenses* (2017)

Red Sun, created in 2012, was retroactively adopted into a versioning. It became a predecessor of *Kragen* (The Collar, 2017, Fig. 2.9a). These two paintings, made five years apart, share few similarities besides the layout and a ghostly central figure. However, while the majority of *Red Sun* has been overpainted in *The Collar*, two small figures in the lower right corner – one woman in a yellow and black striped skirt and another in a long red skirt – are, like their congeners in *Red Sun*, a pastiche of the famous Mao poster *Chairman Mao Is the Red Sun in the Hearts of the People of the World* (1967, Fig. 2.1a). *The Collar* features a large (male) torso wearing a collared shirt and a Western-style suit jacket. This headless figure rises from a mountain range that blends the Yellow River Grand Canyon in China and the Alps. The original German title of the painting, "Kragen," literally means "collar." At first glance, this is a descriptive title that captures only a small detail of the painting. However, Lan was alluding to the Chinese phrase *lingxiu*, which literally means "collar and sleeves" and metonymically "the supreme leader." When Chinese people hear the word *lingxiu*, they immediately associate it with Mao.

The sunflowers in front of the suited figure recall Chinese propaganda posters that depict Mao as the sun and the people as sunflowers turning toward him, for example in *Chairman Mao Is the Reddest, the Reddest, Red Sun in Our Heart* (1967).[37] Ai Weiwei's *Sunflower Seeds* (2010) also uses this trope to signify both the conformity and the power of the Chinese people. Thus, this ethereal and surreal collage, *The Collar*, is, in fact, another portrait of Mao in disguise. The sartorial title, however, conceals the painting's political nature and makes the artwork innocuous in the censor's eye.

In an act of *Selbstverfraulichung* (woman's self-aggrandization, see introduction and chapter 4), Lan inserted herself into the world's most famous painting – da Vinci's *Mona Lisa* (1503–19) – to create *Progressive Lenses* (2017, Fig. 2.9b), which is a sub-version of *The Collar*. The debt to the *Mona Lisa* is most recognizable in the posture and folded hands of the subject. The painting's title refers to both the eyeglasses Lan wears and her forward-looking perspective. This faceless sub-version suggests anonymity and obscurity. It parodies the political art of the Cultural Revolution, which centered and magnified the cult figure. The self-non-portrait fuses the implied Mao from *The Collar* with Mona Lisa, thus conjoining politics and art, East and West, man and woman. Since both Mao

37 Anonymous, 敬祝毛主席万寿无疆 [*Respectfully Wish Chairman Mao Eternal Life*], 1968. Call nr. BG E13/549, Landsberger collection, <https://chineseposters.net/posters/e13-549>.

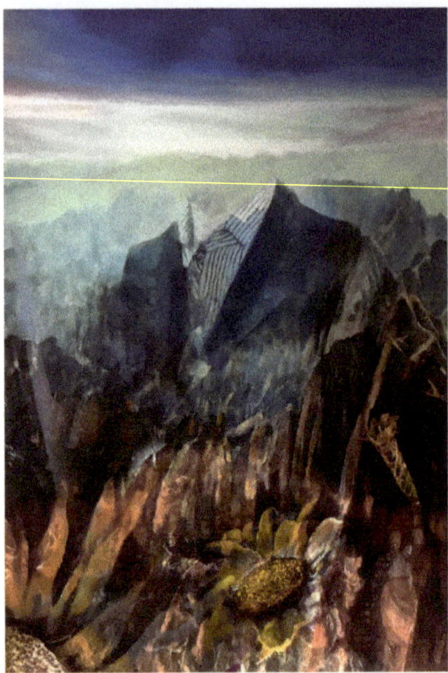

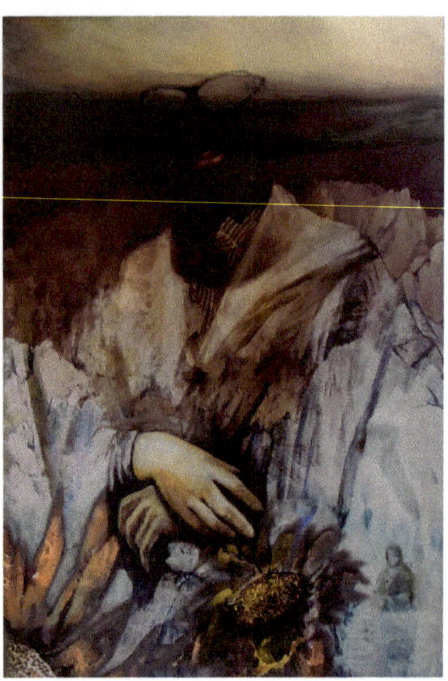

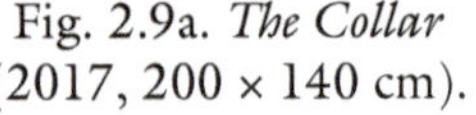

Fig. 2.9a. *The Collar* (2017, 200 × 140 cm).

Fig. 2.9b. *Progressive Lenses* (2017, 200 × 140 cm).

and Mona Lisa have been deified and glorified, each in their own way, the artist's self-inscription aligns with her concept of self-exaltation. She has effaced herself from this version except for her glasses and painted lips. But the collar, the sunflowers, and the faintly visible female figures in the lower right corner, common to both paintings, clearly indicate the connection between this disguised self-portrait and *The Collar*. Like *Red Sun*, her painting of Angela Merkel, *Die Krone* (The Crown, 2018), discussed in chapter 7, is another sub-version of the same Maoist cult poster. Thus, even the portrayal of Merkel, long-time leader of the free world, is linked to Mao iconographies. The artist takes an exaggerated approach, asking whether Merkel, too, resembles an authoritarian leader.

Artistic Influences from Political Pop and Narrative Figuration

Mao's image was not only ubiquitous during his own lifetime but has been obsessively appropriated and reappropriated by avant-garde and Political Pop artists in China as well as by Western artists, most prominently the American Pop artist Andy Warhol and the Icelandic Narrative Figuration artist Erró. The emergency of Political Pop in the early 1990s was a resigned but creative reaction to the violence at Tiananmen in 1989 and the subsequent political repression. Curator Chang Tsong-zung wrote about the sociohistorical conditions under which Political Pop emerged: "In shock, artists came to a sudden realization of their impotence in the face of real politics. The idealism and utopian enthusiasm so typical of new art in the 1980s met its nemesis in the gun barrels of Tian'anmen."[38] Chang and Li Xianting co-curated *China's New Art Post-1989* in Hong Kong from January 31 to February 25, 1993, and the exhibition went on an international tour under a new title, *Mao Goes Pop: China Post-1989*. According to Li, the nucleus of the Political Pop movement consists of artists from the '85 New Wave movement who "adopted a deconstructionist approach matched to a Pop technique, to execute works of comic satire which illustrate their view of influential political figures, particularly Mao, and major political events."[39] The major exhibition of the works of American Pop artist Robert Rauschenberg in Beijing in 1985 had an enormous impact on young artists.[40] The art critic Oscar Ho Hing-Kay points out that Political Pop shows fascination for popular culture, capitalism, and consumerism, but "ironically it is also nostalgic about the ideals, if not the reality, of the Cultural Revolution era," which is why stylistically Political Pop borrows a whole range of "red, bright, and shining" images from the Cultural Revolution era.[41]

The roster of Political Pop artists is long. Wang Guangyi, who came to fame with his Mao images in the *Black and Red Reason* paintings (1987), is a representative figure. In his *Great Criticism* series (1990–2007), he merged and juxtaposed Chinese communist propaganda posters and Western commercial logos to capture the duality of China's hybrid model of a capitalist economy and one-party rule. Qi Zhilong's portraits of young Chinese beauties in the *Consumer Icons* series (1994–) and *Chinese Girl* series (2002–) draw on iconographies of the Cultural Revolution. The Luo brothers' *Welcome the World Famous Brand* (1999) adapts Chinese New Year calendar art but inserts famous Western brands, such as McDonald's sandwiches. Li Xianting points to Ai Weiwei's pioneering role in Political Pop: "If we say that Chinese art after 1989 took Mao into the realm of Pop as a kind of necessity, then we must see Ai Weiwei's Mao

38 Chang Tsong-zung, "Into the Nineties," in *China's New Art Post-1989: With a Retrospective from 1979–1989* (Hong Kong: Hanart T Z Gallery, 1993), i–vii, here i.

39 Li Xianting, "Major Trends in the Development of Contemporary Chinese Art," in *China's New Art Post-1989*, x–xxii, here xx.

40 Li, "Major Trends in the Development of Contemporary Chinese Art," xxi.

41 Oscar Ho Hing-Kay, "1989 and New Art Post-1989," in *China's New Art Post-1989*, viii–ix, here ix.

series from around 1985 as opening that pathway."[42] Already a member of the Stars, Ai was inspired by Warhol's silkscreens from 1972 and created *Mao in Triptych* (1985), *Mao (Facing Right)* (1986), *Mao (Facing Forward)* (1986), and *Untitled (Three Leaders)* (1989).[43] Later, in the LEGO bricks project *Traces Left on Mao's Portrait* (2019), Ai retraced the paint splatters left on Mao's portrait by the three young protestors in 1989, without showing the portrait itself.[44] Yu Youhan made Mao his favorite subject and combined famous Mao photos with folk art in the fashion of Political Pop. The artist brothers Gao Zhen and Gao Qiang created many works critical of the Cultural Revolution and Mao, such as *Miss Mao* (2006) and *Mao's Guilt* (2009). Numerous other Chinese artists have taken up motifs of the Cultural Revolution in their work, including Wang Keping's wood carvings *Long Live!* (1978), *Silence* (1978), and *Idol* (1979); Xu Yihui's *Little Red Book* series (1994–); Yu Hong's *Witness to Growth* (1999–); Li Shan's *Rouge Series* (1989–); Huang Rui's *Chairman Mao 10,000 RMB* (2008); and Wang Ziwei's numerous Mao portraits. Political Pop was the first contemporary art style from China that was embraced by Western collectors and curators, who helped to make some artists millionaires and international celebrities.[45]

Many Western artists portrayed Mao as well, including Andy Warhol, Erró, Gerhard Richter, and Sigmar Polke. Warhol started creating Mao images in 1972, inspired by Nixon's historic visit to China. His Mao paintings show the dictator wearing lipstick and eye shadow, typical of Warhol's portraiture. Warhol made approximately two thousand Mao portraits in all sizes and prices, to make them affordable for anyone. As Arthur Danto writes: "What Warhol had managed to do was to detoxify one of the most frightening political images of the time."[46] Erró painted the collage series *Chinese Paintings* between 1972 and 1980 during the golden decade of Maoism in Iceland. Erró depicts Mao as a world traveler by appropriating Chinese propaganda posters of Mao and placing them at well-known tourist sites such as Oslo's City Hall, the Piazza San Marco in Venice, the Empire State Building, and Piccadilly Circus. In reality, Mao only traveled abroad twice, both times to Moscow. Erró's *Chinese Paintings* were first exhibited in 1975 in Lucerne, Switzerland, and toured Europe; the catalogue was a parody of Mao's *Little Red Book*.[47]

42 Li, "The Stars: The Flag-Bearers of Chinese Modern Art," 259.

43 Dieter Buchhart, Elsy Lahner, and Klaus Albrecht Schröder, *Ai Weiwei: In Search of Humanity* (Munich: Hirmer Verlag, 2022), 60–5.

44 Buchhart, Lahner, and Schröder, *Ai Weiwei: In Search of Humanity*, 88.

45 Wu, *Remaking Beijing*, 202.

46 Arthur C. Danto, *Andy Warhol* (New Haven, CT: Yale University Press, 2009), 113.

47 Paul Saba and Sam Richards, eds., "Erro: Mao's World Tour," *Encyclopedia of Anti-Revisionism On-Line*, October 8, 2019, <https://woodsmokeblog.wordpress.com/2019/10/08/erro-maos-world-tour/>; Andrews, *Painters*

Together with the French visual artist Gérard Fromanger, Erró belonged to the Narrative Figuration movement in the 1960s and early 1970s. Narrative Figuration is not as well-known as some other Western art movements, but the art historian Sarah Wilson points out that Chinese Political Pop artists cited the Narrative Figuration movement as an inspiration: "The link between the [Narrative Figurative] movement (whose images had long been plundered on the internet) and contemporary Chinese painting (like that of Zhang Xiaogang's *Bloodline* series, now fetching millions of dollars) was … explicitly avowed by the Chinese."[48] Zhang Xiaogang's *Bloodline: Big Family* series (1995), for example, recalls Fromanger's photorealistic paintings with red silhouettes.

Narrative Figuration provides a useful context for viewing Lan's work. In 1964, the French art critic Gérald Gassiot-Talabot organized the *Mythologies quotidiennes* (Everyday Mythologies) exhibition, which effectively defined the movement, featuring works by thirty-four artists. These artists rebelled against abstract art, which had been a powerful presence on the international art scene since WWII, and advocated for a new form of figurative composition utilizing images and objects from contemporary society.[49] Gassiot-Talabot explained that Narrative Figuration came about partly as a reaction to American Pop art: "Warhol and his peers force us to make a radical revision of the criteria for esthetic enjoyment inasmuch as they affirm with often delightful cynicism, a conceptual and technical laziness that makes them prefer the means of automatic reproduction to the vagaries and fatigue of the traditional profession."[50] Many Narrative Figuration artists recognized the potential of using pre-existing images in their own work.[51] Jean-Paul Ameline reports:

> The similarities that connect the various figurative trends emerging in Europe and the United States during the 1960s are easily discernible: first, their extensive use of mechanically manufactured images – posters, photographs, comics, art reproductions – making them the source material for the work; secondly, pictorial formatting, through its projection with an episcope and transposition onto canvas, its

---

and Politics in the PRC, 314–42; Sarah Wilson, *The Visual World of French Theory: Figurations* (New Haven, CT: Yale University Press, 2010), 2–3. I thank Joachim Wintzer for helping me identify the Palais des Nations in Genf and Oslo's City Hall.

48 Wilson, *The Visual World of French Theory*, 4.

49 See Jean-Paul Ameline, "Figures and Fictions: The Contribution of Narrative Figuration to the Figurative Revival of the 1960s in Europe," in *The Narrative Figuration*, ed. Jean-Paul Ameline (Milan: 5 Continents Editions, 2017), 10–21, esp. 10, 11, 14.

50 Ameline, "Figures and Fictions," 14.

51 Gauthier, "The Ambivalence of Images: Notes on Pop Figuration," in *The Narrative Figuration*, 24–31, here 28.

> enlargement, cropping, and colourization, as well as possible juxtaposition with other images, or even assemblage. This set of operations of course presupposes some iconographical choices.[52]

Similar operations of reproduction and transposition are essential to Jinyology, the chief difference being that the pre-existing images Lan utilizes are primarily her own paintings.

Like Narrative Figuration artists, she rejects abstract and minimalist art. Her art training in China prepared her to be a painter of figurative and concrete subjects, rooted in realism. Her canvases are crowded, as she tries to maximize the use of the space. On a number of occasions, she has stated: "Minimalismus ist ein Luxus, den ich mir bisher noch nicht leisten kann" (Minimalism is a luxury that I cannot yet afford).[53] But she distills these different subjects or themes, often from both Eastern and Western cultural traditions, to an abstract level through a fragmentary and constructivist collage style that is well suited to her concept of Jinyology. The patchwork composition allows her to handily execute new versionings. It gives her the freedom to move her pieces strategically like a chess player and include ideas that may be contradictory, ambiguous, or dialectical. Her work is peppered with intertextual, cross-cultural references, quotations, and parodies. Like Pop and Narrative Figuration artists, she engages in the "practice of the reprise, the quotation, of playing around with earlier works."[54]

Ameline describes Narrative Figuration as committed art. The leftist artists actively contributed to the 1968 movement in France and opposed the Vietnam War. A handful of these artists were affiliates of specific Communist or Maoist groupings.[55] In the 1960s and 1970s, many Western leftist intellectuals had a rosy picture of the mass revolution in China and greeted Maoism as an alternative to Soviet revisionism and American imperialism.[56] The relationship between Mao's China

52 Ameline, "Figures and Fictions," 16.

53 See, e.g., "Hochdotierter Kunstpreis Löwe von Weilburg geht 2023 an Jiny Lan: Presseeinladung zur Preisverleihung am 17. Dezember 2023 im Rosenhang Museum in Weilburg an der Lahn," Pressetext, November 30, 2023, <https://www.pressetext.com/news/hochdotierter-kunstpreis-l-we-von-weilburg-geht-2023-an-jiny-lan.html>.

54 Gauthier, "The Ambivalence of Images," 29.

55 Wilson, *The Visual World of French Theory*, 6–8; "Gérard Fromanger, leading light of Narrative Figuration painting, 1939–2021," *Art Review*, June 21, 2021, <https://artreview.com/gerard-fromanger-leading-light-of-narrative-figuration-painting-1939-2021/>.

56 See, for example, Richard Wolin, *The Wind from the East: French Intellectuals, the Cultural Revolution, and the Legacy of the 1960s* (Princeton, NJ: Princeton University Press, 2010); Sebastian Gehrig, Barbara Mittler, and Felix Wemheuer,

and Khrushchev's Soviet Union deteriorated around the beginning of the 1960s. Mao was seen as a true, uncompromising revolutionary against imperialism, whereas Khrushchev with his policy of peaceful coexistence became a "traitor" to communism. Although the Narrative Figuration movement emerged at the time of Mao's Cultural Revolution, their art drastically differed from the Red Guard type of personality cult art in China. Most contemporary Chinese artists, especially those who live overseas in voluntary or forced exile, hold a very critical view of Mao. They remain acutely aware of the baneful and crippling – or "castrating" – effect that communist dictatorship has had on the nation and its people.[57]

Coda: Tradition and Innovation

Born in 1970, Lan was six years old when the Cultural Revolution ended. However, Mao's legacy continued to dominate Chinese politics, and the aesthetics of the Cultural Revolution left indelible traces in her work, including her Lei Feng painting, the "Mao-imposters," and the Tiananmen paintings. Her artistic creation resembles that of Political Pop, American Pop art, and Narrative Figuration in appropriating iconographic material and preexisting images. She uses Cultural Revolution posters, photographs, comics, and reproductions of Western art as source material. What is noticeably different is that she also appropriates her own paintings and has developed her personal guiding concept: Jinyology. Similar to the Narrative Figuration artists, her art is socially and politically committed. But Narrative Figuration artists were anti-capitalists and hostile to the commercial art market.[58] Here she resembles more the Political Pop artists and considers success on the art market part of her feminist agenda, to be discussed in chapter 5.

---

eds, *Kulturrevolution als Vorbild?: Maoismen im deutschsprachigen Raum* (Frankfurt am Main: Peter Lang, 2008).

57 To borrow Wolf Biermann's critique of Mao and the East German regime in "In China hinter der Mauer" [In China behind the Wall, 1966], in *Für meine Genossen: Hetzlieder, Balladen, Gedichte* (Berlin: Verlag Klaus Wagenbach, 1972), 76–8. The song itself, released on Biermann's 1973 album, *aah-ja!*, can be heard here: <https://www.youtube.com/watch?v=4JSO5dAa_bk>.

58 "Artist Interview: Gérard Fromanger," Tate, September 2015, <https://www.tate.org.uk/whats-on/tate-modern/world-goes-pop/artist-interview/gerard-fromanger>.

Part Two

Feminist Art

3: The Bald Girls: Feminist Visual and Performance Art

Although there have been other groups of women artists in China as well as artists who self-identify as feminist, the Bald Girls was the first feminist artist collective formed in China.[1] How come a feminist art group did not exist in China until 2012? The answer has to do not only with traditional patriarchy, but also with socialist patriarchy. Reflecting on women's visual art in contemporary China, art historian Shuqin Cui explained why Chinese women artists were reluctant to designate their art as feminist:

> Since the 1990s, Chinese women have approached art as an individual endeavor and artistic experiment that cannot be defined categorically as feminist. In a society where a totalitarian political system and capital-driven market economy dictate the ideology and control the material resources, women in art face various challenges. For someone striving to survive as an artist and have her works recognized, raising the banner of feminism would invite a further push toward the social-cultural periphery.[2]

1 Li Xinmo wrote that since Xiao Lu fired two shots at the *China/Avant-Garde* exhibition in 1989, feminist artists have gradually entered the art scene in China. The list includes He Chengyao, Chen Lingyang, Xiang Jing, Cui Xiuwen and many others. See Li, "中国女权运动与女性主义艺术发展历程," in *Bald Girls: Three Feminist Artists' Exhibit*, 152–3; its English translation, "History of Feminism and Feminist Art in China," appears on 154–5; Luise Guest, "'Space Invaders': Discourses of Gender in Contemporary Chinese Art," in *Stepping Out!*, 27–31; Mei-yin Leung, *The Chinese Women's Calligraphy and Painting Society: The First Women's Art Society in Modern China* (Hong Kong: University of Hong Kong Press, 2005); Doris Sung, "Chinese Women Artists in the Early Twentieth Century," *AWARE (Archives of Women Artists Research & Exhibitions)*, October 12, 2021, <https://awarewomenartists.com/en/magazine/artistes-chinoises-du-debut-du-xxe-siecle/>. In 1998 the Women's Museum in Bonn hosted a rare exhibition dedicated to contemporary art by women from the PRC, *Die Hälfte des Himmels: Chinesische Künstlerinnen der Gegenwart* (Half of the Sky: Contemporary Chinese Women Artists). See Christina Penetsdorfer, "Walking on the Great Wall," in *Stepping Out!*, 36–9, here 36.

2 Cui, *Gendered Bodies*, 194.

Writing about "structural sexism" in China and the marginalization of female artists, Christina Penetsdorfer observes the same reservation toward the term "feminist": "Indeed, most female artists distance themselves from being referred to as such, or even report that they feel annoyed by it."[3] She traces the reasons for this aversion back to the state-decreed "equality" of the genders as suggested by Mao's dictum: "Women hold up half the sky." After Mao's death, according to Penetsdorfer, women have refrained from claiming rights for themselves based on their gender or sex; they doubt that feminism offers a solution to a nondemocratic society that does not safeguard basic human rights.

A look at the relationship between socialism and feminism in the German Democratic Republic (GDR) could further shed light on the lack of feminist aspirations in China. GDR official rhetoric proclaimed that women's emancipation had been achieved.[4] This bogus claim had its origin in the Marxist belief that "the woman question" had been solved by the success of the proletarian revolution, and thus a separate women's movement was not necessary in a socialist country. Karl Marx, Friedrich Engels, and August Bebel regarded the feminist demand for equality as essentially bourgeois.[5] Rosa Luxemburg, co-founder of the German Communist Party (KPD), shared their opinion.[6] Clara Zetkin, the leader of the proletarian women's movement in Germany, concurred: "The place of the working-class woman, the Marxists insisted, was beside the man of her class, not beside the women of other classes."[7] The dominant perception of feminism in the GDR was that it is inevitably bourgeois, separatist, and antagonistic toward men, including working-class men, and thus divisive of the proletariat. In socialist countries, even women whose ideas are essentially feminist generally refuse to be identified as such. Thus, it is not surprising that Chinese women eschew feminism.

In the West, the traditional leftist attitude toward gender as a secondary conflict aggravated women with a feminist consciousness. It was precisely the prioritization of class over sex that motivated a group of incensed and frustrated women activists to break away from the New Left in 1968, catalyzing the birth of second-wave feminism. Even within the women's movement itself, radical feminists and politicos dispute whether they should operate within the framework of the revolutionary leftist movement; as Alice Echols, a professor of gender and sexuality studies,

3 Penetsdorfer, "Walking on the Great Wall," 37.

4 Herta Kuhrig, *Die Gleichberechtigung der Frauen in der Deutschen Demokratischen Republik*. Schriften des DDR-Komitees für Menschenrechte 5 (Berlin: DDR-Komitee für Menschenrechte, 1973), 108.

5 Beatrice Farnsworth, *Aleksandra Kollontai: Socialism, Feminism, and the Bolshevik Revolution* (Stanford, CA: Stanford University Press, 1980), 2.

6 Farnsworth, *Aleksandra Kollontai*, 184.

7 Farnsworth, *Aleksandra Kollontai*, 2.

puts it: "Is the enemy capitalism or men?"[8] The right to abortion, recognition of housework as work, equal pay for equal work, and sexual emancipation are some major feminist concerns.[9]

In China, Xiang Jingyu, the first leader of the Ministry of Women in the CCP, "criticized feminist groups and ideologies as individualistic when they aspired to the Western bourgeois family."[10] In her feminist account of women's emancipation in China, Julia Kristeva documents Chinese women's liberation from the feudal-patriarchal clan by Mao's revolution; nonetheless, the same subjugation of the feminist cause to the revolutionary cause that characterized Western socialism held true for China as well. Following the instruction of the Third International in Moscow, Chinese women communists had to "dissociate themselves from the women's rights movement in which most of them have participated, to defer the feminist cause to the revolutionary cause, and await the resolution of women's problems as an automatic result of the social-political transformation envisaged by the Party."[11] Thus the self-designation of the Bald Girls as a feminist art collective was an anomaly in China. Because Xu, the group's curator, and Jiny Lan were based in Germany, their exposure to Western feminism made them less susceptible to socialist reservations toward feminism. In an interview, Xu pointed out the difference between the Bald Girls and women artists in China:

> The Bald Girls explicitly mention women's rights, which is very different from "women's art" in China. Even in exhibitions of Chinese female artists abroad, none of them explicitly mentioned women's rights and included women's rights in human rights as the Bald Girls did. In 1998, the Frauenmuseum (Women's Museum) in Bonn held an exhibition of Chinese women artists entitled "Women Can Hold Up Half the Sky." This exhibition still focused on women's own psychological feelings, but did not show women's issues from the perspective of politics, culture, and society, and thus lacked a clear sense of female subjectivity.[12]

8 Alice Echols, *Daring to be BAD: Radical Feminism in America, 1967–1975* (Minneapolis: University of Minnesota Press, 1989), 104.

9 Ute Frevert, *Women in German History: From Bourgeois Emancipation to Sexual Liberation* (Oxford: Berg, 1989).

10 Julia Kristeva, *About Chinese Women*, trans. Anita Barrows (New York: Urizen Books, 1977), 114.

11 Kristeva, *About Chinese Women*, 112.

12 See Xu's interview with Bai Yilan, 白一岚, 关于<秃头戈女>的一次访谈 [An Interview about the "Bald Girls"], 画廊网 *Hua lang wang*, April 21, 2014, <http://www.hualangnet.com/?act=app&appid=17&mid=11095&p=view>.

Instead of "a clear sense of female subjectivity," I suggest that what women artists in China lack is political subjectivity or agency. In this chapter, I will analyze Lan's major artistic contributions to the Bald Girls collective, including feminist paintings, performances, and installations.

Half Oranges as Feminist Symbols and the Canceled Performance of *Chinese Apple*

In 2011, Lan modified a few earlier paintings by adding a half orange before the exhibition at Galerie Petra Nostheide-Eycke in Düsseldorf.[13] In *Self-Portrait* (1997–2011, Fig. 3.1a), the artist is seated against a bluish-white background and rests a palette on her leg while raising a paintbrush with her left hand. An orange and a half orange cover her right and left eyes.

In *The Chinese Glass Eye* (1998–2011, Fig. 3.1b), an orange sits squarely in the right eye socket of a woman who holds an eyeball in her left hand. In the self-portrait *Bathing Addition* (2011, Fig. 3.1c), a half orange covers the front of Lan's head. Upon closer inspection, the face is visible through the "panes" of the orange as if she were wearing a diver's mask, suggesting that the orange serves as a lens for viewing the world.

Half oranges, which are also featured in *Red Sun, Black Moon*, hold a personal significance for Lan. The German word for orange is *Apfelsine*, literally "apple from China," since the Europeans brought oranges from China to Europe – an etymology that is reflected in a number of Central and Northern European languages. Apples are associated with Eve and Adam's sin in the Garden of Eden and the tradition of misogyny in Western culture. But in China, too, sexism and misogyny have persisted for thousands of years. So Lan adopted the "apple from China" for her feminist art. She explained that by cutting the orange in half, she symbolically gives half of the responsibility for the primeval sin to men. Hence, half oranges are a feminist symbol in her work.

At the opening of the first Bald Girls Exhibition, the banning of *Red Sun* made the museum director so nervous that he canceled the performance of Lan's project *Chinese Apple* (2012). The project called for Lan's husband Roidl to cut oranges in half and hand them out to audience members in a pretend Garden of Eden. Roidl/Adam was to wear a mask made from a photo of Lan/Eve's face, indicating that he represents both man and woman.[14]

13 "Galerie Nostheide-Eycke präsentiert Jiny Lan," *Rheinische Post*, January 6, 2012, <https://rp-online.de/nrw/galerie-nostheide-eycke-praesentiert-jiny-lan_aid-13846565>.

14 Juan Xu, "Art Vision and Authenticity: Lan Jiny, Avant-Garde Jovial Feminist Artist," in *Bald Girls: Three Feminist Artists' Exhibit*, 42–8, here 45.

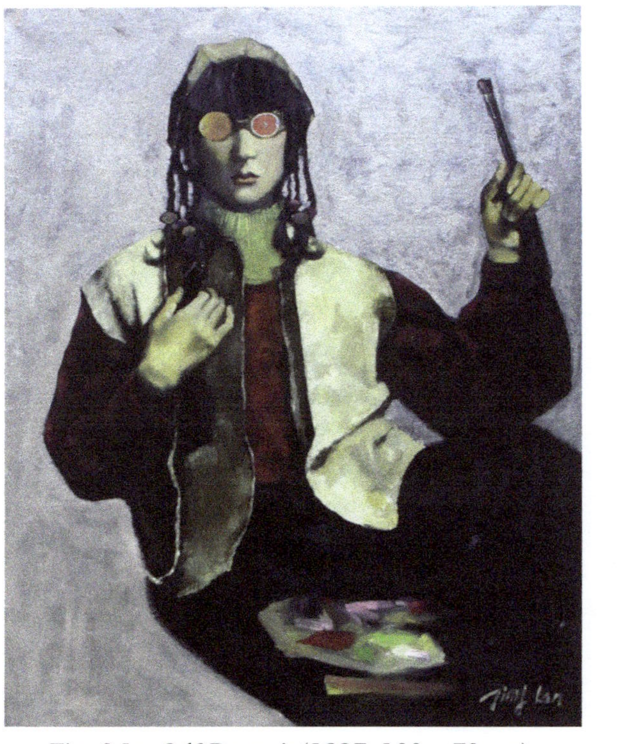

Fig. 3.1a. *Self-Portrait* (1997, 100 × 70 cm).

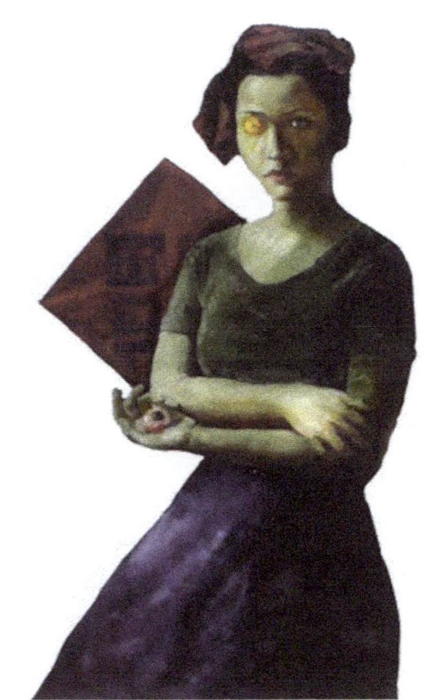

Fig. 3.1b. *The Chinese Glass Eye* (1998–2011, 120 × 80 cm).

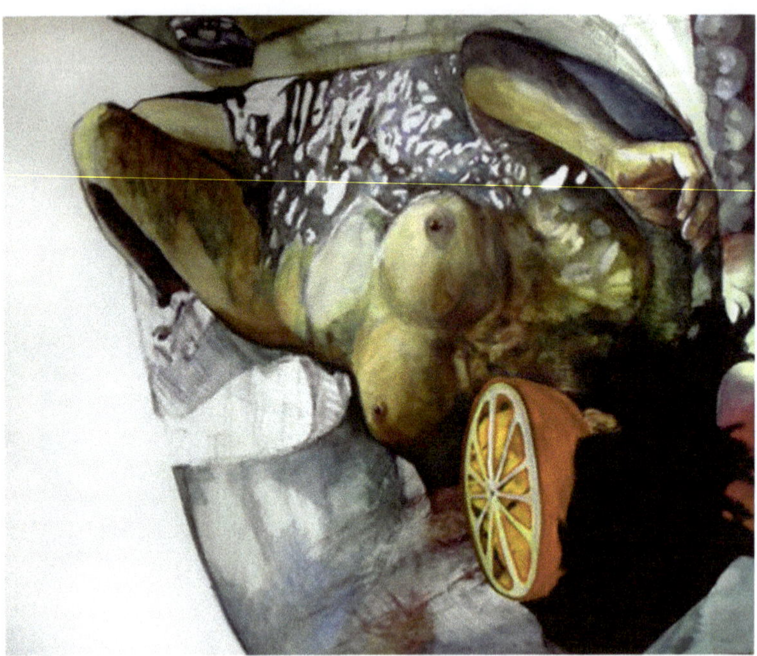

Fig. 3.1c. *Bathing Addition* (2011, 150 × 180 cm).

It was not Roidl's symbolically laden fruit that forced the cancellation of *Chinese Apple*, however. Rather, as a resident of Eden, he would appear unclothed before the audience (Fig. 3.2). Nudity has always touched a sensitive nerve in Chinese society, let alone full-frontal male nudity in public. While nudity is rarely depicted in traditional Chinese painting, art historian Amanda Wangwright demonstrates the prevalence of the female nude in the early twentieth century: "For Republican-period female artists who chose to work in modernist styles, painting the female nude was the norm."[15] The female nudes of Pan Yuliang (1895–1977) are especially well known.[16] Shortly before the Cultural Revolution, however, Culture Ministry officials banned the drawing of nude models in the academy – a ban that lasted until 1977.[17] *The Grand Exhibition of Figure Painting*, held in 1988 at the National Art Museum in Beijing, was the first show dedicated exclusively to the nude subject since the Cultural Revolution. The exhibition marked a shift in the cultural status of figurative art.[18] Thus when Lan was attending college and the art academy in Hangzhou,

15 Amanda Wangwright, *The Golden Key: Modern Women Artists and Gender Negotiations in Republican China (1911–1949)* (Leiden: Brill, 2021), 70.

16 Wangwright, *The Golden Key*, 60–75.

17 Andrews, *Painters and Politics in the PRC*, 392.

18 Cui, *Gendered Bodies*, 50.

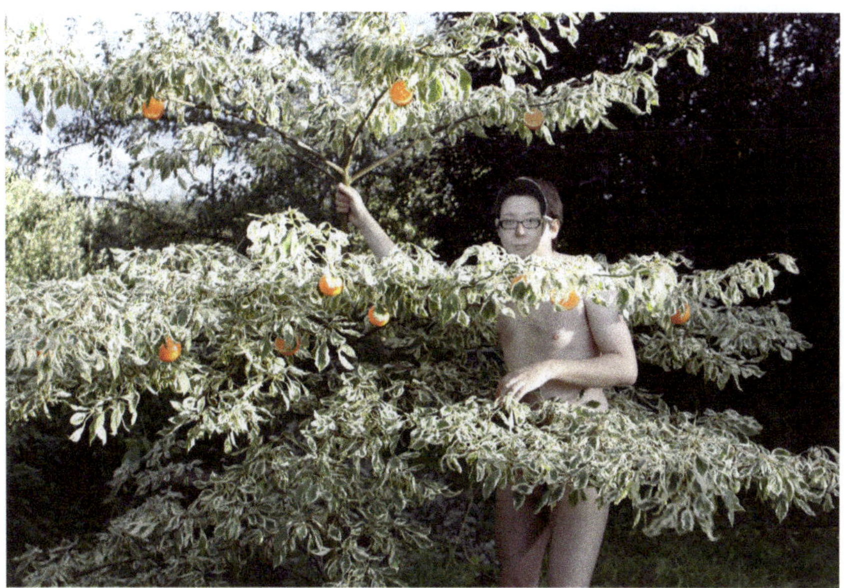

Fig. 3.2. Canceled performance: *Chinese Apple* (2012, photo: Adela Zu Salm Salm).

nudity in art was no longer taboo. However, it is still extremely rare for female artists to depict male nudity. But Lan has painted many male nudes, including her models Alessandro and Moritz, as well as politicians and male artists. She was inspired by the Guerrilla Girls, an anonymous group of women artists who fight against sexism and racism within the art world. Their poster *Do women have to be naked to get into the Met. Museum?* asserts that "Less than 5% of the artists in the Modern Art sections are women, but 85% of the nudes are female."[19] In favoring male nude subjects, she subverts a male gaze into a female gaze and places herself and, by extension, women in a position of control and authority, shifting the power dynamic.

Artist (2011): Solidarity with Ai Weiwei

A third project censored at the first Bald Girls exhibition was an art performance in support of the Chinese dissident artist Ai Weiwei. Lan first performed *Artist* on August 26, 2011, during the opening ceremony of the ASRM art exhibition at the Mauritus Gallery in Wiesbaden, Germany. Ai had been detained in Beijing by Chinese authorities on April 3, 2011,

19 Xu, "Art Vision and Authenticity," 45–6; Cui, *Gendered Bodies*, 51.

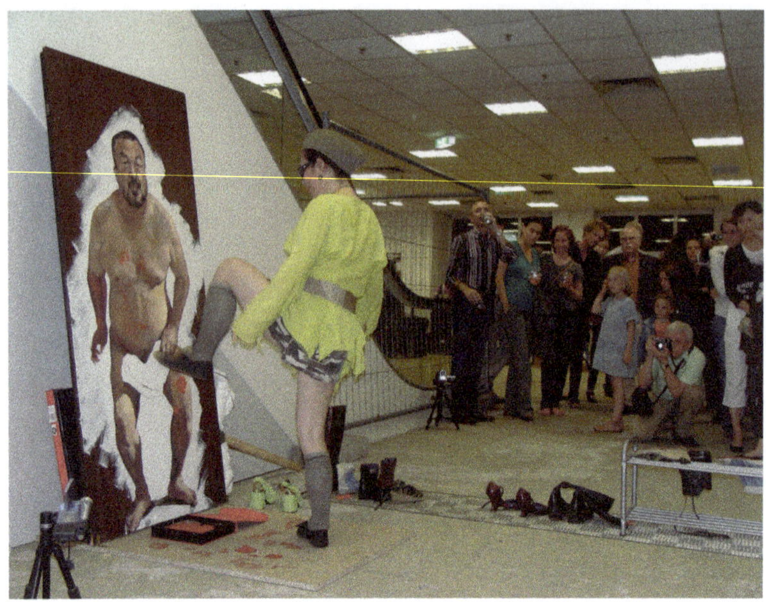

Fig. 3.3. *Artist* (2011, photo: Yuejun Qian).

and was released on June 22.[20] The title "Artist" was chosen because it sounds like the Chinese phrase *A, ti si ta*, which literally means "Ah, kick him to death." On a wooden door, Lan painted a copy of a famous photo of Ai Weiwei naked and holding a white stuffed "grass-mud horse" (*cao ni ma*), an imaginary animal similar to an alpaca, in front of his groin. The pronunciation of the Chinese name of this fictive creature is very close to a word meaning "motherf--ker." Thus, the caption of the photo, literally "Grass-mud horse covering the middle" (*Cao ni ma, dang zhongyang*), can be read as a vulgar slur against the Party Central Committee (*Dang zhongyang*).[21] With Yuejun Qian's assistance, Lan prepared eight pairs of shoes with Chinese characters engraved on the soles, naming the eight crimes of which Ai was accused: plagiarism (扒手), treason (卖国贼), hooliganism (流氓), being idle (不务正业), corrupting public morals (伤风败俗), idiocy (傻X 二百五), breaking taboos (哪壶不开提哪壶), and being a troublemaker (搅局儿). She then put on each pair of shoes, stepped on some red paste used for sealing official documents, and stomped on the

20 "Ai Weiwei's 81-Day Detention," in Ai Weiwei, *Disposition*, ed. Maurizio Bortolotti and Ossian Ward (London: Koenig Books, 2014), 98–109; Buchhart, Lahner, and Schröder, *Ai Weiwei: In Search of Humanity*, 238–67.

21 Xiao Qiang, "The Grass-Mud Horse, Online Censorship, and China's National Identity," December 5, 2012, <https://www.ischool.berkeley.edu/news/2012/grass-mud-horse-online-censorship-and-chinas-national-identity>; 档中央, Chinese Digital Space, <https://chinadigitaltimes.net/space/档中央>.

painted Ai (Fig. 3.3). For the final act, she dealt Ai a blow with her "shoe axe," leaving a gaping hole in his face. On the side of the shoe axe was written the phrase "unwarranted charges" (莫须有 *mo xu you*), signaling that Ai's alleged crimes were not the real reason for his arrest.

As Qian observes, the door was a reminder that Ai Weiwei was under house arrest, and that censorship of an artist is in itself a form of imprisonment; the painted figure of Ai seems to be breaking through the door even though he is trapped in it, unable to get out of the picture. Qian notes that the shoe-axe destroys Ai's face, "but Ai Weiwei has no words. In the face of the axe mark, is it silence? Or is it anger?" Qian points out that Ai was a well-liked artist in Germany and that Lan's performance was intended to draw attention to the plight of avant-garde artists in China today.[22] The performance was not allowed to be repeated at the inaugural Bald Girls show in Beijing in 2012, but photos from the Wiesbaden performance were included in the exhibit catalog. Since Ai's name was blacklisted, however, the catalog only identifies him as "a nude male artist."[23]

"Drown Her in Spit": Solidarity with Mu Zimei

The power dynamic between men and women in China was provocatively challenged in 2003 by a woman from Guangzhou who published a full account of her sexual life online. In her diary *Remains of Love* (*Yi qing shu*, 2003), Mu Zimei recorded in explicit language her encounters with a series of constantly changing sexual partners.[24] She not only detailed her sexual experiences with different men (some of whom she identified by name) but also gave deadpan judgments of their sexual skills. For Lan, Mu's unorthodox action was revolutionary in liberating women from shame about their sexuality and body: "Although Mu Zimei did not consider herself a feminist, she is in my eyes a feminist pioneer in China who openly and unabashedly talks about her sexual experiences and even brags about her sexual conquests." Mu's objectification of men counters the male privilege of objectifying women and replaces the male gaze with a female gaze. Her casual and unrestrained attitude toward sex was unprecedented in China's Confucian society and she became a symbol of women's sexual emancipation.[25] Her con-

22 Yuejun Qian, "Artist (啊, 踢死他)," *Chinese-European Post* 欧华导报Ou Hua Dao Bao, no. 11 (September 2011).

23 *Bald Girls: Three Feminist Artists' Exhibit*, 98.

24 James Farrer, "China's Women Sex Bloggers and Dialogic Sexual Politics on the Chinese Internet," *China aktuell* 4/2007 (2007): 9–44.

25 See Xu, "Art Vision and Authenticity," 45; "Mu Zimei," *China Digital Space*, <https://chinadigitaltimes.net/space/Muzi_Mei>.

troversial diary, censored in China, was later translated into several languages, including French, German, and Polish.[26]

When *Deutsche Welle* invited Mu to a forum in Frankfurt in 2004,[27] Lan sought her out as an artistic collaborator. In a hotel room, Mu undressed and allowed Lan to videotape her as she feigned an orgasm. Seven years later, Lan turned two clips from this session into video installations, *Martyr* (*Xun* 殉, 2011) and *Dirt* (*Chen* 尘, 2011). Mu paid a price for her non-conformist behavior: she was fired from her job as a news editor in Guangzhou and pilloried online. Some netizens wished to "drown her in spit," using a Chinese phrase that expresses disgust. But Mu remained unfazed. "Dirt" plays on the association of the word *chen* with prostitutes or women of easy virtue (*fengchen nüzi*). According to Lan, in Chinese culture and society, prostitutes have an ill reputation, but their male patrons are not condemned. Women alone are required to be chaste, and thus the liberation of women must include their sexual liberation; when sexual liberation is reserved for men alone, it entails the oppression of women. As art historian Shuqin Cui observes, "in the Chinese art tradition, women artists have rarely addressed female sexuality openly and explicitly."[28] This has changed in contemporary Chinese art.

Lan herself provoked online outrage in 2011–12 on the North American Chinese-language website Wenxuecity by posting obscenely erotic op-eds under the pen name Lan Liu'er.[29] These essays formed a performance project she named *Nine and a Half Weeks* after the 1986 Hollywood film, which her college, the Chinese Academy of Art, had screened as part of the curriculum. For the first Bald Girls exhibit, she selected two Chinese texts and projected them onto a nude self-portrait entitled *Portrait mit Fledermaus* (Portrait with a Bat, 2010, Fig. 3.5a) and a black-and-white sketch *Alessandro Kind: Intersection* (2011), respectively. The project became *Nine and a Half Weeks, Part II* (2012, Fig. 3.4a, b). Although the museum director, intimidated by the secret police, canceled the *Chinese Apple* performance, Lan's erotic videos of Mu Zimei as well as the nude paintings were exhibited.

26 Zimei Mu, *Journal sexuel d'une jeune Chinoise sur le net* (Paris: Albin Michel, 2005); *Mein intimes Tagebuch* (Berlin: Aufbau Taschenbuch Verlag, 2007); *Popioly milosci* (Warsaw: Albatros, 2007).

27 潇阳 Xiao Yang, 采访木子美, 用时1小时18分 [To Interview Zimei Mu Took One Hour and Eighteen Minutes], *DW Chinese*, December 3, 2004, <https://www.dw.com/zh/采访木子美用时1小时18分/a-1415268>.

28 Cui, *Gendered Bodies*, 69.

29 Lan's blogsite on wenxuecity.com.

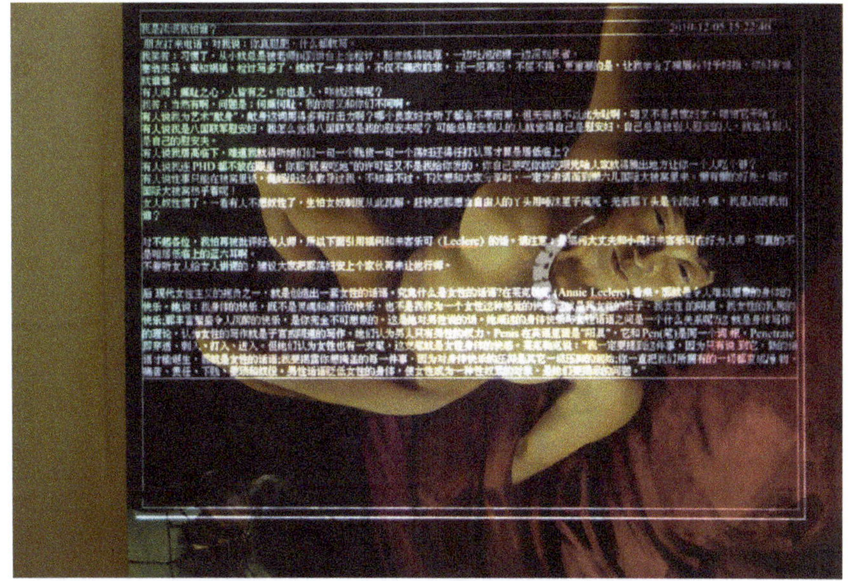

Fig. 3.4a. *Nine and a Half Weeks, Part II* (2012).

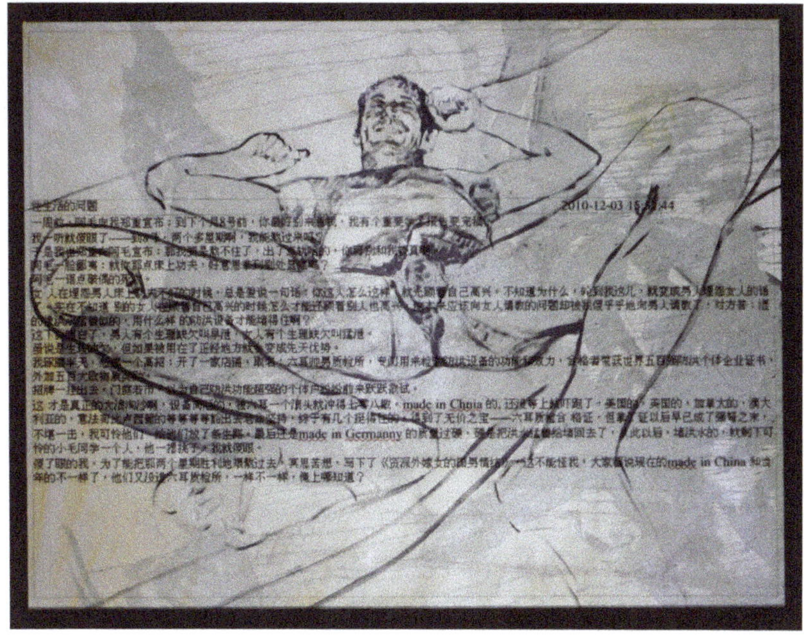

Fig. 3.4b. *Nine and a Half Weeks, Part II* (2012).

Fluid Identity in *(Fe)Male Nude with a Bat* (2010–13)

After the installation *One-Persons-Chorus* in February 2013 (chapter 2), Lan participated in the first charity auction that Christie's organized for Terre des Femmes (TDF) on February 23, 2013, at the Berlinische Galerie. TDF is a German non-profit organization committed to human rights for girls and women. Over fifty artworks would be auctioned on that day and the proceeds would enable TDF to help abused girls and women to receive professional care and free themselves from violent situations. Before the auction, Lan submitted a photo of the painting (Fig. 3.5a), printed in the catalog as No. 37, "Jiny Lan: Portrait mit Fledermaus" (Jiny Lan: Portrait with a Bat, 2010, 150 × 180 cm).[30] It is a self-portrait of a nude Lan wearing a necklace, reclining on a scarlet bed and looking up at the viewer. Green drapery appears in the background. In the upper-left corner a bat hangs from a window frame. Due to perspective the woman appears to be upside down like the bat. Lan was inspired by Aesop's fable "The Birds, the Beasts, and the Bats." When the birds and beasts are battling each other, the bats choose to identify themselves as birds if the birds are winning, and as beasts if the beasts are winning. Whereas the bats in the fable are condemned as opportunists, Lan focuses on their dual identity as mirroring the in-between existence of immigrants like herself and thus uses the bat as a recurrent motif in her paintings.

After submitting the photograph, she regretted donating a female nude in support of a woman's cause because it would imply her complicity in the masculine tradition of objectifying women. She thus decided to add an erect, uncircumcised penis to her self-portrait, as well as to the bat, without notifying Christie's. She envisioned this revision as a performance – *Kleine Veränderung in Kauf nehmen* (Allow A Small Change, 2013). The famous TV presenter Roger Willemsen, who was hosting the auction, offered Lan the opportunity to explain the changes on stage (Fig. 3.6). However, the alterations were not well received, and the work did not attract any bidders.[31] But the president of TDF supported her rationale and asked whether she would be willing to donate the painting to TDF, to be displayed in its Berlin headquarters, and Lan agreed.

30 "Benefiz-Kunstauktion zugunsten Terre des Femmes," auction catalog, Berlinische Galerie, February 23, 2013, <https://www.kunstauktion-tdf.de/2013/images/downloads/Katalog-Benefizauktion-2013.pdf>.

31 Whereas the majority of other artworks were priced in the hundreds or thousands of euros, Lan set the range for her painting higher, at 12,000–24,000 euros; see "Benefiz-Kunstauktion."

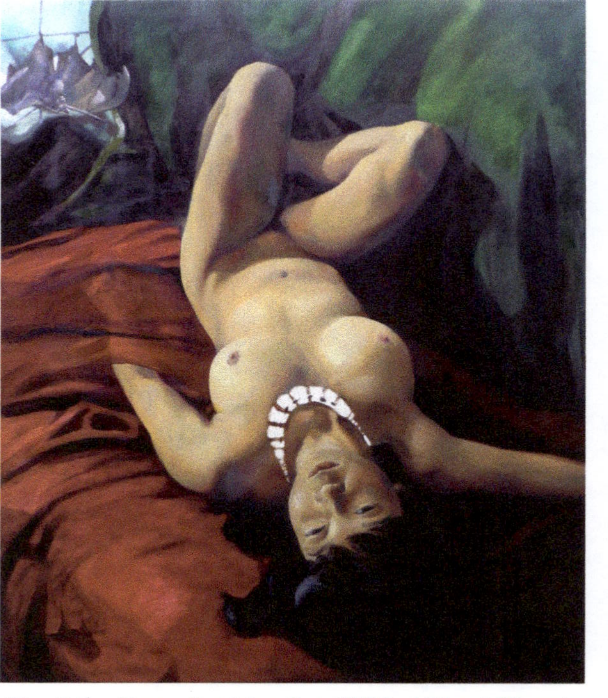

Fig. 3.5a. *Portrait with a Bat* (2010, 180 × 150 cm).

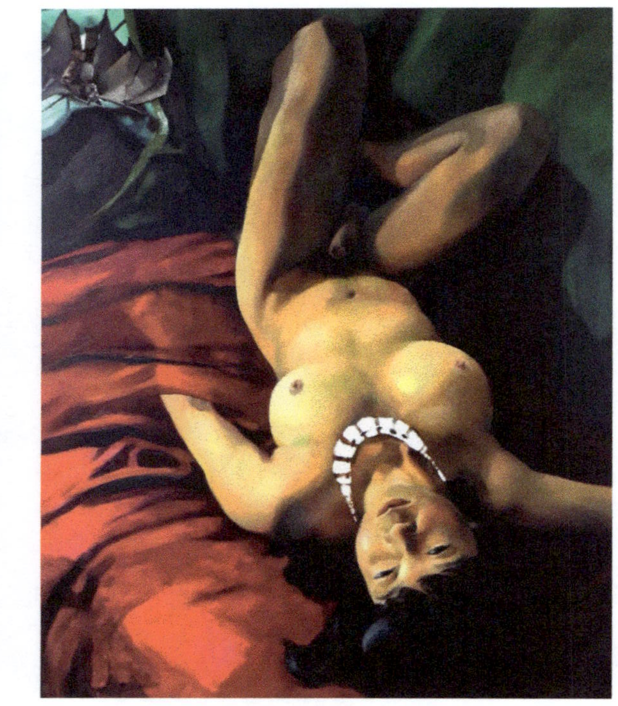

Fig. 3.5b. *(Fe)male Nude with a Bat* (2010–13, 180 × 150 cm).

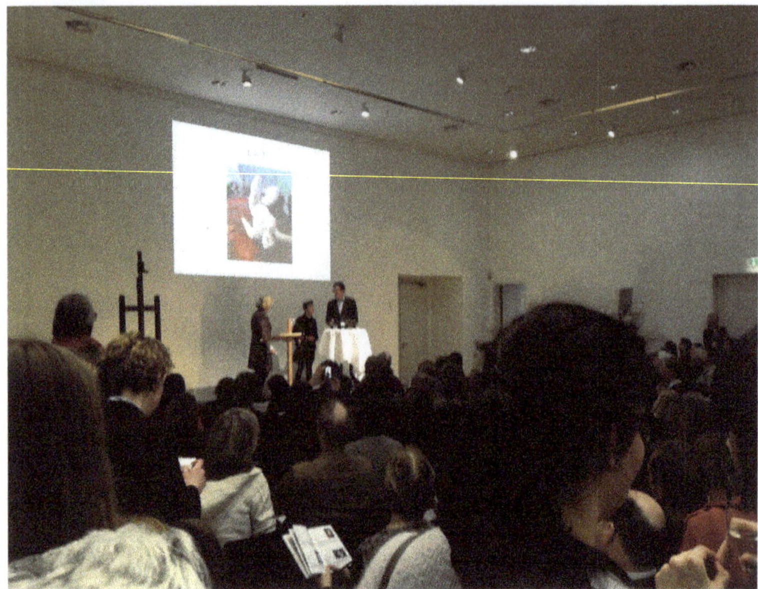

Fig. 3.6. *Allow A Small Change* (2013) at Christie's: Jiny Lan on stage explaining the changes to *Portrait with a Bat* (2010, photo: Moritz Roidl).

The new painting, *(Fe)male Nude with a Bat* (2010–13, Fig. 3.5b), boldly shows a non-binary person wearing nothing but an ornate white necklace. Whereas Lan often adds female physical features to male nudes in her later paintings, here she already combines features of both sexes, thus crossing gender boundaries and visualizing non-binary identities. The eccentric addition of a penis to the bat caused some consternation on the day of the auction, but the bat functions as an allegory of an immigrant, whose interstitial existence shares the bat's "fluid" identity. Thus, the bat appears as a double of the artist in the painting.

Opening a Door: *108+1* (2013) and Female Infanticide

In subsequent years, the Bald Girls continued to draw public attention to rampant sexism and sexual violence in China. The collective's projects often lambasted Chinese patriarchy and the one-child policy, which resulted in sex-selective abortions and female infanticide. On May 25, 2013, the Bald Girls collaborated with Zajia Art Lab on a show in Beijing titled *A Door*, which metaphorically allows one to enter feminist art and consciousness. The German artist Mary Bauermeister, closely associated with the Fluxus movement, was the collective's visiting feminist artist that year. The program included a series of gut-wrenching acts. Li Xinmo, for example, put a razor in her mouth and narrated the story of an artist friend who was raped by her own father. The difficulty in speaking caused by the razor simulated the difficulty in speaking about the traumatizing sexual violence that women in China endure. Li said that young girls are raped by men in positions of power, such as teachers, government officials, and police, but at best one percent of these rapes become known to the public. Li Maizi gave a speech about being an unconventional woman in China: lesbian and bald. Another feminist artist, Yan Yinhong, reenacted a rape by a policeman. Yan later told the *New York Times* that rape in police custody is a widespread but rarely discussed problem in China.[32]

In Lan's performance, *108+1*, she placed 108+1 red balloons on old, heavily used white bed sheets from a maternity ward. She popped the red balloons one after another, and her fellow artist Fenni imitated a baby crying after each pop, which represented a birth. Lan drew a penis on the sheet after each burst to indicate that the baby born was a boy. (The "+1" in the title refers to a token girl.) Lan explained the idea behind this conceptual art project: because the one-child policy prohibited revealing the sex of a fetus before birth, countless women had lain in these bed sheets praying for a boy. Lan found this scenario extremely ludicrous and expressed this absurdity through an equally repetitive and absurd project. This performance aimed to highlight the skewed gender ratio of 108 males to 100 females in China, which is the root cause of the trafficking of women to satisfy men's sexual and reproductive needs. The 2013 Bald Girls show was an excruciating and shocking experience for viewers, but the feminist artists opened a door to expose the painful truth of sexual inequality and violence in China.

Timelag: Who's Your Daddy (2014) and *A Modest Proposal* (2014)

In their first two years (2012 and 2013), the Bald Girls staged shows in China. In their third year (2014), they began to engage in dialogues with international artists, first at the Women's Museum in Bonn, then in Wiesbaden, and later in Bogotá, Columbia. In 2014, the Women's Museum in Bonn invited artists to contribute to a vernissage on *Single*

32 "Bald Girls: 'A Door' Zajia Lab, Beijing," Juan Xu Curator, <https://www.juanxucurator.com/bald-girls-a-door-2013.html>; Tatlow, "In Art, a Strong Voice for Chinese Women"; Didi Kirsten Tatlow, "Raw Scenes, Unspeakable Violations," *New York Times*, June 18, 2013, <https://www.nytimes.com/2013/06/19/world/asia/19iht-letter19.html>.

Moms.[33] Playing on the word "jetlag," the Bald Girls presented *Timelag*, showing how the women's rights movement in China lags behind that in the West.[34] On April 13, Lan performed her work *Who's Your Daddy* in front of a crowd in the museum's courtyard (Fig. 3.7b).[35] On the canvas, spectators saw a larger-than-life Confucius with his legs spread wide apart as if in labor. The image calls to mind the painting *Value-Added Movement 1 – 4A Revision 1a: Alessandro Kind* (2013, Fig. 3.7a), which she completed a year earlier. Naked like Alessandro, Confucius lies on his back with his legs splayed and with his right hand he points to this head. Working on site, Lan painted a vagina over the male genitalia. She then inserted a tube through the vagina from behind the canvas and used a stick to push plastic babies out the front, one at a time. In total, eighty plastic boy dolls emerged, representing eighty generations of Confucius's descendants. Each doll had a number on its head, representing the first-born son of each generation, and on the back of each doll was the name of the descendant.[36] One more doll remained visible in the tube, with the number eighty-one written on its head, representing the latest generation. The genealogy of Confucius's descendants is traced only through male heirs.[37] Lan saw this custom as characteristic of the ingrained feudal thought of Chinese patriarchy, which was articulated in its classical form in Confucian thought.

The face of Confucius in *Who's Your Daddy* is modeled after Ai Weiwei. While Lan respects Ai's civil courage, she sees him as a symbol of gender inequality: "Ai Weiwei is a typical macho, and as a male artist he benefits from his sex, while Chinese women artists do not enjoy the same

33 Claudia Rometsch, "Allein mit Kind – Bonner Frauenmuseum widmet sich der Situation von 'Single Moms,'" *WAZ*, April 19, 2014, <https://www.waz.de/archiv-daten/article9258113/allein-mit-kind-bonner-frauenmuseum-widmet-sich-der-situation-von-single-moms.html>.

34 Juan Xu, "Bald Girls – 'Timelag,'" Juan Xu Curator, <https://www.juanxucurator.com/bald-girls-timelag-2013.html>.

35 Juan Xu, "Who Is Your Daddy? – Performance of 'Bald Girls – Timelag,'" uploaded May 18, 2014, <https://www.youtube.com/watch?v=Rk92wXYAXh0>.

36 朱波 Zhu Bo, 二年级小学生是孔子81代孙 [Second Grade Pupil Is the Eighty-First Generation of Confucius's Descendants], *Sina*, September 11, 2006, <https://news.sina.com.cn/o/2006-09-11/08459989702s.shtml>; Leland Meitzler, "Confucius' Family Tree Finished in 80 Books with Over 2M People Included," GenealogyBlog, September 25, 2009, <https://www.genealogyblog.com/?p=5864>; "Confucius' Family Tree Digitalized," Xinhua, June 13, 2017, <http://www.xinhuanet.com//english/2017-06/13/c_136362834.htm>.

37 Not until 2006 were women included in Confucius's family tree. See, e.g., Jonathan Watts, "Family Tree of Chinese Sage Branches Out to Include Women," *The Guardian*, September 28, 2006, <https://www.theguardian.com/world/2006/sep/28/china.jonathanwatts>.

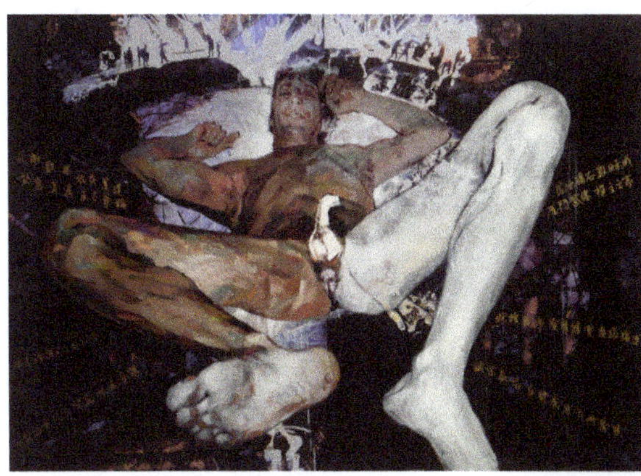

Fig. 3.7a. *Value-Added Movement 1 – 4A Revision 1a: Alessandro Kind* (2013, 140 × 200 cm).

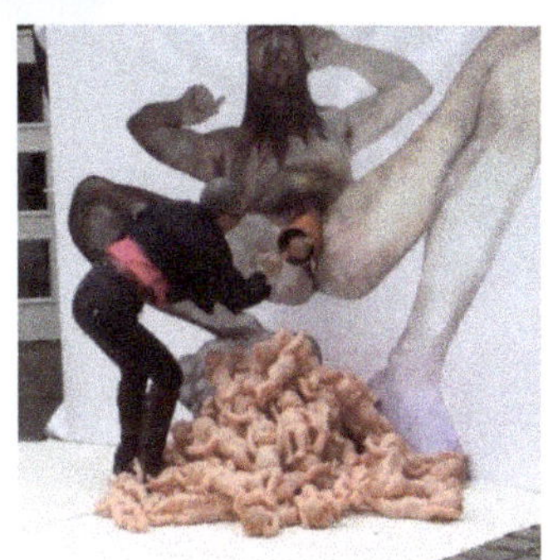

Fig. 3.7b. Installation and performance of *Who's Your Daddy* (2014, photo: Kangping Piao).

privileges in the West." She finds the German media's infatuation with Ai problematic, observing that "Ai Weiwei seems to personify traditional Chinese wisdom for the Western world, as if he were Confucius incarnate." For the title, she borrowed street slang to criticize the patriarchal family lineage. She argues, "'Who's your daddy?' could be a question to which one does not know the answer. Confucius himself was conceived out of wedlock. Many illegitimate children do not know who their father is, but they most likely know who their mother is. The maternal bloodline would be more reliable than the paternal line." This resonates with her matriarchal concept of Jinyology, which traces artistic "bloodline" on the mother's side.

For the exhibition at the Women's Museum in Bonn, Lan devised a second project, *Ein bescheidener Vorschlag* (A Modest Proposal, *Pi fu zhi jian*, 2014, Fig. 3.8). Since traditionally only male heirs could carry on the family name, contributing to sex-selective abortions and infanticide, she made "a modest proposal" to name the newborn after the father or mother based on the roll of a die. She commissioned a factory to make 6,679 dice, corresponding to the number of gynecological clinics in China at the time. On each die, three sides were inscribed with the Chinese

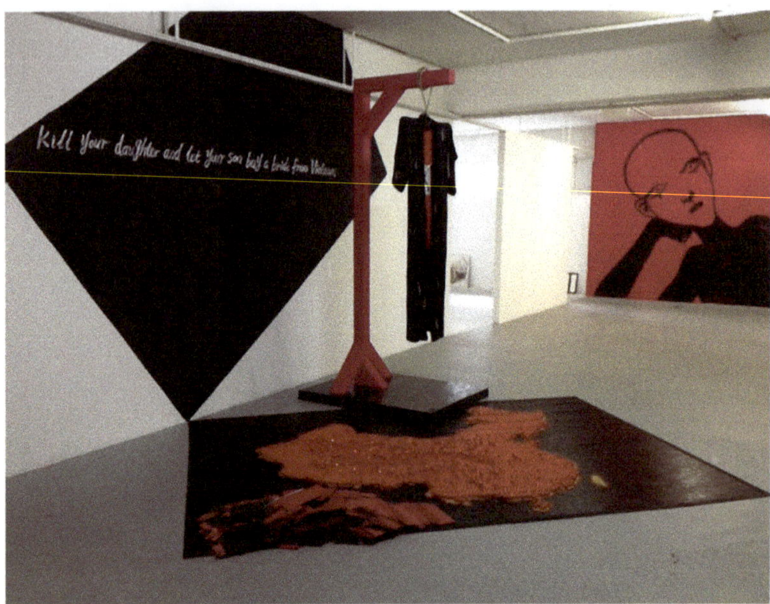

Fig. 3.8. *A Modest Proposal* (2014, 500 × 500 × 350 cm, photo: Kangping Piao).

character for father and three sides with the character for mother. She addressed thousands of envelopes to women's clinics in China and had volunteers donate stamps and mail letters to them. The title "A Modest Proposal" was derived from a satirical essay written by Jonathan Swift in 1729, in which Swift proposes to free poor Irish people of the burden of raising children by selling their offspring as food to the rich. The fictive macabre plan has turned into the horrific reality of female infanticide in China caused by the one-child policy.

At the Women's Museum, small red dice were arranged in the shape of the map of China. A magenta-colored gallows was set up on a black mat and a black Chinese robe hung from the gallows. On the robe was sewn a white cloth bearing the Chinese character 谏 *jian*, which means "proposal," while also alluding to 死谏 *si jian*, a petition addressed to the emperor by a minister who offers his life as a pledge. "Kill your daughter and let your son buy a wife in Vietnam" was written on the wall in English, a reference to human trafficking between China and Southeast Asia.[38] Beneath the robe was a pile of red envelopes and letters proposing legislation that would establish special commissioners to oversee

38 Tom Hancock, "Rural Chinese Men Are Buying Vietnamese Brides For $3,200," *Business Insider*, August 18, 2014, <https://www.businessinsider.com/rural-chinese-men-are-buying-vietnamese-brides-for-3200-2014-8>.

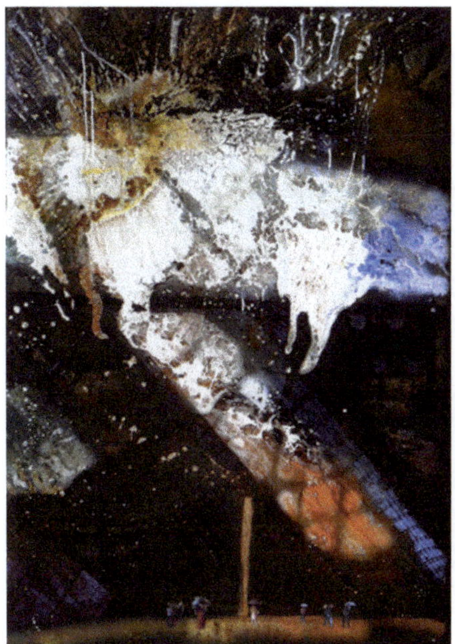
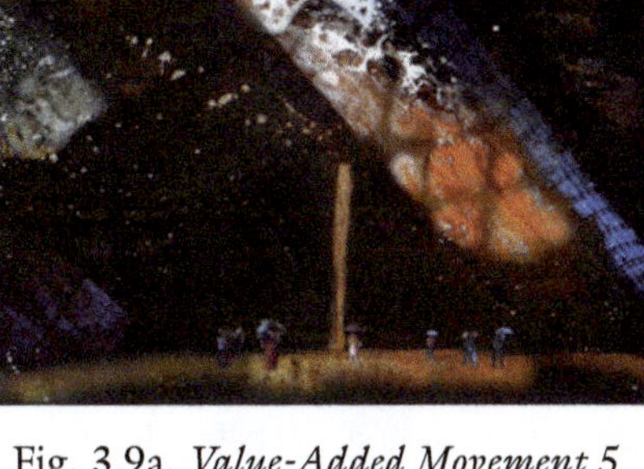

Fig. 3.9a. *Value-Added Movement 5* (2013, 200 × 140 cm).

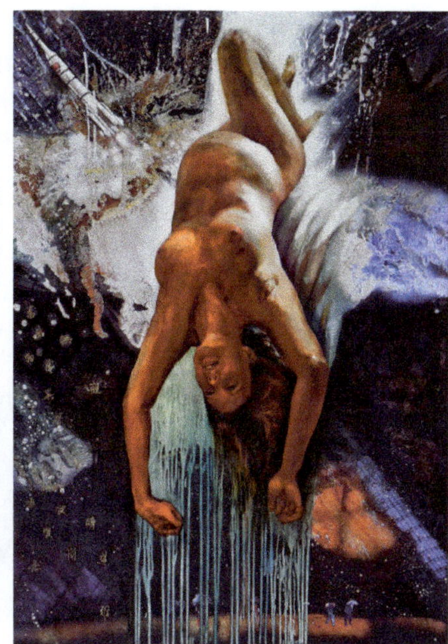

Fig. 3.9b. *Falling Is the Last Motion before Flying* (2014, 200 × 140 cm).

dice-rolling and name registration in maternity wards. The goal was to create the political will to turn Lan's proposal into actual practice. An official in Changfeng County, Anhui Province, where the gender ratio at the time of the Sixth National Census in 2010 was 130 men to 100 women (the normal ratio in China ranged from 103 to 107 males for every 100 females), adopted Lan's idea and launched a pilot project called "Surname Reform," in which parents were awarded one thousand renminbi (ca. 150 euros in 2014) if their child received the mother's surname; the reward system did indeed encourage participation and improve the birth rate for girls.[39] However, it is not easy to effect any bottom-up social change in China.

Befitting the show's theme, "Single Mothers," Lan painted a pregnant mother-to-be in *Value-Added Movement 5: Falling Is the Last Motion before Flying* (2014, Fig. 3.9b) to criticize the stigmatization of single mothers in China. In the painting, a pregnant woman with long blonde hair is tumbling upside down over a waterfall. Chinese characters are

39 安徽长丰试点"姓氏改革", 子随母姓奖千元 [Anhui Changfeng Pilot Project "Surname Reform": Children Given Mother's Surname Are Awarded a Thousand Yuan], *Pengpai News*, August 1, 2014, <https://m.thepaper.cn/newsDetail_forward_1259285>.

inscribed on the left side. In the background a rocket is being launched into outer space. The optimism expressed in the title promises a lifting-up before the woman hits the ground. When asked why she portrayed the woman in free fall, Lan said that in China single mothers are often blamed for lacking *zi zhong*, or self-respect. But the phrase *zi zhong* literally means "a person has self-weight or intrinsic gravity." Hence, she "draws out" the literal meaning of a phrase. The woman is being pulled down by her self-weight. The serial number indicates that the painting is based on *Value-Added Movement* 5 (2013, Fig. 3.9a), which is the fifth of the second-generation abstract paintings with bright splotches of white paint on a dark background. At the bottom of the painting, in a well-lit space, walk several tiny, isolated figures who are holding up umbrellas. Traces of the roof of the Milan shopping mall are detectable.[40]

Fluxus Meets Bald Girls: *Talented Girls in Oil and Salt* (2014) and *Pink Solution* (2015)

Immediately after performing at the Women's Museum in Bonn, on April 16, 2014, the Bald Girls sought "a performative dialogue with Fluxus" in its birthplace, Wiesbaden.[41] Together with German artists, the Bald Girls recreated two classical Fluxus performances: *4'33"* (1952) by John Cage and *Memoriam to Adriano Olivetti* (1962) by George Maciunas. The Bald Girls then performed *Talented Girls in Oil and Salt* (*Cainü youyan*, 2014, Fig. 3.10). The title plays on the similar-sounding four-character phrase *chaimi youyan*: firewood, rice, oil, and salt. The performance connected "talented girls" with household chores to underline how women are bound by traditional societal expectations to perform mundane household tasks and thus cannot realize their full potential. The performers stood on a large white sheet and rubbed one another's naked bodies with pink paint, then tossed firewood, rice, cooking oil, and salt on the sheet. They lay down on the white sheet and wrapped themselves in it while men in protective clothing doused them with soy sauce and rice vinegar until the pink paint and brown soy sauce created blood-like stains on the white sheet. With this project, the feminist artists questioned why men still dominate various fields and industries in China, even though many girls outperform boys in the education system from elementary school to university.

A year later, Lan was inspired to paint *Pink Solution* (2015, Fig. 3.11b) so that the performance would be preserved not only in video

40 The painting was exhibited in 2016 in Paris at the exhibit *Bald Girls – Fempire de Mai*, mentioned below.

41 Juan Xu, "Fluxus Meets Bald Girls," Juan Xu Curator, April 16, 2014, <https://www.juanxucurator.com/bald-girls-meet-fluxus-2014.html>.

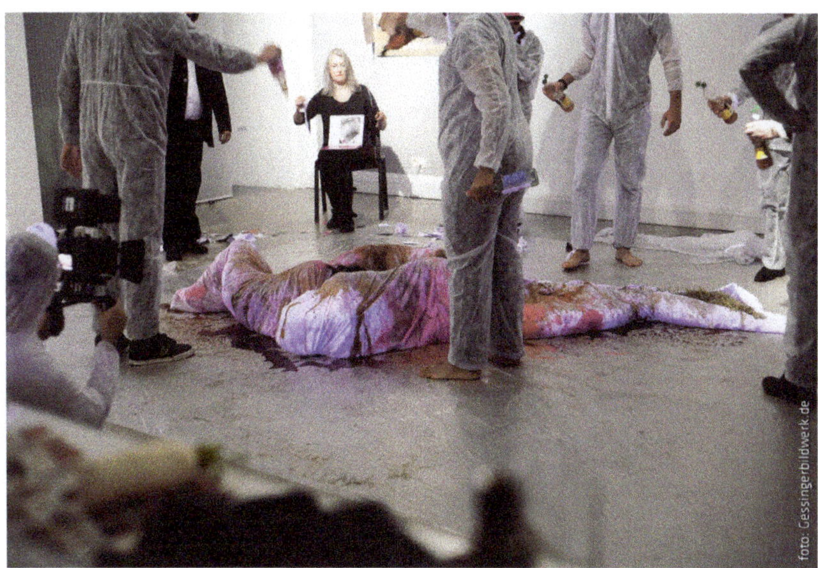

Fig. 3.10. *Talented Girls in Oil and Salt* (2014).

documentation but also on canvas. The glass roof of the shopping mall in Milan, a holdover from the template *Value-Added Movement 5A* (Fig. 3.11a), still flickers through here and there. A multistory building and at the bottom small figures carrying umbrellas, including a large beach umbrella, are figurative elements carried over from the template. Lan's use of incompatible color materials – oil pastels, acrylics, and paints – created a strange tension on the canvas. After painting the two naked bodies in oil pastel, she splashed white acrylic paint, as well as rice, vinegar, oil, and salt on the canvas, controlling their flow and manipulating their shape and thickness in a variation on action painting. Because the oil pastel used to sketch the bodies is resistant to acrylic paint, it blocks the flow of the white acrylic paint and fleshes out the two bodies in vivid contours, withstanding the onslaught of the pink solution while creating a surreal scenario. In the painting, a nude, bald, pink Lan stands over the nude, kneeling Xiao Lu and pours a basin of pink solution onto her neck, which splashes and forms a puddle. The title "Pink Solution" refers literally to the liquid mixture of pink paint and water, and metaphorically to the solution of social problems at the expense of women. The pouring of the pink liquid reenacts the imposition of customary social roles on women.

What appear to be water streaks are, upon closer inspection, four green brushes placed right in the center of the canvas. Lan revealed that they were actual brushes that had been accidentally integrated into the painting. One day, a female worker in her atelier opened the windows to air out the room, but the draft toppled the freshly painted canvas and

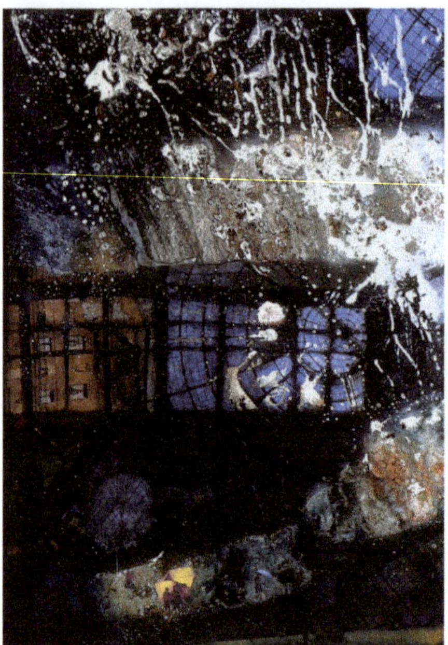

Fig. 3.11a. *Value-Added Movement 5A* (2013, 200 × 140 cm).

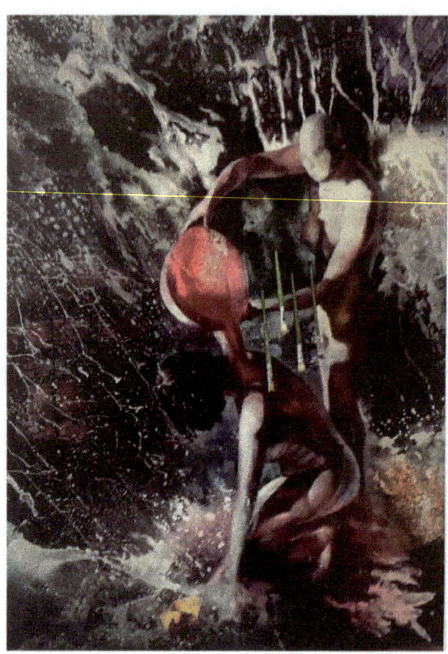

Fig. 3.11b. *Value-Added Movement 5A Revision 1a: Pink Solution* (2015, 200 × 140 cm).

the brushes landed on top. This fortuitous event added a new medium to the painting and presented an unexpected symbol: one could interpret the paintbrushes as a reference to women's talent. Aesthetically, they blend into the painting to the point of being unrecognizable, signifying the invisibility and (self-)effacement of women's talent.

Boys of Plastic vs. Girls of Soap: *Bald Girls – Pink Solution* (2014) in Columbia

From July 31 to August 28, 2014, the Bald Girls collaborated with three artists from Latin America – the Guatemalan artist Regina José Galindo, the Colombian artist Sandra Miranda Pattin, and the Argentinian artist Sol Storni – to put on an art show entitled *Pink Solution* in Bogotá, Columbia. Pink or magenta, a stereotypically feminine color, is the brand color of the Bald Girls, who hope to build "a new peaceful 'Pink World,' a world without suppression and violence."[42]

Lan contributed three projects to the show. First, accompanied by a Spanish interpreter, she went to the Plaza de Bolívar in Bogotá and

42 Juan Xu, "'Pink Solution' – An Unusual Title. What Is It?" May 26, 2014, <https://www.juanxucurator.com/bald-girls-pink-solution-2014.html>.

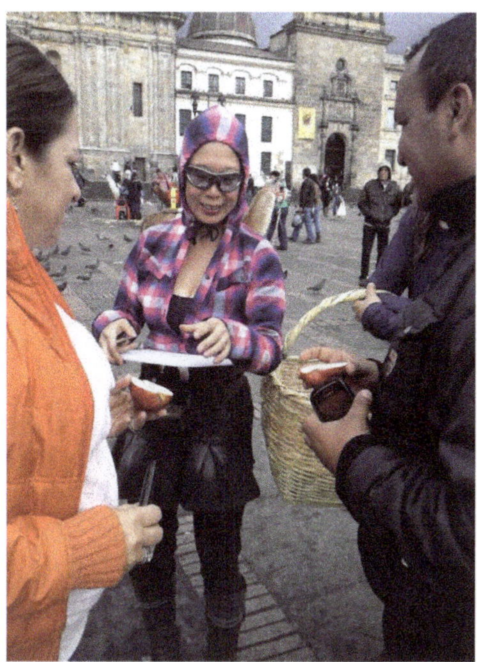

Fig. 3.12. Handing out half apples at the Plaza de Bolívar in Bogotá (2014, photo: Juan Xu).

distributed apples to Sunday churchgoers while saying to them: "Today is Valentine's Day in China. Do you agree that Eve should not carry the original sin alone, and that the original sin should be shared by man and woman?" Then she cut the apples – bought from a local market – in half and handed them out (Fig. 3.12). Worth noting is the title of the performance, *The Tragedy of the Qixi Festival* (*Qixi zhi qi*). The seventh day of the seventh month in the Chinese lunar calendar is the Chinese equivalent to Valentine's Day, a tradition based on the legend of the Cowherd and the Weaver Girl. But Lan points out that this legend was a #MeToo story. In a prototype of the Chinese folktale, a poor young man steals the garments of one of the celestial maidens who are bathing in a river and makes her his wife; she finds the garments and flies back to heaven. The man pursues her into the heavenly realm, but the heavenly king decrees that the couple shall meet only once a year.[43] According to Lan, the Chinese made a romance out of a harrowing tale of rape and a mythical version of human trafficking. In Bogotá, she presented a local version of her half-oranges concept but did not debunk the traditional Chinese myth due to linguistic and cultural barriers.

43 Wolfram Eberhard, *Typen chinesischer Volksmärchen* (Helsinki: Academia Scientiarum Fennica, 1937), 55–7.

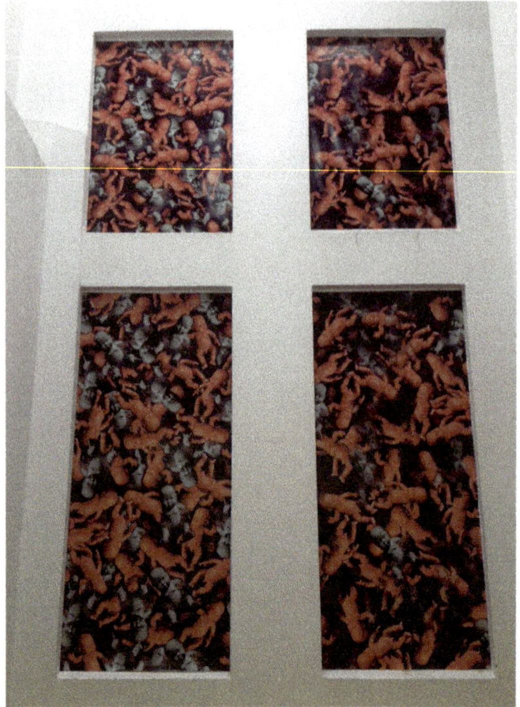

Fig. 3.13: *Survival of the Fittest?* (2014, installation using computer-generated images).

Lan's second contribution was the *Modest Proposal* installation she had shown in Bonn, but she modified the dice to reflect the colors of Colombia's national flag. The third was *Survival of the Fittest?* (*Shi zhe sheng cun*, 2014, Fig. 3.13), which was originally conceived as an installation project: 106 boy dolls made of plastic and 100 girl dolls made of soap would be put into two swimming pools filled with hot water. Once in the water, the soap-girl dolls would dissolve and *perish*, whereas the plastic boy dolls would *survive*. The title "Survival of the Fittest" is thus ironic: the boys are *naturally* better fit for survival because they are made of more enduring material, implying that more favorable conditions are provided to males than to females. This project takes aim at the lack of gender equality in China. Due to the high cost of manufacturing the dolls, Lan made one girl out of soap and one boy out of plastic and used computer-generated images to present the project in Bogotá. Each of the images features a jumble of plastic baby dolls variously colored red and gray. Although the project was not realized in full, this feminist concept won her much praise.

The Seventh Commandment (2015): On Gender and Sexuality

Lan's representation of gender is mostly binary, as the Bald Girls' primary focus is on sexism and sexual violence in China, where women's basic human and reproductive rights are not guaranteed. When challenged about the lack of non-binary representation in her work by a Western college student, Lan explained:

> In China, our struggle is very simple. If you have a vagina, you'll be killed. It was only several years ago that the one-child policy was abandoned. This is very difficult for people in the West to understand. And given the imbalance in the gender ratio, Chinese women are kidnapped and sold as wives. How can you buy a wife? A wife is bought only because she has a vagina. It is very biological. You must have the ability to have a baby. The West is very advanced in the gender debate. It is not yet time to show my Chinese audience the non-binary understanding of gender.[44]

According to curator Xu, "the LGBTQ+ community and the Bald Girls are collaborators and comrades in arms. The definition of gender is similar to that of identity; it is fluid; there are no absolutes, but the Bald Girls are still talking about women; without women, there would be no feminism."[45]

Lan addresses attitudes toward lesbianism in *The Seventh Commandment* (*Di qi jie*, 2015, Fig. 3.14b), which shows an intimate interaction between two women in a churchlike interior space.[46] However, they scarcely appear to be touching. A naked woman with long dark hair is propping herself up with her arms while crouching over another naked woman with a half orange for a head, lying on her side on a fluorescent green surface. Titled after the seventh of the Ten Commandments, which prohibits adultery (Exodus 20:14), the painting thematizes Christianity's aversion to (homo-)sexual lust and illicit passion. The painting is a subversion of *Value-Added Movement 1 – 4A Revision 1b: St. Alessandro Church* (2013, Fig. 3.14a), which uses, according to the artist, Antoni Gaudí's Sagrada Família Basilica in Barcelona as a backdrop. Since the Catholic Church considers homosexuality a sin, the giant eye watching the lesbian couple could be seen as a visualization of religious authorities' disapproval of homosexuals. The eye of the church evokes the surveilling

44 Lan addressed Bryn Mawr College students during their study abroad trip, March 7, 2022, Galerie Tammen, Berlin.

45 My interview with Juan Xu on April 21, 2023 in Berlin.

46 A Chinese collector who is interested in collecting artworks depicting homosexuality purchased this painting for his private art museum in China.

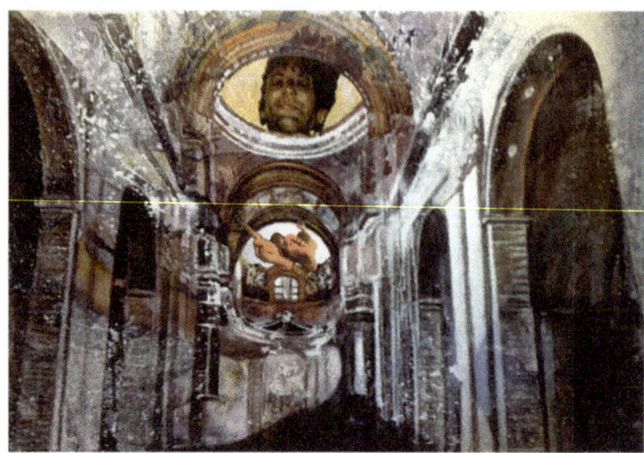

Fig. 3.14a. *Value-Added Movement 1 – 4A Revision 1b: St. Alessandro Church* (2013, 140 × 200 cm).

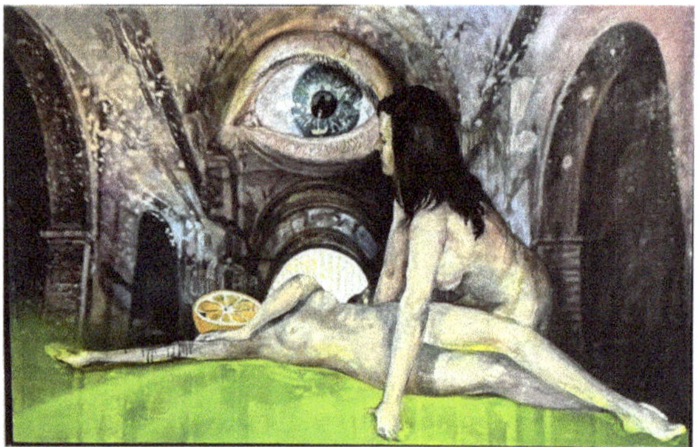

Fig. 3.14b. *The Seventh Commandment* (2015, 100 × 180 cm).

"Skyeye" in *Backward Movement* (2014, Fig. 6.1b). Is the eye interrupting the couple's act? Or is it lustfully voyeuristic?

This painting retroactively sheds light on the earlier painting *St. Alessandro Church*, which depicts a heterosexual couple. The face of a smiling man, eyes closed, appears in an aperture at the top of the building, which is borrowed from *Alessandro Kind* (2013, Fig. 3.7a). Another figure floats in the middle of the painting, supine and foreshortened, feet facing the viewer, clearly a hidden self-reference (cf. Fig. 2.8b). In light of *The Seventh Commandment*, *St. Alessandro Church* could be understood as a critique of religion's disapproval of (hetero-)sexual lust that does not aim at procreation. Lan's "canonization" of Alessandro as a saint is thus sacrilegious and constitutes an affront to the Catholic Church.

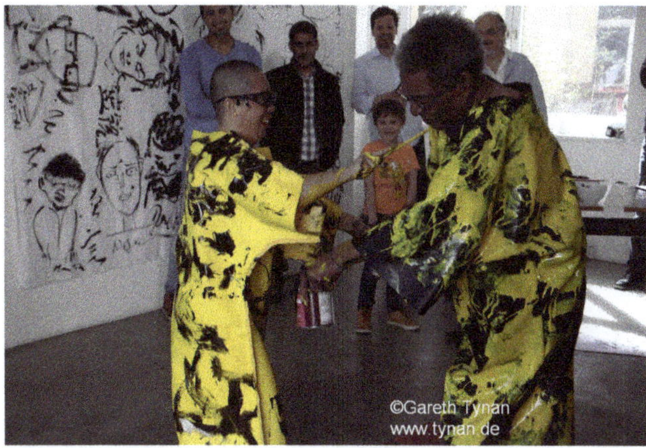

Fig. 3.15. *Lack le (乐) by Low* by Lan and Patterson (2015, photo: Gareth Tynan).

Lack le(乐) by Low (2015): A Performance with Ben Patterson against Racism

As the world witnessed the influx of refugees into Europe in 2015, Xu and a co-curator, Leander Rubrecht, invited five artists, including Fluxus co-founder Ben Patterson, to perform at the art show *Excluded* in Wiesbaden on April 12. Lan and Patterson staged an anti-racism performance with the whimsical title "Lack le(乐) by Low."[47] The African American artist Patterson brushed black paint on Lan's yellow raincoat while uttering anti-Asian slurs, and Lan brushed yellow paint on his black raincoat while reciting anti-Black phrases (Fig. 3.15). In the end, the yellow and black colors were mixed together, and the raincoats became indistinguishable. The artists undressed and stood naked in front of the spectators. This performance aimed to bridge the racial divide and emphasize the humanity of people of all races. *Lack le(乐) by Low* is an anagram that Lan formed by mixing up the letters in "black" and "yellow." *Le* is the pinyin for the Chinese character 乐, which could mean "to taunt" (*qu le*); the full title could be construed to mean "people with lacks or insufficiencies are taunted by people who are low."

Lan and Patterson had planned another collaborative performance titled "Auf die dritte Farbe!" (To the Third Color), but Patterson died in 2016 before it could be presented. The script of the performance suggests an ambience more formal than that of *Lack le(乐) by Low*. Patterson wears a black suit and Lan a yellow dress. Each guest is offered red wine

47 Juan Xu, "Performance Day, 12 April 2015," Juan Xu Curator, <https://www.juanxucurator.com/performance-day-2015.html>.

in a small shot glass. The two performers have similar shot glasses filled with water on a table. They cut their fingers and squeeze a few drops of blood into the water. They exchange glasses and say to each other and to the guests, "Auf die dritte Farbe!" Everyone drinks. The performance blends the Eucharist and the pagan ritual of drinking each other's blood to symbolize kinship. The performers salute the third color, red, which Lan joked is the color of the blood of every human being, except for *blue-blooded* aristocrats. She has not yet given up on this project, which invites groups that have historically been victims of racism to reflect on the possibility that they themselves may hold racist views.

Fempire de Mai (2016): Vis-à-vis with Refugee Integration

During New Year's Eve celebrations at the end of 2015 in Cologne, hundreds of women were mobbed and sexually assaulted by men of North African and Arab origin, most of whom were refugees.[48] In the wake of this outrage, German politicians at the highest level demanded that refugees convicted of crimes be deported faster.[49] In response to the Cologne assaults, Lan presented the performance art project *Vis-à-vis* in Paris on the opening day of *Bald Girls – Fempire de Mai* (May 17–31, 2016), sponsored by the French feminist center L'Espace des Femmes – Antoinette Fouque and the Union des Artistes d'Asie en France. She conceptualized a "Pictures Republic of Jiny" as a fictive

48 See Ralf Bosen, "New Year's Eve in Cologne: 5 years after the mass assaults," *DW*, December 31, 2020, <https://www.dw.com/en/new-years-eve-in-cologne-5-years-after-the-mass-assaults/a-56073007>; Alice Schwarzer, ed., *Der Schock: Die Silvesternacht von Köln* (Cologne: Kiepenheuer & Witsch, 2016); and Christian Wiermer, *Die Nacht, die Deutschland veränderte: Hintergründe, Fakten und Enthüllungen zu den dramatischen Übergriffen der Silvesternacht in Köln* (Munich: riva, 2017).

49 "De Maizière übt massive Kritik an Kölner Sicherheitskonzept," *Süddeutsche Zeitung*, January 5, 2016, <https://www.sueddeutsche.de/panorama/uebergriffe-an-silvester-de-maiziere-uebt-massive-kritik-an-koelner-polizei-1.2806333>; "Cologne Attackers 'Could Face Deportation,'" *DW*, January 7, 2016, <https://www.dw.com/en/german-justice-minister-threatens-foreign-cologne-attackers-with-deportation/a-18964436>; Daniel Herder, Jens Meyer-Wellmann, and Irene Jung, "Sexuelle Übergriffe: Olaf Scholz: Kriminelle Flüchtlinge schneller abschieben," *Hamburger Abendblatt*, January 8, 2016, <https://www.abendblatt.de/hamburg/polizeimeldungen/article206902439/Olaf-Scholz-Kriminelle-Fluechtlinge-schneller-abschieben.html>; "Vizekanzler Gabriel fordert schnellere Abschiebungen," *Der Spiegel*, January 8, 2016, <https://www.spiegel.de/politik/deutschland/koeln-uebergriffe-an-silvester-vizekanzler-gabriel-fordert-hartes-vorgehen-gegen-taeter-a-1071009.html>.

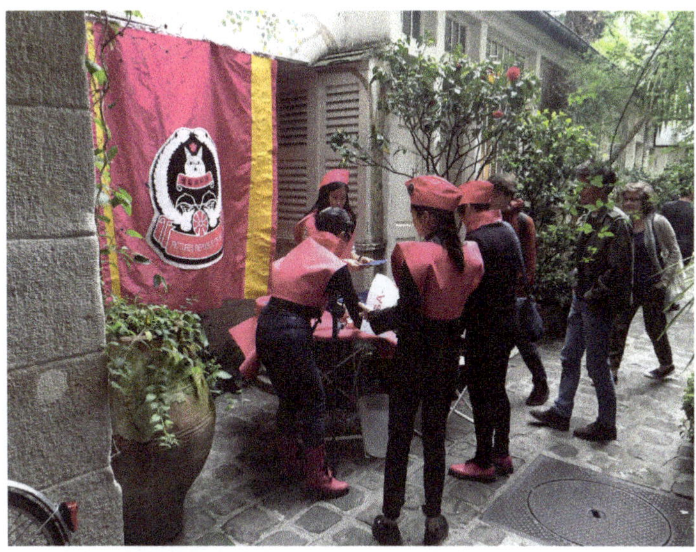

Fig. 3.16. *Bald Girls – Fempire de Mai* (2016, photo: Yuhong He).

country, *Fempire de Mai* (五月媂国 *Wu yue di guo*, The May Female-Empire, Fig. 3.16), with its own national flag, emblem, anthem, uniform, and customs and borders. All visitors to the May Female-Empire had to apply for a visa and to pass through customs at a fictive border. In addition to filling out personal information in the visa application, every applicant had to answer two questions: (1) Are you willing to respect and comply with the rules and regulations of the Pictures Republic of Jiny after entering the country, whose rules may be incompatible with your own culture, traditions, and religion? (2) Are you willing to accept deportation if you find yourself unable to comply with these rules and regulations for whatever reasons after entering the country? Only if both questions were answered in the positive would a visa be granted.[50]

50 秃头戈女 – 五月媂国: 德国华裔当代艺术家蓝镜 (Jiny Lan) 巴黎艺术展 ["Bald Girl – May Love." German-Chinese Contemporary Artist Jiny Lan's Paris Art Exhibition], Union des Artistes d'Asie en France, May 10, 2016, <http://www.uaafparis.com/expositions--25152263772363735272/-jiny-lan>. In an interview, she referred to the "Pictures Republic of Jiny" as the family of her paintings, similar to Jinyology: "This big family of paintings is actually fictitious. It is a new species that I have created, neither human nor animal.... I myself am the god and creator of this republic, and I can make them proliferate in this imaginary world according to my will." See 艾米 Ai Mi, 蓝镜的 "殖拟图像共和国" 在巴黎 [Jiny Lan's "Pictures Republic of Jiny" in Paris], 华语—法国国际广播电台 [Chinese Language – Radio France Internationale], May 27, 2016, <https://www.rfi.fr/cn/中国/20160528-蓝镜的"殖拟图像共和国"在巴黎>.

Lan attributed the failure of the French and German media to report on this performance to the political correctness of the dominant Western media outlets. When the Cologne sexual assaults happened, she, as a feminist artist, not only criticized the behavior of the attackers, but also cited the failure of German official and public discourse to effectively communicate the behavior it expected from immigrants and refugees, lest Germans be seen as patronizing or racist. In June 2016, she repeated the performance in Duisburg during the exhibit *Another Germany* in the Cubus-Kunsthalle in Immanuel-Kant-Park, which featured works by nine Chinese artists living in Germany.[51] To her disappointment, this performance did not receive media coverage either, likely due to the affinity between the performance's message and right-wing political views.

Here Lan's background as an immigrant impacted her perspective. After she came to Germany in 1995, she appreciated, in her words, the "cultural enlightenment" she underwent in Germany. Based on her own experience, she knew that culture shock or clash is inevitable for new immigrants, especially for refugees who did not prepare for their entry into Germany linguistically or culturally. She knew that in China, for example, lewd behavior or sexual harassment in public is not subject to prosecution. Lan used the Chinese proverb, "Unpleasant words must be said up front," meaning that one must be frank and dispel illusions. In this way, one is proactive, not reactive, as German policies toward refugees tended to be. Lan believed that proactive communication of expectations would foster the integration of refugees into German society and ensure their success. She argued that in the absence of sociocultural education, a case such as the Cologne sexual assaults resulted in backlash against refugees in general: it alienated the erstwhile supporters of Merkel's *Willkommenskultur* (welcoming culture), benefited the far-right populist party, the Alternative for Germany (AfD), and impacted the migration policy of Germany and other countries.[52] She calls this performance *Vis-à-vis*: "One cannot bypass some problems or solve them through silence, but must confront them *vis-à-vis*."

As a feminist artist, Lan's first and foremost concern is the global rights of women. In her opinion, multiculturalism and diversity cannot be promoted at the expense of women. She does not see a contradiction between supporting refugees while at the same time criticizing certain problems arising with the refugee influx and within the refugee

51 Anna Ernst, "Das andere Deutschland und das andere China," *WAZ*, June 18, 2016, <https://www.waz.de/staedte/duisburg/das-andere-deutschland-und-das-andere-china-id11928041.html>; Ingo Hoddick, "Chinesische Kunst in der Cubus-Kunsthalle" *Rheinische Post*, June 18, 2016, <https://rp-online.de/nrw/staedte/duisburg/chinesische-kunst-in-der-cubus-kunsthalle_aid-21479323>.

52 Bosen, "New Year's Eve in Cologne."

community. She questioned the self-censorship of the left camp and its failure to communicate rules and expectations for fear of being labeled racist or Islamophobic. She was disappointed that both French and German media chose to ignore her project, provocative as it was, and thereby missed the opportunity for a difficult discussion regarding the *Willkommenskultur* and integration of refugees. Lan explained: "Art is an experiment. Artists have a lot of freedom. They might be ahead of their time, or, contrarily, their ideas might be wrong or absurd. But, as an artist, I want to preserve the right to independently reflect and raise questions for social debate. Any silencing is a form of authoritarianism that I associate with the Cultural Revolution in China." On many occasions she explained that she criticized the left because she did not want the AfD to gain more traction.

The Chained Woman and Covid in *Ping* (2022)

The Bald Girls do not perform or exhibit together every year.[53] The three artists live on different continents: Xiao Lu in Australia, Li Xinmo in Asia, and Jiny Lan in Europe. In 2022, however, the feminist collective celebrated its tenth anniversary with an exhibition titled *Chain Reaction*, held from July 14 to August 6 in Düsseldorf and curated by Xu with co-curator Julia Hartmann. Lan's contributions included the painting *Ping* (Fig. 3.17).

In February 2022, a video of a lone woman chained by the neck to a wall in a shack in Feng County, city of Xuzhou, Jiangsu Province, spread like wildfire on social media, sparking a national scandal that threatened to derail the 2022 Beijing Winter Olympics (February 4–20). The "chained woman" (*Tielian nü*), a mother of eight, was confirmed to be a victim of multiple human trafficking crimes. She was discovered in late January 2022 by a blogger who was visiting the area to document the achievements of the government's poverty alleviation campaign.[54] The blogger's revelation tore open an old wound concerning the abduction and

53 For more performances and activities of the Bald Girls, see the curator's webpage: <https://www.juanxucurator.com/>.

54 Xiaofei Xu, Wayne Chang, Jade Wurapa, and Heather Chen, "A Woman Was Chained and Tortured in China and the Images Put Online. Six People Have Been Jailed," *CNN*, April 8, 2023, <https://edition.cnn.com/2023/04/08/asia/chinese-woman-chained-torture-intl-hnk/index.html>; Chen Jing, "Chained Mother of Eight Brings Attention to Abduction and Sale of Women in Rural China," thinkchina.sg, February 18, 2022, <https://www.thinkchina.sg/chained-mother-eight-brings-attention-abduction-and-sale-women-rural-china>.

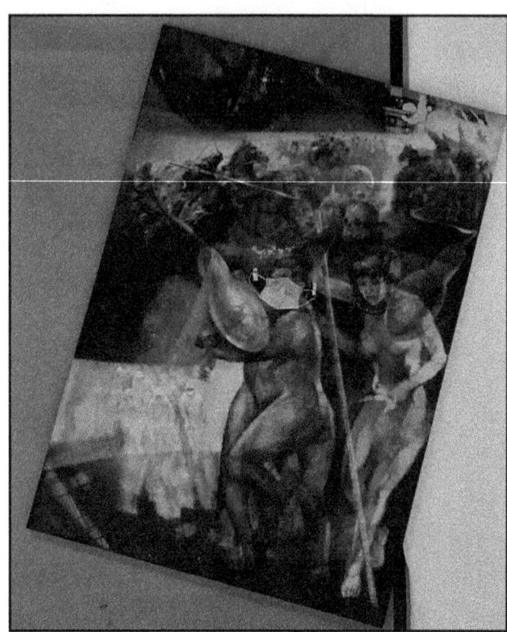

Fig. 3.17. *Ping* (2022, 200 × 140 cm) at the Bald Girls' Tenth Anniversary exhibition (photo: the author).

trafficking of women. The public was outraged by local officials' efforts to censor the news and prevent the truth from coming out.[55]

Lan conceived *Ping* as part of a new series of calligraphic paintings including *Oh, the Humanity!* (Fig. 6.6). The Chinese character hidden in this painting is 平 (*ping*), which has various meanings depending on the context: balance, equality, fairness, or justice. It is also one of the characters in the name of Chinese president Xi Jinping. In the painting, the character *ping* is formed by several visual elements, including two broad, horizontal, white brushstrokes covered in fluorescent paint that glow in

55 Guo Rui, "China's Chained Woman Scandal: Public Anger Persists as Investigations, Censorship 'Raise More Questions,'" *South China Morning Post*, February 25, 2022, <https://www.scmp.com/news/china/politics/article/3168282/chinas-chained-woman-scandal-public-anger-persists>; Mary Hong, "Former Journalist Chooses to Leave China after Being Harassed for Investigating the 'Chained Woman,'" *The Epoch Times*, August 9, 2022 <https://www.theepochtimes.com/china/former-journalist-chooses-to-leave-china-after-being-harassed-for-investigating-the-chained-woman-4649937>; Vivian Wang, "The Secret Campaign in China to Save a Woman Chained by the Neck," *New York Times*, March 5, 2025, <https://www.nytimes.com/interactive/2025/03/05/world/asia/xuzhou-china-chained-woman-incident-activists.html?unlocked_article_code=1.1k4.qBKj.iQS4hmE-iKBx&smid=url-share>.

the dark. The stick in the woman's hand constitutes the vertical stroke in the middle of the character, while two balloon-like sperm represent the remaining strokes. According to Lan, the stick held by the woman is inspired by the statue of the sword-holding Lady Justice in Vienna's Palace of Justice, as well as by the statue of Athena, the goddess of wisdom, who holds a spear in her left hand at the Pallas Athena Fountain, located a short distance away in front of the Austrian Parliament. Lan uses these hidden references to cast the chained woman as a goddess of justice, even though justice has been denied to her.[56] Whereas the blogger's video shows the chained woman to be traumatized and emaciated, her counterpart in the painting is radiant; her depiction is an act of poetic and transcendental justice that restores her beauty and dignity.

Xi Jinping and the chained woman are the protagonists in the foreground of the painting. (During the Bald Girls' tenth anniversary exhibition, Lan taped a surgical mask to *Ping* to cover Xi's face, a tactful move given the presence of hundreds of Chinese visitors representing various political positionalities. Although the masking of Xi's face is an act of self-censorship, it resonates with his zero-Covid policy.) Xi, naked, turns and runs away from the woman, symbolizing how women who are victims of the one-child policy or sexual violence have been abandoned and ignored by the government. A closer look shows another male body conjoined with Xi, allegorizing the collusion between Chinese authorities and men who have bought wives. As the "husband" reaches out to take the chained woman's left hand, he actually grasps another disembodied male hand, possibly that of a human trafficker. Thus, in an eerie and appalling way, the painting pungently sketches the collective patriarchal exploitation of women and the government's indirect responsibility for hundreds of thousands of women who were exploited as the chained woman was.

The irony of the scandal is that the chained woman – a victim of the one-child policy – came to public attention after the government abandoned that same policy in 2016. Meanwhile, countless Chinese families were still reeling from their traumatic experiences with the one-child policy. The slogans promoting the three-child policy often resemble those used to enforce the one-child policy. However, due to the prohibitive cost of raising and educating a child in China and the lack of meaningful government incentives, the effectiveness of the three-child policy is still unknown.[57] The attitude of "lying flat" (*tang ping*), a mentality of nonviolent non-cooperation prevalent among the childbearing generation,

56 On April 7, 2023, the husband of the chained woman was sentenced to nine years in prison, again sparking internet outrage over the light sentence.

57 Susan Greenhalgh, "The Biopolitics of the Three-Child Policy," *Made in China Journal* 9, no. 1 (2024), <https://madeinchinajournal.com/2024/06/06/the-biopolitics-of-the-three-child-policy/>.

worries the government. Thus, *ping*, which can mean "flat" in Chinese, takes on another resonant connotation.

From enforcing compulsory abortion to restricting abortion, family planning policy in China has changed radically. In Lan's words: "First, fetuses were forced to be aborted; now the Chinese government is taking measures to stimulate births. The reality is even more ridiculous than my painting." Lan explained that the skulls above the figures have the proportions of infant skulls and represent aborted fetuses. Above the skulls, a dull-colored crowd waves the red Mao bible. To their right, a martial scene with horses, armed riders, and spears suggests that the Chinese government, fearing another peasant uprising, has turned a blind eye to the purchase and sexual enslavement of women. Men in villages and remote areas are particularly affected by their inability to find wives due to the gender imbalance. They have become the main buyers of trafficked women. Having (male) heirs to carry on the family name is such a critical concern for peasant families that if this wish is not fulfilled, the stability of the state is threatened. Throughout Chinese history, peasant rebellions have often toppled dynasties.[58] Thus, the expedient solution for the government to remedy its own policy failure is to sacrifice women to keep the peasants under control, hence a *pink solution*. On the right, Lan painted a scene from the War of Liberation, the term the CCP uses for the Second Civil War with the Nationalists (1946–49), but as she wryly noted: "It is so ironic to call it the 'War of Liberation' because the Chinese are still oppressed after the 'liberation.'" The population at large bear the brunt of the government's disastrous campaigns and initiatives, such as the Great Leap Forward and the one-child and zero-Covid policies.

Ping includes a reference to another contemporary event that fueled opposition to Party rule. In response to the Covid-19 outbreak, Xi instituted a draconian zero-Covid policy to halt transmission of the virus. In the lower left corner of the painting, a group of policemen or security forces dressed in white protective clothing represents those tasked with enforcing the zero-Covid policy, often by violent means. The enforcers gained notoriety in 2022 during a two-month lockdown of Shanghai and were dubbed *da bai* ("big white" pandemic workers) or White Guards (*bai weibing*).[59] Lan's collage method and symbolic style allow her to juxtapose images in order to present and comment on contemporary events.

58 Frederick Wakeman, Jr., "Rebellion and Revolution: The Study of Popular Movements in Chinese History," *The Journal of Asian Studies* 36, no. 2 (1977): 201–37.

59 Rita Cheng, Qiao Long, and Chingman, "China's 'White Guards' Gain Reputation for Brutal Enforcement of Shanghai Lockdown," *rfa* (Radio Free Asia), May 29, 2022, <https://www.rfa.org/english/news/china/shanghai-whiteguards-05292022070418.html>; Arjun Neil Alim, Kai Waluszewski, and Eleanor Olcott, "'No One Remembers Us': China's 'Big White' Pandemic

During the exhibition, *Ping* was hung in front of the painting of Confucius created for the *Who's Your Daddy* performance in 2014. Chinese patriarchy was literally the hidden background for the shocking story of the chained woman. This juxtaposition is a particularly rich example of how Lan recycles and recontextualizes her artworks to create formal and thematic continuity. Xiao Lu brought from Australia an installation and video project, *Tear Down This Wall* (*Tuidao zhedu qiang*, 2022), alluding to Ronald Reagan's appeal to Mikhail Gorbachev on June 12, 1987. The installation included a piece of barbed wire fence and a metal wall used to quarantine people as part of China's draconian corona measures. A video screen played footage downloaded from WeChat, the largest social media platform in China. Some of the clips had already been censored. Xiao was also encouraged by blog posts that show resistance within China's Great Firewall.[60] Li Xinmo could not travel to Düsseldorf due to Covid measures in China.

The last day of the exhibition culminated in a panel discussion with one of the most celebrated Chinese writers, Geling Yan, in Düsseldorf on August 6, 2022. Yan, a resident of Berlin, published "Mother, oh, Mother" (*Muqing a muqing*) on February 5, 2022, expressing her lament for the chained woman and her exasperation over the lawsuit filed by the woman's eldest son, who accused the blogger of defaming his mother and photographing her without her permission.[61] In early 2020, Yan published an essay mourning the death of Dr. Li Wenliang, the whistleblower who spoke out about the coronavirus and was disciplined by authorities before dying from the virus himself. In "To Borrow Tang Wan's Three Words: Cover-up, Cover-up, Cover-up" (*Jie Tangwan sanzi: man man man*), Yan lambasted the Chinese authorities for censoring Li and another Wuhan doctor, Ai Fen, known as the whistle-giver.[62] This essay was Yan's first public criticism of the Chinese government, and she was not surprised when she herself was censored.[63]

Workers Reel from End of Zero-Covid," *Financial Times*, February 2, 2023, <https://www.ft.com/content/2cc7e36c-ec30-4c8a-8629-369663f82ac8>.

60 "Xiao Lu Participates in 'Bald Girls—Chain Reaction' Exhibition in Düsseldorf," November 4, 2022, <http://xiaoluart.com/index.php?c=show&id=172>.

61 严歌苓Geling Yan, 母亲啊母亲 [Mother, oh, Mother], Women's Rights in China, February 16, 2022, <https://wrchina.org/archives/12751>; Yan, "Mother, Mother," iMedia, May 29, 2025, <https://min.news/en/culture/365cb4bacacf5ae751db29b5fd77b096.html>.

62 Geling Yan's essay is central to Fang Fang's diary entry on March 16, 2020; see Fang Fang, *Wuhan Diary: Dispatches from a Quarantined City*, trans. Michael Berry (New York: HarperVia, 2020), 290–7.

63 "Yan Geling: Well-known Writer on Xuzhou Mother of Eight Criticises Xi Jinping's Censorship," *BBC*, February 15, 2022; "The Price of Free Expression:

Coda: "The Political Is Personal"

The familial and social ramifications of the one-child policy have been a constant concern for the Bald Girls. The chained woman was a shock to Chinese society as a whole and especially to a feminist collective like the Bald Girls. The scandal exposed how politics intrudes into private and personal lives. The chained woman's fate was determined by reproductive policies enacted by the Chinese state. Curator Xu declared that over the past ten years, the Bald Girls had adopted the slogan of Western second-wave feminism, "The personal is political," but now the Bald Girls 2.0 affirm that "The political is personal."[64] The first slogan emphasized an international struggle for women's rights and focused on what women could and should do to obtain sexual equality. The second slogan, however, draws attention to how political decisions impact personal and private lives. Combining the chained woman and Covid, for example, the painting *Ping* suggests the systemic disadvantage of a dictatorship: One-child and zero-Covid were both draconic policies that were ultimately abandoned, leaving dire consequences in their wake. The emergence of the Bald Girls 2.0 seems to mark a shift away from what women can or cannot do to what politics could or should (not) do, from consciousness-raising among women to calling for political reform.

Geling Yan on Censorship," Lecture at Bryn Mawr College, YouTube, November 19, 2024, <https://www.youtube.com/watch?v=5rR1DXAl6TI>.

64 秃头戈女：链锁反应！极具爆炸和冲击力的艺术盛宴 在杜塞尔多夫开幕 [Bald Girls: Chain Reaction! An Art Feast with Explosive Impact Opens in Düsseldorf], *Hua Shang Bao*, July 24, 2022.

4: *Selbstverfraulichung* with the Master's Tools: A Double-Edged Reception of Joseph Beuys

FROM 2006 TO 2009, Lan worked as a part-time China project coordinator at the Museum Schloss Moyland in North Rhine-Westphalia, which houses the world's largest collection of works by Joseph Beuys (1921–86). Beuys, whose Nazi ties and autobiographical fictions made him one of the most controversial artists in the West, exerted a great impact on Lan, who called him her "spiritual mentor." She appreciated his visual style: "When I first saw Beuys's early sketches, I liked their freedom and simple aesthetic. His animal sketches reminded me of Picasso's bulls." Moreover, she argued that Beuys had redefined the role of the artist in society: "He liberated artists from the fate of being craftsmen and allowed them to be intellectuals. What resonated with me a lot was his anti-authoritarianism and his quest for democracy." Like Beuys, Lan became a conceptual (*guan nian*) and performing (*xing wei*) artist, and she has interacted with his work in a number of projects, sometimes imitating Beuys's own performances, and at other times struggling to liberate herself from his influence. This chapter treats her reverent yet critical reception of Beuys as a key to understanding her concept of *Selbstverfraulichung* (a Woman's Self-Glorification).

Pictures of an Exhibition (2006–7): A Phase of Searching

While working at Museum Schloss Moyland, Lan made a series of fourteen paintings titled *Pictures of an Exhibition* (2006–7), which depict visitors viewing and reacting to Beuys's paintings (shown here are four examples used later in *One Person Room* [2013], Fig. 4.1a–d).[1] At that time, Beuys's works were displayed in salon style at the museum, hung

1 The title is borrowed from the Russian composer Modest Mussorgsky's 1874 suite for piano, which in turn is based on pictures created by the artist/architect Viktor Hartmann. Beuys himself attempted to reinterpret Mussorgsky's program music. See Shinya Watanabe, "Searching for EUR-ASIA: Joseph Beuys and Nam June Paik' [*sic*] Life Long Collaboration" (PhD diss., Universität der Künste Berlin, 2017), 185–8.

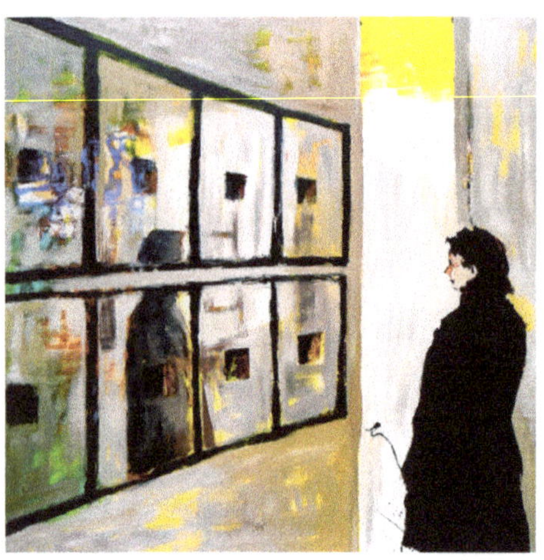

Fig. 4.1a. *Pictures of an Exhibition* (2006–07, 185 × 185 cm), example 1.

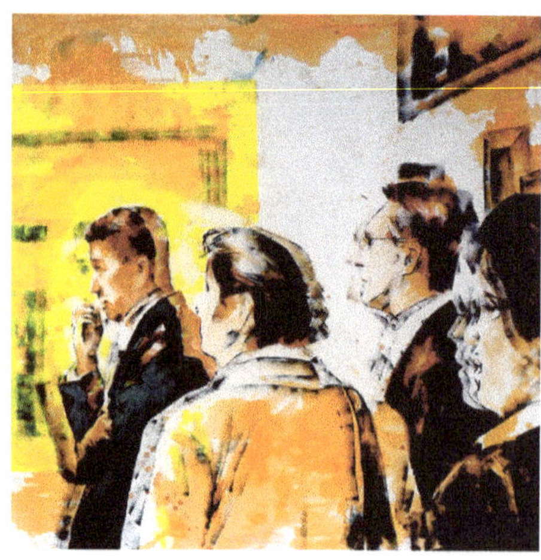

Fig. 4.1b. *Pictures of an Exhibition*, example 2.

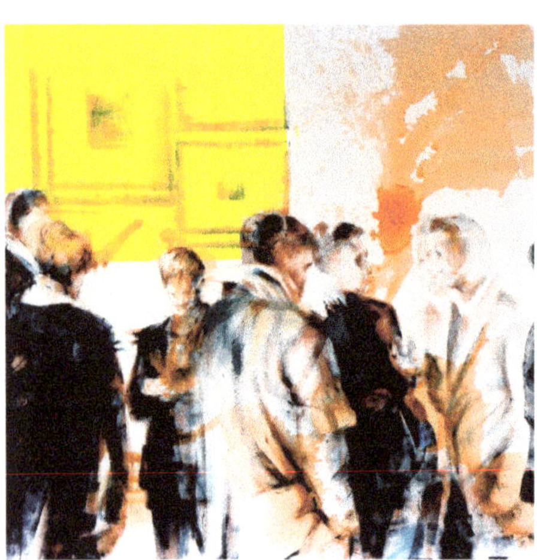

Fig. 4.1c. *Pictures of an Exhibition*, example 3.

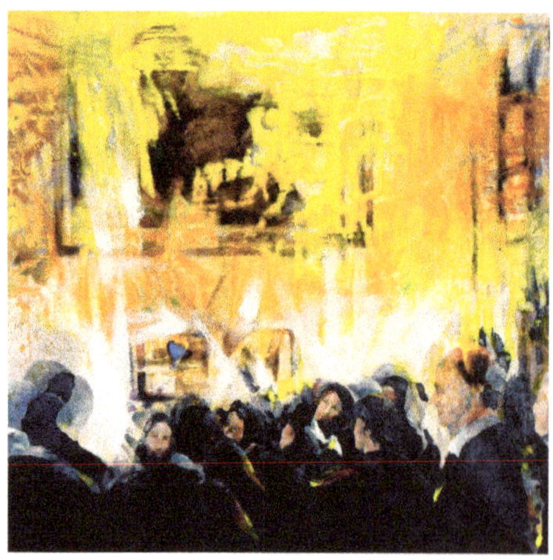

Fig. 4.1d. *Pictures of an Exhibition* example 4.

close together and stacked up to the ceiling. Lan renders Beuys's paintings in a blurred and abstract manner; her focus is on the viewers looking at Beuys's works. Thus, the title "Pictures of an Exhibition" is a double entendre, referring to both Beuys's paintings and her own.

Notable in this series is the predominant use of yellow patches, contrasted with some streaks of orange and other colors. The yellow paints overlay Beuys's works and obscure them. As Yuejun Qian writes in his analysis of this series, yellow has a high-intensity hue, which makes it an invasive color, and it is also frivolous and unstable; therefore, in these paintings, yellow intrudes into other colors, but is also intruded upon by other colors.[2] Yellow has significance for Beuys as well: *Capri Battery* (1985), a project linked to renewable energy, warmth, and the environment, imagines a lemon supplying power to a yellow light bulb. He also depicted himself with a yellow skin tone in *Yellow* (1977), a serigraph in yellow and blue on cardboard. Beuys stands in front of a microphone, suggesting that the yellow coloration could be caused by stage lights shining on him. Thus, the image implies a public event or performance.

The relationship between the artist and the audience was important to Beuys. It likewise became a guiding principle in Lan's work. In her career, Lan often coordinates her exhibitions with a public performance. She sometimes leaves a painting unfinished in the studio in order to complete it during an exhibition by including selected visitors in her artwork. Her participatory art relies on years of experience painting strangers in public places. In the age of AI and fake news, live painting also allows the audience to be her witness. The series *Pictures of an Exhibition* already attests to her interest in the interaction between art and the public.

Fluxus, Social Sculpture, and the First Beuys Exhibition in China

In September 2006, Wang Huangsheng, the director of the Central Academy of Fine Arts (CAFA) Museum in Beijing, visited Museum Schloss Moyland while attending the exhibition *Today's German Art* in Düsseldorf. Lan introduced him to the German museum curator, which led to discussions about the possibility of exhibiting Beuys in China, and Lan herself accompanied German representatives on two trips to China. Ultimately, however, no works from Museum Schloss Moyland could be shown in China, in part due to ongoing legal disputes between the

2 钱跃君 Yuejun Qian, 茫然地寻找人生之路 – 赏析旅德女画家蓝镜绘画 [Dazedly Searching for the Path of Life – Appreciation of the Paintings by Jiny Lan, a Chinese Artist in Germany], Wenxuecity, January 14, 2021, <https://bbs.wenxuecity.com/art/133198.html>.

museum and Beuys's widow, Eva Beuys.[3] But the wish to bring Beuys's works to China was not abandoned.

In 2009, Lan became acquainted with Juan Xu, who knew that the art collector Michael Berger, based in Wiesbaden, owned many of Beuys's multiples and other important Fluxus artworks. In the winter of 2010, Yu Xingze, an art teacher from the School of Architecture of CAFA who also studied art in Düsseldorf, invited Berger to the CAFA Museum. The possibility of a Beuys exhibition in China was back on the table. In April 2011, Wang Huangsheng, Yu Xingze, Xu, and Lan went to Wiesbaden to see Berger's Beuys collection and decided to plan an exhibition in China. After Wang and Yu returned to Beijing, they invited two Chinese experts on Beuys, Professor Zhu Qingsheng from Peking University and Professor Yi Ying from CAFA, to be the main curators and enlisted Xu, Lan, and Yu as co-curators. The founder of the Shanghai How Art Museum, Zheng Hao, was a collector of Beuys. His museum contributed many Beuys works to the exhibition.[4] Berger also sold about three hundred Beuys multiples to How Art Museum. "These are always edition objects (*Auflagenobjekte*), not originals," he explained. "But in China the image (*das Bild*) counts. The content, knowledge, inscription, and the essence of the image are more important than whether it is number 1, 31, 32, or 34."[5]

Berger was an important sponsor of Fluxus artists. He hosted the Korean American artist Nam June Paik for ten years in his house, and the African American musician and artist Benjamin Patterson lived for twenty years in a parsonage Berger owned in Wiesbaden. Berger also pointed out the importance of women artists in Fluxus: "Fluxus was the first art movement where women had the big say. Japanese women artists Yoko Ono, Takako Saito, Mieko Shiomi, and Shigeko Kubota, who was the wife of Nam June Paik, were all important members."[6] He introduced Lan to Patterson and the Fluxus movement.

3 See for example, Christiane Meixner, "Museum Schloss Moyland: Streit um Beuys-Erbe," *Der Tagesspiegel*, August 22, 2010, <https://www.tagesspiegel.de/kultur/museum-schloss-moyland-streit-um-beuys-erbe/1908330.html>.

4 Wang Huangsheng, "Joseph Beuys and China," *Social Sculpture: Beuys in China* 社会雕塑: 博伊斯在中国, a bilingual edition ed. Wang Huangsheng (Beijing: 中国青年出版社 China Youth Publishing House, 2013), 18–20.

5 Phone interview with Michael Berger on December 3, 2024.

6 Phone interview with Berger. See also Megan Butcher, "Fluxus: The Significant Role of Female Artists" (Honors diss., Pace University, 2018), <https://digitalcommons.pace.edu/cgi/viewcontent.cgi?article=1185&context=honorscollege_theses>; Martha Schwendener, "Yoko Ono and the Women of Fluxus Changed the Rules in Art and Life," *New York Times*, October 27, 2023, <https://www.nytimes.com/2023/10/27/arts/design/fluxus-artists-japan-society-yoko-ono.html>; "Out of Bounds: Japanese Women Artists in Fluxus,

The Fluxus idea of changing society through art in a manner that is as serious as it is humorous, as provocative as it is parodic, inspired Lan greatly. When she heard about Fluxus and its anti-authoritarian and irreverent approach to art, she felt a sense of relief and liberation: "What I did intuitively as a child was validated as art. I became more confident in what I was doing: it IS art, and it has a name." She had found a theorization of her early artwork. Her Lei Feng painting already embodied the use of humor and sarcasm by hiding images of pigs in a portrait of the model Chinese soldier. She seemed to have a spiritual kinship, a *Geisteswahlverwandtschaft*, with Fluxus. Intrigued by the Fluxus idea of blurring the distinction between different media and materials, Lan also created mixed-media art, which had no place in the academic art training she received in China. She recalled: "The professors at the China Academy of Art did not allow us to draw with charcoal pencils, only with pencils. Color had to be applied one brushstroke at a time. No splashing, spattering, rubbing (frottage), or other techniques were allowed either. Professors trained students' basic skills and did not permit 'clever' ways to produce effects."

Beuys was loosely attached to the Fluxus movement. Thomas Kellein, an art historian and director of the Kunsthalle Bielefeld, has shown how Beuys appropriated and co-opted Fluxus. He argues that Beuys's self-association with Fluxus, beginning in 1963 with his second "stable exhibition" at the van der Grinten farm in Kranenburg, served as a launching pad for his international reputation. In contrast to George Maciunas, whose *Fluxus Manifesto* (1963) framed the movement as a project to dismantle high art, Beuys applied the elastic term to his own radically expanded notion of art, namely, that "everyone is an artist."[7] He believed in the importance of transforming society through human creativity, and his democratic and anti-elitist concept of art blurs the line

---

October 13, 2023–January 21, 2024," Japan Society, <https://japansociety.org/gallery/out-of-bounds-japanese-women-artists-in-fluxus/>; Rachel Christopher, "The 4 Japanese Female Artists Who Changed The Game," *Japan Nakama*, February 13, 2014.

7 Thomas Kellein, "Zum Fluxus-Begriff von Joseph Beuys," in *Joseph Beuys-Tagung: Basel 1.–4. Mai 1991*, ed. Volker Harlan, Dieter Koepplin, and Rudolf Velhagen (Basel: Wiese, 1991), 137–42 . See Claudia Mesch and Viola Michely, "Editors' Introduction," in *Joseph Beuys: The Reader*, ed. Claudia Mesch and Viola Michely, with a foreword by Arthur C. Danto; additional translation by Nickolas Decarlo, Kayvan Rouhani and Heidi Zimmerman (Cambridge, MA: MIT Press, 2007), 1–25, here 19–20; Thomas Kellein, "I Make Jokes! Fluxus through the Eyes of 'Chairman' George Maciunas," in *Fluxus* (London: Thames and Hudson, 1995), 7–26. Kellein also notes an irony in this confrontation: whereas Fluxus's visibility arguably waned after 1965, Beuys's stature grew as he garnered international recognition.

between art and life.[8] Through the concept of social sculpture (*soziale Plastik*), Beuys expressed the social obligation of art and the desire to change society through art. This view overlaps with the beliefs of avant-garde and Narrative Figuration artists in the West. It also aligns with the credo of Chinese avant-garde artists after the Cultural Revolution. As Li Xianting writes of the Stars group, "artists need to be involved in society; when their lives are tied with the people's, this brings life to art."[9]

The first Beuys solo exhibition in China finally took place at the CAFA Museum in Beijing from July 9 to November 15, 2013. It overlapped with a solo Andy Warhol exhibition at CAFA (September 29–November 15), allowing Chinese viewers to experience the works of two radically different icons of contemporary Western art on the same day.[10] The curators initially thought of naming the exhibition "We Are the Revolution," after the famous life-size photograph of Beuys striding toward the camera (*La Rivoluzione siamo noi*, 1972). Fearing censorship by Chinese authorities, however, they settled on the anodyne title "Social Sculpture: Beuys in China."[11] In fact, an important dimension of social sculpture was Beuys's strong advocacy for a "people's referendum" and "direct democracy." Claudia Mesch writes: "As Beuys implemented it, the exchange of individual opinions within an open public dialogue and debate comprised social sculpture; a functioning and unmediated public sphere therefore became the realization of social sculpture. Beuys

8 Writing about Beuys's involvement with the Green Party in its early days, Lukas Beckmann quotes Beuys as saying: "Thinking is sculpture. A thought is the product of human creativity.... A thought that is born of creativity is already a work of art, a sculpture.... In thinking, this future becomes the focus of a Social Sculpture, which has yet to take shape as a society suited to humankind.... The essential capital of a society is human creativity. Art = Capital." Lukas Beckmann, "The Causes in the Future," trans. S. Linberg and R. Brenner, in *Joseph Beuys: Mapping the Legacy*, ed. Gene Ray (New York: Distributed Art Publishers, 2001), 91–111, here 96–7.

9 Li Xianting, "About the Stars Exhibition," in *Stars 79–80*, 252–5. This is translated from the Chinese article entitled 关于星星美展, originally published in *Meishu*, no. 3 (1980).

10 Wang, "Joseph Beuys and China," 20.

11 The exhibition consisted of 307 items, primarily everyday objects, posters, photographs, postcards, newspaper clippings, and handwritten notes. Over two thousand visitors came on the first day. Beuys's expanded notion of art opened the eyes of many Chinese artists and visitors to how art could be created using techniques other than drawing and painting. Since then, many performance art projects and installations in China have shown a Beuysian influence, for example through the significant use of blood, nails, hair, and animals. See Sun Linlin, 为什么人人都爱谈论博伊斯 [Why do people love talking about Beuys], *Sina*, December 11, 2013, <https://collection.sina.com.cn/plfx/20131211/1024136590.shtml?from=wap>.

advocated the 'grassroots' process of *Volksabstimmung* or people's referendum as a way to inject true public debate into the political process."[12] But "people's referendum" and "direct democracy" are seditious concepts in China, where a civil society with a true public sphere is lacking. Not surprisingly, the Chinese exhibition did not touch on Beuys's explicit advocacy for political reform, democracy, and radical individual freedom and self-empowerment. Beuys's notion of social sculpture was presented to the Chinese audience selectively.

In their article about the exhibition, Xu and Lan relate Beuys's theory of social sculpture to the concept of rational self-interest developed by the American mathematician John Nash. They explain that social sculpture holds significance for China because the concept proposes cooperation and social warmth as a means to effect social change. The authors cite social problems in China: economic striving at the cost of the environment, and a tainted market that permitted the selling of poisoned infant formula and waste oil, resulting in a collapse in social trust. Thus, they see Beuys's social sculpture and Nash's theory of equilibrium as practical ideals for Chinese society to pursue during the globalized, capitalistic information era.[13] In an interview, Lan mentioned that Beuys's concept of social sculpture played a role in the founding of the Bald Girls: "Influenced by the thoughts of 'social sculpture,' I made the decision to connect my own art with social issues tied to reality. These thoughts coincided with the intention of a curator and two other artists. So, the group came together very quickly."[14]

Beuys left a singular impression on Chinese art. As Wang Huangsheng writes: "Since the cultural opening in late 1970s, especially the '1985 Art Movement,' Beuys has been influencing the contemporary Chinese art field, and has been widely discussed and quoted as a social spirit, a unique art behavior and form."[15] Wang Guangyi, Wang Youshen, and Shang Yang acknowledged the influence Beuys had on them. The Political Pop artist Wang Guangyi said that Beuys with his mysteriousness made an even

12 Claudia Mesch, "Institutionalizing Social Sculpture: Beuys's Office for Direct Democracy through Referendum Installation (1972)," in *Joseph Beuys: The Reader*, 198–217, here 199.

13 庸现/蓝镜 Juan Xu and Jiny Lan, 信息资本主义时代的博伊斯 – "社会雕塑"与"理性利己"的博弈 [Joseph Beuys in the Capitalistic Information Era – Struggle between "Social Sculpture" and "Rational Self-interest"], in *Social Sculpture*, 100–13; "Beuys in China. CAFA Art Museum Beijing," Juan Xu Curator, <https://www.juanxucurator.com/beuys-in-china-2013.html>.

14 Partl, "Jiny Lan: The Right to Speak via Art."

15 Wang, "Joseph Beuys and China," 19; see also 赵炎 Zhao Yan, 博伊斯对中国当代艺术界的影响 [Beuys's Influence on China's Contemporary Art Scene], 东方早报*The Oriental Morning Post*, October 2, 2013, <https://collection.sina.com.cn/plfx/20131002/1008128826.shtml?from=wap>.

greater impact on him than Andy Warhol. Wang compared his own use of millet as a material with Beuys's choice of felt.[16] Wang Youshen printed an issue of *Beijing Youth Daily*, the newspaper he worked for, onto a piece of clothing (*Newspaper Clothing*, 1991). This invokes Beuys's famous multiples of *Felt Suit* (1970). Wang Youshen also wore the garment when buying a copy of another newspaper. *Newspaper Clothing* shows the pervasiveness of news in our life and the intrusion of mass media into private life.[17] Shang Yang said that during his first trip to Europe in 1993, he saw a lot of contemporary art but Beuys touched him the most. Shang sought to infuse classical vibes into the contemporary spirit and he found that same tendency in Beuys: "I saw in [Beuys's] works this 'classical quality,' be it fat, felt, steel furniture, a vest, or a rose. They are connected with the most important qualities of the human spirit. Beuys repeatedly presented memory, gratitude, pain, and spiritual journey in his own way.... Even though Beuys pursued a radical break with the old art system, his works still evince the core classical spirit."[18] Philip Tinari discussed at length Ai Weiwei's turn from Marcel Duchamp toward Beuys, from the readymade toward social sculpture.[19] In short, Beuys's concept of art influenced contemporary Chinese artists enormously by expanding their understanding of art and encouraging them to use art to intervene in social politics.

One Person Room (2013) and *Signer in Hangzhou* (2013): At the Shanghai Biennale

In the spirit of Beuysian conceptual art, Lan orchestrated a transnational performance project, *One Person Room*, during the Shanghai Biennale (October 2012–March 2013) in order to highlight the imbalance in economic and cultural development through globalization.[20] To that end, she arranged viewing rooms in four places in China and Germany: the Power Station of Art and the Jingxing Textile Factory, both in Shanghai,

16 王广义 Wang Guangyi, 沃霍尔PK波依斯, 我更喜欢谁? [Warhol PK Beuys, Who Do I like Better?], *Sina*, November 21, 2016, <https://collection.sina.com.cn/ddys/zh/2016-11-21/doc-ifxxwrwh4812498.shtml>.

17 "Wang Youshen," *Shanghai Art*, <http://www.shanghart.com/texts/wys1.htm; https://www.shanghartgallery.com/galleryarchive/work.htm?workId=5695>.

18 赵野 Zhao Ye, 尚扬:当代绘画的困境 [Shang Yang: Dilemma in Contemporary Painting], *Sina*, December 22, 2018, <http://k.sina.com.cn/article_6647956963_18c3fc5e300100gndf.html>.

19 Philip Tinari, "A Kind of True Living: The Art of Ai Weiwei," *Art Forum* 45, no. 10 (2007), <https://www.artforum.com/print/200706/a-kind-of-true-living-the-art-of-ai-weiwei-15365>.

20 This performance was a counterpart to the exhibit *One-Persons-Chorus* in Düsseldorf, discussed in chapter 2.

the NRW-Forum in Düsseldorf, and the Bochum-based machine factory Bomafa Armaturen. In this way, viewers would encounter her art in either a workplace setting or a traditional art museum.[21] Each of the four viewing rooms was furnished with a couch and a single picture from *Pictures of an Exhibition* (Fig. 4.1a–d). Only one viewer at a time was allowed in a room. Viewers could lock the door and remain inside for as long as they wished. German volunteers all exited the room quickly. Chinese volunteers at the garment factory, however, stayed inside for as long as two hours. But Lan learned that the workers were using the couch to catch up on sleep. This discovery became a highlight of the project – a result that was unexpected, but, in retrospect, not surprising. Lan's experiment of giving temporary privacy and individual freedom to Chinese migrant workers who live in crowded dorm rooms and work long factory shifts pointedly ended with the workers enjoying rest instead of art.

This comparative performance yielded a concrete example of developmental inequalities between China and Germany in the age of globalization. The working conditions for employees in the Bochum factory were much better than those for migrant workers at the Shanghai garment factory. Chinese workers earned excruciatingly low wages for long hours of work. Although China is often seen as a beneficiary of globalization, one cannot neglect its human cost. According to Lan, it does not matter whether the clothing belongs to a high-end or an average brand: Chinese workers receive about the same piece rate. As a result, the leisure to appreciate art is a luxury beyond the reach of Chinese migrant workers.

At the Shanghai Biennale, Lan also witnessed the Swiss artist Roman Signer's installation, *Kugel mit blauer Farbe* (Ball with Blue Paint, 2012, Fig. 4.2a), at the Power Station of Art in Shanghai, a museum of contemporary art housed in a decommissioned power plant.[22] In *Ball with Blue Paint*, Signer suspended a huge wooden ball filled with blue paint at the top of an eighty-meter-tall chimney. He had Chinese workers build a spiral staircase leading to the place from which the ball would drop. The spiral staircase allowed a few handpicked people, including Lan and Swiss curator Simon Maurer, to climb up and watch the ball fall. Everyone had the same thought: What if the force of the falling ball causes the chimney

21 "Kunst in der Fabrik vernetzt die Welt," *WAZ*, May 17, 2013, <https://www.waz.de/staedte/wattenscheid/kunst-in-der-fabrik-vernetzt-die-weltid7964805.html>; Visitors to the German art museum were able to Skype with workers at the Chinese factory, and visitors to the Chinese art museum could Skype with German factory workers. Lan's concept was to connect producers and consumers in a global supply chain.

22 Simon Maurer, 蓝镜与西格纳的"对画": 献给罗曼 · 西格纳八十周岁生日 [Jiny Lan and Roman Signer's Painterly Dialogue: A Chinese Artist's Dedication to the 80th Birthday of Roman Signer], 国家美术 [National Arts], July 17, 2018, <https://mp.weixin.qq.com/s/dvNbZsfu2rzF6L7NfZOxMw>.

to implode? As Maurer wrote: "I clearly remember I was prepared to give my life for a piece of art at that moment."[23] The hawser suspending the ball was set aflame, and when the ball hit the ground, the blue paint splattered in a striking geometric pattern. *Ball with Blue Paint* exemplifies Signer's penchant for explosive projects that incorporate the unexpected into the final artwork.[24]

Lan captured this experience in *Signer in Hangzhou* (2013, Fig. 4.2c), a crucial painting that begat a number of sub-versions, including the painting of Beuys discussed below. Like the ball, a naked woman is bound and suspended in mid-air, anticipating the trussed Beuys. She is hogtied, suggesting sadomasochistic practices. Her shaved head is raised and her expression is calm. Perhaps this enigmatic figure conveys the excitement the artist felt at the time as one of the eyewitnesses to the suspenseful experiment. The man in the dark green t-shirt sitting below the trussed woman is Roman Signer. The nearly concentric circles in the background replicate the spiral staircase that runs along the wall inside the chimney. *Signer in Hangzhou* shows paint spreading out of the ball not only in blue, but also in red. In fact, Signer had originally considered using a more conspicuous red color but feared that its symbolic associations might trigger an intervention by Chinese authorities. Lan's painting thus fulfills Signer's unrealized wish.

Signer in Hangzhou depicts Signer as a guest in the Hangzhou home of Xiao Feng, the longtime director of the China Academy of Art (CAA, not to be confused with CAFA in Beijing). The two naked kneeling men who serve as furniture have fetishistic overtones. They are actually carryovers from Lan's earlier paintings, such as *Value-Added Movement 6: Behind the Mountain There Is Another Mountain, Behind the Heaven There Is Another Heaven* (*Shan wai you shan, tian wai you tian*, 2013, Fig. 4.2b).[25] These two men have not been painted over and serve as legs for

23 Maurer, "Jiny Lan and Roman Signer's Painterly Dialogue."

24 According to an artist profile of Signer by the gallery Hauser & Wirth, "Signer's work explores the relationships between sudden energy releases and calm, between order and chaos, and the existence of form in the apparently formless. Physical forces like gravitation and motor energies are both a challenge to the artist and the instruments he relies on to realize his sculptural ideas. In his work, classical sculptural materials have been usurped by sand, water and ordinary objects. Meticulous planning and incalculable chance interact, generating 'poetic' visual installations with their own highly developed individual aesthetic." <https://www.hauserwirth.com/artists/2805-roman-signer>.

25 This painting was part of the exhibition *Ausserhalb und Wittendrin*, see Thomas Nitsche, "Ausstellung in Haus Herbede," *WAZ*, January 23, 2014, <https://www.waz.de/staedte/witten/article8908015/austellung-in-haus-herbede.html>.

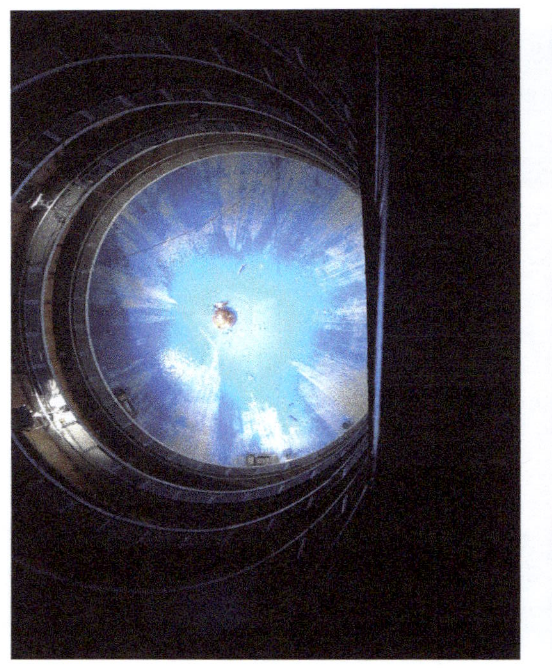
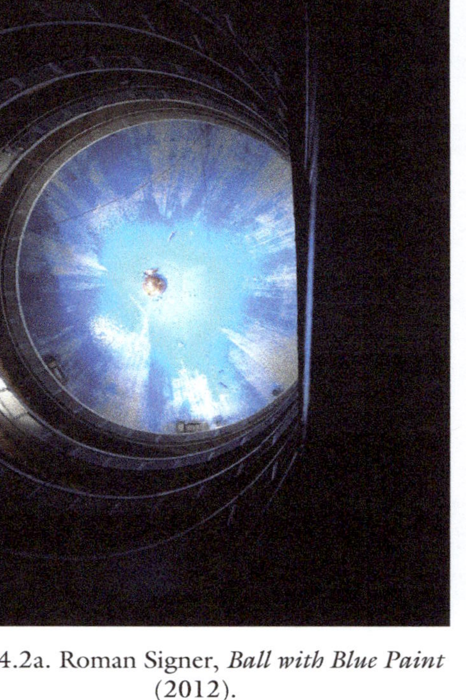
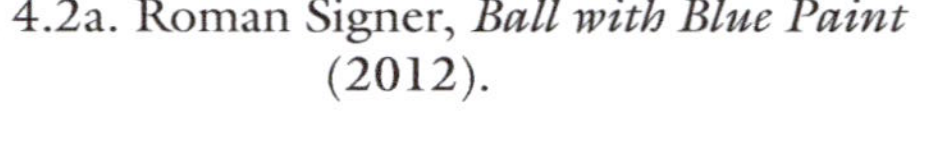

Fig. 4.2a. Roman Signer, *Ball with Blue Paint* (2012).

Fig. 4.2b. *Value-Added Movement 6: Behind the Mountain There Is Another Mountain, Behind the Heaven There Is Another Heaven* (2013, 200 × 140 cm).

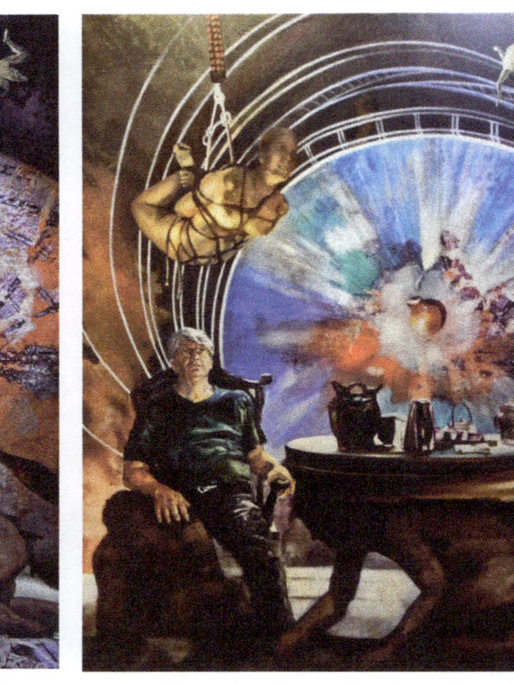

Fig. 4.2c. *Signer in Hangzhou* (2013, 200 × 140 cm).

the chair and tea table.[26] Their submissive posture suggests subservience to the male artist, as Lan explained: "I was very impressed by the whole Shanghai project. Everyone – engineers, cameramen, curators – served the artist unconditionally. So many people were involved in a costly project that had no practical use value. So the kneeling men are a metaphor for service to art."

Although *Signer in Hangzhou* and the Beuys portrait discussed below are visually connected, Signer and Beuys seem to possess very different artistic visions. The Signer project with its teams of engineers and builders decrees absolute submission to art and the artist. This is an inversion of Beuys's democratic concept that "everyone is an artist." Thus, Signer's project is wholly un-Beuysian. It is not social art but rather a Hollywood stunt. However, Lan greatly admired Signer's project. Is this the level of power and control that she aspires to? Her incorporation of quasi-religious hymns to herself in a performance described later in this chapter seems to suggest so.

Suspending Judgment: *"You didn't get that from me!"* (2018–19)

In 2018, Lan painted Joseph Beuys; one year later she revised the work and entitled it, *"You didn't get that from me!"* (Fig. 4.3). The sled in the lower right corner of the painting is a pastiche of Beuys's most famous multiples. The sled refers to the "Tartar legend" that Beuys created about his wartime experiences. In the spring of 1941, Beuys volunteered for the German Air Force and was deployed as a rear gunner in a Ju 87 Stuka dive-bomber. On March 16, 1944, his airplane crashed on the Crimean Front, close to Znamianka.[27] Beuys claimed that Tartars found him unconscious in the snow, wrapped him in fat and felt so as to warm and resuscitate him, and pulled him on a sled into their felt tent, where they nursed him back to life. In reality, there was neither snow nor nomadic Tartars near Znamianka at the time, and Beuys was rescued by German soldiers on the day of the crash and taken to a military hospital.[28] But the sled, fat, and felt associated with the Tartar legend would become signature props in his conceptual art long before the myth was debunked. Defenders of Beuys explained his self-mythologization by tracing it back

26 Maurer, "Jiny Lan and Roman Signer's Painterly Dialogue."

27 "Joseph Beuys," Saylor Academy, <https://resources.saylor.org/wwwresources/archived/site/wp-content/uploads/2011/05/Joseph-Beuys.pdf>.

28 Caroline Rupprecht, *Asian Fusion: New Encounters in the Asian-German Avant-Garde* (Oxford: Peter Lang, 2020), 162–3; cf. Peter Nisbet, "Remarks on a Beuys Story," in *Joseph Beuys: Mapping the Legacy*, 5–18; Jörg Herold, "Ein Tag im Leben des Joseph B.," *FAZ*, August 7, 2000.

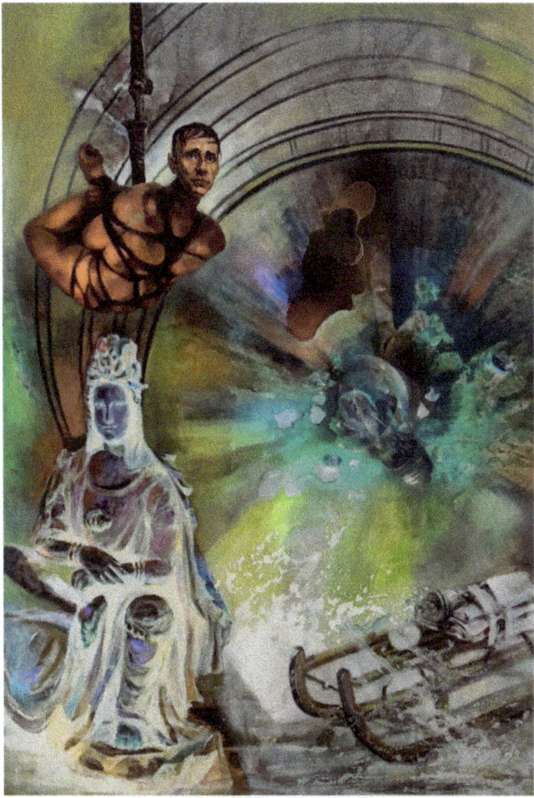

Fig. 4.3. *"You didn't get that from me!"* (2018–19, 200 × 140 cm).

to a change in his subconscious mental reality after a near-death experience and justified it as an exercise of artistic freedom.[29]

In 1969, Beuys used sleds in two installation projects: *The Sled* and *The Pack*. *The Sled* is equipped with a roll of felt, a flashlight, and a dried lump of fat – life-sustaining items that provide warmth, light, and nourishment. *The Pack* consists of twenty-four sleds spewing out of the back of a Volkswagen van. Beuys wrote that in the critical moment after his plane crash in the wilderness, rescuers driving a modern vehicle like a Volkswagen could not have reached him as quickly as nomads using a primitive form of transport, such as a sled.[30]

29 Rupprecht, *Asian Fusion*, 163.

30 "There, where a catastrophe has taken place…, the wounded might only be reachable with this kind of instrument, not with a more highly developed vehicle. In a state of emergency, one has to reach back to primitive means." Quoted in "Sled," Pinakothek der Moderne, <https://pinakothek-beuys-multiples.de/product/sled/?lang=en>.

In the painting, Beuys is hogtied and hanging from a frayed rope, creating suspense as to whether it will break. The spot where Signer's ball hit the ground is replaced by a light bulb, which is a pastiche of Beuys's multiples of a yellow-painted light bulb wired up to a fresh lemon, an installation he created while recuperating from a lung illness on the Italian island of Capri in 1985, a year before his death. Beuys called this work *Capri Battery*, and its depiction of a renewable energy source links it to his ecological activism. In Lan's painting, the light bulb appears to be bursting, since the fragments appear to be in motion. However, an actual light bulb would not have this explosive power, which is in fact a visual effect borrowed from *Signer in Hangzhou*.

Beuys dangles above a representation of what Lan calls the Buddhalisa: a fusion of the Buddha and Mona Lisa, thus of East and West, that could be seen as an allegory of Eurasia. Beuys's construction of Eurasia as the site where East meets West is an appealing concept for a Chinese German artist. Beuys was influenced by the anthroposophist Rudolf Steiner, who advocated for "cooperation between East and West as a route to greater social harmony" and reimagined Europe and Asia as a unified entity: Eurasia.[31] His Eurasian projects originated with his self-mythologizing Tartar legend, set in the Crimea – technically located in Europe but historically part of the Mongol Empire that spanned Central Asia. Among his works related to Eurasia were an installation and a performance project. In the sculpture *Der Eurasier* (The Eurasian, 1958), a small figure wrapped in gauze stands at the corner of a rectangular piece of felt, holding a shepherd's staff and surveying the steppe as if he is about to undertake a shamanistic journey across the empty plain to return with healing powers.[32] Beuys performed *The Eurasia Siberian Symphony* in October 1966 in Copenhagen and Berlin. The ninety-minute-long action featured a blackboard and a taxidermy hare and was described in the Copenhagen art journal *Billedkunst* as follows: "On the board [Beuys] drew a cross which he then half erased; underneath he wrote 'Eurasia.'… The division of the cross is the split between East and West, Rome and Byzantium. The half cross is the United Europe and Asia, to which the rabbit is on its way." Through the symbolic erasure of half of the cross, Beuys erased the division of Europe and Asia in order to reimagine the two as one. Beuys explained that the hare is a peaceful animal that hops around the entire

31 Victoria Walters, "Joseph Beuys and EURASIA," *Tate Papers* 31 (2019), <https://www.tate.org.uk/research/tate-papers/31/joseph-beuys-eurasia>; Rupprecht, *Asian Fusion*, 167. Beuys's performance of *Eurasia Siberian Symphony* was reported in *Billedkunst* (Copenhagen), no. 4, 1966; see Lucy R. Lippard, ed., *Six Years: The Dematerialization of the Art Object from 1966 to 1972* (Berkeley: University of California Press, 1973), 16–18.

32 Rupprecht, *Asian Fusion*, 167.

Eurasian continent and archetypically represents "incarnation in Europe and re-incarnation in Asia."[33] Beuys's conception of Eurasia included a strong political dimension. He and Nam June Paik collaborated for many years on their utopian vision, called EURASIA, which aimed to eliminate borders and overcome the divisions created by modernity. In 1967, he founded the utopian Free Democratic Socialist State EURASIA, which evolved into the German Student Party, also known as Fluxus Zone West, an important precursor of the Green Party.[34] In 1979, Beuys became a founding member of the Green Party.[35]

If the rope holding Beuys breaks, he will fall and crush Buddhalisa, here standing for his own artistic legacy of Eurasia. Buddhalisa is spectrally depicted in inverted tones like a film negative, giving the figure an illusory quality. The imperiled state of Beuys hints at his polarized reception already during his lifetime. Benjamin Buchloh was among Beuys's fiercest critics. In his oft-reprinted essay "Beuys: The Twilight of the Idol," first published in 1980, Buchloh challenged Beuys's public persona as a progressive and leftist intellectual who supported a new postwar German identity that reckons with the National Socialist past.[36] Buchloh argued that the goal of Beuys's "myth of origin" was "pardoning and reconciling [the new German spirit] prematurely with its own reminiscences of a responsibility for one of the most cruel and devastating forms of collective political madness that history had known."[37] He identified an essential contradiction in the artist's work: "The aesthetic conservatism of Beuys is logically complemented by his politically retrograde, not to say reactionary, attitudes. Both are inscribed into a seemingly progressive and radical humanitarian program of aesthetic and social evolution."[38]

By 2001, Gene Ray could observe a more balanced critique of Beuys developing:

33 Watanabe, "Searching for EUR-ASIA," 74–8.

34 Watanabe, "Searching for EUR-ASIA," 181–3.

35 Beckmann, "The Causes in the Future," 91–111; Michael Sontheimer, "Gründung der Grünen vor 40 Jahren. Pfarrer, Grafen und Bauern mit (Sonnen-) Blume," *Der Spiegel*, March 15, 2019, <https://www.spiegel.de/geschichte/die-gruenen-sind-40-wie-die-partei-1979-gegruendet-wurde-a-1257396.html>. The project most closely associated with Beuys's ecological activism was the large-scale urban greening project *7000 Eichen – Stadtverwaldung statt Stadtverwaltung* (7,000 Oaks – City Forestation instead of City Administration), launched in 1982 at documenta 7. The planting of seven thousand oak trees in Kassel, Germany, brought about a lasting change in the city's urban landscape while raising ecological awareness.

36 Benjamin Buchloh, "Beuys: The Twilight of the Idol," in *Joseph Beuys: The Reader*, 109–26.

37 Buchloh, "Beuys: The Twilight of the Idol," 115.

38 Buchloh, "Beuys: The Twilight of the Idol," 123.

> Beuys's reception while he was alive was notoriously polarized. That situation is improving, in that critical responses more nuanced than all-or-nothing denigration or idolatry have now established themselves in the literature. Troubled by his private history, his public persona, or his politics, some observers of postwar and contemporary culture remain reluctant to admit the impact of his work, and alternatively many others are still unable or unwilling to be at all critical about the object of their adoration.[39]

But Hans-Peter Riegel's biography of Beuys, published in 2013, revealed that the artist's ties to Nazism ran much deeper than he himself had admitted.[40] Drawing on Riegel, Caroline Rupprecht declares that Beuys's notion of Eurasia is "deeply regressive,"[41] for it appears dangerously close to Hitler's *Drang nach Osten* (push for eastward expansion). She argues that Beuys's Orientalist turn to Eurasia, depicted as pristine territory, is an escapist denial of his witnessing the beginning of the Shoah: from May to December 1941, he was stationed within walking distance of the Posen concentration camp, the first to be built in German-occupied Poland.[42] The revelation in Riegel's biography prompted Rupprecht to call for an end to the idealization of Beuys: "Until today, in the English-speaking world, Beuys's Nazi leanings have been either downplayed or completely denied, and he is still marketed in the art world as a leftist, progressive artist – it's time for a change."[43]

Lan takes an eclectic approach to Beuys's legacy. "I am against deification or demonization of Beuys," she stated. "In my painting, I created a tense feeling on purpose, and froze the scene at an uncertain moment, in order to emphasize the two sides of a person or a thing. Highlighting various possibilities is a running thread in my works. I like to think dialectically." In this vein, while she acknowledges Beuys's significant influence on her, she is irritated by the Beuys cult maintained by his students and others who reject any criticism of him. In an interview with the *TAZ*, she said: "Beuys was always against authority and bureaucracy. But his students present themselves in an authoritarian way, claiming: We understand Beuys better than others. What if Beuys's public image falls apart and his myth is dismantled?"[44] Thus, she titled her painting "You didn't get that from me!," imagining Beuys rebuking his students who have

39 Gene Ray, "Preface," in *Joseph Beuys: Mapping the Legacy*, 1–4, here 1.

40 Hans Peter Riegel, *Beuys: Die Biographie*, 3 vols (Hamburg: Aufbau, 2013). Cited in Rupprecht, *Asian Fusion*, 162.

41 Rupprecht, *Asian Fusion*, 158.

42 Rupprecht, *Asian Fusion*, 149–81.

43 Rupprecht, *Asian Fusion*, 181.

44 Max Florian Kühlem, "Joseph Beuys hängt am rissigen Seil," *taz*, July 20/21, 2019, <https://taz.de/Joseph-Beuys-haengt-am-rissigen-Seil/!5609356/>.

capitalized on his influence and fostered a Beuys cult. To idolize Beuys as a godlike authority seems to contradict his own anti-authoritarian message. By showing Beuys in a torturous posture, Lan's painting captures the paradox of his habitual rebellion against authority and his own penchant for authority, seen in his autobiographical fictions and self-stylization as a messianic figure.[45] By suspending Beuys, Lan suspends her judgment of Beuys, reflecting her personal and artistic indebtedness to Beuys and her dialectical views of a complex cultural-historical icon.

Responses to Beuys: *How to Explain Pictures to the Dead Beuys* (2021)

From September 3 to October 9, 2021, Galerie Tammen in Berlin hosted Lan's solo exhibition *Found in Translation*.[46] Challenging the common notion that some meaning is always "lost in translation," Lan emphasizes the effectiveness of translation as a process of discovery, contending that translation can also add value and generate meaning: "I translated some of Beuys's materials from the museum into Chinese. During the process of translation, I learned a lot. If you are a passive recipient of a translation, you lose something; but if you actively translate, you find something." As usual, a performance accompanied her exhibition. On September 14, 2021, the day before the start of Art Week in Berlin, Lan appeared as Beuys redivivus, imitating his best-known shamanic performance, *Wie man dem toten Hasen die Bilder erklärt* (How to Explain Pictures to a Dead Hare, 1965). Beuys began his performance by locking himself alone inside the gallery, allowing visitors to observe him only through the windows. After coating his head with honey and gold leaf, he held a dead hare in his arms and spoke to the animal about art. With this seemingly nonsensical and anti-intuitive performance, Beuys tried to communicate that understanding art is not a rational, cerebral thought process, but an intuitive, perceptive, non-materialistic, and transcendental one that

45 Buchloh criticizes Beuys's "compulsive self-exposure as the messianic artist." See Buchloh, "Beuys: The Twilight of the Idol," 122.

46 Max Florian Kühlem, "Versuch über die Selbstverfraulichung," *taz*, September 14, 2021, <https://taz.de/Versuch-ueber-die.../!5796117/>; "Jiny Lan – Found in Translation," Galerie Tammen, <https://presentation.next.art-butler.com/de/showrooms/cd0a8f34-f4db-4fbc-902d-cbb9fb9274b0>. Lan featured Beuys in a number of paintings including *Axiom der korrekten Beinhaltung* (Axiom of Correct Leg Posture: Beuys, the Hare, the Castle, and the Museum, 2021), *Versuch über die Selbstverfraulichung* (A Woman's Attempt at Self-Deification, 2021), and *Die Redereien des Joseph Beuys sind unterbewertet* (The Oratory of Joseph Beuys Is Undervalued, 2021). Due to recurrent elements and similar themes, I will not include a discussion of them.

involves alienation, creativity, and vision.[47] He intended to criticize overthinking and over-rationalization. His eccentric, seemingly irrational, and shamanic act of communicating with a deceased hare pitted Eastern mysticism against Western rationality.

Lan mimicked this famous performance in *Versuch über die Selbstverfraulichung oder wie man dem toten Beuys die Bilder erklärt* (Experiment about a Woman's Self-Glorification or How to Explain Pictures to the Dead Beuys, 2021, Fig. 4.4). Similarly to Beuys, she began her performance by locking herself in Galerie Tammen, while talking to "the dead Beuys" about her artwork in Chinese. Visitors could only observe her through windows as she cuddled a sculpture of a wooden hare with a gilded human head representing Beuys. Instead of honey and gold leaf, she wore headphones, sunglasses, and "two pants," since the top she wore was converted from a pair of pants, alluding to the phrase "Who wears the pants?" The title introduces a word she coined, "Selbstverfraulichung," which she explained as follows: "The word 'verherrlichen' [literally, "to glorify"] has 'Herr' in it, which originally referred to God or master. It is more acceptable for men to praise themselves or to be praised. But when a woman praises herself, it is considered inappropriate and indecorous. That is why I invented the word 'Selbstverfraulichung' and conceived the performance as a glorification of myself." To this end, she invited Luigi Grosso, one of the restorers of Titian's *Wisdom*, whom she met during her exhibition at the Library of St. Mark in Venice in 2019, to collaborate with her. Grosso is also an opera singer, and during Lan's performance in Berlin he sang religious hymns whose lyrics had been altered to praise Lan profusely. Colmar Schulte-Goltz, Lan's gallerist and a connoisseur on the German television show *Bares für Rares* (Cash or Trash), read a German translation of the eulogistic lyrics. According to Lan, this provocative, "blasphemous" art performance angered some devout Christians among the visitors.

Lan distances herself from Beuys's refashioning of himself as a shaman. As a member of the Manchu ethnic minority, she is familiar with the shamanic rituals that are common in northern China. Beuys's Western appropriation of shamanism inspired her to take advantage of her ethnic identity by posing as an Eastern shaman. She quips: "Shamanism comes from Asia. Beuys drew inspiration for his anthroposophy from Oriental wisdom. I can dress like a shaman. Am I not more authentic?" Beuys imagines himself as the intermediary of Eastern mysticism for a Western audience. Lan intends to present herself as a more "authentic" cultural

47 "Joseph Beuys' Aktion 'wie man dem toten Hasen die Bilder erklärt' (Gespräch)," KunstSpektrum, January 27, 1983, YouTube, <https://www.youtube.com/watch?v=kVSbAJO4D1k>.

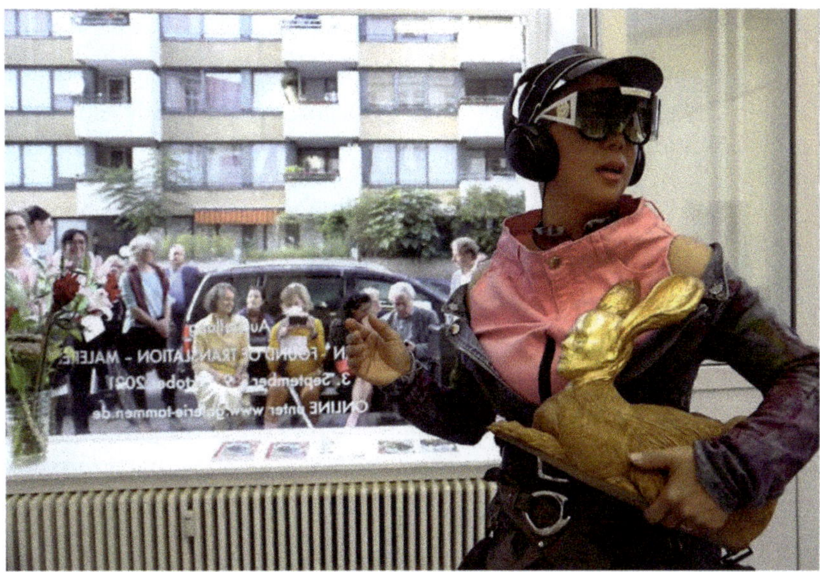

Fig. 4.4. Performance: *Experiment about a Woman's Self-Glorification or How to Explain Pictures to the Dead Beuys* (2021, photo: Yang Xia).

representative from the East. Female shamans recur in her works, such as *Jede ist eine Schamanin* (Every Woman Is a Shaman, 2021).

One could view Lan's imitative performance approvingly, as a clever pastiche. But, critiquing Western feminism's replication of the structural racism of white patriarchy, Audre Lorde wrote: "*For the master's tools will never dismantle the master's house.* They may allow us temporarily to beat him at his own game, but they will never enable us to bring about genuine change."[48] Lorde's observation about the limitations of Western feminist theory could also apply to Lan's feminist art. She desires to exceed and replace male artists, but her imitative approach remains tethered to the existing canon. In her feminist confrontation with German male artists she is still playing by the men's rules.[49] A similar conundrum is embedded in the idea of Jinyology itself: it is not a dismantling of the idea of patriarchal succession but a regendering of it.

48 Audre Lorde, "The Master's Tools Will Never Dismantle the Master's House," in *Feminist Postcolonial Theory: A Reader*, ed. Reina Lewis and Sara Mills (New York: Routledge, 2003), 25–28, here 27.

49 See also Jiny Lan, "Lob der alten weißen Männer," *Cicero: Magazin für politische Kultur*, December 2, 2020, <https://www.cicero.de/kultur/cancel-culture-lob-alte-weisse-maenner-dieter-nuhr-christian-lindner>.

Coda: The "Buddha's Palm" and the Literal Meaning of *verfraulichen*

In retrospect, the concept of *Selbstverfraulichung* is already embodied in the paintings *Red Sun*, *Progressive Lenses*, and *One-Persons-Chorus*, in which Lan inserted herself, disguised as Jiang Qing or Mona Lisa, as the object of idolization. There, too, a tension is apparent between Lan's feminist art and the master's tool of *Selbstverfrau/herrlichung*. Her work is only as radical as the master's tools allow, since the essence of her inventiveness is an extension and appropriative pastiche of the master's language and work. Sun Wukong, the rebellious Monkey King, is her favorite alter ego (chapter 1), but he is not invincible. In a famous episode in the classic Chinese novel *Journey to the West*, Sun Wukong wagers that he can jump out of the Buddha's palm. He loses the bet, and the Buddha punishes him by burying him under the Five Finger Mountain for five hundred years. Perhaps Lan cannot leap out of the Buddha's palm either.

Yet, the verbatim meaning of the neologism "verfraulichen" is to make someone a woman. As discussed in the next chapter, Lan has visualized male artists as female: Baselitz is pregnant and "delivers" Lan, his Oedipal child; Markus Lüpertz is adorned in an empress's robe; Kiefer's posture resembles that of a woman in labor; and Sigmar Polke wears only a pair of high-heeled pumps. Lan often imagines a role reversal between male and female artists: What if a woman artist created a sculpture of a porcelain urinal signed "R. Mutt," as Marcel Duchamp did? What if she splattered paint like Jackson Pollock, and what if she raised her middle finger in front of Tiananmen like Ai Weiwei? Would she receive similar accolades? The answer is very likely no. Therefore, women artists have no choice but to elevate themselves.

5: Contending with the "Painter Princes" of Germany: Lan's *Masterpieces* (2018–19)

In the second half of the nineteenth century, the title "Malerfürst" (painter prince) was often bestowed on successful salon painters.[1] Today, the German media habitually apply this term to Markus Lüpertz and Georg Baselitz.[2] Lüpertz himself hated this feudal label and retorted: "At which court?"[3] Baselitz also perceived this label as a kind of mock-

1 Group Exhibit *Malerfürsten*, curated by Doris H. Lehmann and Katharina Chrubasik, September 28, 2018–January 27, 2019, <https://artfacts.net/exhibition/malerfuersten/889291>; "Malerfürsten: Die wahren Herrscher," *Fresko: Das Magazin für Kultur- und Kunstgenießer* 3/2018, <https://www.fresko-magazin.de/malerfuersten/>.

2 Alexander Bartl, "Georg Baselitz – Malerfürst und Einsiedler: profil zu Besuch im Atelier am Ammersee," Profil.at, February 25, 2009, <https://www.profil.at/home/georg-baselitz-malerfuerst-einsiedler-besuch-atelier-ammersee-234809>; Tilman Urbach, "Malerfürst Markus Lüpertz: 'Die Welt dreht sich nur um mich,'" *Welt*, March 10, 2009, <https://www.welt.de/kultur/article3349313/Die-Welt-dreht-sich-nur-um-mich.html>; Rachel Corbett, "The Painter Prince: Markus Lüpertz," Michael Werner, June 2017, <https://www.michaelwerner.com/news/the-painter-prince-markus-lupertz>; Ingeborg Ruthe, "Markus Lüpertz ist einer der letzten deutschen 'Malerfürsten,'" *Berliner Zeitung*, April 25, 2021, <https://www.berliner-zeitung.de/kultur-vergnuegen/kunst/markus-luepertz-ist-einer-der-letzten-deutschen-malerfuersten-li.154042>; "Der letzte Malerfürst: Künstler Markus Lüpertz wird 80," *Berliner Kurier*, April 24, 2021, <https://www.berliner-kurier.de/panorama/der-letzte-malerfuerst-kuenstler-markus-luepertz-wird-80-li.154912>; Till Briegleb, "Einer der letzten Malerfürsten," *Süddeutsche Zeitung*, October 9, 2022, <https://www.sueddeutsche.de/meinung/georg-baselitz-nationalsozialismus-pinakothek-der-moderne-1.5671460?reduced=true>; Ulf Paschardt, "Georg Baselitz: Der Anti-Spießer," *Welt*, January 23, 2023, <https://www.welt.de/kultur/plus243129615/Georg-Baselitz-zum-85-Geburtstag-Der-Anti-Spiesser.html>; Katharina Rustler, "Umstrittener Malerfürst Georg Baselitz tobt sich im KHM Wien aus," *Der Standard*, March 4, 2023, <https://www.derstandard.at/consent/tcf/story/2000144140041/umstrittener-malerfuerst-georg-baselitz-tobt-sich-im-khm-wien-aus>.

3 "Markus Lüpertz hasst Bezeichnung 'Malerfürst,'" *Tiroler Tageszeitung*, March 17, 2016, <https://www.tt.com/artikel/11265248/markus-luepertz-hasst-bezeichnung-malerfuerst>; "'Malerfürst': Genie Markus Lüpertz feiert

ery.[4] Perhaps for this very reason Lan cast eight postwar German blue-chip male artists as "painter princes" in her portrait series *Meisterwerke* (Masterpieces, 2018–19), which features Joseph Beuys, Georg Baselitz, Markus Lüpertz, Jörg Immendorff, Anselm Kiefer, Sigmar Polke, Gerhard Richter, and A. R. Penck. Characteristic of her work is the pastiche of representative works of the German male artists portrayed. Lan is inspired by the German conceptual artist Hans-Peter Feldmann's method of manipulating and recontextualizing classical works of art. Lan's gallerist, Colmar Schulte-Goltz, views her pastiches as a gesture of homage to famous male artists in the tradition of the "Hommes illustres," but it is also a critical engagement with their legacy.[5] Lan's classification of her own artworks as "masterpieces" is part of her *Selbstverfraulichung*.[6]

In her portrait *Markus Lüpertz. Imperator LV* (2018, 5.1a), Lüpertz stands at the center and wears an ornate red costume, which Lan based on the regal robe worn by Empress Wu Zetian of the Tang Dynasty in the television drama *The Empress of China* (*Wu mei niang chuan qi*, 2014, Fig. 5.1b).[7] Whereas she sometimes modeled her work after propaganda posters, here she utilizes a movie poster, similar to Narrative Figuration artists who took their source images from posters, photographs, comics, and other commercial productions. Lan painted a rooster standing on Lüpertz's bald head. But the rooster has the fanned tail of a white peacock. Lan once again visualizes a Chinese idiom, "rooster's head and phoenix's tail" (*ji tou feng wei*). This phrase means that it is better to be the head of a chicken rather than a plume in the tail of a phoenix; metaphorically, it is better to have the power to make decisions than to appear

seinen 75. Geburtstag," *Welt*, April 23, 2016, <https://www.welt.de/regionales/nrw/article154537719/Genie-Markus-Luepertz-feiert-seinen-75-Geburtstag.html>.

4 Susanne Beyer and Ulrike Knöfel, "Meine Bilder sind Schlachten," *Der Spiegel* 4/2013, January 20, 2013.

5 Colmar Schulte-Goltz, in *Jiny Lan*, exhibition catalog (2020).

6 These large-format paintings were exhibited from June 16 to September 22 at the Ludwiggalerie Schloss Oberhausen and at the Library of St. Mark during the fifty-eighth Venice Biennale from September 7 to November 4, 2019. See Martin Kleinwächter, "Ludwiggalerie: Bei Jiny Lan erscheint Gerhard Richter im Wasser-Spiegelbild," *WAZ*, July 8, 2019, <https://www.waz.de/staedte/oberhausen/article226419401/Jiny-Lan-in-Oberhausen-Mittlerin-zwischen-den-Kulturen.html>; Ludwiggalerie, "Jiny Lan verschifft ihre 'Malerfürsten' nach Venedig," *WAZ*, August 23, 2019, <https://www.waz.de/staedte/oberhausen/article226863819/Jiny-Lan-verschifft-ihre-Malerfuersten-nach-Venedig.html>; Nicole Büsing and Heiko Klaas, "Jiny Lan," in *Portfolio –Genealogies: Jiny Lan*, exhibition catalog (2019), 28–31, here 31.

7 武媚娘傳奇 [Legend of Wu Mei Niang], eslite, <https://www.eslite.com/product/1004184982438035>.

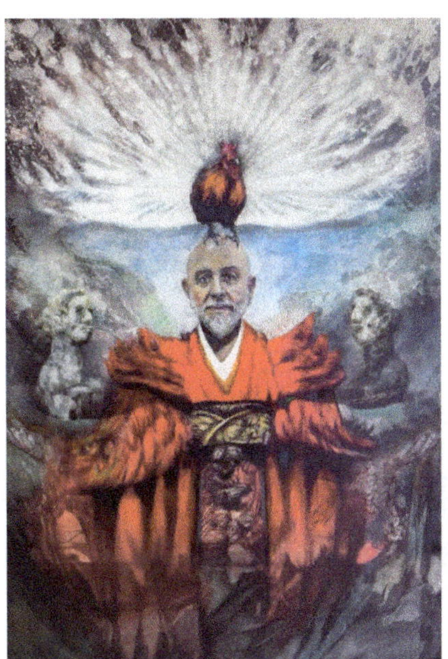

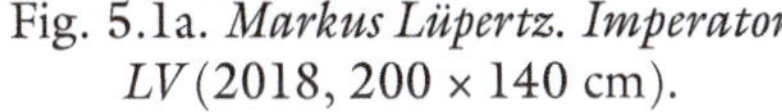

Fig. 5.1a. *Markus Lüpertz. Imperator LV* (2018, 200 × 140 cm).

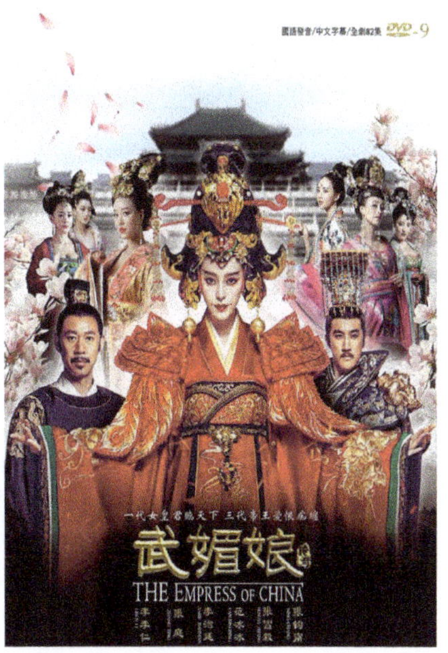

Fig. 5.1b. Television poster of *The Empress of China* (2014).

splendid while carrying out someone else's orders. This symbolic fusion of animals matches Lüpertz, who was the rector of the Art Academy in Düsseldorf for twenty-two years (1987–2009). He possesses decision-making power like the rooster's head, and his phoenix-like elegance is manifest in his penchant for good clothes.[8]

The painting is a statement about Lüpertz, but it also speaks to life as an artist in general: An artist enjoys great honor and respect from society but also faces society's expectations and its gaze, like a peacock in a zoo. The scene is similar to the depiction of Angela Merkel wearing a weighty headdress in *The Crown* (Fig. 7.1a), suggesting that honor is accompanied by the burden of responsibility. The symmetric composition shows how Lüpertz had to perform many balancing acts in his administrative role. The two busts flanking him pastiche his brand of archaic sculptures and classical themes.

8 When Lüpertz went to China, he was voted as one of the most handsome men by a Chinese fashion magazine; see 马库斯·吕佩尔茨在中国亮相湖北美院美术馆![Markus Lüpertz in China at the Art Museum of Hubei Academy of Fine Arts], September 12, 2017, 中国艺术现场 [China Art Scene] <https://www.sohu.com/a/191500160_541698>; 吕佩尔茨告诉你高颜值的优质大叔是如何炼成的 [Lüpertz Tells You How a Handsome Man Is Made], *Sohu*, September 27, 2017, <https://www.sohu.com/a/194969102_348004>.

Lan titled this painting "Imperator LV." Lüpertz is called "Lü dashi" or "Master Lü" in China. It is a typical Chinese cultural practice to assign to a foreigner a Chinese surname that resembles the sound of the foreigner's surname, in this case Lü 吕. On a keyboard, the Chinese character 吕 is typed LV, like the initials of the fashion icon Louis Vuitton, a coincidence that, in Lan's opinion, perfectly suits Lüpertz's chic appearance. She depicted him as an emperor of fashion and jokingly calls him the "Empress of Louis Vuitton." She also had in the back of her mind the German instrumental band Sutcliffe's song "Ming Imperator." The creative process of titling a painting shows the verbal games Lan plays, which rely on intercultural knowledge and multilingualism.

In *Penck Solution* (2019, Fig. 5.2b.), she rendered the émigré East German painter Ralf Winkler (pseudonym A. R. Penck) as a mirror reflection of Tintoretto, the great Italian Renaissance painter. "There are about four hundred years between Tintoretto and A. R. Penck," she noted. "In those four hundred years, the definition of a good painting has changed dramatically, but what has not changed is the idea of what a good painter should look like: an (old) white man, preferably with a beard."[9] The title "Penck Solution" plays on *Pink Solution* (Fig. 3.8b). To the left is a cartoonish pink figure. This small figure appropriates Penck's famous "stick man," often depicted with a large penis. On the right, she copied the central figure from Tintoretto's early masterpiece *The Miracle of St. Mark Freeing the Slave* (1548), specifically the floating saint dressed in a pink garment. The background of the upper part of the painting is also pink.

Penck Solution is a sub-version of Lan's painting of her mother, *Fluss- und Bergzerstörer* (River- and Mountain Destroyer / *Jiang shan huo shui*, Fig. 5.2a).[10] In *River- and Mountain Destroyer*, her mother is dressed in a dark embroidered gown and appears to have a white mane of hair. Lan, dressed in black, stands before her, doll-sized, with her arms stretched out and her head tipped back. This painting evolved from the Merkel painting, and all three of these paintings can be traced back to a Mao cult

9 Cited in Büsing and Klaas, "Jiny Lan," 31.

10 The title "River- and Mountain Destroyer" refers to a well-known phrase in China, *Fubei daxia de jiangshan*, which literally means "the rivers and mountains that our fathers conquered" and was used by the second and third generations of communist cadres to justify their privileges. According to Lan, her father also liked to emphasize, to her irritation, that he was part of the conquering force that helped the communists come to power. Therefore, she jokingly called her mother the "river- and mountain destroyer" to satirize her father's self-importance. Lan painted the portrait of her mother on Mother's Day in 2018. See 蓝镜 Jiny Lan, 母亲大人, 您一路走好!旅德华人追忆父母往事 [Mother, RIP! A Chinese in Germany remembers her parents], *Chinesische Handelszeitung*, August 27, 2018, <https://deouhuashang.de/作者专栏/5451/>.

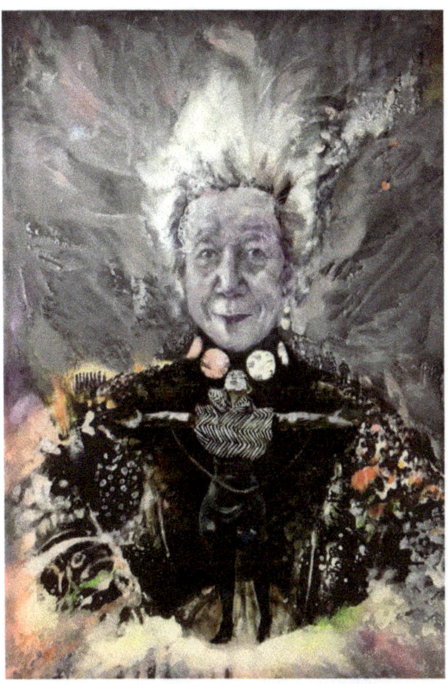

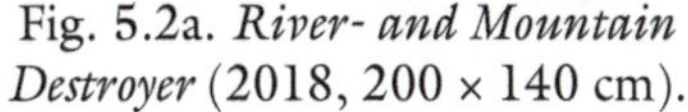

Fig. 5.2a. *River- and Mountain Destroyer* (2018, 200 × 140 cm).

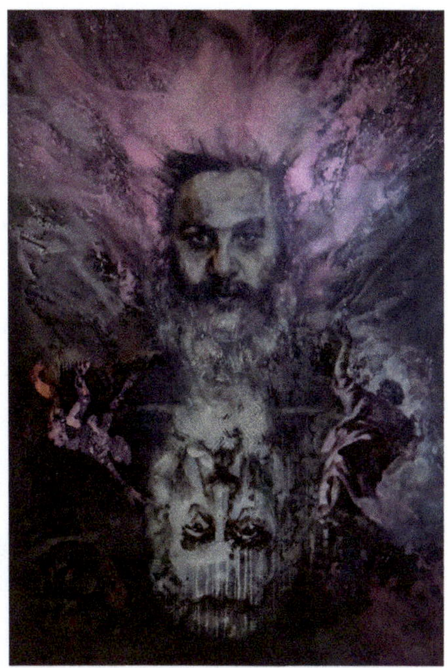

Fig. 5.2b. *Penck Solution* (2019, 200 × 140 cm).

poster, as discussed in chapters 2 and 7. Thus, although *Penck Solution* is a stand-alone painting, it stands in a web of interrelated pictures that explain its visuals: It belongs to the series of *Masterpieces* and at the same time to a Jinyological versioning that started with a Mao poster.

The artists depicted in the *Masterpieces* series all lived in a time of great upheavals in Germany and in the art world. Jack Cowart writes about neo-expressionists in Germany, "Their crusades come at a time of hot professional debate between abstract and figure, the history of expression and new expressive motifs."[11] Similar to the Narrative Figuration artists in France, these German artists rejected pure abstract art and embraced neo-expressionism and neo-figuration. Sigmar Polke, for example, founded the Capitalist Realist movement in the 1960s with Gerhard Richter and Konrad Fischer-Lueg as a witty and ironic response to socialist realism and Pop art.[12] In her painting of Polke, Lan appropri-

11 Jack Cowart, "Expressions," in *Expressions: New Art from Germany; Georg Baselitz, Jörg Immendorff, Anselm Kiefer, Markus Lüpertz, A. R. Penck*, ed. Jack Cowart and Siegfried Gohr (Munich: Prestel-Verlag in association with the Saint Louis Art Museum, 1983), 9–25, here 13.

12 Ingo Arend, "Kapitalistischer Realismus, Porträts und die Berghain Novelle," Edition Block, July 30, 2011, <https://www.getidan.de/kolumne/

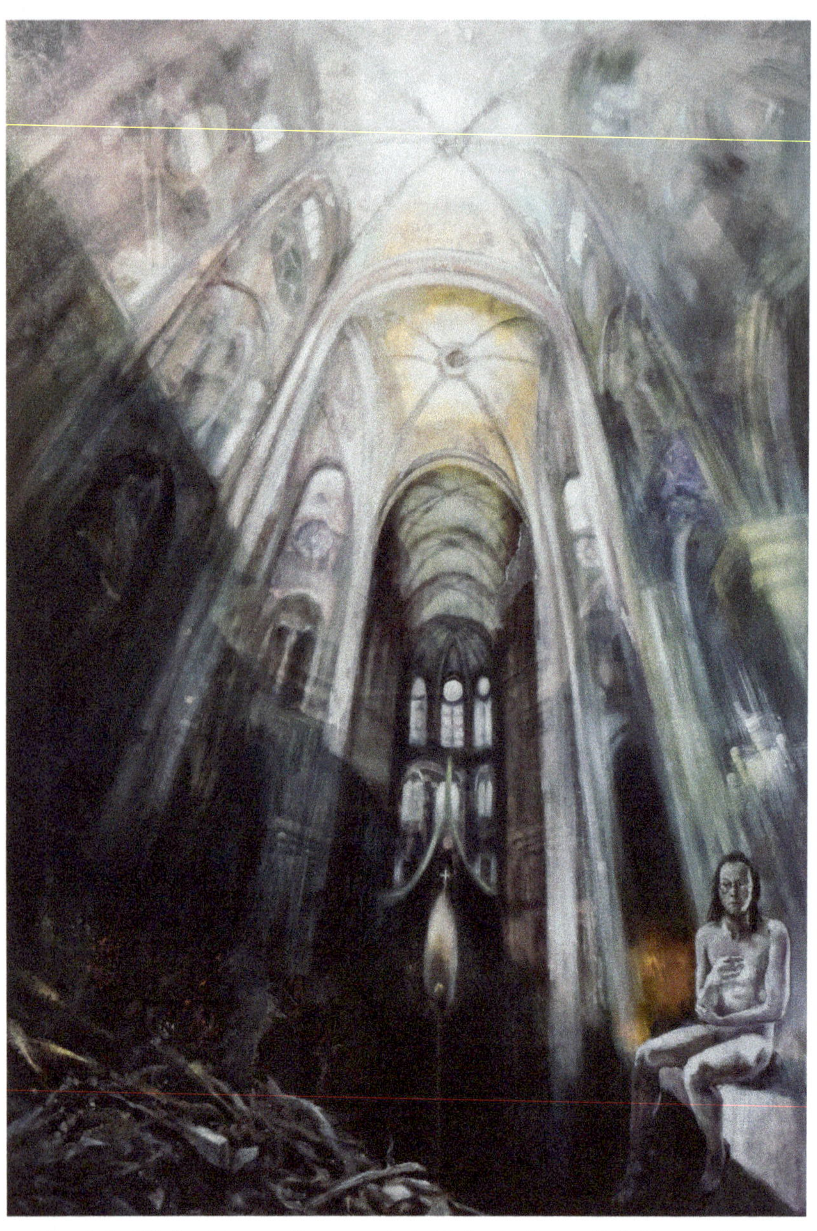

Fig. 5.3. *Higher Powers Commanded: Make the Lower Left Corner Black!* (2019, 200 × 140 cm).

ates his famous artwork—*Höhere Wesen befahlen: rechte, obere Ecke schwarz malen!* (Higher Powers Commanded: Paint the Upper Right Corner Black!, 1969). She flipped the upper right corner to the lower left corner and titled her portrait imitatively: *Höhere Wesen befahlen: untere, linke Ecke schwarz machen* (Higher Powers Commanded: Make the Lower Left Hand Corner Black!, 2019, Fig. 5.3).

Polke's original painting consists of a white canvas with the upper right corner painted black and the title of the painting at the bottom, hand-lettered in typewriter style. He painted it in the wake of the 1968 student movement, where "higher powers" were challenged, if not toppled. Since irony and wit define Polke's style, the title is to be understood jokingly; higher powers would not issue such a command, and if they did, they should be called into question. With this tongue-in-cheek abstract painting, Polke parodied the Hard Edge school of painting and challenged the authoritative status of abstract art. He pondered the origin of artistic expression: Is it divine or is it man-made?[13] The fact that Lan places Polke in a church appears logical given his evocation of higher powers. The tall church interior and the burning match indicate that the Polke painting is based on *Value-Added Movement 5: Out of Sagrada Família* (2015, Fig. 8.3b), but Lan changed Sagrada Família to Notre-Dame de Paris. A heap of debris in the lower left corner alludes to the fire that destroyed the roof of the cathedral in 2019. A naked Polke in high-heeled pumps sits forlorn in an empty, damaged church.

Among the eight postwar German artists Lan chose as subjects, Jörg Immendorff (Fig. 6.5a) was the one who identified most strongly with Maoist ideology. At the Düsseldorf Art Academy, he developed a close working relationship with Joseph Beuys, whose concept of social sculpture impacted Immendorff tremendously. He was active in the West German radical left during the late 1960s, participating in protests against the Vietnam War. With several other artists, he formed Red Cell Art (Rote Zelle Kunst) at the Academy in the early 1970s. He also involved himself with the K-Gruppen (Communist groups), especially the Communist Party of Germany (KPD). His Maoist paintings combined accessible visuals in socialist realist style with slogan-like texts to address class struggles against capitalism and imperialism. He also engaged in the Maoist practice of self-criticism and chastised himself for failing to demonstrate political engagement in his earlier art. Later, he developed a friendship with

---

rundgang/ingo_arend/28524/kapitalistischer-realismus-portrats-und-die-berghain-novelle>; Hilton Kramer, "Signs of Passion," in *Zeitgeist*, 15–19.

13 "Höhere Wesen befahlen: rechte, obere Ecke schwarz malen!," Van Abbe Museum, <https://vanabbemuseum.nl/en/collection/hohere-wesen-befahlen-rechte-obere-ecke-schwarz-malen>.

A. R. Penck in Dresden, and both thematized the inner German border, believing that art could overcome German separation.[14]

Comparing the eight *Masterpieces* with representative works of the artists depicted shows differences between Lan's figurative art and that of the German new expressionist artists. Donald Kuspit describes the figures in the German new figurative paintings as usually phantomlike, relatively identityless, nondescript, anonymous, expressive, and abstract, and notes that this abstraction of the (human) figure could be seen as an allegory of "the abstract power of society that flows through it, dominating [the figure] totally."[15] Lan's figures are to the contrary realistic, concrete, and often identifiable. Different from German neo-expressionists, Lan does not distance herself much from Pop art. In the series of *Masterpieces*, she adopts an iconic approach, chooses the most famous male artists, and maintains that male artists are granted more privileges in the art world than their female counterparts. Her feminist critique of the German art scene is echoed in art historian Lisa Saltzman's observation: "It is abundantly clear that neo-expressionism, as it took shape and cohered as a practice and perceived movement, was an almost exclusively male domain."[16]

Provoked by Georg Baselitz: *Water Flows Downward. This Is a Fact* (2019)

Lan's painting of Beuys suspended in mid-air, *"You didn't get that from me!"* (2018–19, Fig. 4.3), ended up being the first in the *Masterpieces* series. Back then, she had not yet envisioned a series featuring "painter princes," an idea that emerged when she began her painting of Georg Baselitz. A remark by Baselitz, who said in a 2013 interview with *Der Spiegel*, "Frauen malen nicht so gut. Das ist ein Fakt" (Women do not paint that well. That is a fact), got under her skin. Baselitz based his claim on the lower market value of women artists.[17] It is true that women's artwork sells for less, but the conclusion to be drawn from this fact should

14 Lauren Graber and Daniel Spaulding, "The Red Flag: The Art and Politics of West German Maoism," in *Art, Global Maoism and the Chinese Cultural Revolution*, ed. Jacopo Galimberti et al. (Manchester: Manchester University Press, 2019), 109–27.

15 Kuspit, "New German Painting: The Discovery of Expression," 2.

16 Lisa Saltzman, *Anselm Kiefer and Art After Auschwitz* (Cambridge: Cambridge University Press, 1999), 49.

17 Beyer and Knöfel, "Meine Bilder sind Schlachten," 105; Kühlem, "Joseph Beuys hängt am rissigen Seil"; Francesca Romana Audretsch, "Künstlerin Jiny Lan: Spiegelbilder für selbstherrliche Malerfürsten," *Monopol: Magazin für Kunst und Leben*, June 14, 2019, <https://www.monopol-magazin.de/jiny-lan>.

not be that their work is inferior, but that the monetary valuation of art is distorted by sexism in the art world. For centuries, women were excluded from professional art training. In Germany, for example, women were not allowed to study at public art academies until 1919, after the Weimar Constitution granted them legal equality with men.[18] Although conditions for women artists have improved considerably, their work still does not command the same prices as that of their male colleagues. There are exceptions, however, such as the German artist Käthe Kollwitz and the American painter Agnes Martin. Martin's paintings fetched even higher prices than Baselitz's.[19] Still, it is generally much easier for a male artist to elevate himself (*selbstverherrlichen*) or to be elevated by others. In China, too, women's art suffers from a lack of social recognition, institutional support, and market endorsement, as Shuqin Cui observes.[20] Cui comments on the challenges women artists face on the art market:

> An artist must work rigorously to have her work acknowledged and her name known to the art world. To win recognition, artists have to rely on market valuations and sales as well as exhibitions. Women artists are lagging in the art market. Measured by prices and transactions, works by women artists occupy two ends: fairly stable sales for a few prominent artists but scattered sales for the majority. According to the Yachang index, works listed for auction by women artists represent only 5 percent of the total, and no woman ranks in the top sixty in the category of contemporary art.[21]

This is exactly what provoked the Guerrilla Girls to fight against sexism and racism in the art world (chapter 3).

Throughout his interview with *Der Spiegel*, Baselitz made aggressive and derisive comments about almost everything: the German media, German museums, museumgoers, German writers, and female and male artists. After declaring that women cannot paint as well as men, he acknowledged that this is not due to "a genetic defect." But instead of offering a sociological explanation for this difference, he tried to rescue himself by explaining male artists' alleged superiority in terms of their own "defect": "Male artists are often on the verge of imbecility; a woman is most likely not like that. Women are excellent at science, just like men."

18 Eugen El, "Und ob Frauen malen können," *Schirn Magazin*, June 9, 2016, <https://www.schirn.de/magazin/schirn_tipp/kuenstler_frauen_vortrag_julia_voss_faz/>.

19 Julia Voss, "Besser malen!," *Frankfurter Allgemeine Zeitung*, May 23, 2015; see also Friederike Oertel, "Gleichberechtigung: Viel zu günstig," *Die Zeit*, January 31, 2018.

20 Cui, *Gendered Bodies*, 191.

21 Cui, *Gendered Bodies*, 192.

But then Baselitz made the essentializing claim that women lack the "brutality" necessary to produce great art: "Of course, there is quite a bit of brutality in art. Not a kind of brutality against other people, but brutality against existing things. … Men have no problem with that, they do it." In a final bid to redeem himself, Baselitz confessed, "but you have to know: I love women."[22]

Lan took issue with Baselitz and painted *Wasser fließt nach unten. Das ist Fakt* (Water Flows Downward. This Is a Fact, 2019, Fig. 5.4a). It is adapted from *Falling Is the Last Motion Before Flying* (2014. Fig. 3.9b). Baselitz inherits the physical features of the mother-to-be, a pregnant belly and breasts – a representational choice that strikes back at Baselitz by forcing him into a woman's body. Baselitz tumbles head first over a waterfall, holding a paintbrush in his left hand. A disapproving female face peers out from behind the waterfall, and as in the pre-version, at the top a spaceship blasts off.

Baselitz's plunging posture evokes the defining characteristic of his own oeuvre.[23] In 1969, he began painting his subjects upside down in order to achieve a certain degree of abstraction. Richard Shiff commented on Baselitz's inversion technique: "Turning a commonplace image upside down introduced a blunt, illogical difference from the visual norm, establishing the autonomy of Baselitz's art. Irony, parody, caricature, and debasement would be recognized as avant-garde or countercultural tactics, but nothing so simple and fundamental as physical inversion. Baselitz's gesture was without classification."[24] Lan's practice of inversion, however, originated from her early inclination for camouflage. Moreover, the viewing options for Lan's paintings are not limited to two directions; she sometimes mounts her artwork on a motorized wheel so that the painting can be viewed from different angles.

The sub-version, *Baselitz Delivery* (2019, Fig. 5.4b), invites such a viewing: Lan and Baselitz, fused at the waist by a barren tree and pitted against each other, are rotating, as if in a struggle or wrestling match. Tree limbs grow out of the conjoined bodies. Water falls in the background. Although the woman wears a white face mask, the yellow boot identifies her as Lan. A red fox can be discerned on Baselitz's torso. The title implies that Baselitz has delivered or "begot" Lan, suggesting an oedipal relationship of attraction and rivalry. It could also mean she delivers a

22 Beyer and Knöfel, "Meine Bilder sind Schlachten," 105; see also the defense of Baselitz in the German feminist magazine *Emma*: "Pascha: Georg Baselitz, Maler," *Emma*, March/April 2013, <https://www.emma.de/artikel/pascha-georg-baselitz-maler-266266>.

23 Richard Calvocoressi, "A Source for the Inverted Imagery in Georg Baselitz's Painting," *The Burlington Magazine* 127, no. 993 (1985): 894–9.

24 Richard Shiff, "Georg Baselitz Grounded," *Negotiating History: German Art and the Past* 8, no. 1 (2002): 52–65, 109–10, here 55.

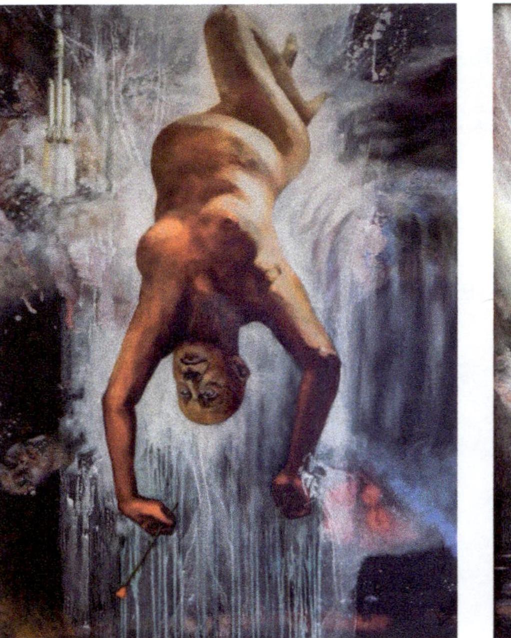

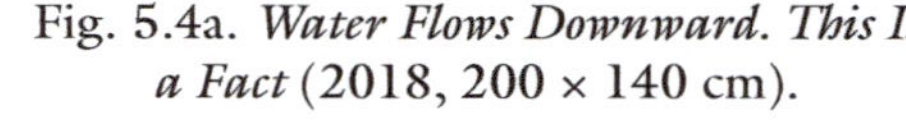
Fig. 5.4a. *Water Flows Downward. This Is a Fact* (2018, 200 × 140 cm).

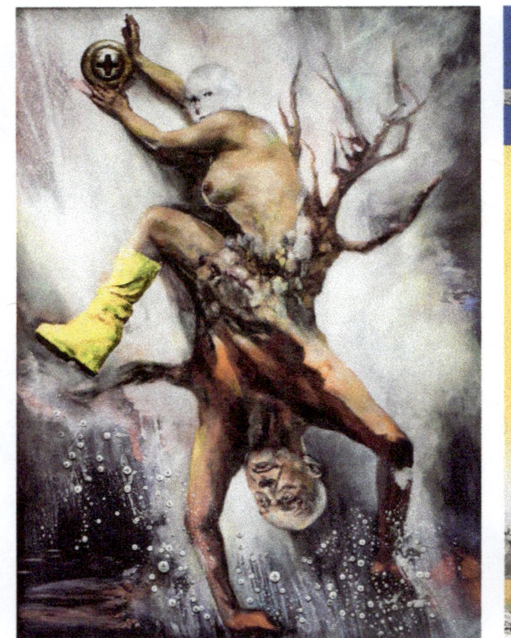

Fig. 5.4b. *Baselitz Delivery* (2019, 200 × 140 cm).

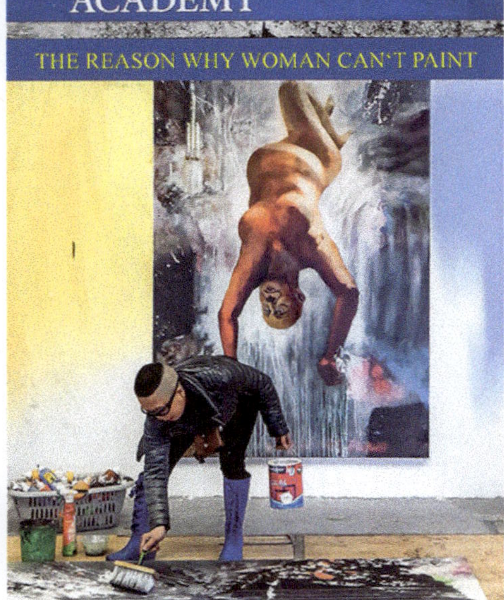

Fig. 5.4c. *The Reason Why Woman Can't Paint* (2019, poster: Julia Beusch; photo: Sebastian Drüen).

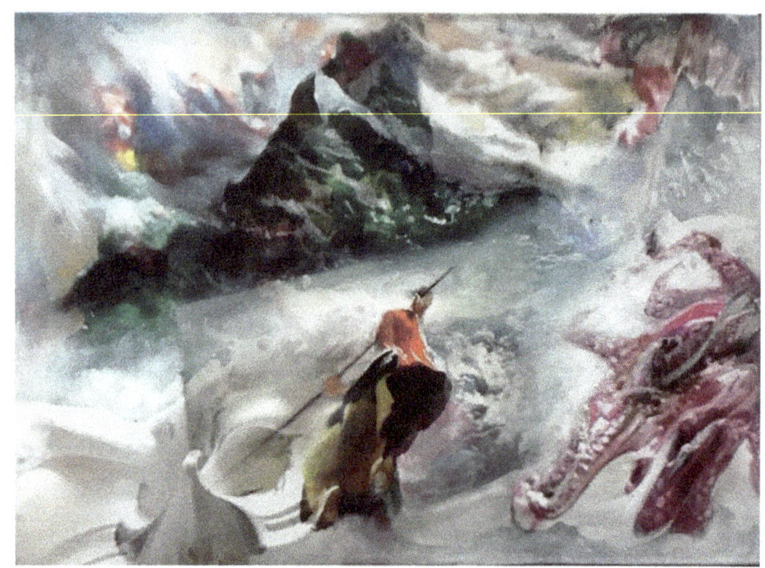

Fig. 5.5a. *Always Watch One's Back* (2020, 50 × 70 cm).

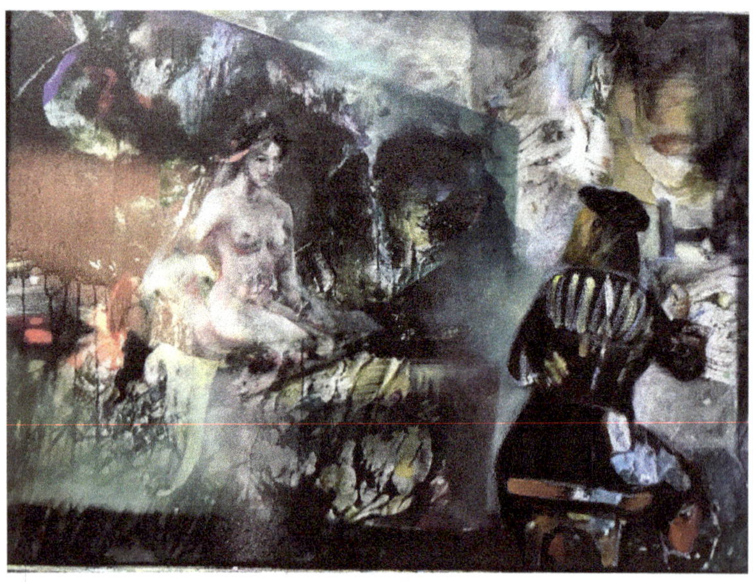

Fig. 5.5b. *The Muse* (2020, 50 × 70 cm).

blow to him by overriding him, in an act of *Selbstverfraulichung*. Lan is turning the head of a large screw with her hands, while the lower half of the painting is filled with countless screws.[25] The painting is mounted in a way that allows rotation and inversion of the painting and enables multidirectional viewing.[26]

Lan continued to explore the claim that "women do not paint so well" and created works that suggest reasons for this perception that go beyond women's alleged lack of brutality. On the occasion of Baselitz's major retrospective, *Baselitz Academy*, which took place at the Gallerie dell'Accademia in Venice from May 8 to October 6, 2019, she created an electronic flyer, *The Reason Why Women Can't Paint* (2019, Fig. 5.4c; cf. Fig. 2.7). The poster shows Lan bending down to paint a canvas on the floor of a gallery, with *Water Flows Downward. This Is a Fact* mounted on the wall behind her. She deliberately positions herself in such a way that the painted Baselitz appears to be groping her from behind with his outstretched hand, thereby proposing #MeToo issues in the art world as an alternative reason "why women can't paint." She also wonders why some male artists accept female students into their art programs and even marry their female students: "What would their female students and later wives think [of Baselitz's remark]?"

Lan went on to paint a series of seven more paintings in response to Baselitz's disparaging remark, titled *Baselitz's Question*, and included them in her exhibition *Tauriform Destiny* in Riegel am Kaiserstuhl (August 30–October 14, 2020).[27] In *Die Hinterhältigkeit* (Always Watch One's Back, 2020, Fig. 5.5a), she depicts a woman artist wielding a long-handled brush kneeling before a canvas to paint a stormy scene as a large pink octopus approaches her from behind. The representation of the octopus as a sexual predator recalls the Japanese artist Hokusai's erotic woodblock print *The Dream of the Fisherman's Wife* (1814). The title "Hinterhältigkeit" means "deviousness" and may also be read as

25 When black cloth was nailed over her paintings following a major dispute, she decided to channel her anger and frustration through painting screws in her artworks.

26 *Baselitz Delivery* was one of thirty-nine paintings displayed in her solo exhibition *Prospektiv* in the Wasserburg Haus Graven from July 12 to September 13, 2020; see *Jiny Lan @ Langenfeld / One-Woman-Show "Prospektiv,"* curated by Kunst-Raum Schulte-Goltz-Noelte, <https://artspaces.kunstmatrix.com/de/exhibition/1924176/jiny-lan-langenfeld-one-woman-show-prospektiv>; Segovia-Buendia, "Malerin Jiny Lan spielt mit Kontrasten."

27 "Mal humorvoll, mal provokant, immer kritisch: Jiny Lan stellt in Riegel aus," *Badische Zeitung*, August 21, 2020, <https://www.badische-zeitung.de/mal-humorvoll-mal-provokant-immer-kritisch>; Michael Haberer, "Angedeutete Klarheit: Die chinesische Konzeptkünstlerin Jiny Lan stellt in der Galerie Messmer aus," *Badische Zeitung*, September 3, 2020, <https://www.badische-zeitung.de/angedeutete-klarheit>.

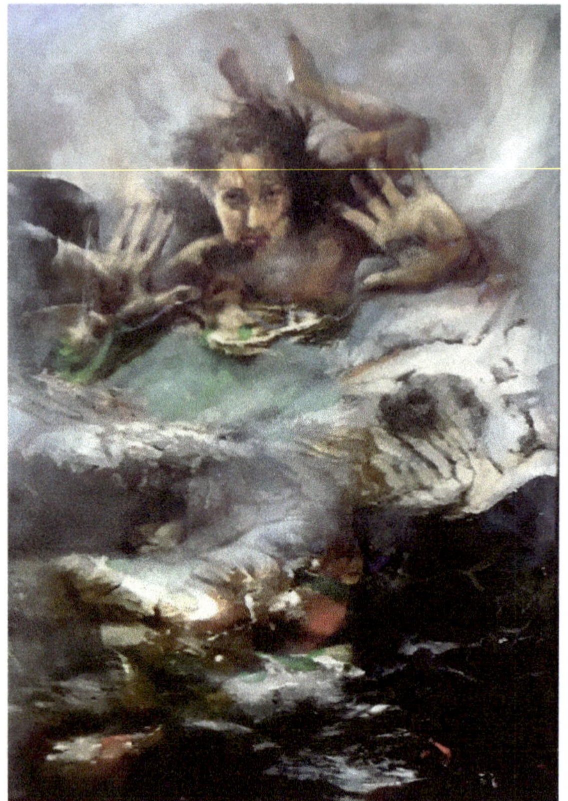

Fig. 5.5c. *Glass Pane* (2020, 70 × 50 cm).

a pun on "Hintern halten," meaning "to grab someone's *derrière*." In another painting in this miniseries, *Die Muse* (Vermeer Muse, 2020, Fig. 5.5b), Lan appropriates Johannes Vermeer's *The Art of Painting* (1666–68). Unlike in Vermeer's original painting, where the male artist is painting a fully clothed model, Lan's artist is copying a large painting of a naked woman kneeling on a bed. The faces of other women are visible in the background, indicating that women, especially naked beauties, have always served as muses for men. *Die Glasscheibe* (Glass Pane, 2020, Fig. 5.5c) depicts a nude woman swimming underwater toward the viewer. Her palms are outstretched and she appears to be pressing against a glass partition. A disembodied hand pushes back against one of her hands from the other side of the partition. This painting aptly visualizes the "glass ceiling" as another reason why women fail to achieve the same status as male artists.

Anselm Kiefer in China and *The German Crib* (2018)

The fifth "Masterpiece" in the series, *Die deutsche Krippe* (The German Crib, 2018, Fig. 5.7), was prompted by the scandal surrounding the first exhibition of Anselm Kiefer's works in China. From November 19, 2016, to January 8, 2017, Kiefer's works were shown at the CAFA Art Museum in an exhibition titled *Coagulation*, curated by Beate Reifenscheid, director of the Ludwig Museum in Koblenz and a visiting professor at the Tianjin Academy of Fine Arts from 2015 to 2018. Reifenscheid is committed to artistic exchange between Germany and China, where she enjoys high esteem, but the Kiefer exhibition was unusual because it had been organized without the artist's consent. Shortly before the opening, Kiefer issued a statement calling for the show's cancellation: "Throughout my career I have been heavily involved in all my major international exhibitions and it is a matter of deep regret and frustration that the organizers of my first show in China have seen fit to exclude me from this process."[28] In an interview with the *Süddeutsche Zeitung*, Kiefer said that he had been treated as if he were a dead artist and that he felt "raped" (*vergewaltigt*),[29] an expression that exasperated Lan.

Speaking to the *New York Times*, Reifenscheid explained that early in the planning stages, organizers made several attempts to contact Kiefer and were ultimately told that he could not spare the time to participate.[30] She said that it is generally desirable for an artist to participate in planning an exhibition, but if the artist declines, it should still be possible to show works owned by museums and collectors: "Curators must respect the artist but be able to work for the wider public's benefit. If all artists and their art dealers could control when, where, and why their art is displayed in

28 "Curator of Anselm Kiefer Show in China Speaks Out against Artist's Criticism of Exhibition," *Artforum International*, February 14, 2017, <https://www.artforum.com/news/curator-of-anselm-kiefer-show-in-china-speaks-out-against-artist-s-criticism-of-exhibition-66554>.

29 Kai Strittmatter, "Kunst: Eklat mit Erfolg," *Süddeutsche Zeitung*, December 2, 2016, <https://www.sueddeutsche.de/kultur/kunst-eklat-mit-erfolg-1.3277590>; Johnny Erling, "Kunstskandal: Anselm Kiefer und China haben ein Problem," *Welt*, November 24, 2016, <https://www.welt.de/kultur/article159733166/Anselm-Kiefer-und-China-haben-ein-Problem.html>; Heinz-Norbert Jocks, "Versuch über die Selbstverfraulichung: Ein Atelierbesuch bei Jiny Lan," exhibition catalog, May 16, 2021, <https://s774dc82513f14d00.jimcontent.com/download/version/1630077020/module/11601294994/name/Jiny%2520LAN%2520Essay%2520von%2520HNJ%2520v05.pdf>.

30 Amy Qin, "Chinese Museum Mounts an Anselm Kiefer Show, Over the Artist's Objections," *New York Times*, November 22, 2016.

museums after it's sold, the public interest would not be fully served."[31] One of Reifenscheid's colleagues, the critic and curator Klaus Honnef, argued that Kiefer and his gallerists refused to participate in the exhibition for financial reasons, a claim that Kiefer's galleries denied.[32]

The dispute over the exhibition came as a surprise to Wang Huangsheng, director of the CAFA Art Museum, who said that by the time the museum learned of the conflict between Kiefer and the other organizers, it would have been too costly to cancel the show. The artworks were already in Beijing. Eighty of the eighty-seven works, including paintings, sculptures, installations, and videos, were provided by Maria Chen Tu, a German collector of Taiwanese descent. Tu loaned the Kiefer acquisitions from her collection to Bell Art, a Hamburg-based organization that mostly imports Chinese art to Western countries.[33] Another five works were loaned by private collections to the Ludwig Museum, where Reifenscheid was director.[34] Because the display of works borrowed from private collectors was in accordance with international law, the museum went ahead with the show, which drew many more visitors than expected, partly due to the scandal.

German media were predictably critical of the decision to proceed with the exhibition, but the response was even stronger in China, where social media users launched a massive attack on the CAFA Art Museum, arguing that it was unethical to display Kiefer's works without the artist's permission.[35] Lan, however, defended the exhibition, citing its political significance. She noted that Wang and Reifenscheid rushed to put together the show because of the global political situation. The world was facing major ideological conflicts: Donald Trump had won his first presidential election two weeks before the exhibit opened, while in Europe the Syrian refugee crisis gave a leg up to far-right political parties, and in China, populism and nationalism were also on the rise. According to Lan, Kiefer, who had long warned of the dangers of populism and nationalism,

31 "Curator of Anselm Kiefer Show in China Speaks Out."

32 "Curator of Anselm Kiefer Show in China Speaks Out."

33 Bell Art was founded by Chinese businessman Ma Yue and Wilderich Graf von Schall-Riaucour. In 2019, Bell Art was liquidated; it was also involved in a scandal when a trove of artworks by famous German artists disappeared and later turned up moldering in a warehouse in southern China; see Stefan Dege, "Renowned German artworks disappear in China," *DW*, November 21, 2019, <https://www.dw.com/en/artworks-by-renowned-german-artists-disappear-in-china/a-51353568>; "$300 Million Worth of Work by Anselm Kiefer and Other German Artists Has Mysteriously Gone Missing in China," *Artnet*, November 20, 2019, <https://news.artnet.com/art-world/300-million-art-china-germany-1709529>.

34 "Curator of Anselm Kiefer Show in China Speaks Out."

35 Erling, "Kunstskandal."

had the authority to address the present moment.[36] His "Sieg Heil" salutes, performed in front of different landmarks in Europe, made him an iconic representative of Germany's *Vergangenheitsbewältigung* or coming to terms with the Nazi past. As Saltzman remarked: "It is Kiefer more than any other postwar German painter who grapples not only with the aesthetic question of what it means to paint but with the ontological question of what it means to paint as a German."[37]

In 1969, Kiefer, a student of Beuys, had traveled to Switzerland, France, and Italy to photograph himself giving the Hitler salute as part of his thesis project at the Düsseldorf Art Academy. He called these photographs "heroische Sinnbilder" (heroic symbols), later recontextualized in his 1975 project *Besetzungen* (Occupations).[38] Kiefer conceived this project in order to understand why so many Germans fell for Hitler: "I do not identify with Nero or Hitler, but I have to reenact what they did just a little bit in order to understand the madness. That is why I make these attempts to become a fascist."[39] Thus Kiefer launched his career by jolting an all-too-easily lulled German society into confronting its Nazi past. According to art historian Daniel Arasse, "Kiefer was the first to tackle the representation of Nazism head-on, using his own body."[40] Before the 2019 European Parliament elections, Lan painted *Verhandlung* (Negotiation, 2019, Fig. 5.6), in which she placed a silhouetted Anselm Kiefer giving his fascist salute within a giant hand making the "ok" sign, as if to give her own endorsement to Kiefer's controversial but epochal act.[41] The title "Negotiation" captures how postwar German artists negotiate their identity between the paternal generation of *Täter* and *Mitläufer* (persecutors and fellow travelers) and the oedipal sons rebelling against their "fathers."

One year prior to this affirmation of Kiefer's art, however, Lan had sharply criticized Kiefer for his "management" of his art. In *The German*

36 See also 蓝镜 Jiny Lan, 也说说基弗风波中收藏家的利益 [On the Interests of Collectors in the Kiefer Affair], published in 中国美术报 [Art News of China] and 凤凰艺术 [Phoenix Art], November 24, 2016, <https://m-news.artron.net/news/20240918/n962568.html>. When Lan finally met Kiefer in person during his *Rue de Ponthieu* exhibition in Paris in 2022, they did not talk about this unpleasant past.

37 Saltzman, *Anselm Kiefer*, 50.

38 Anselm Kiefer, "Occupations 1969," *Interfunktionen* 12 (1975): 133–44; Christian Weikop, "'Occupations': A Difficult Reception," Tate, 2016, <https://www.tate.org.uk/research/publications/in-focus/heroic-symbols-anselm-kiefer/difficult-reception-occupations>; see also Saltzman's nuanced discussion of Kiefer's reenactment of being a Nazi in *Anselm Kiefer*, 54–62.

39 Quoted in Saltzman, *Anselm Kiefer*, 60.

40 Daniel Arasse, *Anselm Kiefer* (New York: Harry N. Abrams, 2001), 33.

41 Cf. Liu Ying, "Lan Jing, a famous and formidable Chinese female painter in Germany," *Hua Shang Bao*, April 16, 2019.

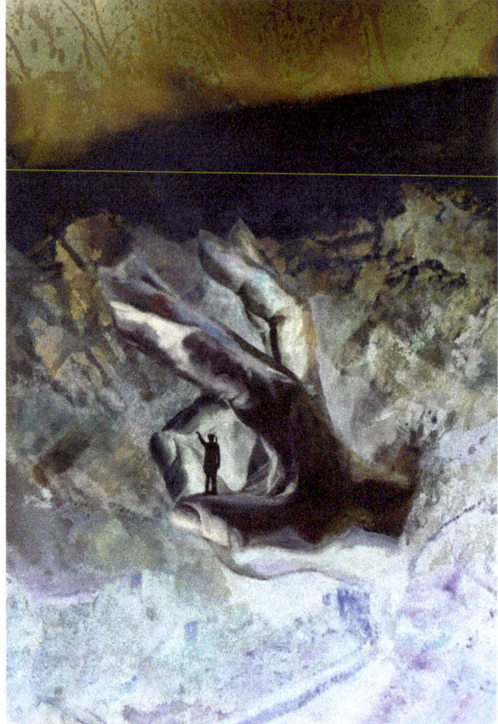

Fig. 5.6. *Negotiation* (2019, 200 × 140 cm).

Crib, she painted an image of Kiefer sitting in front of the Reichstag, the "real" wings of which are visible beyond the edges of the painting within the painting, creating a mise-en-abyme effect. Kiefer's complaint that he felt "raped" by the CAFA exhibition so enraged Lan that she placed the head of an eagle, a symbol of power, predation, and masculinity, at his groin, and a flood of pink baby dolls pours forth between his feet. She forcefully rejected his claim of violation: "He felt 'raped' when a Chinese museum exhibited expensively acquired works without his collaboration. I say: No, he has trivialized rape. With his authority and reputation in the art world, he could easily destroy a museum like CAFA. How can such a powerful man be 'raped' by the Chinese?" The eagle conjures up Kiefer's famous painting *Icarus—March Sand* (1981). In the Greek myth, Icarus was punished by the gods when the sun melted his wax wings. Kiefer's Icarus, as Saltzman points out, is the artist's self-portrayal as a victim: "By representing Icarus as palette, Kiefer inserts himself, as son and artist, into his work. Moreover, he inscribes himself as a victim, victim of the historical legacy, of the paternal legacy, against which he has tried so

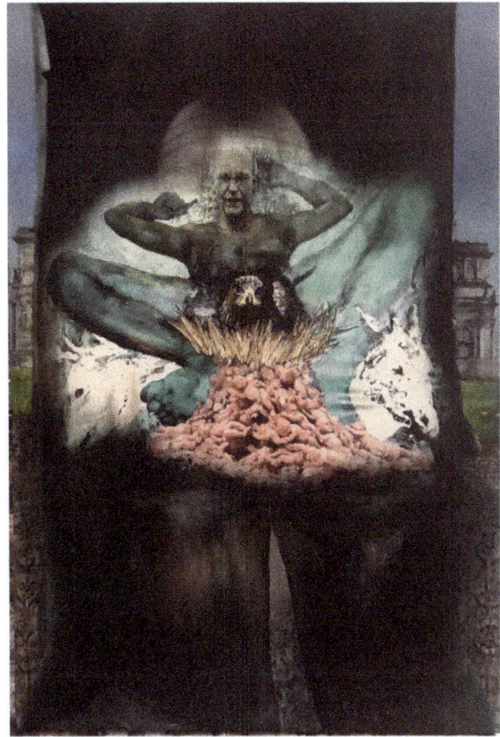

Fig. 5.7. *The German Crib* (2018, 200 × 140 cm).

hard to articulate and negotiate his own identity."[42] Saltzman complicates the straightforward interpretation of Kiefer as an oedipal son who rebels against "a historically tainted father" by critiquing Kiefer's sense of his own victimhood.[43] In Kiefer's comparison of the unauthorized exhibition of his work to rape, a tinge of that victim mentality shows through.

In *The German Crib*, Kiefer's splayed and disproportionately long legs, as well as the large pile of identical dolls, recall Alessandro reclining with legs spread in *Alessandro Kind* (2013, Fig. 3.7a) or the parturient posture of Confucius/Ai Weiwei in *Who's Your Daddy* (Fig. 3.7b). A juxtaposition of the images confirms their iterative relationship. All of them point proudly with their right index finger at themselves. Whereas Alessandro seems to be showing off his masculinity, in *Who's Your Daddy* Lan criticizes the idolization of patriarchal hierarchy in Chinese society, and her representation of Kiefer making the same proud gesture could express her objection to patriarchal worship in the art world.

42 Saltzman, *Anselm Kiefer*, 65; Andreas Huyssen, "Anselm Kiefer: The Terror of History, the Temptation of Myth," *October* 48 (1989): 25–45.

43 Saltzman, *Anselm Kiefer*, 50.

The German Crib incorporates a dialectical view of Kiefer. On the one hand, the cow is a deferential pastiche. In 2010, Kiefer exhibited six large-format paintings of grazing cows at the Villa Schöningen in Potsdam under the title *Europa*, as a show of support for the European Union as a peace project.[44] The title "The German Crib" refers to Germany's zero hour, the rebirth of German democracy after the war, and Kiefer's crucial role in ending the evasive silence about German guilt. On the other hand, the hanging canvas depicted in *The German Crib* is shaped like a person's back, with folds suggesting buttocks; if the slit that is already tearing through the eagle, the dolls, and Kiefer continues upward, the glass dome symbolizing democracy will be torn apart. In the upper left corner, a slight tear in the canvas creates a sense of tension and unease, similar to the cut in the rope in Lan's painting of Beuys. During the early part of Kiefer's career, an important task for Germany was to figure out how to address National Socialism. Today in the West, resurgent populism, nationalism, and racism threaten democracy. Lan feels that highly acclaimed artists like Kiefer should look directly at the current world situation and use their immense influence to fulfill the social and political responsibilities they so brilliantly assumed in their younger days. She declares: "If they fail to do so, they should step down from their princely throne, as the tear in the cloth suggests."

The Cult of Gerhard Richter: *Judgment Day* (2019)

A series of *Masterpieces* would not be complete without Gerhard Richter, Europe's most commercially successful contemporary artist.[45] Lan's painting *Judgment Day* (2019, Fig. 5.8a), in which Richter is symmetrically multiplied and gradually blurred, imitates his own techniques: photorealism, multiples, posters, overpainting, and blurring. Richter uses squeegees to apply thick layers of pigment, methodically creating abstract compositions of intense color schemes and indeterminate forms that open up endless possibilities for the viewer to explore.[46]

44 Tim Ackermann, "Villa Schöningen: Anselm Kiefer macht die Kuh zum Kosmos," *Welt*, October 4, 2010, <https://www.welt.de/kultur/article10065291/Anselm-Kiefer-macht-die-Kuh-zum-Kosmos.html>.

45 "German Painter Most Expensive Living Artist," *Art Forum*, March 27, 2002, <https://www.artforum.com/news/german-painter-most-expensive-living-artist-163757/>; "Gerhard Richter – the Most Expensive Living Artist in Europe," *ArtWizard*, February 10, 2023, <https://artwizard.eu/gerhard-richter--the-most-expensive-living-artist-in-europe-ar-134>.

46 "Gerhard Richter – Abstractions," *Artsy*, 2015, <https://www.artsy.net/artist-series/gerhard-richter-abstractions>; Rosie Lesso, "How Does Gerhard Richter Make His Abstract Paintings?" *The Collector*, December 8, 2022, <https://www.thecollector.com/how-does-gerhard-richter-make-his-abstract-paintings/>.

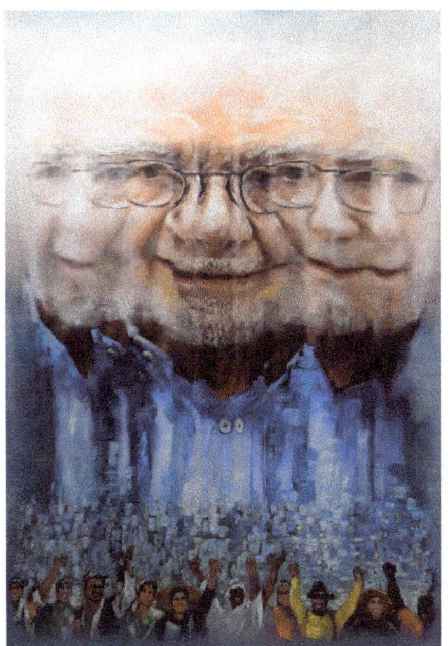

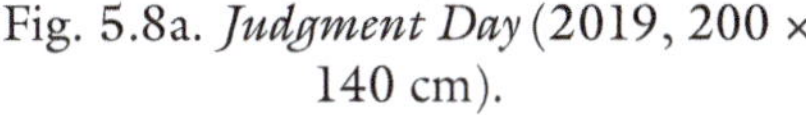

Fig. 5.8a. *Judgment Day* (2019, 200 × 140 cm).

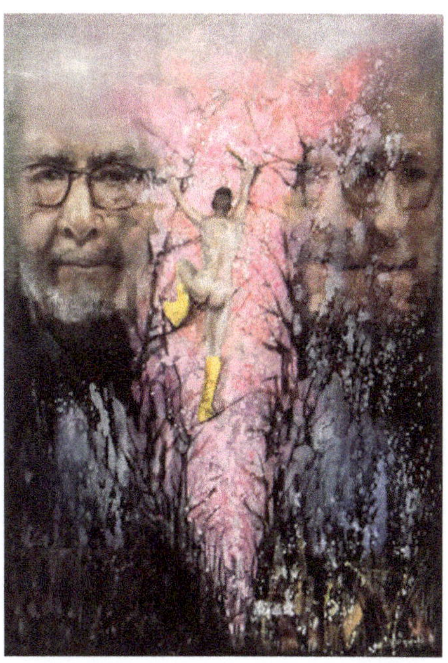

Fig. 5.8b. *New Perspectives on Modern Masters* (2019, 100 × 70 cm).

With the English title "Judgment Day," Lan plays on Richter's name, which means "judge." The painting is modeled on the same Cultural Revolution propaganda poster as *Red Sun* (Fig. 2.1b). The personality cult posters are often organized along a horizontal axis, with Mao's bust occupying the upper section and a row of people lining up below, facing the spectator and waving the Mao bible. By configuring the Richter painting like a Mao poster, Lan shows the capitalist equivalent of a personality cult, or in this case, an artist cult. The crowd in the Richter painting also represents people from different continents, raising their arms and cheering Richter in the same way that people cheered Mao. What they are holding, according to Lan, are green dollar bills, but she points out that "Richter's artworks are literally regarded as hard currency or gold, more valuable than dollars."[47] This is evident in a recent spate of Richter forgeries, one of which involved Lan's former Berlin gallerist, Michael Schultz (1951–2021), who was arrested in 2019 for repaying his debt to an art collector with a Richter painting that was soon proven to be fake.[48]

47 See Ralph Wilms, "In der Ludwiggalerie trifft Charme-Attacke alte Malerfürsten," *WAZ*, June 14, 2019, <https://www.waz.de/staedte/oberhausen/article226161863/Charme-Attacke-trifft-Malerfuersten.html>.

48 "Arrested and released for health reasons, German Dealer Michael Schultz is accused of having deceived clients with false documentation," Association for

Lan's desire to emulate Richter is conveyed in the sub-version *New Perspectives on Modern Masters* (2019, Fig. 5.8b). It transforms the figure of Richter on the central axis into a pink zone where a small naked woman is climbing a tree. The closely cut hair and yellow boots indicate that the climber is Lan herself. She is climbing the ladder of the art world to reach the height of Gerhard Richter. Pink, a color associated with girls, indicates that the uphill struggle she faces stems from bias against female and minority artists in the (art) world. In the lower right corner, Lan explains, is the Cologne Cathedral, with the Hohenzollern Bridge nearby. Richter, who lives in Cologne, designed a stained-glass window for the cathedral. Echoing her battle with Baselitz, Lan humorously depicts herself as the proportionally tiny climbing artist reaching for the "painter prince" at the top of the art world.

Coda: Becoming a Pearl: The Diasporic Artist as *Fremdkörper*

In another painting in the *Baselitz's Question* series, *Becoming a Pearl* (2020, Fig. 5.9a), Lan places a sexualized woman inside an oyster shell to thematize her objectification and consumability. The painting shows the woman in silhouette, lying in a nacreous shell-like rock formation, propping herself up on her elbows. The abstract background suggests flowing water. Another empty rock-shell formation is visible in the background. Similarly, in *A Thousand Years of Humility – Part 2* (2020, Fig. 5.9b), a bound nude woman lies sleeping in a shell-like rock formation in the middle of a rapidly flowing stream. On a rock above the stream a woman dressed in red reclines under overhanging greenery.

The image of a bound woman represents the restriction and bondage of women throughout history. But after a thousand years of keeping themselves humble, it is time for women (artists) to cast off that bondage.[49] Lan's choice of the oyster shell as a sexual symbol was inspired by a fellow female Chinese student's pronunciation of *Muschel* (clams) as *Muschi* (slang for "vulva"). A foreign student's accented German led to the association of clams with the female genitalia and spawned bawdy jokes among (male) students. Thus, the symbolic associations of the oyster in Lan's work extend to the immigrant experience, linguistic confusion, and vulgar sexism.

Research into Crimes against Art, blog entry, October 25, 2019, <https://art-crime.blogspot.com/2019/10/arrested-and-released-for-health.html>; "Kunstskandal: Die falsche Marilyn," *Focus Magazin* 36, August 28, 2020.

49 *Becoming A Pearl* is a cropped sub-version of Part 2 of the triptych *A Thousand Years of Humility* that zooms in on the shell in the earlier painting. Sometimes in Lan's Jinyology a sub-version is created by reproducing only one section of a previous version.

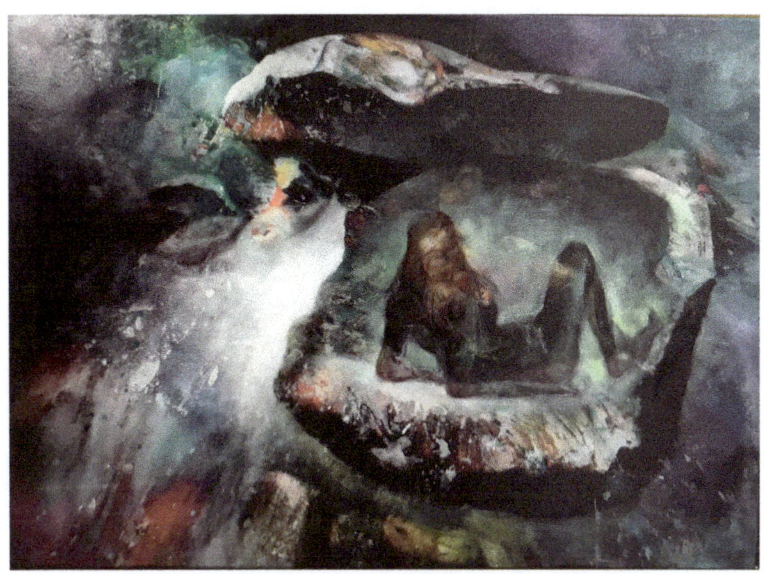

Fig. 5.9a. *Becoming A Pearl* (2020, 50 × 70 cm).

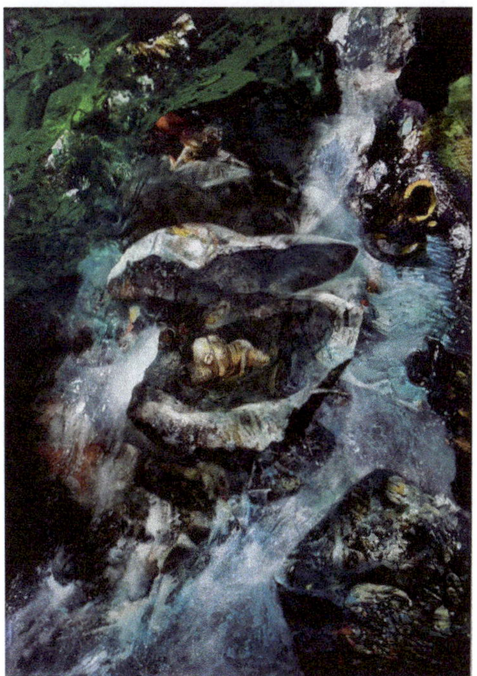

Fig. 5.9b. *A Thousand Years of Humility – Part 2* (2020, 280 × 200 cm).

Lan's biographical trajectory, her immigrant and diasporic status, and her language and cultural heritage made her an outsider and an exotic figure in the German art world. Describing the intersectional challenges that an Asian woman artist faces in the West because of her gender and race, Lan compares herself to a *Fremdkörper* (foreign matter), similar to the irritant that enters an oyster. The irritating "foreign matter" has the potential to "become a pearl." However, to become a pearl is also to lose one's rough edges and potential to irritate. It could be said that the male German artists singled out by Lan have also been transformed by fame and honor from erstwhile "irritants" into "pearls." The title "Becoming a pearl" inadvertently reveals Lan's wish to become like the targets of her own criticism, evoking the bat that wants to be on the winning side (chapter 3).

Rather than inventing a radically different visual language, or a new mode of intersectional feminist painting, Lan's approach remains bound to the existing canon. Her portraits are "portraits of power," revealing a self-contradiction between her purported anti-authoritarianism and her reliance on powerful and famous public figures to promote herself. Art critics in Europe and the United States have been commenting on artistic co-opting of the market for decades. The American artist, Damien Hirst, for example, has been crowned the "self-promotion king" who exemplifies the current tendency for the art scene to degenerate into little more than a form of PR and ruthless capitalist self-promotion.[50] Ai Weiwei's costly projects and publicity stunts aroused consternation due to his privilege and poor taste.[51] With *Selbstverfraulichung*, Lan walks a fine line between self-marketing on the one hand and feminist striving on the other.

50 Abigail R. Esman, "Damien Hirst at Gagosian Worldwide: See Spot Show Off," *Forbes*, January 12, 2012, <https://www.forbes.com/sites/abigailesman/2012/01/12/damien-hirst-at-gagosian-worldwide-see-spot-show-off/>; Jack Malvern, "Collectors Lose Thousands on Damien Hirst Artworks," *The Times*, September 14, 2018, <https://www.thetimes.com/culture/art/article/collectors-lose-thousands-on-damien-hirst-artworks-k5vp3tp0t>.

51 Jed Perl, "Noble and Ignoble Ai Weiwei: Wonderful Dissident, Terrible Artist," *The New Republic*, February 1, 2013, <https://newrepublic.com/article/112218/ai-wei-wei-wonderful-dissident-terrible-artist>; Lorena Muñoz-Alonso, "Ai Weiwei Brings His Controversial Life Vest Installation to Vienna," *Artnet*, July 14, 2016, <https://news.artnet.com/art-world/ai-weiwei-refugee-jacket-installation-vienna-557324>; Nitasha Dhillon, "Ai Weiwei's Photo Reenacting a Child Refugee's Death Should Not Exist," *Hyperallergic*, February 2, 2016, <https://hyperallergic.com/272881/ai-weiweis-photo-reenacting-a-child-refugees-death-should-not-exist/>; Anya Zhang, "Ai Weiwei: Blurring the Lines between Artistry and Absurdity," *Havard Political Review*, September 6, 2023, <https://harvardpolitics.com/ai-weiwei-blurring-the-lines-between-artistry-and-absurdity/>.

Part Three

Political Art

6: Modernizing or Moldering: Criticism of Autocracies

LAN'S ARTWORK OFTEN comments on contemporary political affairs and international politics. The contemporary world is not divided into communist, capitalist, and non-aligned blocs, but into autocracies and democracies, with different shades of illiberalism and liberalism in between. Russia's pseudo-democracy, China's atheist pseudo-communism, and Iran's theocracy do not have much in common. What unites them is their anti-Americanism and their forceful preservation of autocratic rule. At a time when the systemic rivalry between autocracies and democracies has intensified, Lan is wary of the polarization taking place within democracies to the advantage of autocracies. Her lived experience under both political systems leads her to criticize autocratic regimes and those in the West who sympathize with or condone authoritarian leaders. This chapter groups paintings that are critical of illiberal regimes, especially China, but also Russia, North Korea, and Iran.

Backward Movement (2014): A Painting with a "Skyeye"

Echoing the Tiananmen series, Lan's *Value-Added Movement 3A Revision 1a*: *Backward Movement* (2014, Fig. 6.1b) criticizes China as a surveillance state. In 2005, the Chinese government created a mass surveillance system called Skynet that included over 20 million cameras located in cities across China. By 2015, the Beijing Public Security Bureau had mandated full coverage in the capital, and other Chinese cities followed suit.[1] Thus, at the time Lan painted *Backward Movement* (2014), the Skynet was spreading across China at an accelerating rate, transforming the country into a notorious surveillance state. In 2014, Xi introduced

1 "Beijing: Skynet Is Watching," *The Week*, February 8, 2013, 9; Cao Yin, "More 'Eyes' Fight Crime in Crowds," *China Daily*, October 5, 2015, <https://www.chinadaily.com.cn/china/2015-10/05/content_22091634.htm>; Zheping Huang, "Absolutely Everywhere in Beijing Is Now Covered by Police Video Surveillance," *Quartz*, October 7, 2015, <https://qz.com/518874/absolutely-everywhere-in-beijing-is-now-covered-by-police-video-surveillance>.

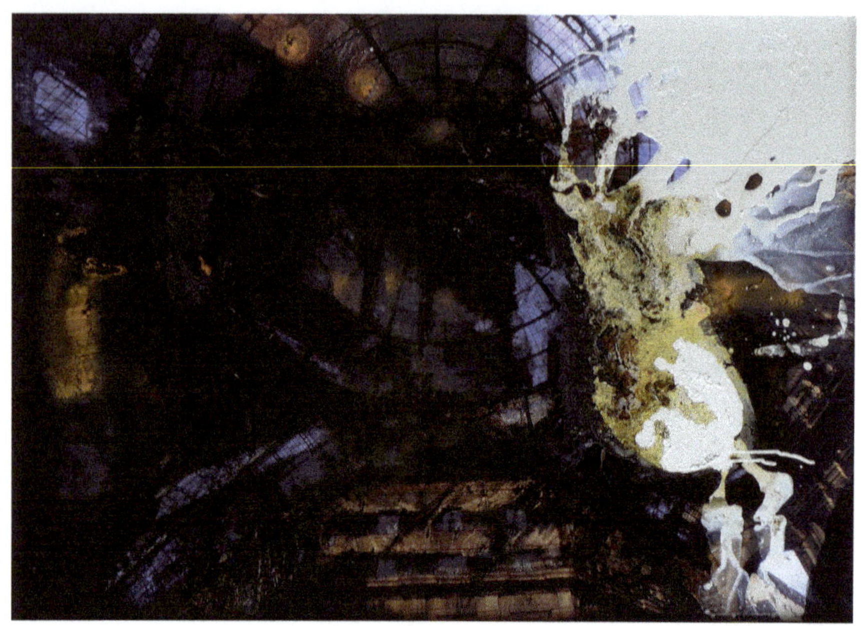

Fig. 6.1a. *Value-Added Movement* 3A (2013, 140 × 200 cm).

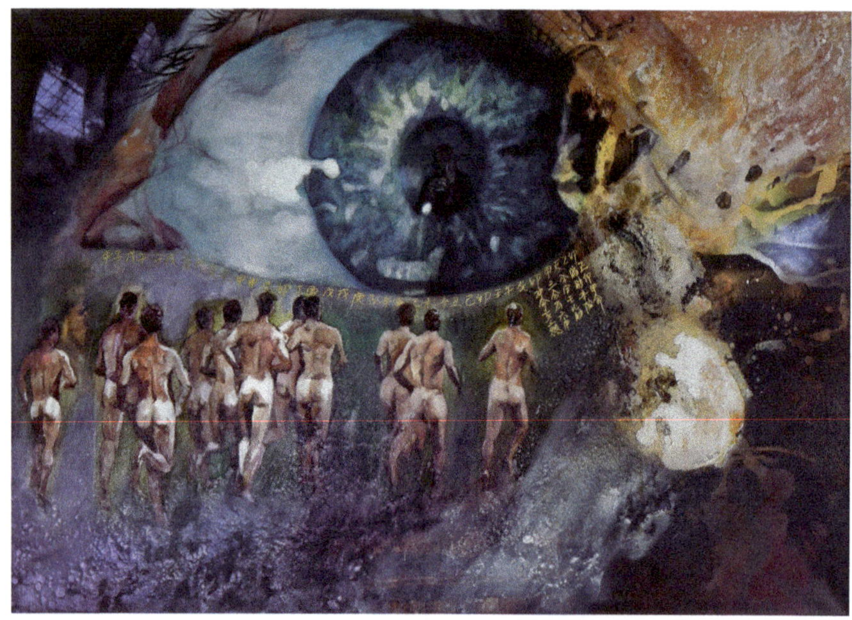

Fig. 6.1b. *Backward Movement* (2014, 140 × 200 cm).

new regulations that further restricted journalistic activity and tightened control over the news media.[2]

The abstract ancestral version, *Value-Added Movement 3A* (2013, Fig. 6.1a), shows elements of the Milan shopping mall roof and a multistory building. Splotches of white paint cover much of the right edge. In *Backward Movement*, the concave interior of the blue glass ceiling of the mall has been partially repainted with a giant convex naked eye, a "Skyeye." A dozen naked men run toward the Skyeye, their nude bodies heightening the sense of voyeurism associated with surveillance. A male figure in the iris peers menacingly at these men through a camera, representing the human agents who employ mechanized digital surveillance to assist the government in monitoring and recording the activities of citizens. The disproportion between the all-encompassing eye and the small, naked runners highlights the vulnerability and exposure of citizens in a dystopian society. Chinese text runs along the lower lid of the Skyeye. The right edge of the painting includes colorful blotches on a dark, cosmic background. This is a carryover from the pre-version that resembles a fire pit. Lan explains that the fire refers to the myth of Prometheus, who stole fire from the gods to give to mankind and was subsequently punished by Zeus. The painting thus contrasts primitive technology with modern high-tech. But while humanity has benefited from primitive technologies, it runs the risk of being controlled and manipulated by today's ultra-high technology. The painting captures the dialectical relationship between man and technology and the reversible power dynamic between them. The situation was exacerbated during the pandemic when, for example, the Chinese government falsely classified "troublemakers" as infected with Covid in order to control political movements and social protests.[3]

The Happiness of Two Rabbits (2017) and Pseudo-Democracy

Continuing her rage against political fossilization in China, Lan created *The Happiness of Two Rabbits* (2017, Fig. 6.2) as a response to the Nineteenth National People's Congress (NPC) of the CCP, which in October 2017 passed an amendment to the constitution that canonized

2 Michael Forsythe, "Chinese Government Tightens Constraints on Press Freedom," *New York Times*, June 19, 2014, <https://www.nytimes.com/2014/06/20/world/asia/chinese-government-tightens-constraints-on-press-freedom.html>.

3 Nectar Gan, "China's Bank Run Victims Planned to Protest. Then Their Covid Health Codes Turned Red," *CNN*, June 15, 2022, <https://edition.cnn.com/2022/06/15/china/china-zhengzhou-bank-fraud-health-code-protest-intl-hnk>.

Xi Jinping Thought as the Party's new ideology. While in the NPC, the largest parliament in the world, agendas are passed (almost) unanimously, its counterpart in Germany, the Bundestag, is a place of heated debate. According to Lan, unanimous votes are celebrated on national television in China but would be considered absurd in the West. She satirized this unanimity by painting countless thumbs-up on mountainous terrain under a blue sky in *The Happiness of Two Rabbits*. The inspiration for putting thumbs on a mountain came from the Chinese idiom *man shan bian ye*, which means "over all the hills and fields," implying that something pervades the gaze and offers an impressive sight.

A closer look reveals two rabbits with long ears hidden among the upturned thumbs. Lan titled the painting *The Happiness of Two Rabbits*, referring to the use of rabbits as a figure for Chinese people, as in the meme "Every hare has a dream of China becoming a powerful country" (*Meige tuzi douyou yige daguo meng*). This phrase originated in the popular webcomic *Year Hare Affair* (*Na'nian natu naxie shi'er*, 2011), drawn by Lin Chao, which represents nations as animals to illustrate modern China's history and international relations.

The reason why Lin Chao chose the hare, rather than the proverbial panda or dragon, as an allegorical figure for the Chinese is that "hares are herbivorous animals that are usually considered cute, docile, and populous, but can still inflict nasty bites and kicks when irritated. [The hare] represents the author's view that the People's Republic of China is traditionally not so aggressive in foreign policies but can still pack a punch when required."[4] Lin's populist depiction of characters and events boosted patriotic feelings, especially among younger Chinese viewers. But another web series, *Kuang Kuang the Little Rabbit* (*Xiao tuzi kuang kuang*, Wang Bo, 2011), uses the rabbit to represent average Chinese people suffering under the tyranny of the state, personified as a tiger. The hare, when overly oppressed, fights back and attacks the tiger. Conceived as a New Year's greeting for 2011, ushering in the Year of the Rabbit and bidding farewell to the Year of the Tiger, this cartoon satirized a series of social and political scandals and was quickly banned in China.[5] In short, *Year Hare Affair* and *Kuang Kuang the Little Rabbit* attach opposing allegories to the hare: the former sees the Chinese government as meek and peaceful, but when provoked, it strikes back at other countries; the

4 Victor Mair, "Year Hare Affair," *Language Log*, April 15, 2018, <https://languagelog.ldc.upenn.edu/nll/?p=37717>.

5 Mair, "Year Hare Affair"; Amber Boczar, "The Power of Creativity: How Web-Based Parody Encourages Chinese Civil Participation," *International ResearchScape Journal* 3 (2015), Article 1; «小兔子哐哐»在中国大陆被封杀 ["Kuang Kuang the Little Rabbit" Is Banned in Mainland China], *DW*, January 28, 2011, <https://www.dw.com/zh/小兔子哐哐在中国大陆被封杀/a-14800946>.

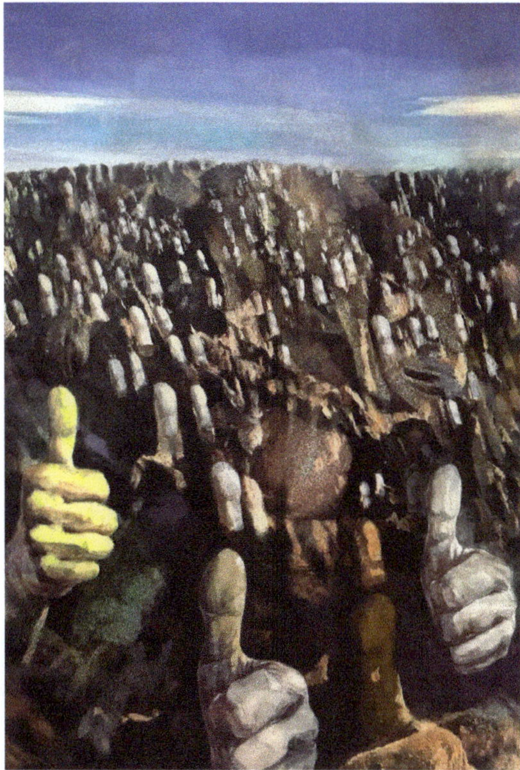

Fig. 6.2. *The Happiness of Two Rabbits* (2017, 200 × 140 cm).

latter sees the Chinese people as meek and peaceful, but when severely victimized, they fight back against their own government.

The two rabbits in Lan's painting stand for the compliant and nationalistic Chinese, which accounts for their inconspicuous presence in the painting. Without close scrutiny, the two rabbits would have been overlooked and mistaken for thumbs. The painting suggests that in a society that lacks freedom of the press and speech, it is difficult to form an individual opinion that differs from the one that the NPC has formed for the collective.[6] Similar to *One-Persons-Chorus* (chapter 2), *The Happiness*

6 The painting was originally titled "Like." Journalist Segovia-Buendia wrote about the painting: "The only thing our society apparently still pays attention to is approval via social networks" (das einzige, worauf unsere Gesellschaft noch zu achten scheint – die Anerkennung über die sozialen Netzwerke?), see Cristina Segovia-Buendia, "Malerin Jiny Lan spielt mit Kontrasten," *Rheinische Post*, July 13, 2020, <https://rp-online.de/nrw/staedte/langenfeld/langenfeld-malerin-jiny-lan-spielt-mit-kontrasten_aid-52110201>.

of Two Rabbits conveys the uniformity of the Chinese political landscape and the absence of a civil society and public sphere. In 2018, the presidential term limit was removed from China's constitution, allowing Xi to continue to rule indefinitely. The vote was virtually unanimous, with 2,958 delegates voting in favor, two against, three abstaining, and one invalid—another "rubber-stamping exercise."[7] Since 2011, the government has been promoting the Chinese version of democracy, the so-called whole-process people's democracy (*quan guocheng minzhu*), which does not involve free elections but pretends to consult ordinary people on policymaking. This democratic rhetoric functions as a ploy to maintain absolute control of one-party power and avoid the fate of the Soviet bloc countries.[8] In March 2023, despite his disastrous zero-Covid policy and its hasty and embarrassing abandonment, Xi secured a unanimous endorsement for his unprecedented third term.[9]

The *1989* Series: The Year in Review (2019–22)

The Chinese constitutional amendment was a manifestation of the authoritarian political trend in Beijing, followed by the Hong Kong Extradition Bill (2019) and the Hong Kong National Security Law (2020). Beijing's increasing encroachment on Hong Kong prompted Lan to lament: "Hong Kong *was* my favorite city, which combined Eastern and Western cultures in a very pleasant way – unfortunately, I have to use the past tense here." The year 2019 was also the thirtieth anniversary of the Tiananmen Square massacre, which inspired Lan to start her *1989* series. In *1989–2019* (2019, Fig. 6.3a), a bright yellow umbrella takes center stage, with Tiananmen lurking behind it. Yellow umbrellas stand for the fight for democracy in Hong Kong. During protests against the Chinese government's interference in Hong Kong's 2014 elections, yellow umbrellas shielded people from the sun and rain, and later from the tear gas and pepper spray used by Hong Kong

7 "China's Xi Allowed to Remain 'President for Life' as Term Limits Removed," *BBC*, March 11, 2018; Chris Buckley and Steven Lee Myers, "China's Legislature Blesses Xi's Indefinite Rule. It was 2,958 to 2," *New York Times*, March 11, 2018, <https://www.nytimes.com/2018/03/11/world/asia/china-xi-constitution-term-limits.html>.

8 Matthew Loh, "China Says It's Running on a New Version of Democracy that Doesn't Rely on Elections. Experts Say It's Just Another Mind Game," *Business Insider*, October 22, 2022, <https://www.businessinsider.com/china-whole-process-democracy-expert-explainer-mind-game-2022-10>.

9 Rhoda Kwan, Amy Hawkins, and Agencies, "Xi Jinping Handed Unprecedented Third Term as China's President," *The Guardian*, March 10, 2023, <https://www.theguardian.com/world/2023/mar/10/xi-jinping-handed-unprecedented-third-term-as-chinas-president>.

police to disperse the crowds. The demonstrations became known as the Umbrella Movement. More yellow umbrellas dot the bottom of the painting where marching demonstrators are drenched in greenish-blue water, recalling the blue-dyed water that Hong Kong police sprayed at the demonstrators to render them identifiable.[10] But the water also evokes the protesters' "be water" strategy, inspired by Bruce Lee's advice to "be like water, making its way through the cracks."[11] A nude woman appears to be performing a jackknife dive. Lan identifies this as a representation of herself: being aquaphobic, she often depicts herself in water to express uncomfortable, suffocating feelings. The diving figure could also be interpreted as Lan plunging into the movement to show her spiritual solidarity with the protesters.

In the background of *1989–2019* hovers the Basilica di San Marco in Venice, which provides the Western dimension in this painting. The two humanoid terra-cotta soldiers on the right represent the totalitarian Qin dynasty that unified China in the third century BC but also established a tradition of dictatorial, paternalistic rule. By using the terra-cotta soldiers and Tiananmen as symbols, Lan suggests the continuity of authoritarian rule from China's beginnings to the present. In *1989–2019*, Tiananmen is overshadowed by the prominent yellow umbrella, implying that the Hong Kong pro-democracy movement had gained great momentum and visibility, as well as international support. But this was about to change, as the sub-versions of the painting show.

In 2020, Covid-19 spread beyond China and became a worldwide pandemic. For *1989–2020* (2020, Fig. 6.3b), Lan ran the pre-version through the color inversion app on her mobile phone, converting black to white, bright yellow to dark blue, and turquoise to hot pink. Dark blue is the color of the European Union, representing a constant political contrast to China in Lan's work. The Bundestag replaces the Basilica di San Marco on a white background, and a blue umbrella, again showing Tiananmen, partially screens the diver. Next to the diving woman's knee, Lan painted the famous Yellow Crane Tower, a symbol of Wuhan, the city where Covid-19 first broke out. A second Yellow Crane Tower is visible on the Wuhan Yangtze River Bridge, another symbol of Wuhan. A third Yellow Crane Tower is placed inside the German Bundestag, and a fourth outside the Bundestag on its side wing. The multiplication of the Yellow Crane Tower mimics the contagious transmission of the coronavirus.

10 "Hong Kong: Blue-dyed Water Fired at Protesters Defying Ban," *BBC*, August 31, 2019, <https://www.bbc.co.uk/news/av/world-asia-49536000>.

11 Erin Hale, "'Be Water': Hong Kong Protesters Adopt Bruce Lee Tactic to Evade Police Crackdown," *Independent*, January 6, 2020, <https://www.independent.co.uk/news/world/asia/hong-kong-protest-latest-bruce-lee-riot-police-water-a9045311.html>.

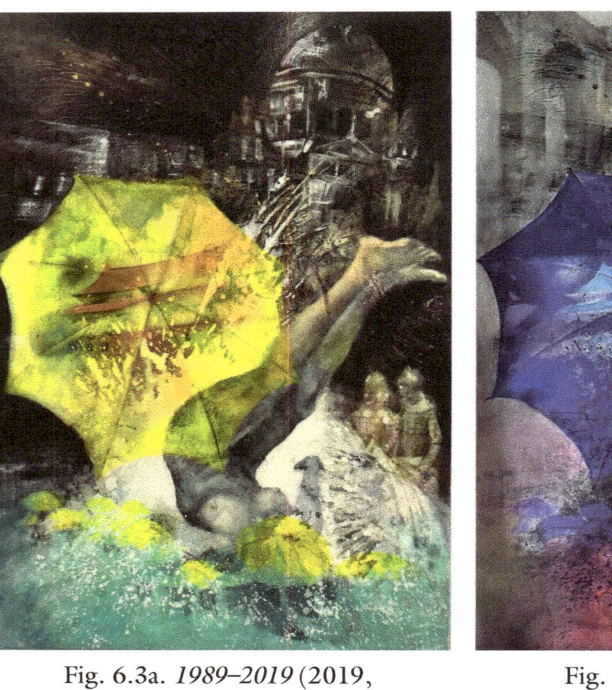

Fig. 6.3a. *1989–2019* (2019, 140 × 100 cm).

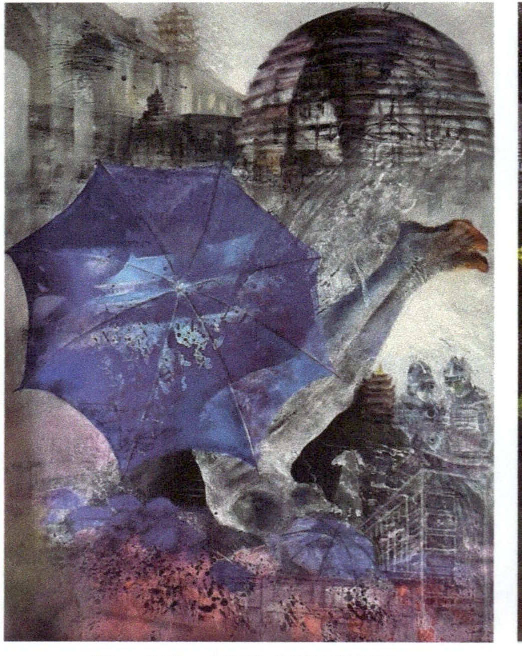

Fig. 6.3b. *1989–2020* (2020, 140 × 100 cm).

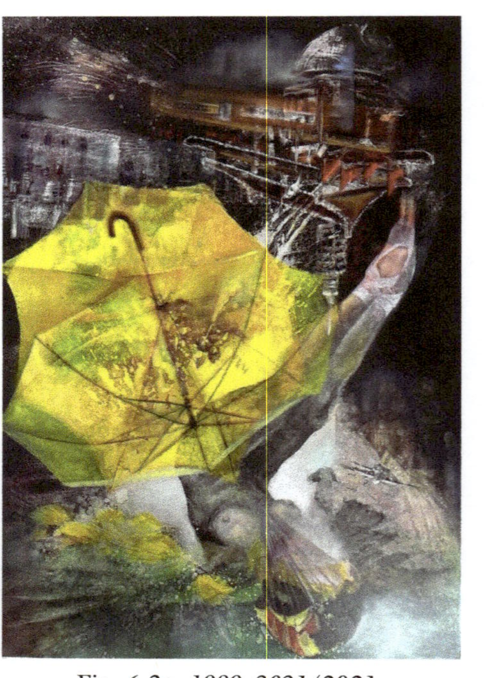

Fig. 6.3c. *1989–2021* (2021, 140 × 100 cm).

In the lower right corner, Lan shows the Wuhan Institute of Virology, which was at the center of the controversy over the origin of Covid-19. The two terra-cotta soldiers above the institute have been replaced by two masked virologists from the lab. Placing the Bundestag's glass dome above the Wuhan Institute of Virology is also very pungent. The dome of the German parliament symbolizes political transparency. This contrasts with the mystery that shrouds the Wuhan Institute of Virology. The Bundestag and Tiananmen, symbols of German and Chinese political power, show the artist's constant desire to contrast liberal Germany and illiberal China. In both *1989–2019* and *1989–2020*, Tiananmen lurks behind the umbrella, showing the (in)visible hand of Beijing in Hong Kong and Wuhan. The jackknife diver represents the feeling of suffocation and drowning under the CCP's authoritarian rule.

The sequel *1989–2021* (2021, Fig. 6.3c) is a more colorful sub-version of *1989–2019*. Here Tiananmen does not appear on the umbrella but has been inverted and visibly fitted to the bottom of the Basilica di San Marco. In contrast, the protesters have retreated behind the yellow umbrella. They wear helmets, gas masks, and goggles, essential protective gear for rallies in Hong Kong. The yellow umbrella is now doubled by its own mirror image and has reproduced itself, yet the second yellow umbrella is *knocked over*, just as the eponymous movement has been *knocked down*. Through these images, the painting asserts that by 2021, Beijing will no longer hide its role in Hong Kong affairs after crushing the city's democracy movement. When the painting is viewed right side up, the woman is now soaring in the sky with a parachute around her missing head and wings above her arms. But the parachute also looks like a helmet and mask over her head. A fighter jet is visible next to her, foreshadowing an ominous future for Hong Kong. These three iterative paintings from 2019 to 2021 trace the political crisis in Hong Kong and the suppression of the democratic movement there, a premature retreat from the promise of "one country, two systems."

1989–2022 (2022, Fig. 6.4) marks a visual break from the iteration of the earlier *1989* paintings. The gray color palette suggests that 2022 resembles a dream and, for many, a real nightmare. The painting juxtaposes events in China, on the left, and in Ukraine, on the right. Inside the tunnel-like underpass, some vague figures can be seen holding blank pieces of paper. A bridge, inconspicuously placed over the underpass, alludes to the Sitong Bridge in Beijing. On October 13, 2022, Peng Lifa, later called the "Bridge Man," hung white banners bearing slogans in red paint on the Sitong Bridge while a loudspeaker played a recorded message calling for strikes and the removal of Xi Jinping. The banners protested endless Covid tests, lockdowns, human rights abuses, lack of press and speech freedom, the new cultural revolution, and the cult of personality: "Say / No to Covid test, yes to food / No to lockdown, yes to freedom

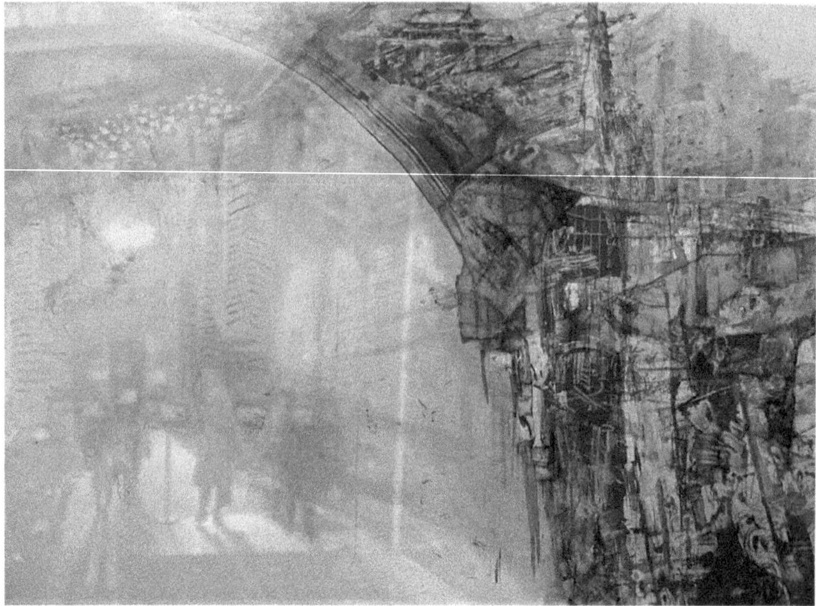

Fig. 6.4. *1989–2022* (2022, 100 × 140 cm).

/ No to lies, yes to dignity / No to cultural revolution, yes to reform / No to great leader, yes to vote / Don't be a slave, be a citizen / Remove dictator and national traitor Xi Jinping."[12]

Hailed by many inside and outside China as a lone hero, Peng was arrested that same morning and "evaporated" from public view. For a while, the Chinese word for "bridge," *qiao*, became a sensitive word, and bridges were monitored by security guards. Peng's actions, however, eventually ignited the November 2022 White Paper protests. Though short-lived, these exhilarating protests demonstrated the widespread discontent among young people despite tight ideological and political control. The right side of the painting is saturated with demolished buildings, wreckage, and debris in Ukraine. Lan bases a lot of her content on images she finds online. But she indicated that she modeled the tanks in this painting not on Russian tanks but on tanks used in Beijing in 1989. Placing the Gate of Heavenly Peace and the tanks that crushed Tiananmen protestors in the midst of destruction in Ukraine, she swapped out Moscow for Beijing, making the authoritarian regimes interchangeable. A pictorial

12 This translation of the text of Peng's banners was displayed (along with the original Chinese text) on a sign at the University of Melbourne in Australia. See Frances Mao, "China's 'Bridge Man' Inspires Xi Jinping Protest Signs around the World," *BBC*, October 18, 2022, <https://www.bbc.co.uk/news/world-asia-china-63295749>.

representation of a traumatic period, *1989–2022* bleakly depicts the fateful year of 1989, the Covid pandemic, the White Paper protests, the war in Ukraine, and, implicitly, the arrests, deaths, and suffering caused by dictators. The paintings in the *1989* series capture historical events on canvas and function as mementos that resist amnesia.

Hong Kong Is Becoming Modern (2020): Is Hong Kong Modernizing or Moldering?

A disguised reaction to the 2019–20 protests in Hong Kong sparked by the extradition bill, *Hongkong wird modern* (Hong Kong Is Becoming Modern, 2020, Fig. 6.5b) is a sub-version of *Monkey Goes to Heaven* (2018, Fig. 6.5a). In 2018, Lan had painted the German artist Jörg Immendorff in her series of "painter princes" (chapter 5). In *Monkey Goes to Heaven*, a tunnel-like structure frames a view of Hong Kong over which a transparent portrait of Immendorff is painted. When Lan met Immendorff in the last few years of his life, he was suffering from ALS (Lou Gehrig's disease), an incurable disease that prevented him from painting. Chancellor Gerhard Schröder appointed Immendorff to paint his portrait and he completed it with the help of his assistants. A Chinese friend advised him to go to Hong Kong to try Chinese medicine, and Immendorff eagerly followed up. In Lan's painting, Hong Kong is located at the end of a tunnel, representing light and a beam of hope. Immendorff was a staunch Maoist in his youth, and the painting bears some resemblance to a Maoist poster, with sunshine-like rays emanating from Immendorff's head.

Immendorff's mouth is shaped by a dinghy in *Monkey Goes to Heaven*, while in the sub-version *Hong Kong Is Becoming Modern* the dinghy is topped with a roof that evokes Tiananmen, another steganographic allusion to Beijing's long arm in Hong Kong. The boat itself could refer to a famous propaganda song from the Cultural Revolution that praises Mao as the Great Helmsman: "Sailing the Seas Depends on the Helmsman" (*Dahai hangxing kao duoshou*, 1964). At the top of *Monkey Goes to Heaven*, a monkey stares at the viewer. Immendorff considered the monkey his alter ego, and monkeys populate his paintings and sculptures. At bottom right, a humanoid figure wearing a monkey mask rides a zebra with black and yellow stripes. The monkey mask evokes Immendorff's serigraph *Man with Monkey Mask and Brush in Snow Globe* (2000). The zebra's black and white stripes represent the Taoist philosophy of yin and yang. Lan painted the zebra yellow to allude to racist "yellow peril" (*gelbe Gefahr*) rhetoric as well as her own race.

When *Hong Kong Is Becoming Modern* was hung at Galerie Tammen in Berlin, German cabaret artist, comedian, and photographer Dieter Nuhr,

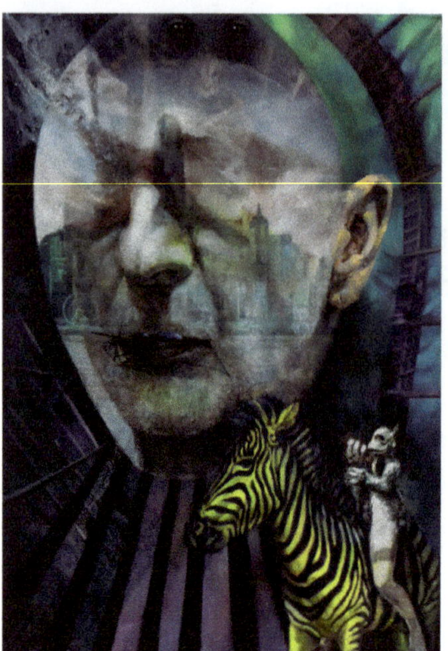

Fig. 6.5a. *Monkey Goes to Heaven* (2018, 200 × 140 cm).

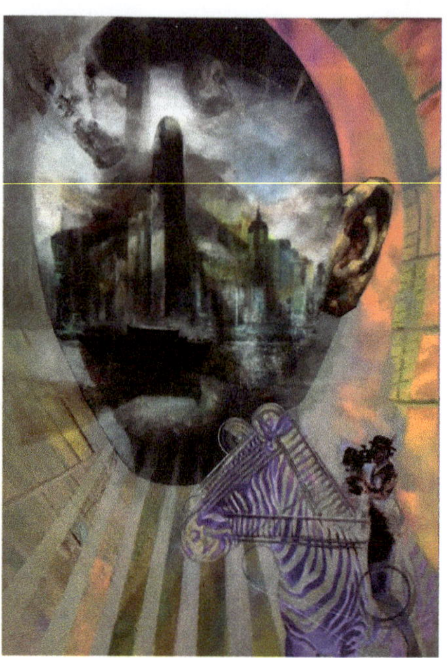

Fig. 6.5b. *Hong Kong Is Becoming Modern* (2020, 200 × 140 cm).

whose atelier is next door to Lan's in Düsseldorf, gave a public presentation about the painting. He explained that the German title – "Hongkong wird modern" – is oxymoronic, since Hong Kong was already a mega-modern city; the title was actually adapted from the slogan "München wird modern" (Munich is becoming modern). In preparation for the 1972 Olympics, Munich was rebuilt, and posters all over the city proclaimed the motto. But a passerby mistook the adjective "modérn" (modern) for the verb "módern" (to rot or molder).[13] The change in accentuation turned a progressive slogan – "Munich is becoming modern" – into a gloomy prophecy of the city's eventual decay or downfall – "Munich is going to molder."

This subtext applies to the recent political deterioration in Hong Kong. The Chinese name for Hong Kong is *xiang gang*, literally "fragrant harbor," and if Hong Kong loses its credibility as a major financial center and a stronghold of democracy and the rule of law, foreign investors may pull out, turning the "fragrant harbor" back into a "stinky harbor" (*chou gang*), a term that first appeared in the 1960s. The image of Hong Kong is apocalyptic. Debris falls on Hong Kong from the upper left corner. The face of the monkey in *Hong Kong Is Becoming Modern* has been obscured.

13 Dieter Nuhr, "Jiny Lan: Hongkong wird modern – präsentiert von Dieter Nuhr," Galerie Tammen, January 30, 2021, <https://vimeo.com/506453623>.

The monkey's nose has become a surveillance camera, as has a building in the upper left corner. The upper part of Immendorff's face is invisible and the new contours are reminiscent of Hitler. In the lower right corner, as Nuhr observed, is Charlie Chaplin, who directed and starred in the anti-Nazi film *The Great Dictator* (1940). He rides a zebra wearing a harness of pullies, looking through a film camera. By framing Hong Kong within the facial contours of Hitler and reinforcing the message with a reference to *The Great Dictator*, the artist draws a parallel between Nazi Germany and Communist China. Although Lan remains aesthetically indebted to the agitprop style of the Communist regime, politically and ideologically she develops her own *Gegenpropaganda* or counterpropaganda to work through the radical political changes in Hong Kong.

Sexual and Territorial Invasions in *Oh, the Humanity!* (2022)

After thirty-five years of the one-child policy (1980–2015) led to an aging population and a low birth rate, the Chinese government passed a law in 2016 allowing all couples to have two children. When the new policy failed to produce the expected increase in births, the government introduced the three-child policy in 2021.[14] Officials are now scratching their heads, looking for ways to boost the fertility rate. The radical policy reversal inspired Lan to paint couples, both human and animal, making love for reproductive purposes in *Oh, the Humanity* (2022, Fig. 6.6). One year after the three-child policy was enacted, Putin invaded Ukraine. Lan links China's encroachment on women's reproductive rights to Russia's war against Ukraine, as the sexual penetration of one authoritarian regime coincides with the territorial penetration of another.

Oh, the Humanity! was carefully planned. To condemn the Russian invasion of Ukraine, Lan decided to paint a tetraptych depicting the two Chinese characters 战争 *zhan zheng*, which together mean "war."[15] This

14 Oiwan Lam, "China's New Three-Child Policy Gives Birth to Ironic Jokes on Social Media," GlobalVoices, June 2, 2021, <https://globalvoices.org/2021/06/02/chinas-new-three-child-policy-gives-birth-to-ironic-jokes-on-social-media/>; Andrew Mullen, "Three-Child Policy," June 5, 2021, *South China Morning Post*, June 5, 2021, <https://www.scmp.com/economy/china-economy/article/3136092/chinas-three-child-policy-why-was-it-introduced-and-what-does>; Ming Zhang, Chi Zhang and Yuxin Liu, "From One-Child Policy to Three-Children Initiative: A Feminist Critique of the Population Planning Policies in China," *Communication, Culture and Critique* 17, no. 2 (2024): 103–11.

15 See Manying, 蓝镜访谈 | 秃头戈女十周年 [Interview with Jiny Lan: Bald Girls' Tenth Anniversary], 德国中文书店 [The Chinese Bookstore in Germany], July 15, 2022, <https://mp.weixin.qq.com/s/nrISt5suX-HF_79i43oaNQ>.

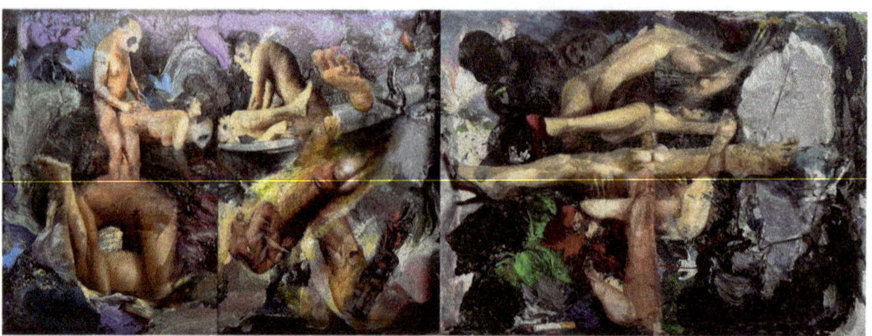

Fig. 6.6. Tetraptych *Oh, the Humanity!* (2022, 200 × 280 cm × 2), consisting of two humanoid Chinese characters, *Zhan Zheng* (war).

tetraptych is part of her calligraphic series, which embeds or hides one or more Chinese characters in a painting. She began by using skin-colored paint to write the Chinese characters for "war" on a palette she had used for an earlier work, creating a "genetic" continuity with her other paintings through paint. (The painting is ultimately a descendant of the original *Adam/Eve* paintings in Lan's Jinyology, but because its creation begins with paint left over from another composition, its exact pedigree is difficult to trace.) She took photographs of the Chinese characters on the palette, divided the characters into four segments, and printed them on four canvases. Through overpainting she shapeshifted the strokes of the Chinese characters into men and women having sex in a variety of postures, based on pornographic images she found in various sources. The strokes may appear abstract to viewers who do not read Chinese, but they are very concrete to Chinese speakers, reflecting a dialectical relationship between the abstract and the figural. The strokes overlap with concrete human figures or body parts, but the human beings also configure abstract Chinese characters as a whole, creating a unique (calli)graphic, humanoid, and neo-expressionist artwork.

Among these heterosexual copulating couples are some panda-headed figures. Pandas are selective in their choice of sexual partners, so zookeepers must use various incentives to coax them into mating. The Chinese government's adoption of measures to stimulate the birth rate resembles how zookeepers entice pandas to breed. According to Lan, the one-child policy enforced from 1979 to 2015 has been replaced by compulsory lovemaking; in the past women were forced to get abortions, but women are now discouraged from terminating a pregnancy unless it is medically necessary. She wants to satirize these draconian government decisions. By fusing lovemaking with the characters for "war," the painting invokes the pacifist slogan "Make Love, Not War," made famous by Yoko Ono and John Lennon's 1969 performance *Bed-Ins for Peace*. Hence, *Oh, the*

Humanity! protests not only the Russian war but also China's top-down love-making decree. The cold colors of the chaotic palette convey a sense of grime, impassivity, and alienation.

The painting *Oh, the Humanity!* is characteristic of her work: figural, graphic, provocative, composite, multicultural, and appropriative. She borrowed the title from a famous moment in radio history: On May 6, 1937, journalist Herbert Morrison was covering the landing of the German airship *Hindenburg* in New Jersey. When the dirigible unexpectedly caught fire and crashed, Morrison spontaneously shouted, "Oh, the humanity!" The collage is full of symbols. On the left edge of the *Zhan* diptych, an old man sketched in gray hangs from a tree, indicating the high suicide rate among the elderly in China, especially in rural areas. Due to the one-child policy, a single child has to support four grandparents. Since the government exploits the Confucian morality of filial duty by making care for the elderly the responsibility of individual families rather than the state, elders whose overburdened or neglectful families are unwilling or unable to provide care cannot rely on a social welfare system. This situation compels the elderly to end their own lives.[16] In the *Zheng* diptych, Lan revealed that she sketched the bearded face of the author of *War and Peace*, Leo Tolstoy, with grinning teeth, from a large blob of white paint. To its left, Auguste Rodin's *Thinker* broods in stark contrast to other blurred, empty heads, made not to think but to follow orders; below, a black lion representing virility is profiled. Lan also recycles images from her other works, such as the foot from *Feet of Heavenly Freedom* (Fig. 2.8b) and the phallus from *Alessandro Kind* (Fig. 3.7a).

The tetraptych was exhibited in the *Humanity: Art Positions – Berlin China Show* at the CSR.ART contemporary showroom in Berlin from June 30 to July 30, 2022.[17] Lan originally painted it for the tenth-anniversary exhibition of the Bald Girls, to be held a few weeks later in Düsseldorf. But in light of the Russian war and the US Supreme Court's decision to overturn *Roe v. Wade*, ending the right to abortion on the federal level, she decided to exhibit it earlier. She stated: "Whether in the United States or in China, whether it is a one-, two-, or three-child policy, women pay the ultimate price." The exhibition also included the series *Fortpflanzen* (Reproduction, 2022), small-format paintings that depict animals copulating. These are byproducts of *Oh, the Humanity!*,

16 See Michael R Phillips, Xianyun Li, and Yanping Zhang, "Suicide Rates in China, 1995–99," *The Lancet* 359 (2002): 835–40.

17 SSC-Redaktion, "ÜBERSCHAU #03 shows HUMANITY with positions of contemporary Chinese art in the CSR Contemporary Show Room," *Deeds. News*, July 1, 2022, <https://deeds.news/2022/07/uberschau-03-shows-humanity-with-positions-of-contemporary-chinese-art-in-the-csr-contemporary-show-room-30-06-16-07-2022/?lang=en>.

as Lan used leftover paint from that project to paint them. In this way, Jinyology continues through palette, paint, and motif.

A Warning against Illiberalism: *Pushkin Storm* (2022)

In the wake of Putin's invasion of Ukraine, Lan painted *Pushkin Storm* (*Puxijin fengbao*, 2022, Fig. 6.7), a triple portrait of dictators from (former) communist regimes. Alexander Pushkin is a household name in China and his work has been anthologized in Chinese textbooks. The painting's title echoes that of Pushkin's short story "Snow Storm" (1830). Lan wittily turns his name into an acronym, standing for Putin (Pu), Xi (Sh), and Kim Jong-un (Kin), whose profiles can be seen on the right side of the riverbank against a stormy sky; Kim is on the left, Putin in the middle, and Xi on the right. The base layer of the canvas originated from an enlarged print of a photographed pre-arranged palette. The artist then created an apocalyptic sky of dark clouds with patches of white, yellow, red and pink, and filled with intricate lightning bolts that trace out the faces of the three authoritarian leaders. Red flames may indicate explosions and provide a reminder that all three states are nuclear powers.

The buildings that flank the watercourse are typical mid-rise, five-story tenement buildings in Berlin. Lan seems to be asking what role Germany should play vis-à-vis the dictators who loom large on the eastern side of the river, which formed part of the boundary in divided Berlin. Although the painting creates a division between the eastern and western sides of the river, the deeper division is not a geographical one, but a political and ideological one between democracy and authoritarianism. Putin and Xi assert that there is "no one-size-fits-all" type of democracy and claim to rule successful democracies.[18] Using a meteorological metaphor, Lan seems to be asking: Will Western democracy withstand the storm of Putin-Xi-Kim?

Winnie the Sham (2022): Remembering Mahsa Amini

On September 16, 2022, an Iranian woman, Jina Mahsa Amini, died in police custody in Tehran three days after she had been arrested by the morality police for wearing her hijab "improperly." Widespread protests erupted across Iran, demanding an end to the authoritarian clerical rule of the mullahs. Women burned their headscarves or cut their hair in

18 Robin Wright, "Russia and China Unveil a Pact Against America and the West," *The New Yorker*, February 7, 2022, <https://www.newyorker.com/news/daily-comment/russia-and-china-unveil-a-pact-against-america-and-the-west>.

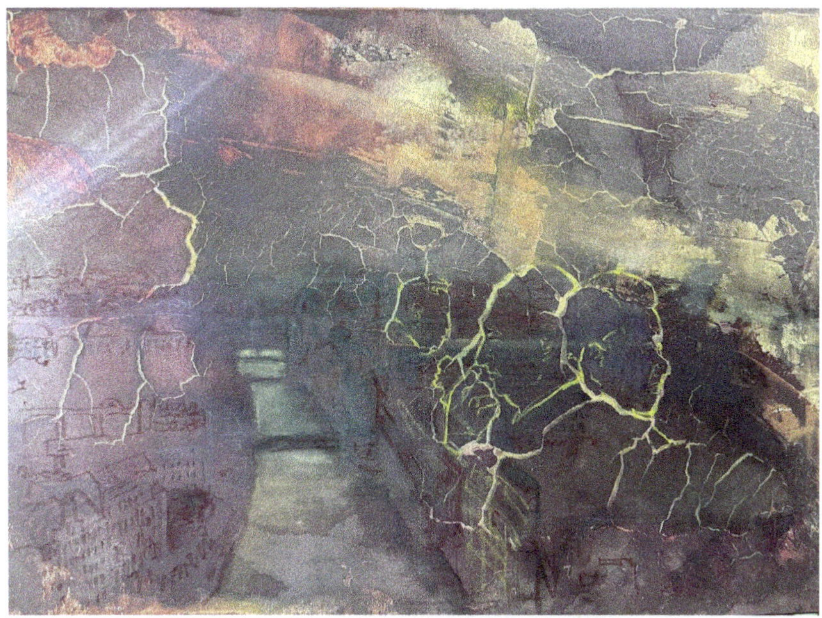

Fig. 6.7. *Pushkin Storm* (2022, 100 × 140 cm).

public to protest Amini's death. Lan painted *Unschuldige Frau* (Innocent Woman, 2022, Fig. 6.8a) and later *Winnie the Sham* (2022, Fig. 6.8b) to show her solidarity with the Iranian protesters. In both paintings, Amini reveals her long, beautiful, and exuberant hair. *Innocent Woman* seems to be covered with streaks of foam tinted pink, green, and blue. At the center, a woman with long dark hair resembling Amini looks to her left; above and to the right, another woman with long, purplish hair faces in the same direction. This painting sold quickly. According to the artist, "pretty women always sell fast."

Winnie the Sham, painted in a fantastic style, shows Amini with lush Medusa-like hair looking at the viewer and holding up two bottles of shampoo, as if making a commercial – something impossible in Iran. An orange, Lan's symbol of feminism, covers Amini's left eye. Her body appears to be on fire, referring literally to the fires that protesters lit to burn headscarves, or metaphorically to the fire that her death sparked and that spread throughout Iran. Scattered to her right are rose petals, symbolizing Iranians' love for her. On the far left, the right hand of a real-life painter sketches Winnie the Pooh, but we do not see the paintbrush, only the shadow of the brush and the shadow of the hand, from which another brush extends toward Amini's forehead. The surreal, anatomically impossible arrangement of the hand, shadows, and brushes connects Winnie the Pooh and Amini.

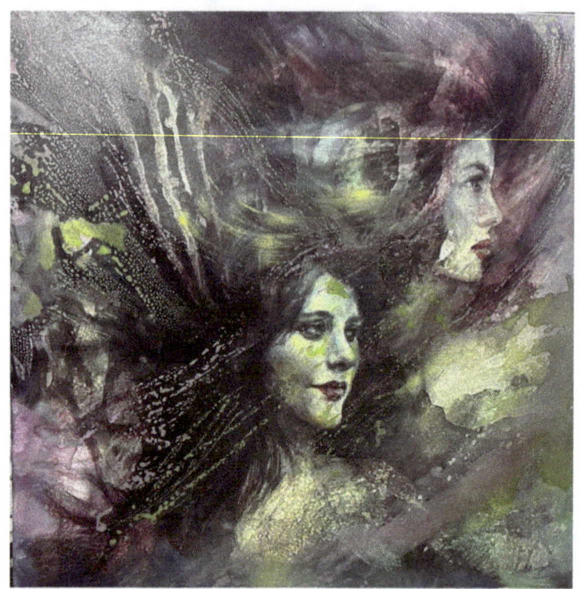

Fig. 6.8a. *Innocent Woman* (2022, 100 × 100 cm).

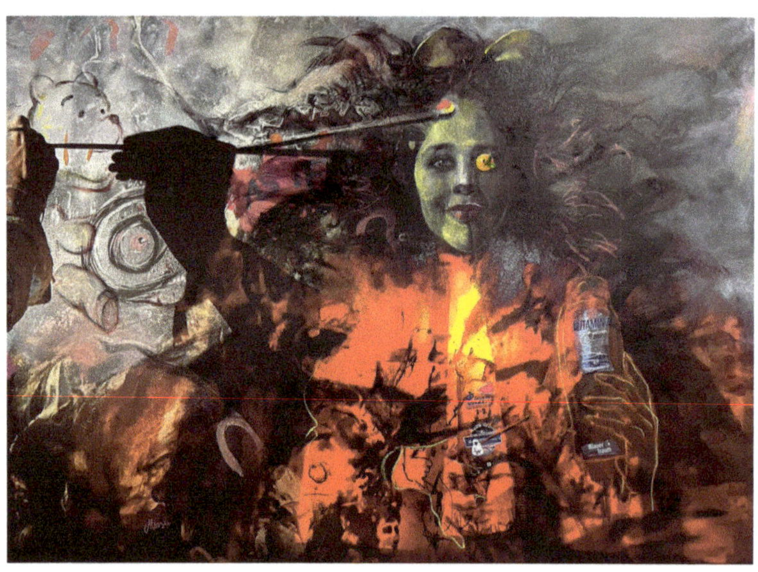

Fig. 6.8b. *Winnie the Sham* (2022, 100 × 140 cm).

Although Winnie the Pooh and Amini may seem unrelated, they represent criminal offenses in China and Iran respectively. The image of Winnie the Pooh was banned in China due to memes comparing Xi to the cartoon bear. By linking Xi in the background and Amini in the foreground, the artist seems to suggest that the Chinese government is indirectly implicated in the oppression of women in Iran, because by supporting the theocratic government in Iran, it is sustaining the despotic Iranian regime. On March 21, 2021, as part of China's Belt and Road Initiative, the Chinese and Iranian governments signed a twenty-five-year strategic cooperation agreement in Tehran, which did nothing to ease the long-standing tensions between each country and the US.

The confusing interplay of the real and the fantastic in the painting mimics the bewildering and intricate relationship between China and Iran. The two regimes are almost diametrically opposed in many aspects. The Communists are secular but at least pay lip service to gender equality. But the supposedly progressive and modern government in China has formed a bizarre alliance with a reactionary theocratic regime based on their shared authoritarianism and anti-Americanism. This could shed some light on the title "Winnie the Sham." Xi is the sham who expresses certain values in China while supporting a regime that contradicts those values. The words "AS IF" – as in "as if it were true" – can be read to the right of the shadowy hand, echoing the "sham" in the title.[19] A horse's head can be discerned over Amini's right shoulder. Horses, especially the dashing mustang, are associated with the Wild West, a free spirit, and energy.

With a diegetic hand painting Winnie, *Winnie the Sham* contains a canvas within a canvas. On the secondary canvas, Winnie the Sham is starkly sketched without his usual warm, orange-colored fur and charming smile. The bear sits, stunned and worried, looking over at Amini, who is in full color on the main canvas, standing tall, defiant, and triumphant. She dominates the picture, bursting out of the painting. Compared to Amini, Winnie the Sham is lackluster and insignificant. By taking great care in portraying Amini while sketching Winnie the Sham in a dismissive manner, the artist shows different levels of emotional investment in the two. Painted in the midst of the Iranian protest movement, when emotions were running high, *Winnie the Sham* clearly alludes to the potential ripple effect of the protests. In the painting, the bear looks over at Amini with a startled expression, as if worried about what might happen to him. In fact, the White Paper protests did occur in China later that

19 I thank Martin Rosenstock for interpreting the painting and the title with me.

year, although they were quickly suppressed without the majority of the domestic population getting wind of them.[20]

The banned image of Winnie the Pooh and the impossible shampoo advertisement led Lan to reflect on the dialectical relationship between art and politics: "The creator of Winnie the Pooh would never have thought in his wildest imagination that his creation would be banned in China. Even if an artist (in the West) thinks that their art has nothing to do with politics, it could still be politicized and censored in an autocracy." Winnie the Pooh and Amini have innocence in common, but in theocratic Iran and autocratic China, the innocent are declared guilty. Through art, Lan empowers and immortalizes a victim of the Iranian regime and criticizes the collusion of two unlikely bedfellows.

Question Heaven (2023): The Right to Question Authority

Lan's permanent exhibition *Himmelsfragen* (天问 *Tian wen*, Question Heaven, 2023) at the Rosenhang Museum in Weilburg, Germany, aptly exemplifies her political art. This project won her the prestigious Löwe von Weilburg Prize, awarded by the museum, accompanied by a cash award of sixty thousand euros. The installation juxtaposes the Chinese character 问 *wen* (to ask or to question) with two paintings containing the Chinese characters 圣 *sheng* and 旨 *zhi*, which together mean "the emperor's decree." Asking questions or challenging authority is a civil right that is denied to people living in an Orwellian society, where the common people "doublethink" and obey the emperor's decrees. Echoing Lan's 2022 painting *Ping* about the chained woman and the zero-Covid policy, *Question Heaven* continues to address authoritarian rule and advocate for democracy and freedom of speech.

For this project, Lan revised an existing exhibition at the Rosenhang Museum that featured a few dozen life-size terra-cotta soldiers excavated from the necropolis surrounding the tomb of Emperor Qin. In the necropolis, all of the soldiers faced in the same direction, awaiting the emperor's orders, but Lan arranged them facing each other in two loose rows, with several more statues in the middle space to resemble the inside strokes of 问 *wen* (Fig. 6.9). Now they stand face to face, as if in the middle of a parliamentary debate in the British House of Commons.

20 Billy Perrigo, "Why a Blank Sheet of Paper Became a Protest Symbol in China," *Time*, December 1, 2022 <https://time.com/6238050/china-protests-censorship-urumqi-a4/>; Yaqiu Wang, "Silenced in China, Grassroots Activists Commemorate the White Paper Protests Abroad," *The Diplomat*, November 29, 2023, <https://thediplomat.com/2023/11/silenced-in-china-grassroots-activists-commemorate-the-white-paper-protests-abroad/>.

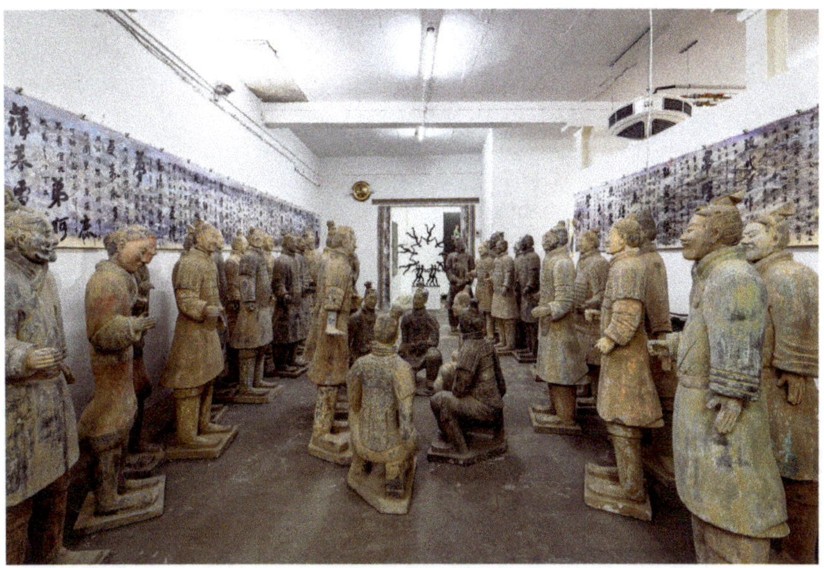

Fig. 6.9. Terra-cotta soldiers face-to-face in *Question Heaven* (2023, photo: Sebastian Drüen).

The square corresponds to the Chinese character 口 *kou*, which means "mouth." This rearrangement of statues from the iconic terra-cotta army humanizes and animates the once-mute soldiers, allowing them to speak and ask questions. Altering the standard layout of the terra-cotta army demonstrates Lan's interrogative, experimental, subversive, and iconoclastic response to convention.

To complete the character 问 *wen*, the artist invites visitors to imagine the two long walls of the gallery as the outer strokes of the character. Hanging on the side walls are two scroll paintings around twelve meters long, each depicting a landscape of mountains and rivers, in Chinese *jiang shan*. But this Chinese phrase has a second meaning: country. Together with Yuejun Qian, Lan laboriously transcribed Qu Yuan's long poem "Questions to the Heavens" (天问 *Tian wen*), whose title is commonly translated as "Heavenly Questions," onto the scrolls. Qu Yuan (339–278 BC) was the earliest patriotic poet in China. He was a key advisor to King Huai, who was the ruler of Chu, the largest and most populous of the seven major kingdoms during the Warring States period (475–221 BC). Thanks to his literary skills, Qu often drafted decrees for the king. However, a jealous opponent slandered him by telling the king that whenever Qu drafted a successful decree, he would brag that the king could not have done it on his own. As a result, King Huai demoted Qu. When the Kingdom of Chu lost battles against the Kingdom of Qin, Qu advised the king not to go to Qin to negotiate. But the king refused to listen and died as a hostage in Qin, and his son sent Qu into exile. In despair, Qu wrote "Questions to the Heavens," which consists of 172 questions on a wide range of topics, including the political realities of his beloved country and the decline of his once prosperous and cultured land, which would eventually succumb to Qin in 223 BC. Emperor Qin was the first to unify China, and the tradition of authoritarian rule he established continues to this day. He was a despot, notorious for burning books and burying Confucian scholars alive; he had the terra-cotta army built to protect him in the afterlife.

Today, Qu is hailed as a patriotic poet, and the Dragon Boat Festival is celebrated in his memory. Using history as an allegory for the present is a common practice among writers and artists.[21] By choosing to inscribe Qu's "Questions to the Heavens" onto a Chinese landscape, Lan points to the lack of opportunities to "question authority" in China. Questioning authority is punishable in a totalitarian society. Like Qu, who wrote his poem in exile, Lan lives abroad and always thinks of her native country and the plight of its people, especially women and dissidents. Following in Qu's footsteps, she asks questions that would have landed her in prison in China.

Her concept organically integrates the exhibition space. The room containing the 问 *wen* exhibit houses the two wall paintings and the terra-cotta figures arranged in a square. In addition, the artist conceived a second, vertical *wen*, maximizing the potential of the exhibition space: at the end of the room, a doorway outlines the outer strokes of *wen*, and a more or less square-shaped sculpture from another room in the museum that is visible through the doorway supplies the inner strokes.

Complementing the double *wen* are two paintings on the other end of the same room, depicting the characters 圣 *sheng* (emperor) and 旨 *zhi* (decree), forming the phrase "the emperor's decree" (Fig. 6.10a, b). The characters are invisible in daylight because the strokes are covered with fluorescent paint and only light up in the dark. In the painting *Emperor*, water pours down from the top of the painting, flowing over an outstretched hand holding a transparent sphere containing a Buddha-like figure wearing glasses and lipstick. Xi himself is often compared to an emperor, and the Buddha figure in the bubble calls to mind the Xi-Buddha in *Alternative Fiction* (2021, see Fig. 8.3d). The bubble may refer to the bloated personality cult around Xi, but if the bubble bursts, what will happen to the Xi-Buddha? That is an open question.

The painting *The Decree* is a sub-version of part three of the triptych *A Thousand Years of Humility* (*Qian nian qian xun*, 2020, Fig. 6.10c), which has a colorful and highly textured surface that includes some metal hardware. *The Decree* inherits its overall structure from Marcel Duchamp's

21 Chinese artist Yu Hong also cites this poem by Qu Yuan in her painting *Questions for Heaven* (2010).

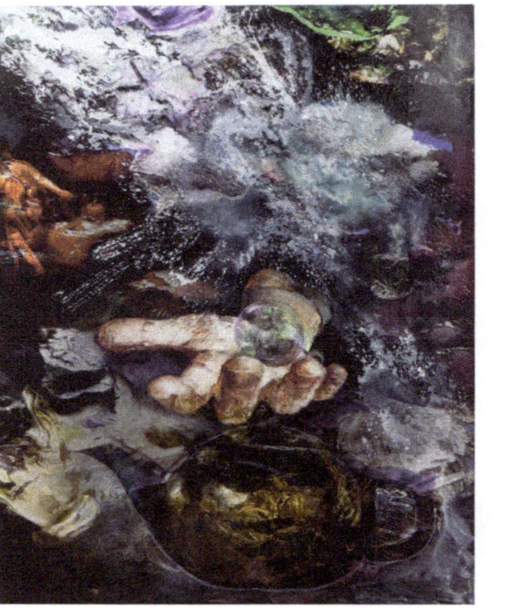

Fig. 6.10a. *Emperor* (2023, 190 × 150 cm).

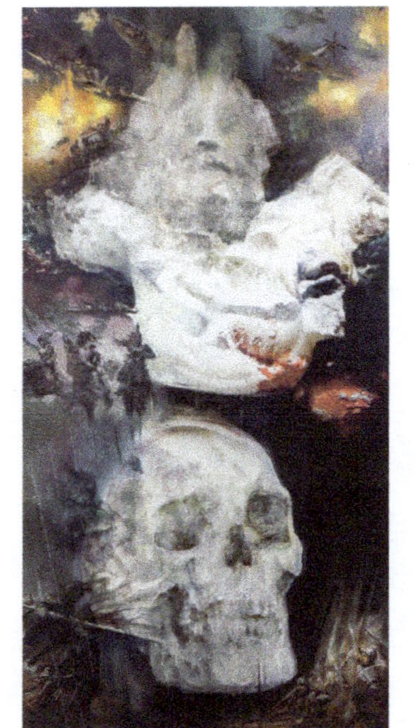

Fig. 6.10b. *The Decree* (2023, 280 × 140 cm).

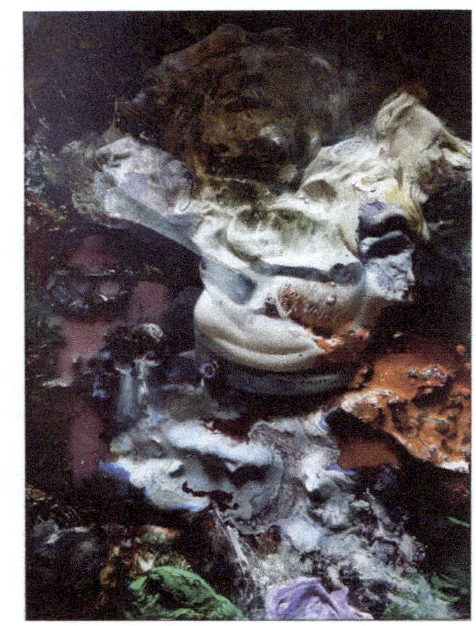

Fig. 6.10c. *A Thousand Years of Humility – Part 3* (2021, 280 × 200 cm).

readymade *Fountain* (1917), as the signature "R. Mutt" near the center of the painting indicates. The pastiche of Duchamp in *A Thousand Years of Humility* expresses Lan's feminist critique of the male-dominated art tradition. By re-contextualizing the toilet in a painting about the emperor's will, the artist capitalizes on the symbolic power of this profane object to piss at the emperor's will and advocate for democracy and freedom of speech. The character 旨 *zhi* consists of two parts. The upper part 匕 *bi* means "dagger," and in Lan's painting it is topped by a godlike bust, a replica of the head of the Old Gaul depicted in François Rude's sculpture *La Marseillaise* (The Departure of the Volunteers of 1792, 1833–36), on the Arc de Triomphe in Paris (Fig. 6.10b). Lan said that drawing plaster casts of this ancient warrior was standard training for art students in China.[22] The lower part 日 *ri* means "sun," but in place of the sun, which could implicitly refer to Mao, there is a human skull. The character *zhi* is flanked by martial scenes: cavalry and swordsmen below could indicate wars in the poet Qu Yuan's time, and fighter planes and explosions at the top refer to wars in our own time. As in her earlier painting *Oh, the Humanity!*, the artist again thematizes Putin's war in Ukraine because, as she puts it, "wars are started by emperors' decrees."

Coda: Counterpropaganda and the Palm of the Xi-Buddha

The works discussed in this chapter span from 2013 to 2023. They consistently target autocratic regimes and repel propaganda with counterpropaganda. The prize-winning permanent installation, *Question Heaven*, summarizes Lan's stance toward autocratic regimes. It pits a double *wen* (to question) against "the emperor's decree," which is no longer glorified or obeyed but questioned, as protests in Russia, Iran, and China attest. The decree shines forth from apocalyptic scenes of war and death. The ruler is "deified" as Buddha or a godlike figure, but his vulnerability is captured by the bubble and the urinal; soldiers no longer face forward but turn to each other to question and debate; the Chinese nation is asking "heavenly questions." The White Paper Movement showed that the Chinese people have not yet lost their will. They called out "the emperor"; they called out his "imperial decree" promulgating the zero-Covid policy. But can the anti-authoritarian Chinese escape from the palm of the Xi-Buddha? That, too, is an open question. Mr. Peng Lifa, the "Bridge Man" who protested against Xi's reign, certainly did not.

22 常见石膏像介绍 – 马赛曲石膏像故事背景与艺术鉴赏 [Introduction to Common Plaster Statues – *La Marseillaise* Background and Artistic Appreciation], <https://meishu.7139.com/4951/09/115.html>.

7: Only Possible in a Democracy: Paintings of German Chancellors

An experienced portraitist, Lan frequently depicts prominent political figures while embedding visual commentary upon their politics. Lan's initial version of her full-sized portrait of Gerhard Schröder (2016) marked the first time that she painted a German chancellor. Although she did not exhibit the work publicly for years, it inspired her to continue painting chancellors. Her portrait of Angela Merkel foregrounded one of the chancellor's most important legacies, namely her response to the refugee crisis in 2015. The permanent loan of the painting to the FDP chairman, Christian Lindner, catapulted her to the vicinity of the political establishment. Immediately following the surprising victory of the SPD candidate, Olaf Scholz, in the federal election of 2021, Lan painted him as a *Glückspilz* (literally, lucky mushroom) or "lucky duck." In 2021, she started the series *Ein Offener Prozess* (An Open Process), which is dedicated to candidates who lost the federal election. Donald Trump's refusal to acknowledge defeat following the 2020 US presidential election showed how democracy is threatened when the losing candidate does not concede peacefully, and the series celebrates German politicians who observe the rule of law.

Through her portraits of contemporary politicians, Lan places herself in the long tradition of court painters who portrayed powerful rulers; she is one of several artists who have painted German chancellors, including Bernhard Heisig, an East German artist, who painted Helmut Schmidt, and Jörg Immendorff, who painted Gerhard Schröder. In contrast to the official portraits produced by Heisig and Immendorff, Lan's figurative and symbolic portraits bear a formal resemblance to the propaganda posters of the Cultural Revolution. The subject occupies the center of the painting, facing the viewer head-on – not in partial profile as in some commissioned portraits of chancellors. Thematically, however, these paintings have little in common with Chinese agitprop art. They portray Germany's political leaders in an irreverent and sometimes critical manner.

From a Mao Poster to the Merkel Portrait: *The Crown* and Its Versioning

In January 2018, Lan painted a non-commissioned portrait of Merkel, *Die Krone* (The Crown, Fig. 7.1a), clothing her in a traditional costume worn by royal women at the Qing Dynasty court that consists of an elaborately embroidered dress and a hairstyle known as "two handfuls of hair" (*erbatou*). Lan modeled her Merkel painting on an oil painting of the Empress Dowager Cixi (Fig. 7.1b)[1], a concubine of Emperor Xianfeng who bore his only son and effectively ruled China from behind the curtain from 1861 to 1908, leaving a contentious legacy. Whereas Chinese historiography emphasizes that the Empress Dowager was a cold-blooded, despotic regent who contributed to the decline of the Qing dynasty, Lan holds a more sympathetic, feminist view of Cixi.[2]

Lan painted *The Crown* after Merkel won her fourth federal election in 2017. The work addresses Merkel's refugee policy, which dominated political debates during her third and fourth terms. In 2015, Merkel famously urged her nation to take on the challenge of accepting refugees from war-torn Syria with the words "Wir schaffen das!" (We can do it!). As a result, over one million refugees entered Germany in 2015 and 2016. But reactions to her momentous decision were deeply divided in Germany. Lan's portrait mirrors the nation's ambivalent response, investing the chancellor with nobility and a hint of autocracy.

In the painting Merkel wears an elaborate, colorful, flowered headdress, which on closer examination is composed of a diverse crowd of upside-down human figures, representing the uprooted and displaced refugees; the responsibility for their welfare weighs heavily on the German chancellor. The dangling tassel to the left of the headdress bears the colors of the German flag. The decorative pattern that adorns the shoulders of the royal gown is actually formed by refugees filing up from the southwest and southeast, the actual directions from which refugees came to Germany. Further scrutiny reveals a steganographic image concealed on Merkel's left arm: a boat loaded with refugees and battered by ocean waves. The small orange patches may represent the life vests some refugees wore. Over Merkel's right shoulder appears the Chinese character 令 *ling*, which signifies a supreme command or an imperial edict, alluding to Merkel's "We can do it!" exhortation.

1 Hubert Vos, H. I. M., *The Empress Dowager of China, Cixi (1835–1908)*, Harvard Art Museums/Fogg Museum, Bequest of Grenville L. Winthrop, Photo © President and Fellows of Harvard College, 1943.162.

2 See also the expatriate Chinese author Jung Chang's recent biography of Cixi, *The Concubine Who Launched Modern China: Empress Dowager Cixi* (New York: Alfred A. Knopf, 2013).

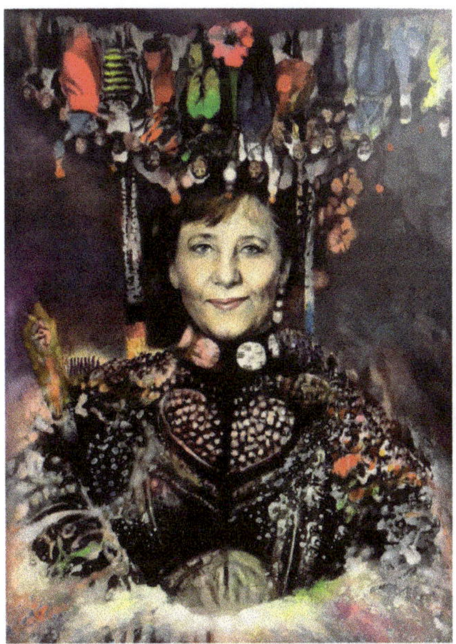

Fig. 7.1a. *The Crown* (2018, 140 × 100 cm).

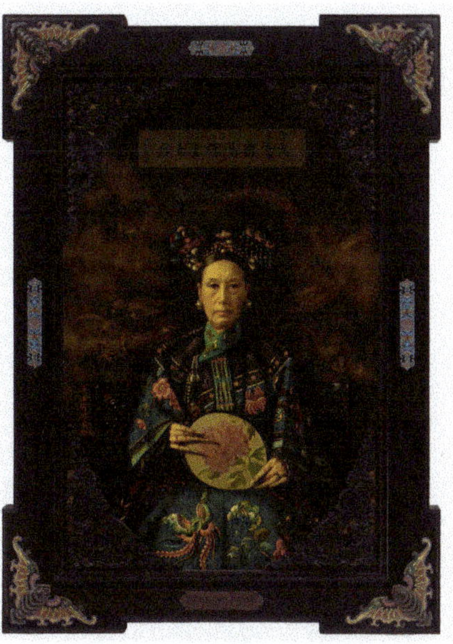

Fig. 7.1b. *The Empress Dowager, Cixi* (1905–6, 170 × 124 cm), Harvard Art Museums/Fogg Museum, Bequest of Grenville L. Winthrop.

The painting recalls the frontispiece to the first edition of Thomas Hobbes's *Leviathan* (1651), although the similarity between the two is accidental.[3] *Leviathan* depicts a crowned giant whose torso is composed of a myriad of puny, de-individualized subjects. Out of the swarming masses, a monster, the Leviathan, is created: the state, ruled by a monarch who keeps his antisocial, violent, and egotistical citizens in check. The inscription above him proclaims: "There is no power on earth to be compared to him." Fearing that England would remain mired in civil war, Hobbes wrote *Leviathan* to justify authoritarian rule as a means of ending chaos. His was not a democratic conception of society. Similarly, the word *ling* is a reminder of the criticism that Merkel's style of decision-making received. Merkel frequently used the word "alternativlos" (or "there is no alternative [TINA]") to explain her decisions, for example on the Greek debt and the refugee crises. Her "dogma of 'alternativelessness'" has been described by critics as "dangerous for a liberal democracy."[4]

3 I thank Martin Rosenstock for pointing me to the frontispiece.

4 Tobias Lill, "Wiederwahl als CDU-Chefin: So gefährdet Merkels Dogma von der 'Alternativlosigkeit' die Demokratie," *Business Insider*, December 6, 2016, <https://www.businessinsider.de/politik/die-alternativlose-merkel-will-die-cdu-auch-weiter-fuehren-dabei-ist-ihre-bilanz-als-parteichefin-alles-andere-

The composition of *The Crown* forms an hourglass shape that invites inversion of the painting (Fig. 7.2b). When the painting is rotated, the viewer sees a group of people who are depicted in the famous propaganda poster *Chairman Mao Is the Red Sun in the Hearts of the People of the World* (Fig. 2.1a), which shows Mao being revered by people of different nationalities. Lan is a fierce critic of both Mao and Chinese patriarchy. She has compared the appeal that Mao's China allegedly had for "the people of the world" to the attraction of the capitalist West:

> That the people of the world would happily come to "us" was a dream during Mao's time, but unfortunately, this scene could only be depicted in propaganda. History has already shown that Mao's ideology is not feasible. Global solidarity was not created by communist ideology, but the people of the world do come to capitalist countries with joy, which is very ironic.... But the scenario is also reversed: instead of the people of the world carrying Mao, the ruler of a democracy has to carry the people who come.

Back in 2012, Lan appropriated the same Mao poster in the painting *Red Sun*, in which she irreverently replaced Mao with his wife, Jiang Qing (Fig. 2.1b). Similar to Jiang Qing, who was blamed for the Cultural Revolution, the Empress Dowager was accused of causing the fall of the Qing dynasty. Rather than whitewashing Jiang Qing or the Empress Dowager, the artist called attention to the sexism and misogyny behind such historiographical narratives. Although Lan was skeptical of Merkel's refugee policy, she was also concerned that the chancellor would be held responsible for Germany's future. Indeed, the blame game started after the CDU lost the 2021 federal election, as discussed below.

In 2014, Lan painted a sub-version of *Red Sun* that replaced Mao/Jiang Qing with a colorful, donkey-shaped piñata suspended from a tree. Exchanging the dictatorial figure for a piñata was a satirical move. She named the painting *Zehntausend bescheidene Vorschläge* (Ten Thousand Modest Proposals, 2014, Fig. 7.2a). "Ten Thousand" translates the Chinese word 万 *wan*; the cry "Long Live Chairman Mao" (*Mao zhuxi wansui*) literally means "a wish that Chairman Mao will live ten thousand years." Lan also plays on the German word *Vorschläge*, which means

---

als-gut-2016-12/>; see also Berthold Kohler, "Merkel und die Flüchtlinge: Die härteste Prüfung," *FAZ*, October 15, 2015, <https://www.faz.net/aktuell/politik/merkel-und-die-fluechtlinge-die-haerteste-pruefung-13858882.html>; Andreas Reckwitz, "Deutschland nach Angela Merkel: Alternativlosigkeit ist Gift," *Zeit*, 20, 2019, <https://www.zeit.de/kultur/2019-01/deutschland-angela-merkel-populismus-demokratie-liberalismus>; Dirk Kurbjuweit, *Alternativlos: Merkel, die Deutschen und das Ende der Politik* (Munich: Carl Hanser Verlag, 2014).

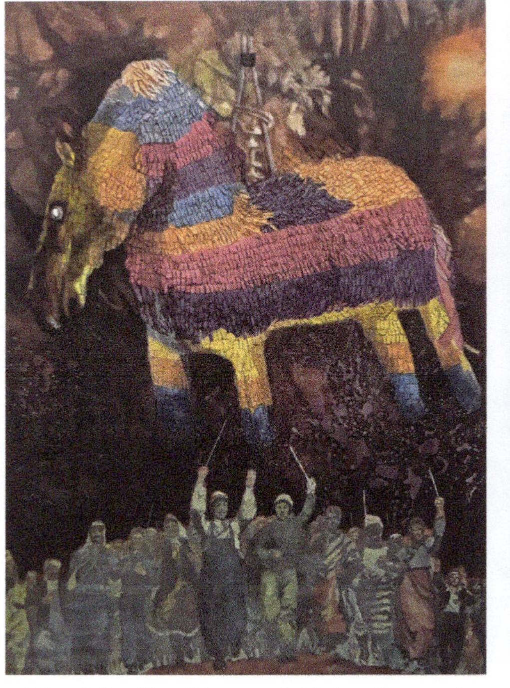

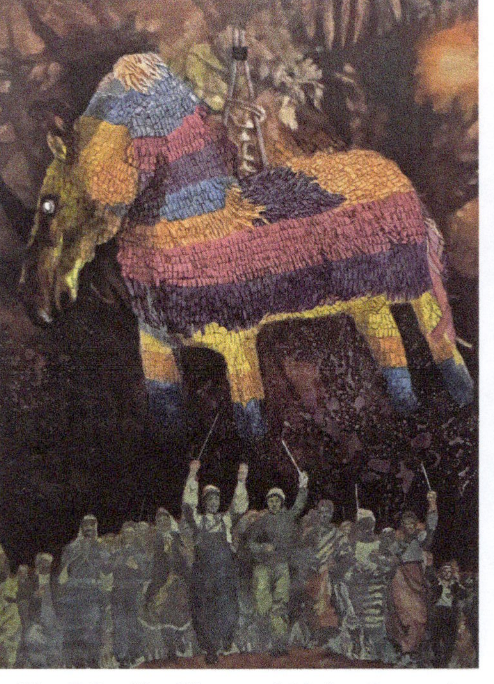

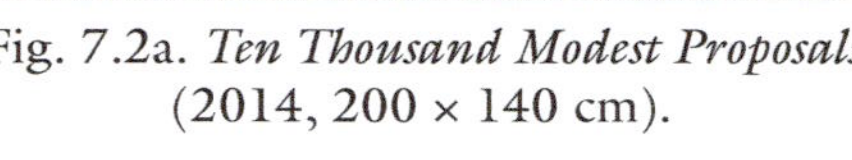

Fig. 7.2a. *Ten Thousand Modest Proposals* (2014, 200 × 140 cm).

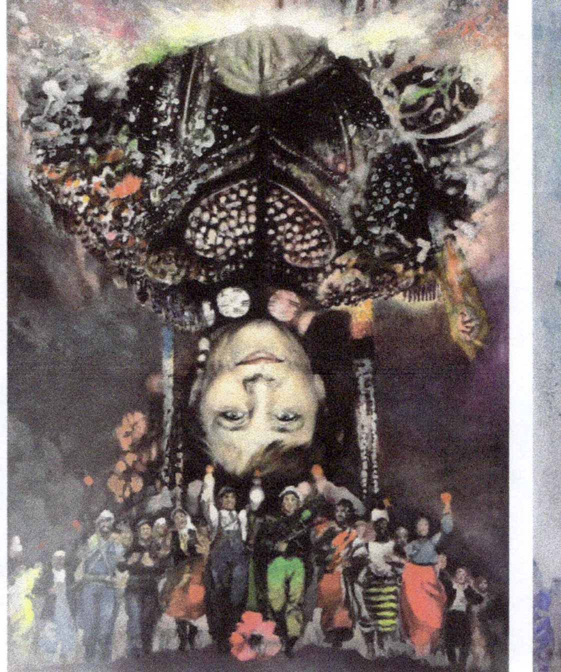

Fig. 7.2b. *The Crown* upside down (2018, 140 × 100 cm).

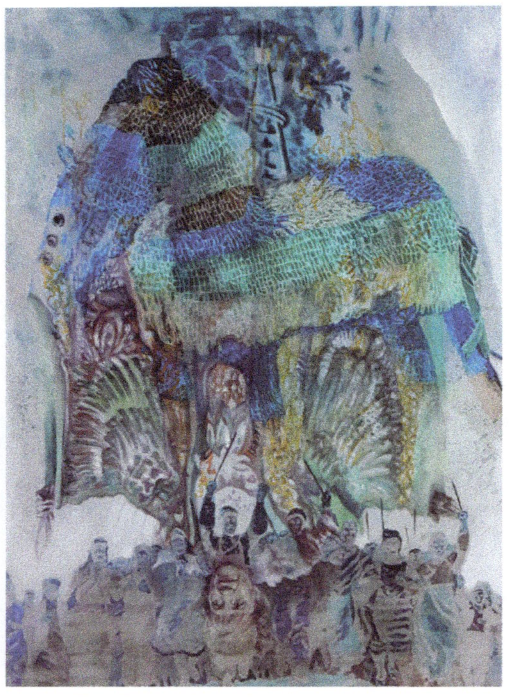

Fig. 7.2c. *Grand Blueprint* (2021, 140 × 100 cm).

"proposals" but contains the word *Schlag*, which means a "hit" or a "blow." With this title, she insinuates that the dictator should be struck ten thousand times. In the painting, the people of the world raise their sticks to hit the dictator-piñata. Once the figure is broken or destroyed, rewards will be distributed and life will improve. Such is the "modest proposal" that Lan communicates to viewers. The painting embodies her stance against the authoritarianism, communism, and radical leftism that fueled the Cultural Revolution. This painting became the template for *The Crown*. But Lan overpainted the piñata so heavily that viewers are unable to trace the lineage without guidance. She pointed out that the piñata's tail, now marked with the Chinese character *ling*, has become the imperial edict hanging over Merkel's right shoulder.

The main inspiration for *The Crown* came from the artist's memories of her childhood. She spent much time in the countryside at the home of her maternal grandmother, whose family had a connection to the Qing court. Growing up, Lan saw relics of a bygone era: a headdress, Manchu platform shoes worn by court ladies, belts, embroidered satin shoes, and ceramic utensils that an average Chinese family would not have owned. During the Cultural Revolution, her grandmother hid the Qing court paraphernalia from the Red Guards. When little Lan saw the headdress, she did not understand why a woman would wear such a heavy and cumbersome object. Her grandmother replied: "It is a symbol of dignity and status. Not every woman could wear it."[5] Lan realized early on that honor almost always comes with a burden, and this childhood memory inspired her to paint Merkel wearing a heavy Qing-style headdress "populated" by refugees. The painting conveys that Merkel's welcoming of refugees has earned Germany honor and respect from other countries but has also created a significant challenge. The artist drew on her cultural heritage and visual reservoir to illustrate the challenge facing Germany. Artistically, the sinicized portrait of Merkel is a refreshing example of cultural hybridization. Ideologically, however, Merkel's exotic appearance creates an alienating effect that invites viewers to reflect on her historic decision.

Lan painted *The Crown* a few months after Merkel's attempt to form a "Jamaica coalition" – so called because the party colors of the conservative CDU (black), the Greens, and the liberal FDP (yellow) match those of the Jamaican flag – failed. In November 2017, FDP leader Christian Lindner pulled out of the negotiations with his much-quoted line, "It is

5 张丹红 Danhong Zhang, 闲话德国:默克尔还是慈禧 [Germany Gossip: Merkel or Cixi], *DW*, March 26, 2018, <https://www.dw.com/zh/闲话德国默克尔还是慈禧/a-43101961>; Danhong Zhang, "Zwei Provokateure und ein Merkel-Portrait," *DW*, March 23, 2018, <https://www.dw.com/de/mein-deutschland-zwei-provokateure-und-ein-merkel-portrait/a-43064523>.

better not to govern than to govern wrongly."[6] Since Lan herself had manifested a rebellious streak since childhood, Lindner's rebellion against Merkel struck her as an act of disobedience "similar to the Monkey King's rebellion against the Queen Mother of the West," a famous episode in *Journey to the West*. Lan met Lindner at a vernissage by Dieter Nuhr. After she painted *The Crown*, she showed it to Lindner, who was very impressed by its "potent artistic expression and provocativeness."[7] Lan offered him a permanent loan of the painting, which he accepted.

Lan conceived the delivery of the painting to Lindner as a small performance. On March 15, 2018, the day after Merkel was sworn in for her fourth term as chancellor, Lan brought the painting to the Bundestag in a transparent wrapping so that everyone could see it. "A parallel act would have gotten me ten years in prison in China," she chuckled. Security guards stopped her, but after checking with Lindner, they let her through. For Lan, this personal experience illustrated the cultural and political contrast between her native and adopted countries: "First of all, there is no opposition party in China. And to hang a painted portrait of the current chancellor in the office of the opposition party leader – as a joke or a provocation – is something impossible in China." Lindner would certainly not hang a conventional portrait of Merkel in his office, but the outlandish, Chinese-influenced portrait of Merkel in the image of the Empress Dowager held a special attraction for an opposition politician like him. Lindner found it "fascinating to hang in his office this portrait of the chancellor in such an enticing artistic representation, imbued with a message and associated with an empress who has the power to command unconditional obedience" – obedience that his party was not willing to provide.[8]

In October 2018, after disastrous state elections in Hesse and Bavaria for the CDU and CSU, Merkel announced that she would not seek another term. In 2021, Merkel's last year in office, Lan painted a second portrait of the chancellor – *Grand Blueprint* (*Hongwei lantu*) – which is also based on the piñata painting. This time she reversed the color scheme of the original, using a photo app to create an inverted color print of the

6 Jefferson Chase, "The FDP's Christian Lindner: the Coalition Killer," *DW*, November 20, 2017, <https://www.dw.com/en/the-fdps-christian-lindner-the-coalition-killer/a-38629508>; Tim Szent-Ivanyi, "Jamaika-Sondierungen: Darum ließ Christian Lindner Jamaika platzen," *Frankfurter Rundschau*, November 20, 2017, <https://www.fr.de/politik/darum-liess-christian-lindner-jamaika-platzen-11002956.html>; "Jamaikia-Sondierungen gescheitert, 'Es ist besser, nicht zu regieren, als falsch zu regieren,'" *Welt*, November 20, 2017, <https://www.welt.de/politik/article170761256/Es-ist-besser-nicht-zu-regieren-als-falsch-zu-regieren.html>.

7 My email communication with Lindner on October 22, 2021.

8 Zhang, "Zwei Provokateure und ein Merkel-Portrait."

piñata painting and achieving hues befitting the title "Grand Blueprint" (Fig. 7.2c).[9] In *Grand Blueprint*, Merkel wears an elaborate robe with wings painted on the sleeves; her arms spread wide, holding a spearhead. Her body merges with an inverted piñata. This painting, which like *The Crown* is invertible by design, arguably presents two opposing views on the acceptance of refugees. When the piñata is hanging upright, it expresses the right-wing view that "the people of the world" place a burden on the welfare state. Lan said: "After the refugee crisis, the piñata assumed a different layer of meaning; since a piñata contains sweets and gifts, it could symbolize Germany as the welfare state." The sticks that the people of the world previously used to beat the dictator-piñata are now aiming at the welfare state, suggesting that the influx of refugees is putting the welfare state under duress. Numerous newspapers reported that Germany's expenditures on welfare benefits more than doubled in 2016.[10] In 2017, German interior minister Thomas de Maiziere said that Germany was providing much greater benefits than other states in the EU, making it "too attractive to human smugglers"; he wanted to see equal benefits paid to asylum-seekers across the EU.[11]

But when the painting is turned, the people of the world are seen to be holding up paintbrushes that touch Merkel's shoulders and arms. Merkel wears an imperial robe adorned with phoenix feathers, suggesting majesty and power. Lan revealed that Merkel's posture is modeled on the portrait of Pope Innocent X (c. 1650) by the Spanish painter Diego Velázquez. This disguised artistic reference indicates Lan's ambition to paint a definitive statement about Merkel's legacy, namely that refugees and immigrants like her are together painting a grand blueprint for Germany's future. Indeed, studies have shown that Germany has

9 I thank my daughter Cindy S. Yang, an aspiring artist herself, for pointing out to me that the second Merkel painting (Fig. 7.2c. *Grand Blueprint*) inverts the colors of Fig. 7.2a, *Ten Thousand Modest Proposals*. This led me to discover Lan's use of the photo app, which the artist confirmed.

10 Ruth Bender, "Germany Sees Welfare Benefits Costs More Than Double," *The Wall Street Journal*, September 5, 2016, <https://www.wsj.com/articles/germanys-welfare-bill-rises-169-as-refugee-numbers-grow-1473077920>; "Number of migrants claiming benefits in Germany surges by 169 percent," *Reuters*, September 5, 2016, <https://www.reuters.com/article/world/number-of-migrants-claiming-benefits-in-germany-surges-by-169-percent-idUSKCN11B11J/#:~:text=BERLIN%20(Reuters)%20%2D%20The%20number,well%20in%20a%20weekend%20election>.

11 Rebecca Staudenmaier, "De Maizere Calls for Reduction in Refugee Benefits," *DW*, September 9, 2017, <https://www.dw.com/en/refugee-benefits-in-germany-are-quite-high-interior-minister-de-maiziere-says/a-40426704>.

already achieved some success in integrating refugees into its economy and labor force.[12]

The era of Merkel, who served almost as long as Helmut Kohl (1982–98), ended in 2021. It appears that Merkel's refugee policy will dominate her legacy. During her chancellorship, her party, the CDU, made a "left turn" that allowed the far-right party, the AfD, to rise and fill the vacuum on the right. But as commentators have pointed out, while Merkel's refugee policy benefited the AfD, the rise of populism was a global phenomenon.[13] Merkel made it clear that helping refugees was not a mistake, because the alternatives would probably have been worse.[14] But German politicians, including Merkel, agree that the "loss of control" (*Kontrollverlust*) of 2015 should not be repeated.[15]

Within the ranks of the Christian Democrats, however, some party members did not wait for historians to pass judgment after the CDU lost the 2021 federal election. In October 2021, during the "Germany Day"

12 Siobhan Dowling, "Germany Welcomed Refugees. Now It's Reaping the Economic Benefits," *Al Jazeera*, June 20, 2019, <https://www.aljazeera.com/economy/2019/6/20/germany-welcomed-refugees-now-its-reaping-the-economic-benefits>; Eva Degler and Thomas Liebig, "Finding their Way: Labour Market Integration of Refugees in Germany," OECD (Organization for Economic Co-operation and Development), March 2017, <https://www.oecd.org/els/mig/Finding-their-Way-Germany.pdf>. Jan Klauth, "Abschluss im deutschen Sinne – Die wahre Zwischenbilanz der Flüchtlings-Integration," *Welt*, July 19, 2024, <https://www.welt.de/wirtschaft/plus252426032/Arbeitsmarkt-Abschluss-im-deutschen-Sinne-Die-wahre-Zwischen-Bilanz-der-Fluechtlings-Integration.html?utm>.

13 Sekou Keita and Helen Dempster, "Five Years Later, One Million Refugees Are Thriving in Germany," Center for Global Development, December 4, 2020, <https://www.cgdev.org/blog/five-years-later-one-million-refugees-are-thriving-germany>; Lenora Chu, "The Crisis Chancellor: How Merkel Changed Germany – and the World," *The Christian Science Monitor*, September 20, 2021, <https://www.csmonitor.com/World/Europe/2021/0920/The-crisis-chancellor-How-Merkel-changed-Germany-and-the-world>.

14 Angela Merkel, *Freiheit: Erinnerungen 1954–2021* (Köln: Kiepenheuer & Witsch, 2024), 508–35.

15 Bernd Riegert, "EU-Flüchtlingspolitik: 2020 ist nicht 2015," *DW*, March 3, 2020, <https://www.dw.com/de/eu-fl%C3%BCchtlingspolitik-2020-ist-nicht-2015/a-52623823>; "Merkel räumt Fehler in Flüchtlingskrise 2015 ein," *Wirtschaftswoche*, September 19, 2016, <https://www.wiwo.de/politik/deutschland/selbstkritische-rede-merkel-raeumt-fehler-in-fluechtlingskrise-2015-ein/14567568.html>; "Kramp-Karrenbauer: Müssen alles daransetzen, dass sich so was wie 2015 nicht mehr wiederholt," *Welt*, February 11, 2019, <https://www.welt.de/politik/deutschland/article188611621/Kramp-Karrenbauer-Muessen-alles-daransetzen-dass-sich-so-was-wie-2015-nicht-mehr-wiederholt.html>.

sponsored by the youth organization of the two political parties CDU and CSU (Die Junge Union Deutschlands or JU), many CDU speakers criticized Merkel, explicitly or implicitly. The JU chairman of North Rhine-Westphalia, Johannes Winkel, attacked Merkel's refugee and energy policies. In his words, Merkel's leadership style, with its strategy of "asymmetric demobilization," has "systematically destabilized and gutted the CDU." He demanded "an internal reckoning with the past sixteen years." Carsten Linnemann, head of the influential Mittelstands- und Wirtschaftsunion (MIT, Middle Class and Economic Association), also criticized Merkel for governing from the chancellery and bypassing party discussion. Jens Spahn took a swipe at Merkel, saying that "the expression 'there is no alternative' should never be heard again at CDU party conventions."[16] All of these comments were only possible in a democracy. And it was also in a democracy that Lan could paint Merkel the way she did.

Olaf Scholz as *Glückspilz: Pre-Judgment* (2021)

As soon as it became clear that SPD candidate Olaf Scholz had been elected Germany's next chancellor, Lan began painting him. Because the SPD was initially trailing the opposition in opinion polls, Scholz is fancifully depicted as a "lucky mushroom" (Fig. 7.3). His head forms the stalk of a brightly colored mushroom in a garden teeming with verdant growth. Faces of two political rivals appear in the background. The portrait features green and yellow, the party colors of the Greens and the FDP, two of the three partners in the so-called traffic-light coalition. Apart from a little red on Scholz, the SPD color is mostly absent, cleverly conveying the fact that many German voters voted for Scholz rather than the SPD. Even the SPD party leaders – Saskia Esken and Norbert Walter-Borjans, who defeated Scholz in the party's internal leadership election in December 2019 – chose him as the SPD's candidate for chancellor. They were aware that they themselves could not count on much support outside of the SPD. Only Scholz stood a chance of winning the federal election; the party had already faced an uphill battle in the run-up to

16 Filipp Piatov, "CDU-Politiker üben scharfe Kritik an der Kanzlerin – Tag der Merkel-Abrechnung: 'Partei destabilisiert und entkernt,'" *Bild-Zeitung*, October 16, 2021, <https://www.bild.de/politik/inland/politik-inland/cdu-politiker-kritisieren-kanzlerin-scharf-tag-der-merkel-abrechnung-77977890.bild.html>; Tobias Schrörs, "Die Abrechnung der Jungen Union," *FAZ*, October 16, 2021, <https://www.faz.net/aktuell/politik/bundestagswahl/abrechnung-mit-parteispitze-beim-deutschlandtag-der-ju-17588603.html>; Maximilian Conrad, "From the Eurozone Debt Crisis to the Alternative for Germany," *Frontiers in Political Science* 2, no. 4 (2020).

the election, trailing far behind the Christian Democrats and the Greens in the polls. However, as the current finance minister, Scholz had won public praise for his pragmatic and forceful handling of the pandemic in Germany, which boosted his approval ratings.

But, as *Der Spiegel* observed, "luck also played a not insignificant role."[17] Dimly visible to the left of Scholz is a laughing Armin Laschet, the CDU candidate. In the summer of 2021, Laschet was leading in the polls but was caught giggling during a visit to the town of Erftstadt in North Rhine-Westphalia after the area suffered one of the deadliest floods Germany had seen in a century.[18] This discredited him in the eyes of many German voters.[19] In the painting, Laschet is surrounded by a landscape that resembles the devastated area he visited. The helicopter and boat in the upper left corner recall the intense rescue efforts during the disaster.[20] To the right of Scholz is the Green candidate for chancellor, Annalena Baerbock; the stack of books in front of her alludes to the plagiarism accusations she faced before the election.[21] Scholz, by contrast, did not experience comparable negative media scrutiny. He responded to voters' yearning for a degree of continuity by imitating Merkel's famous rhomboid hand pose when asked in the *Süddeutsche*

17 Markus Feldenkirchen, Christoph Hickmann, Veit Medick, and Christian Teevs, "Resurrection of the SPD: The Unexpected Rise of Germany's New Chancellor, Olaf Scholz," *Spiegel International*, December 10, 2021, <https://www.spiegel.de/international/germany/resurrection-of-the-sp-the-unexpected-rise-of-germany-s-new-chancellor-olaf-scholz-a-15ccec2d-e9bf-4f2e-9824-409d25128d59>.

18 "Merkel 'Successor' under Fire for Laughing at Flood Visit," *DW*, July 18, 2021, <https://www.dw.com/en/merkel-successor-criticized-for-laughing-during-flood-visit/a-58305436>.

19 Philip Oltermann, "German Election Frontrunners Fail to Impress with Flood Response," *The Guardian*, August 9, 2021, <https://www.theguardian.com/world/2021/aug/09/german-election-frontrunners-fail-impress-flood-response>.

20 "To the Rescue: How Helicopters Played a Leading Role in German Flood Relief Efforts," Airbus.com, November 18, 2021, <https://www.airbus.com/en/newsroom/stories/2021-11-to-the-rescue-how-helicopters-played-a-leading-role-in-german-flood-relief>.

21 The accusations concerned Baerbock's book *Jetzt: Wie wir unser Land erneuern* (Berlin: Ullstein, 2021). Rina Goldenberg, "German Green Party Candidate Annalena Baerbock under Fire," *DW*, July 7, 2021, <https://www.dw.com/en/german-green-party-candidate-annalena-baerbock-under-fire/a-58192858>; Antonia Zimmermann, "German Greens' Baerbock Admits Mistakes in Plagiarism Row," *Politico*, July 8, 2021, <https://www.politico.eu/article/german-greens-leader-baerbock-self-critical-in-plagiarism-debate/>.

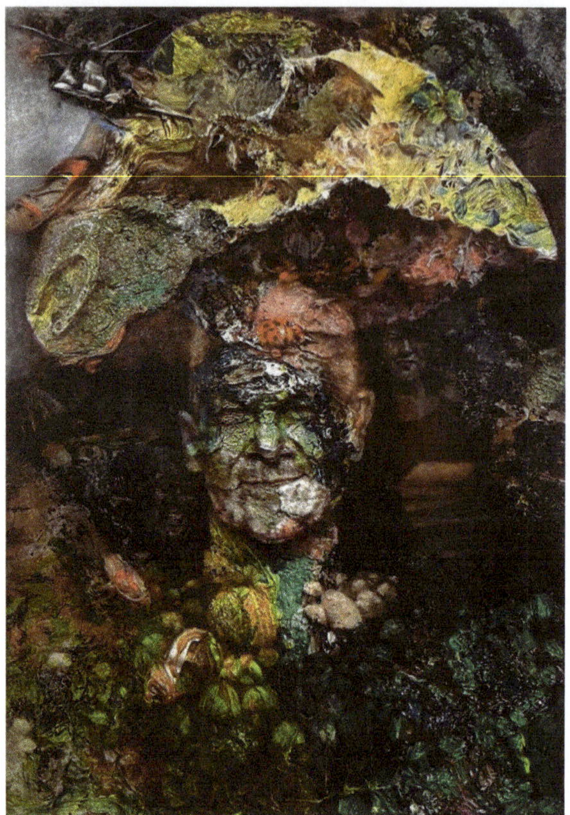

Fig. 7.3. *Pre-Judgment* (2021, 140 × 100 cm).

Zeitung's special "interview without words" to answer the question "Can you be chancellor?"[22]

Lan humorously depicted Scholz as a "lucky mushroom." As *Der Spiegel* wrote, Scholz's victory was "perhaps the most unlikely victory postwar Germany has ever seen."[23] The painting is adorned with German symbols of good luck: a pig reclining under the mushroom cap, a ladybug sitting on Scholz's forehead, a four-leaf clover landing naturally on the mushroom, and a horseshoe on the edge of the mushroom cap. On

22 Peter Riesbeck, "Wird Scholz mit Merkels Raute Kanzler?" *Kleine Zeitung*, September 21, 2021, <https://www.kleinezeitung.at/politik/aussenpolitik/deutschland_wahl/6036528/SPDKandidat-kopiert-Kanzlerin_Wird-Scholz-mit-Merkels-Raute-Kanzler>; Dagmar Rosenfeld, "Mit der Raute sendet Scholz eine kalkulierte Botschaft," *Welt*, August 20, 2021, <https://www.welt.de/debatte/kommentare/article233257443/SPD-Kanzlerkandidat-Mit-der-Raute-sendet-Scholz-eine-kalkulierte-Botschaft.html>.

23 Feldenkirchen, "Resurrection of the SPD."

Scholz's left cheek, a minute, sooty black figure stands for a chimney sweep, another emblem of luck.[24] The life-saving function of the helicopter and the rescue boats renders them symbols of luck as well. The bird above Scholz could be interpreted as a phoenix, because Scholz miraculously rose from a very uncertain political future after his defeat in the SPD internal election in 2019. The many small mushrooms on Scholz's shoulder could represent party colleagues who got a career boost from his success. The Chinese cabbage, both napa cabbage and bok choy, at the bottom of the painting is a witty allusion to China. The use of fungi and cabbage evokes Italian painter Giuseppe Arcimboldo's *The Four Seasons* (1563–73), in which human-like heads are composed of fruits, vegetables, flowers, and plants,[25] or the Spanish Narrative Figuration artist Eduardo Arroyo's *Six Lettuces, a Knife and Three Peelings* (1965), where a lettuce serially transforms into the head of the young Napoleon Bonaparte.[26] The Scholz portrait is a collage of related symbols, some of which are barely discernible. It captures pictorially the political drama of the 2021 federal election, the first to feature three candidates with realistic chances of becoming chancellor. The painting hung in one of Lindner's offices and incurred criticism from mainstream German media for "unflatteringly" depicting the chancellor-elect as "the stem of a mushroom," like "a dwarf standing in the forest."[27]

When Lindner became Germany's finance minister in the Scholz cabinet in 2021, Lan painted *Exakt* (Exact, 准 *zhun*, 2022, Fig. 7.4c). *Exact* contains the Chinese character 准 *zhun,* which means "precise" and "accurate" – qualities expected of the office of the minister of finance. This painting belongs to the versioning starting with *Value-Added Movement*

24 I thank Kathleen Ibe Berube for pointing out that the chimney sweep is a symbol of luck during my Zoom lecture on these chancellor paintings at the University of Minnesota on October 14, 2022; "Warum bringen Schornsteinfeger Glück," *SWR*, March 19, 2022, <https://www.swr.de/wissen/1000-antworten/warum-bringen-schornsteinfeger-glueck-106.html>.

25 I thank Mila Ganeva for mentioning Arcimboldo's work during the lecture at the University of Minnesota.

26 Wilson, *The Visual World of French Theory*, 10.

27 Eva Quadbeck, "Kunstwerk von Jiny Lan: Warum Olaf Scholz bei Christian Lindner überm Schreibtisch hängt," Redaktionsnetzwerk Deutschland (RND), July 11, 2024, <https://www.rnd.de/politik/warum-olaf-scholz-bei-christian-lindner-ueberm-schreibtisch-haengt-FWSM4BJPB5FA5O4QJY5PJJNXOE.html>; Maximilian König, "Ein Kunstgeschmack, der Fragen aufwirft," *RND—Der Tag*, July 11, 2024, <https://www.rnd.de/politik/ein-kunstgeschmack-der-fragen-aufwirft-PKI4BUHUGBD27K7ZNBG6APPB3M.html>; Jds, "Christian Lindner: Das Bild über seinem Schreibtisch wirft Fragen auf": *Schwäbische Zeitung*, July 19, 2024, <https://www.schwaebische.de/politik/christian-lindner-fdp-finanzministerium-jiny-lan-2699299>.

7A (2013, Fig. 2.8a). One of the early sub-versions was *San Giovanni Battista* (2013, Fig. 7.4a), which retains bits of the Milan shopping mall glass roof, spatters of white paint, and one of the two women walking in the rain, representing the artist herself. *San Giovanni Battista* places her with the Swiss curator Simon Maurer, whose head appears at the top of the painting, inside the Church of San Giovanni Battista in Mogno, Switzerland. San Giovanni Battista was designed by the Swiss architect Mario Botta, who has also designed buildings in a number of Chinese cities.[28] Lan retained the church's elegant gray hue and striped masonry.[29] Many Chinese characters are written on the boldly striped masonry of the walls and floor. They are random texts she copied from a Chinese almanac. The alternating light and dark gray stripes resemble stylized rays of light, a pattern seen frequently in Lan's work; it derives from cult posters of Mao, which typically depict the dictator as the sun emitting light.

In 2020, Lan created a sub-version *Doppelbelichtung* (Double Exposure, 2020, Fig. 7.4b), which the Bundestag purchased for its art collection. *Double Exposure* is a painting of a forest scene, with a splash of green liquid in the center. The sun is low in the sky and very bright. The title of the painting, however, indicates two sources of light: one above and one below. Although two natural light sources violate the law of nature, Lan brings two entities, be they God and man or nature and man, into harmonious co-existence. The striped masonry from the pre-version now appears as tall trees and the long shadows they cast, creating a pattern of dark and light stripes on the forest floor.

The painting *Exact* projects an ideogrammic design onto the interior of the Church of San Giovanni Battista. The strokes of the Chinese character, which are aligned with the contours of the church's buttresses and walls, are unobtrusively embedded in the image. But they were painted in blue phosphorus and thus visible in low light, another type of steganography (Fig. 7.4d). At the back of the space, rising out of the shadows, stands the Victory Column in Berlin. Yellow highlights on the floor create a cruciform shape leading up to the column. In so doing, the painting again conflates open and enclosed spaces, blurring the line between inside and outside.

Lindner is Lan's most high-profile supporter. He endorsed Lan's work in 2020: "I am very happy that an artist like Jiny Lan has chosen

28 E.g., the Lu Xun Academy of Fine Arts in Shenyang, the Tsinghua University Art Museum, and the Humanities and Social Sciences Library of Tsinghua University.

29 For a photo of the church, see "The New Stone Age: Church of San Giovanni Battista," Phaidon, <https://www.phaidon.com/agenda/architecture/articles/2019/october/07/the-new-stone-age-church-of-san-giovanni-battista/>.

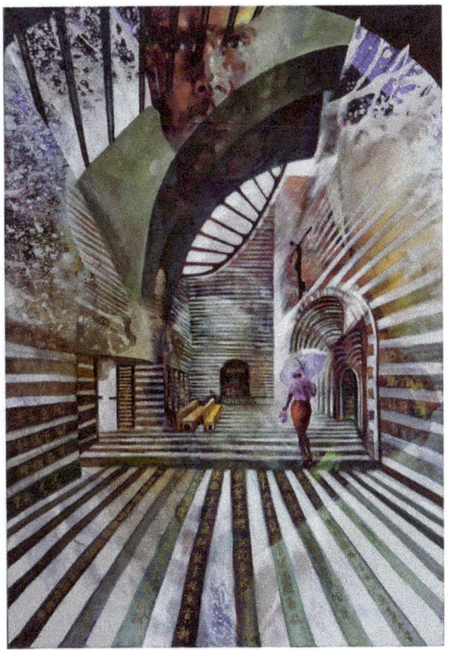

Fig. 7.4a. San Giovanni Battista (2013, 200 × 140 cm).

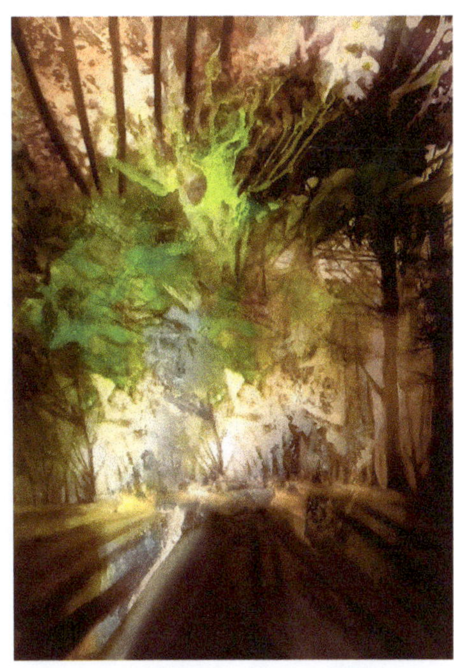

Fig. 7.4b. *Double Exposure* (2020, 140 × 100 cm).

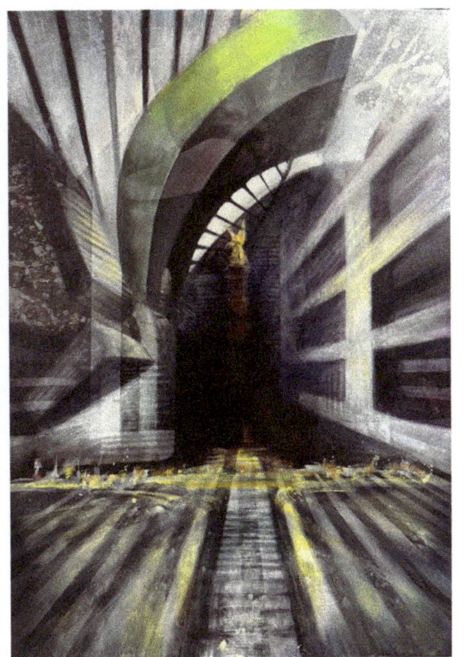

Fig. 7.4c. *Exact* (2022, 140 × 100 cm).

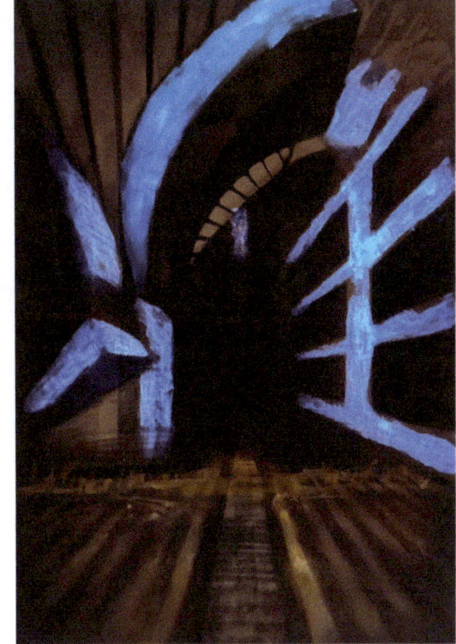

Fig. 7.4d. *Exact* viewed in low light.

Germany as her second home. Her critical soul has found a place where she can thrive freely.... It is a stroke of luck for me to know Jiny Lan and to have the opportunity to get intensively involved with her art. Her cultural and social works of art often open up new dimensions for me."[30] As the head of the FDP and the Federal Minister of Finance from 2021 until his dismissal in 2024, Lindner attended almost every one of Lan's exhibitions. In his offices, both public and private, he has hung Lan's paintings. Journalists have seen them and they have been featured in German mainstream media. Lindner gave the opening speech at the exhibit *Question Heaven* (chapter 6).[31] He is also one of the donors to the Jiny Lan Art Foundation. When the German art magazine *Monopol* asked him who he would choose to paint his portrait should he become chancellor, he answered: "I doubt this would concern me. But I would love to see one by the Chinese artist Jiny Lan."[32] Lan calls Lindner one of her fans.[33] By increasing Lan's public exposure, Lindner's support has created much desired opportunities for her.

Schröder the Acrobat: *Atlas...* (2016–21) and the German-Russian-Chinese Nexus

Scholz, who officially assumed the chancellorship on December 8, 2021, was immediately tested by the Russian invasion of Ukraine on February 24, 2022. Under his leadership, the traffic-light coalition government has shown unwavering support for Ukraine. The change this represents in the relationship between Germany and Russia, and in particular between the SPD and Russia, has opened a new chapter in German history. The war in Ukraine boils down to a contest between democracy and autocracy. Under these circumstances, ex-chancellor Gerhard Schröder of the SPD became the face of the "Putinversteher," someone who understands

30 Christian Lindner, in *Jiny Lan*, exhibition catalog (2020), 32.

31 Christian Lindner, "Vorwort," in *Jiny Lan:* 天问 / *Himmelsfragen*, exhibition catalog (Weilburg: Rosenhang Museum, 2023), n.p.; Uwe Röndigs, "FDP-Lindner, das Geld und die chinesische Kunst," Mittelhessen, October 5, 2023, <https://www.mittelhessen.de/lokales/kreis-limburg-weilburg/landkreis-limburg-weilburg/fdp-lindner-das-geld-und-die-chinesische-kunst-2916902>.

32 "Mit Christian Lindner: FDP-Chef und Kunstfreund," *Monopol* 2/2019, special issue: *Art Karlsruhe Spezial 2019*, n.p.

33 "Art News: Künstlerin Jiny Lan zählt FDP-Chef Christian Lindner zu ihren Fans," *Bunte* 48/2024, 104; see also "Treffpunkt: 'Rauchst du? Trinkst du? Nimmst du Drogen?,'" *Welt*, March 2, 2025.

Putin.[34] His close alliance with Putin and his lucrative business with the autocratic Russian regime became a lightning rod for public criticism.[35]

In October 2016, Lan met the ex-chancellor at a dinner, and her gallerist, Michael Schultz, suggested that she paint Schröder. According to Lan, Schröder offered to sit in her atelier and model for her, but she politely declined and asked for a photo, not wanting to be influenced by his presence. But a painting of Gerhard Schröder, depicted naked with breasts and blue skin, was unacceptable to her gallerist, as she could have foreseen (Fig. 7.5a, b). At the time, Schröder was still a very powerful man, and Lan's irreverent treatment of the ex-chancellor could have damaged the career of the gallerist and the artist herself. Thus, the gallerist's reaction placed a pragmatic limit on her artistic freedom. The painting disappeared into Lan's basement, and Schröder received instead a black IKEA coffee table on which Lan had painted Schröder's face as it appeared in her original portrait, but in a green tint, looking off into the distance (Fig. 7.6). Schröder was very pleased. Had he known how Lan had originally depicted him, he would not have felt so flattered. The original painting was not seen in public until 2021, when it was included in Lan's exhibition *Found in Translation*.[36] The exhibit catalog reproduces the Schröder portrait in both upright and inverted positions, and the reading of the painting varies according to its orientation, as discussed below.

Schröder appears as a nude hermaphrodite, with two halves of a globe forming his breasts. The femininity Lan attributes to Schröder is part of her feminist critique of his macho personality and his relationships with women. Known as the "Audi Chancellor" for his four marriages, which evoke the four interlocking "wedding rings" of the Audi logo, he has now taken a fifth wife, So-yeon Schröder-Kim, a South Korean interpreter, who is twenty-six years his junior. Both Schröder's posture and his feminized features link this painting to the earlier *Falling Is the Last Motion Before Flying* (2014, Fig. 3.9b), as well as her subsequent portrait of Baselitz (Fig. 5.4a). For the Schröder portrait, Lan turned the pregnant belly into a small blue-purplish fox, alluding to his shrewdness. All

34 Sarah Hucal, "German Term 'Putinversteher' Goes International," *DW*, April 6, 2022, <https://www.dw.com/en/german-term-putinversteher-goes-international/a-61381725>.

35 Ben Knight, "The History of Nord Stream," *DW*, July 23, 2021, <https://www.dw.com/en/the-history-of-nord-stream/a-58618313>; Katrin Bennhold, "The Former Chancellor Who Became Putin's Man in Germany," *New York Times*, April 23, 2022, <https://www.nytimes.com/2022/04/23/world/europe/schroder-germany-russia-gas-ukraine-war-energy.html>.

36 *Jiny Lan: Found in Translation*, Ausstellung in der Tammen Galerie – Berlin, September 3–October 9, 2021, exhibition catalog, ed. Mette Kleinsteuber and Werner Tammen (Berlin: Katalogdruck, 2021).

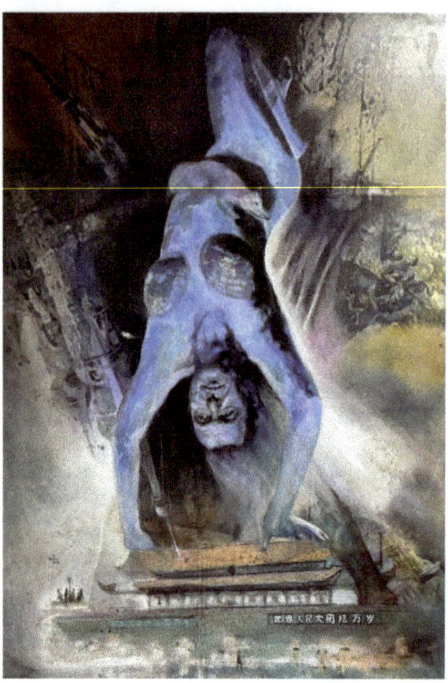

Fig. 7.5a. *Atlas...* (2016–21, 200 × 140 cm).

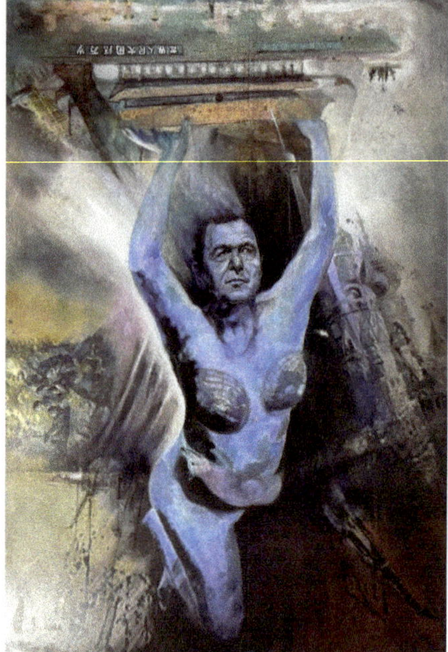

Fig. 7.5b. *Atlas* ... inverted.

of these paintings can be traced back to the same source: *Value-Added Movement* 5 (2013, Fig. 8.3a = Fig. 3.9),[37] from which *Alternative Fiction* (Fig. 8.3d) is also derived.

In *Atlas* ..., Schröder is surrounded by four architectural symbols: Tiananmen, the Brandenburg Gate, the US Capitol, and Red Square, representing the political centers of China, Germany, the US, and Russia. To the right of Tiananmen is a tiny depiction of the Quadriga on the Brandenburg Gate, and to its left is a tilted US Capitol. Half of the Capitol is covered in shadow, symbolizing America's political division during Trump's presidential campaign. Diagonally across from the Capitol is Moscow's Red Square. The juxtaposition of the two centers of power illustrates the attraction between Trump and Putin, but also the confrontational relationship between Russia and the US. The tip of the spire of St. Basil's Cathedral in Red Square seems to pierce the roof of Tiananmen, suggesting connection and contact, but also conflict and friction between Russia and China. Since it was Schröder's notorious high-profile involvement with Russian natural gas giants that drew censure, Lan placed vessels equipped for the construction of the Nord Stream

37 Images are occasionally duplicated within this book to facilitate comparisons and provide context.

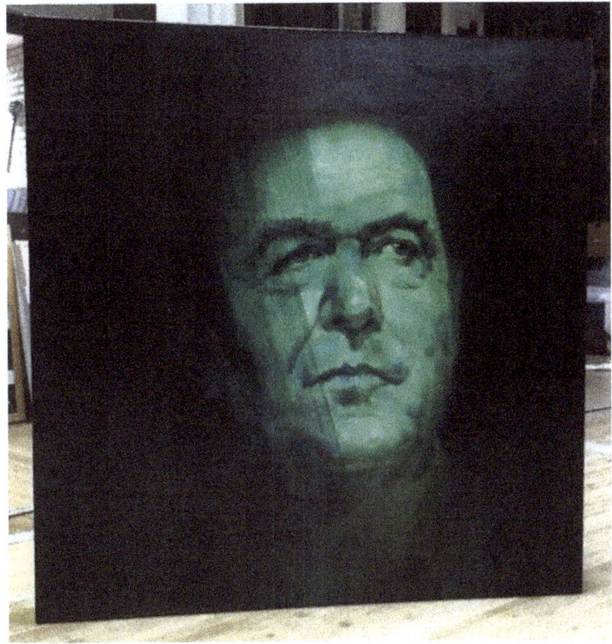

Fig. 7.6. Schröder portrait on a small IKEA tabletop (2016, 55 × 55 cm).

pipelines both below and opposite Red Square. To show the importance of natural gas for heating German households, she added in 2021 a family of four against the backdrop of a giant steel pipe, similar to the pipelines laid on the bottom of the Baltic Sea. The color of Schröder's skin takes on the blue color of burning natural gas, and the blue flame rising from his hair also suggests a jet of natural gas.

After the Russian attack on Ukraine, Schröder became *persona non grata* in the SPD. His role in the development of the Nord Stream pipelines illustrates why Germany became so dependent on Russian gas and why Schröder's actions stirred so much controversy in Germany. On September 8, 2005, during the last weeks of Schröder's chancellorship (1998–2005), the basic agreement between Gazprom, Wintershall, and E.ON Ruhrgas was signed in the presence of Schröder and Putin, announcing a new North European Gas Pipeline (later renamed "Nord Stream") running directly from Russia to Germany through the Baltic Sea, bypassing transit countries including Ukraine and Poland. On December 9, 2005, soon after Schröder left office, Putin called Schröder to urge him to accept the company's nomination for chairman of Nord Stream's supervisory board. Schröder agreed and also made it known that he wanted to make money. After the 2011 nuclear disaster in Fukushima, Japan, Merkel announced that Germany would phase out nuclear power.

Schröder lobbied hard for Nord Stream 2, an additional pipeline running parallel to Nord Stream 1 to double sales of Russian natural gas. In 2017, Schröder also became a member of the supervisory board of the Russian energy company Rosneft. Owing to Schröder's endorsement and lobbying, Russian gas accounted for 55 percent of Germany's natural gas supply from the moment Nord Stream 1 opened until Russia invaded Ukraine. After the invasion, Schröder reacted defiantly to criticism of his involvement with Gazprom, initially refusing to resign from his lucrative positions. He even defended Putin, claiming that NATO's post-Cold-War eastward expansion had provoked the Kremlin and accusing Ukraine of "saber-rattling."[38]

In her portrait of Schröder, Lan criticizes Schröder's morally questionable actions and his self-serving collaboration with an authoritarian regime. Lan titled the painting *Atlas …*, including the ellipsis to suggest that the work was open to interpretation. In Greek mythology, Atlas is the titan who was condemned to carry the celestial sphere. He is usually depicted holding the celestial globe or the terrestrial globe either on his shoulders or over his head. Lan uses the mythical figure as an allegory for world leaders like Putin, Xi, Trump, and Schröder, who, especially in today's world of strongman politics, play important roles; they (should) shoulder great responsibilities. Lan initially named the painting "Atlas Shrugged," after the 1957 novel by Russian American author Ayn Rand, because "Schröder literally shrugged his shoulders, when criticized for his actions."

If Russia has the natural resources that Germany requires, China provides the market on which the nation depends. Similar to Atlas holding up the heavens, Schröder in Lan's painting is holding an inverted model of the Tiananmen gate. When the painting is rotated, he appears to perform a handstand on Tiananmen like an acrobat (Fig. 7.5b). The invertibility of the painting allows the artist to illustrate the mutually supportive relationship between Schröder and Beijing. While serving as chancellor from 1998 to 2005, Schröder visited China six times and secured huge deals for German companies. His first state visit in 1999 came shortly after the accidental NATO bombing of the Chinese embassy in Belgrade,

38 Bennhold, "Former Chancellor"; Daniel Delhaes, "Gerhard Schröder – Auftritt nur für echte Freunde," *Handelsblatt*, September 25, 2008; Knight, "The History of Nord Stream"; Luke Harding, "Schröder Faces Growing Scandal over Job with Russian Gas Giant," *The Guardian*, December 12, 2005, <https://www.theguardian.com/world/2005/dec/13/russia.germany>; Christian Schweppe and Adrian Arab, "Brisante Nähe," *Welt*, December 15, 2017, <https://www.welt.de/politik/deutschland/plus171601464/Brisante-Naehe.html>; Felix K. Chang, "Legacy of Ostpolitik: Germany's Russia Policy and Energy Security," Foreign Policy Research Institute, May 8, 2014, <https://www.fpri.org/article/2014/05/legacy-of-ostpolitik-germanys-russia-policy-and-energy-security/>.

and he was the first Western politician to arrive in China to apologize for the mistake. In 1999, he supported China's entry into the World Trade Organization (WTO), which China officially joined in 2001. He also proposed to include China in the G8 forum. During his chancellorship, he even advocated lifting the arms embargo on China that Western countries had imposed after the Tiananmen massacre in 1989, a stance that left him isolated in his own Red-Green government.[39]

As a US-China trade war loomed, Schröder warned against demonizing Beijing. His political decisions were guided by a pragmatic concern for Germany's economic interests; as he put it: "I don't think much of a values-based foreign policy. Our interests should drive our foreign policy."[40] In numerous interviews and articles, he has remained consistent in his views on China: Germany and the world need China's cooperation on all key issues of world politics; China is still a developing country, despite its recent rapid growth; and the CCP rightly prioritizes the fight against poverty over freedom of expression. Furthermore, an export-dependent country like Germany has different economic and political interests than the US, and Schröder warns "against being drawn into a new Cold War with Beijing out of misunderstood transatlantic loyalty."[41] He also echoes his predecessor Schmidt, who argued that Germany is a mid-sized power and should not raise a moralizing finger in its foreign policy.[42] These views are compatible with the "change through trade" foreign policy.[43]

Lan's blunt portrayal of Schröder demonstrates her disagreement with his value-free foreign policy. As a former participant in the 1989 student movement, Lan boldly expresses her disillusionment with the Chinese Communist Party. The representation of Tiananmen in *Atlas* ... includes the two phrases that appear in front of the building. But although "Long Live the Solidarity of the People of the World" is clearly visible on the

39 "China-Besuch: Schröders schwerer Gang," *Spiegel*, May 11, 1999; "Schroeder Calls for China to Join G8, WTO," *CNN*, November 13, 1999; "Schröder Isolated in China Stance," *DW*, April 15, 2005; Andreas Lorenz, "Hugging the Panda: Gerhard Schröder Opens Doors for German Companies in China," trans. Christopher Sultan, *Spiegel International*, November 6, 2009.

40 Noah Barkin, "Germany's Schroeder Warns against Demonizing China," *Reuters*, November 16, 2018, <https://www.reuters.com/article/business/germanys-schroeder-warns-against-demonizing-china-idUSKCN1NL1UL/>.

41 Gerhard Schröder, "Wer das glaubt, hat China nicht verstanden," *t-online*, February 3, 2022, <https://tendenzblick.net/altkanzler-gerhard-schroeder-wer-das-glaubt-hat-china-nicht-verstanden/>.

42 Schröder, "Wer das glaubt, hat China nicht verstanden."

43 Chang, "Legacy of Ostpolitik"; Holger Schmale, "'Wer Handel treibt, schießt nicht aufeinander,'" *Frankfurter Rundschau*, July 12, 2018, <https://www.fr.de/politik/wer-handel-treibt-schiesst-nicht-aufeinander-10959225.html>.

right, the words on the left – "Long Live the PRC" – are provocatively obscured with white paint. Through her artwork, Lan also denounces authoritarianism and embraces democratic values; from her perspective, Western leaders such as Schröder have illusions about autocratic regimes because they have not lived in one.

An Open Process (2021–): Liminal Portraits Fusing Chancellors and Would-Be Chancellors

As an immigrant from China to Germany, Lan is particularly interested in the democratization of the Federal Republic of Germany since 1945. This interest is reflected in *An Open Process*, in which she painted candidates who have lost German federal elections. She began with a canvas print of a federal election winner's portrait and then slowly overpainted the original to gradually morph the image of the winner into that of the candidate who lost the election. Following the 2017 *Bundestagswahl* (federal election), for example, she transformed the winning candidate, Angela Merkel, into Martin Schulz (Fig. 7.7). Lan contends that the candidates who lost elections should also be remembered and honored, because accepting electoral defeat, especially in a close race, is a precondition for a stable democracy. Thus, the losing German candidates deserve all the more recognition and remembrance. Without them, democracy would not function. Lan originally experimented with the idea of gradually darkening the loser's portrait until it became hardly recognizable, indicating that the failed candidate had fallen into oblivion. Liminal images of the rivals express a fantastic symbiosis of political opponents in democracy. The title "An Open Process" refers to the open-ended election process, as well as to the openness and transparency of the process. These are hallmarks of democracy that are taken for granted in Germany but unattainable in China, a sustained concern of the artist.

Coda: Artistic Freedom Cannot Be Taken for Granted

This chapter focused on Lan's portraits of German chancellors: Angela Merkel, Gerhard Schröder, and Olaf Scholz. Difficult and complex world issues such as Schröder and his *Schulterschluss* (rubbing elbows) with authoritarian leaders, Merkel and the arrival of large numbers of refugees, and Scholz's unexpected ascent to chancellorship in an adverse political landscape are tackled painterly with brushstrokes and always with China in mind and in sight. Lan placed a nude, feminized Schröder on top of Tiananmen, dressed Merkel in the attire of the controversial Empress Dowager Cixi, and camouflaged the "lucky" Scholz as a mushroom stem

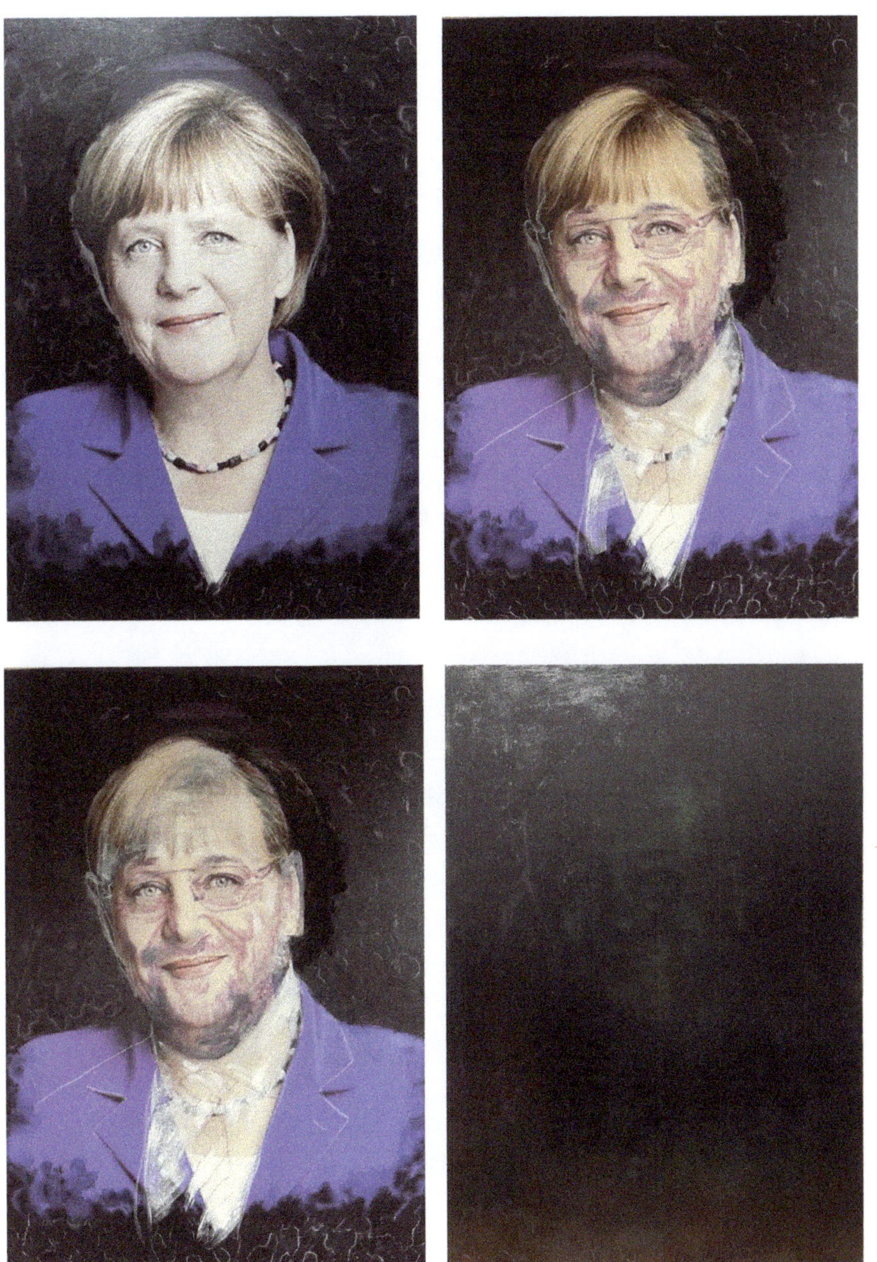

Fig. 7.7. *An Open Process* (2021, 140 × 100 cm):
Angela Merkel and Martin Schulz.

rising amid leaves of Chinese cabbage. These works demonstrate her continued interest in using art as a weapon to intervene in political discourses. They are intriguing visual statements that open dialogues with German and international politics.

In authoritarian regimes, art is politicized and instrumentalized, but in Western democracies, an artist can use art to critique politicians and their policies. Nevertheless, in the absence of official censorship there are other forces that may compel an aspiring artist to refrain from showing or publishing art that is critical of powerful persons. Lan's gallerist feared that her initial portrait of Schröder might be bad for business and convinced her to keep it private. Yet when it was finally shown publicly at the exhibition *Found in Translation* (September 3–October 9, 2021), during the heated debate about Nord Stream 2, the media did not report on the painting, despite the fact that Lindner posed for pictures in front of it. The press might have ignored the portrait because criticism of Schröder was already widespread in German media, and the painting had lost its initial pungency.

8: Visualizing Sino-European Politics: Transcultural Art about the New Silk Road

Lan's career has coincided with the rule of Chinese president Xi Jinping. She came into the public eye during the first Bald Girls exhibition in March 2012, and on November 15 of that year Xi became the leader of the CCP. Two weeks later, while visiting the exhibition *Road to Rejuvenation* at the National Museum of China on November 29, Xi proclaimed the "Chinese dream," which aims to revitalize the nation, advance the country's prosperity, and promote the people's happiness.[1] In March 2013, he became China's president. In an effort to realize the ambitious and Herculean Chinese dream, he began advocating the Belt and Road Initiative (BRI), also known as the New Silk Road. He announced the land-based Silk Road Economic Belt program during a visit to Astana, Kazakhstan, in September 2013, and one month later, he introduced the 21st Century Maritime Silk Road program in Jakarta, Indonesia. Taken as a whole, the BRI is an intercontinental infrastructure project that will build a vast network of roads, railways, ports, power grids, oil and gas pipelines, and industrial and commercial facilities connecting China with Asia, Europe, and Africa.[2] Despite controversy and criticism, the world's largest infrastructure project was well underway before the pandemic hit. It is also a sociopolitical and cultural phenomenon to be reckoned with. As a bridge between China and Europe, the New Silk Road can function as a metaphor for Sino-European relations.

The BRI plan includes endeavors to increase China's soft power, such as the Silk Road International Cultural Expo (SRDICE),[3] an annual affair intended to promote cultural exchange and encourage cooperation between countries along the New Silk Road. SRDICE was grandly launched in September 2016 in Dunhuang, Gansu Province, a

1 "Xi Jinping Visits 'The Road to Rejuvenation' Exhibition in 2012," china.org.cn, October 23, 2014, <http://www.china.org.cn/china/2014-10/23/content_33853481.htm>.

2 "What does Xi Jinping's China Dream mean?," *BBC*, June 6, 2013, <https://www.bbc.com/news/world-asia-china-22726375>; counterintuitively, "Belt" refers to land routes and "Road" to sea routes.

3 "Dunhuang Silk Road International Cultural Expo," chinaculture.org, <http://en.chinaculture.org/special_reports/SilkRoadExpo>.

city in north central China located on both the ancient and the modern Silk Roads. Nearby are the Mogao Caves, a UNESCO World Heritage Site that houses many Buddhist statues and frescoes, some dating back to the fifth century CE. Lan was one of around fifteen hundred foreign guests invited to participate in the inaugural expo. Subsequently, the Mogao Caves in Dunhuang and the (New) Silk Road were featured in a number of her works. This chapter focuses on paintings that capitalize on the historic Silk Road while criticizing the vanity of the BRI. Pursuing the theme of the New Silk Road, this chapter groups artworks that can be described as Eurasian and bicultural and that yield insight into the challenges that face the EU and its most important trading partner, as well as its "systemic rival," China.[4] The paintings function as visual commentaries about European and Chinese politics that impact Sino-European relations.

Venice Silk Road

In 2019, during the show *Portfolio – Genealogies* at the Library of St. Mark in Venice, Lan improvised a "Silk Road" on site. The path to the reading room passes through a large vestibule whose ceiling is adorned with Titian's *Wisdom* (1564). Because the fresco was under repair at the time, temporary walls were erected in the vestibule to create a narrow corridor leading to the reading room. Lan had the idea to turn the corridor into an imaginary Silk Road by lining it with murals. The library's curator allowed her to install *Jinyology – Silk Road* (2019, Fig. 8.1a) in the corridor while the Titian restoration was underway. The historic Silk Road stretched thousands of kilometers from Xi'an (Chang'an), one of China's ancient capitals, through the Taklamakan Desert in Xinjiang and the Pamir Mountains in Tajikistan to the eastern shore of the Mediterranean, where the Venetian merchant Marco Polo began the overland portion of his journey to China in the thirteenth century. Lan thus built a new, symbolic Silk Road in Venice, the native city of the historic Silk Road's most famous traveler.

Lan mounted two giant composite paintings on the two walls of the corridor. Each painting consists of ten canvases that can be arranged in any order. (The paintings could not be photographed in situ due to the size of the artwork and the narrowness of the corridor.) The paintings

4 Hans von der Burchard, "EU Slams China as 'Systemic Rival' as Trade Tension Rises," *Politico*, March 12, 2019, <https://www.politico.eu/article/eu-slams-china-as-systemic-rival-as-trade-tension-rises/>; Cesluk-Grajewski Marcin, "China: From Partner to Rival," *Briefing: What Think Tanks Are Thinking*, European Parliament Research Service (EPRS), October 2, 2020, <https://www.europarl.europa.eu/thinktank/en/document/EPRS_BRI(2020)659261>.

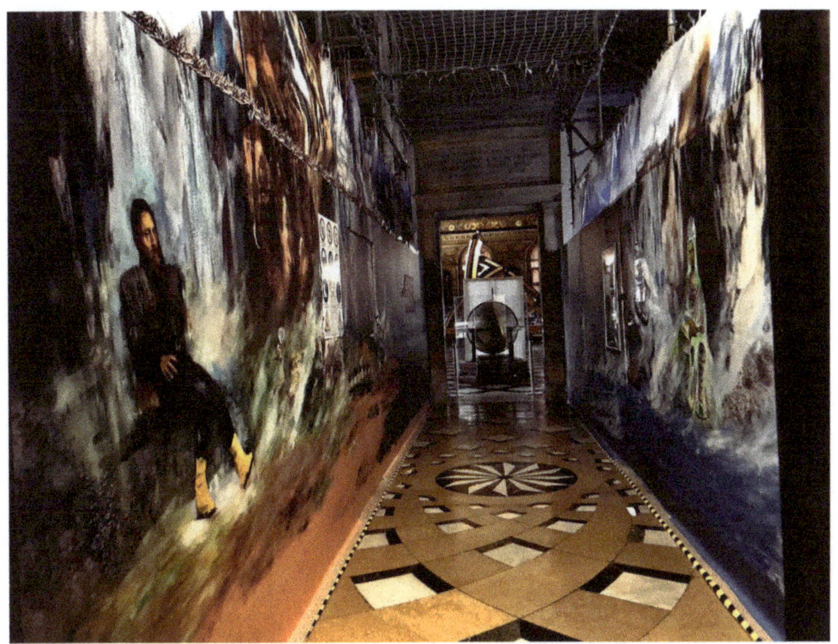

Fig. 8.1a. The corridor leading to the reading room of the Library of St. Mark; Titian is visible on the left.

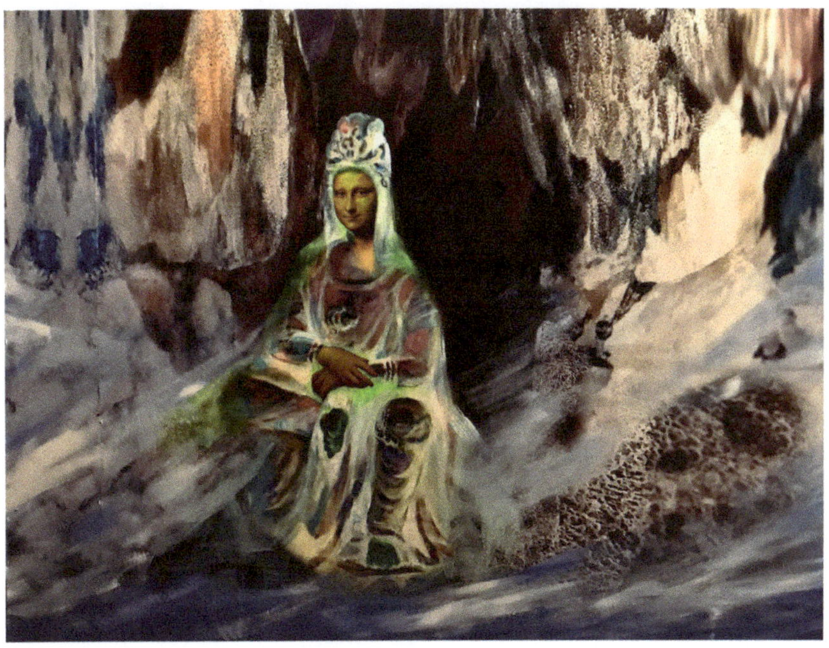

Fig. 8.1b. Buddhalisa.

depict the Alps and China's Yellow River Grand Canyon. By dissecting the European and Asian landscapes into puzzle pieces and rearranging them, she literally interweaves Europe and Asia into a tangled, inseparable unity. Lan's fusion of Buddha and Mona Lisa, Buddhalisa, representing the combination of Eastern and Western traditional culture, was painted on the right wall of the corridor (Fig. 8.1b). Buddhalisa's left foot is planted on the floor while her right leg is folded in the Buddha pose. Buddhalisa appears also in Lan's Beuys portrait (2018–19, Fig. 4.3). On another panel, Lan painted Titian, but he is dressed in her clothes, including a black top with padded shoulders, a belt, black trousers, and her signature yellow boots, an outfit that she often wears in public (Fig. 8.1a). Thus, in a move characteristic of her creative process, she merges herself with Titian to produce a composite, androgynous figure. By grafting the old master's head onto her own body, she envisions herself as a female Titian who aspires to become a famous and influential artist, or alternatively, she envisions Titian as a masculinized Jiny Lan, playfully inserting herself into the lineage of old masters.

The Empty City Strategy (2016): Attending the BRI Cultural Expo in Dunhuang

The painting Lan exhibited at the first BRI Cultural Expo is titled *The Empty City Strategy* (*Kong cheng ji*, 2016, Fig. 8.2c). The title refers to a military ploy in which defenders trick an enemy into retreating by pretending that a deserted city is well guarded. In the classic Ming novel *Romance of the Three Kingdoms*, Zhuge Liang, chancellor of the kingdom of Shu Han, repels an enemy army by sitting at the gate of an abandoned city and calmly playing a stringed instrument. In fact, Phoenix New City, which hosted the expo, was virtually empty when Lan visited it – in preparation for the first SRDICE, the Chinese government had built a brand-new city, including a five-star hotel, a cinema, and a theater, and expanded the Dunhuang airport. Lan remembered the event well:

> There were no ordinary citizens or local residents in the city when we went. The only people we saw were security guards and cleaning personnel. Employees at the airport and hotels were brought in from other places. When I entered one of the buildings, to my surprise, a big screen greeted me by name. This was the legendary facial recognition technology. It shows that high-tech has entered daily life in China. It was a mind-boggling experience for me.

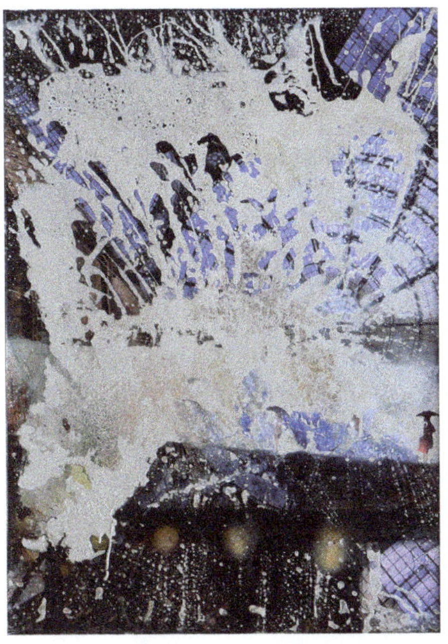

Fig. 8.2a. *Value-Added Movement 6A* (2013, 200 × 140 cm).

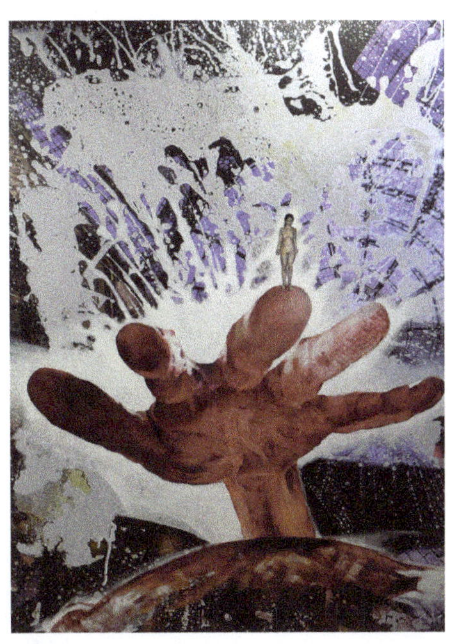

Fig. 8.2b (= Fig. 1.5). *Midlife Hand* (2013, 200 × 140 cm).

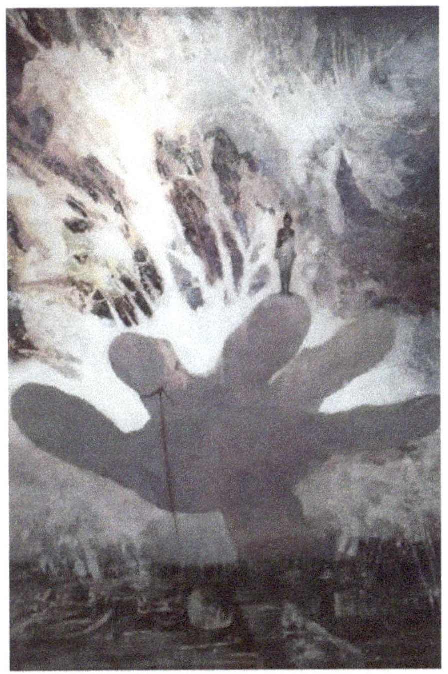

Fig. 8.2c. *The Empty City Strategy* (2016, 200 × 140 cm).

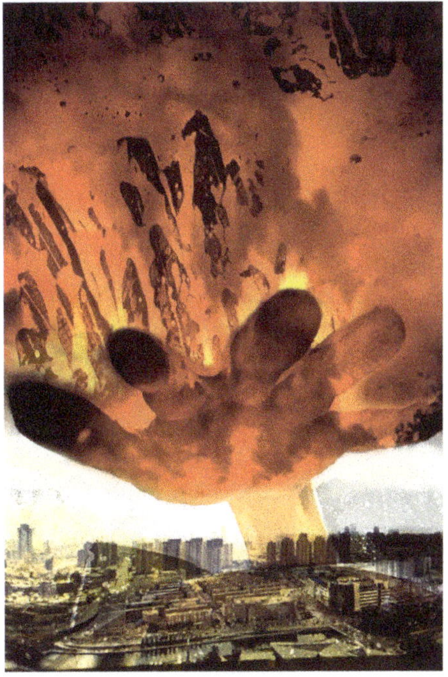

Fig. 8.2d. *Red Nirvana* (2016, 200 × 140 cm).

The international guests were given a grand reception that included accommodation in the best hotels, exquisite meals in high-end restaurants, virtuoso performances, and visits to tourist sites, all at the expense of the Chinese government. The Chinese hosts spared no expense to impress their foreign guests with their hospitality, wealth, and power. However, Lan is skeptical about the results of such a costly endeavor. Despite the dazzling gala shows, foreign guests were put off by a propagandistic film about the BRI that was screened at the expo.[5]

The Empty City Strategy caught the attention of Professor Jeanine Meerapfel, film director and the president of the Academy of Fine Arts in Berlin, who was also present at the expo.[6] In the painting, a large spectral hand stretches out over a hazy cityscape, with an inconspicuous Buddha lying on his side in a state of nirvana. Above the hand, streaks and splotches of white paint cover the dark background. The huge hand makes it clear that this painting belongs to the same versioning as *Midlife Hand* (2013, Fig. 8.2b = Fig. 1.5). The template for the hand series is *Value-Added Movement 6A* (2013, Fig. 8.2a), an ancestral painting half-covered with blotches of frothing white paint. Beneath the froth the glass dome of the shopping mall in Milan can be discerned. A small female figure holding an umbrella and a red shopping bag walks toward the center of the painting, implicitly on a street in Beijing.

This series embodies Lan's therapeutic autobiographical art, which enabled her to gradually work through her past trauma (see chapter 1). Compared to *Midlife Hand*, *The Empty City Strategy* appears murky and hazy, as if the past has been shrouded in a dream-like memory. The pale hand could imply that the impact of sexual trauma on Lan's life had diminished. Dunhuang, a city known for its ancient culture, religion, and art, has taken the place of the penis, suggesting that Lan's artistic pursuits were beginning to flourish. As an invited participant in the international expo, she joined the ranks of recognized artists and entered a productive phase. A red thread is knotted around the index figure, invoking the Chinese phrase 心系祖国 *xin xi zuguo* – literally, a string binds one's heart to one's country. For Lan, who visited China regularly before her parents passed away, Germany and China, her adopted and native countries, became indispensable elements of her existential reality and sources of artistic inspiration.

Another sub-version, *Red Nirvana* (*Hongse niepan*, 2016, Fig. 8.2d), shows a large, glowing red hand stretching out over a bright cityscape. Below the hand the sky is white, but above the hand it is filled with a fiery cloud, so that the hand and the sky appear to be engulfed in flames. The title refers to a phoenix's self-immolation and rise from the ashes and,

5 Meerapfel, "Jiny Lans poetisch-provokative Kunstwelt."

6 Meerapfel, "Jiny Lans poetisch-provokative Kunstwelt."

metaphorically, the artist's emergence from a painful past. The woman standing on the middle finger, present in the previous versions, is no longer visible; perhaps she has been reborn through fire. Dunhuang, the city in *The Empty City Strategy*, has been replaced by a modern city, which the artist identified as Shanghai. Allegorically, the replacement of Beijing with Shanghai, China's economic hub, could be interpreted as China's "rebirth," or the "reincarnation" of the "red" country after 1989, when the nation suppressed the memory of Tiananmen and sought to defuse political dissent through economic self-legitimation.

Message in Art (2017) and Uli Sigg: Gatekeeper to the Chinese Art Temple

The Mogao Caves inspired Lan to paint a sub-version of *Out of Sagrada Família* (2015, 8.3b) in the versioning of *Value-Added Movement 5* (2013, Fig. 8.3a = Fig. 3.9). It depicts the interior of the Basílica de la Sagrada Família in Barcelona. At the bottom center, a large burning match stands on the floor. Several small figures holding up umbrellas are walking about. The upper part of the interior is filled with light. In *Botschaft in der Kunst* (Message in Art, 2017, Fig. 8.3c), a giant statue of Gautama Buddha is transposed into the nave of the Basílica de la Sagrada Família. The enormous columns of the cathedral sketch the contours of an immense Buddha. The fusion of the Catholic church Sagrada Família with a Buddhist temple is an example of Lan's transcultural aesthetic. The group of people walking in the rain at the bottom of the paintings appears to be walking inside the temple-church now, thus conflating interior and exterior spaces, a common flourish in her creations. This temple is a temple of art, because the man in the painting is none other than Uli Sigg, a Swiss patron of contemporary Chinese art. He is the world's most important collector of avant-garde art from post-1978 China. In addition to serving on the advisory committees of museums such as the Museum of Modern Art in New York and the Tate Gallery in London, he established the Chinese Contemporary Art Award (1997) and the Art Critic Award (2007). In the painting, Sigg holds up his palm, in which a Chinese door knocker is embedded, indicating his function as a gatekeeper.

Sigg is a key figure in Sino-European affairs, a staunch advocate of China and of international trade with China, and someone the Chinese government does not want to alienate or antagonize. He pioneered the first joint venture between China and the West for the Schindler Elevator Company in 1980, paving the way for foreign investment in China. From 1995 to 1998, he served as Swiss ambassador to China, North Korea, and Mongolia, working from his office in Beijing. Observing that neither individuals nor Chinese institutions were systematically collecting

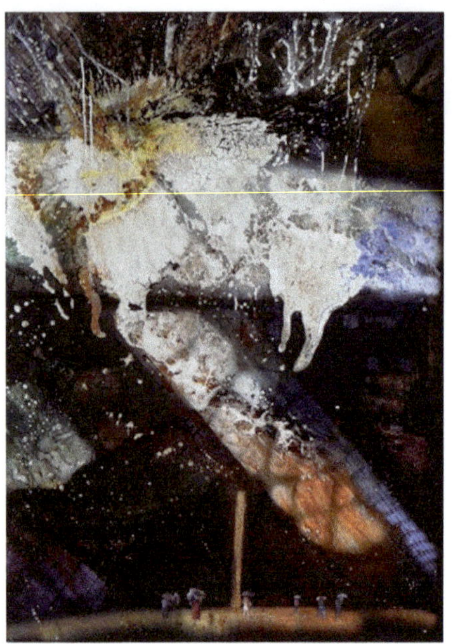

Fig. 8.3a (= Fig. 3.9). *Value-Added Movement 5* (2013, 200 × 140 cm).

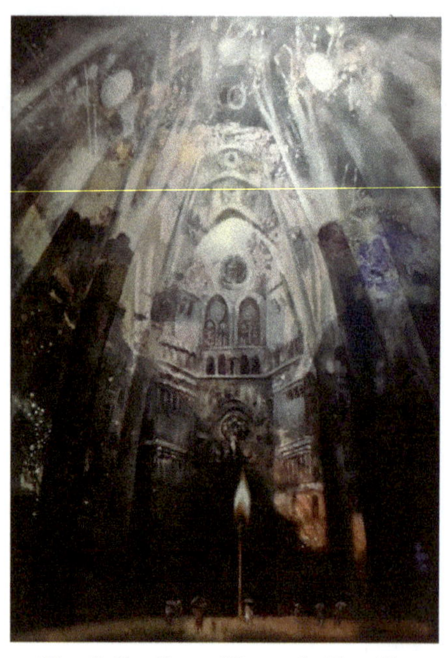

Fig. 8.3b. *Out of Sagrada Família* (2015, 200 × 140 cm).

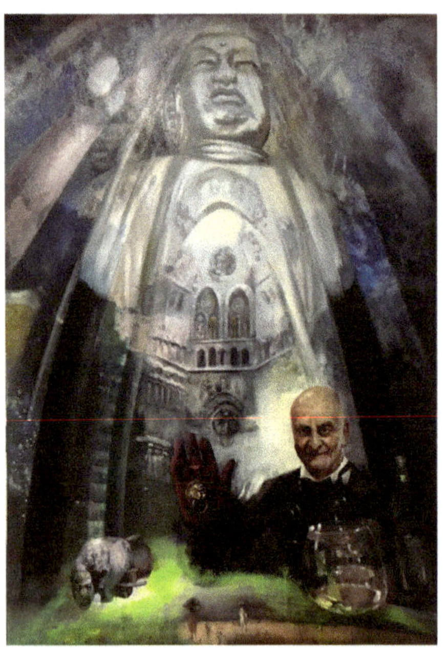

Fig. 8.3c. *Message in Art* (2017, 200 × 140 cm).

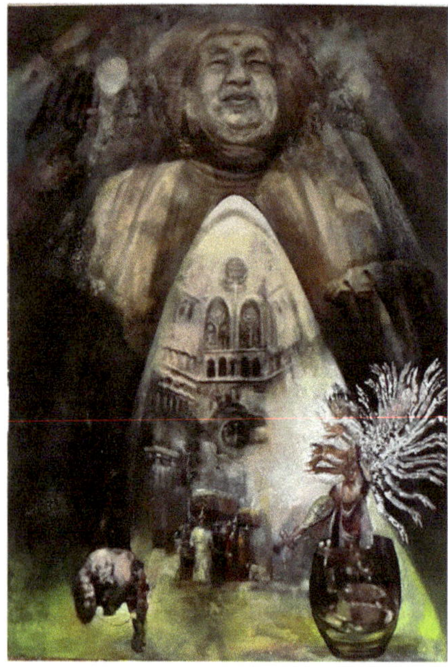

Fig. 8.3d. *Alternative Fiction* (2021, 200 × 140 cm).

Chinese contemporary art, Sigg, an astute connoisseur, gradually amassed an encyclopedic collection of Chinese contemporary art.[7]

Justly, *Message in Art* presents Sigg as a guardian and champion of Chinese contemporary art in the Western world. In the lower left corner of the painting, some of the artworks in Sigg's collection are on display, including an urn, or perhaps a jar in Ai Weiwei's *Whitewash* (1995–2000) installation. Sigg was instrumental in elevating Ai to superstar status.[8] The mask-like face suggests the Chinese avant-garde artist Geng Jianyi's *The Second State* (1987) or Fang Lijun's *Series 2: No. 2* (1991–92), featuring bald-headed men making bored faces. In 2012, Sigg donated 1,463 works by 325 contemporary Chinese artists to the M+ Museum for Visual Arts in Hong Kong because no Mainland art museum was able to exhibit his entire collection, which includes censored or censorable works and artists. Sigg chose Hong Kong after receiving a promise from the Carrie Lam government that all the donated works would be exhibited, but the passage of the city's National Security Law in 2020 made the M+ Museum vulnerable to censorship. As of April 2022, four artworks had been removed from view: Ai Weiwei's *Study of Perspective – Tiananmen* (1997), Wang Xingwei's *New Beijing* (2021), Zhou Tiehai's *Press Conference III* (1996), and Wang Guangyi's *Mao Zedong: Red Grid No. 2* (1989).[9] Many visitors from Mainland China left the M+ Sigg exhibition in tears, a phenomenon Sigg had not witnessed at other art exhibitions.[10]

7 My interview with Uli Sigg in Berlin on April 30, 2023.

8 Uli Sigg, "Confusionism," in Ai Weiwei, *Ways Beyond Art*, ed. Elena Ochoa Foster and Hans Ulrich Obrist (London: Ivorypress, 2009), 12–13; Sigg, "How People Collect Contemporary Art: My Typology of Collecting Styles," in *China's Avant-Garde, 1978–2018*, ed. Daria Berg and Giorgio Strafella (New York: Routledge, 2023), 49–51.

9 Maximilian Kalkhof, "How the Top Collector of Chinese Art Evades Censors in New Hong Kong Museum," *WorldCrunch*, January 27, 2022; Vivienne Chow, "Uli Sigg's Formidable Collection at M+ Is a Beacon of Hope in a Changing China – Even If a Particular Ai Weiwei Work Is Notably Absent," *Artnet*, November 11, 2021, <https://news.artnet.com/art-world/ai-weiweis-hong-kong-m-plus-museum-opens-2033529>; Tessa Solomon, "M+ Museum Pulls Three Politically Charged Works from Display, Spurring Speculation of Censorship," *ARTnews*, April 21, 2022, <https://www.artnews.com/art-news/news/m-plus-museum-pulls-political-artworks-censorship-charges-1234626173/>; Vivienne Chow, "The M+ Museum Has Removed Three Political Paintings by Chinese Artists as Beijing Continues Its Clampdown on Hong Kong," *Artnet*, April 21, 2022, <https://news.artnet.com/art-world/political-chinese-paintings-removed-m-plus-hong-kong-2102659>.

10 My interview with Uli Sigg in Berlin on April 30, 2023.

Alternative Fiction (2021): Courtly Dynamics Past and Present

Already in *Message in Art*, the facial features of the Buddha resemble those of Xi Jinping, a resemblance made even clearer in its sub-version, *Alternative Fiction* (2021, Fig. 8.3d), and Xi now wears a bindi.[11] The Xi-Buddha is seated with his right arm raised, his palm facing outward, and his left hand resting on his thigh. The rose window above the chancel is patterned after the Chinese national emblem. The concept of Xi as a "living Bodhisattva" is in fact not far-fetched. Unlike Mao, Xi considers Buddhism and Daoism as part of the national heritage that China should preserve.[12] In 2016, a venerable abbot called Xi a "Bodhisattva incarnate."[13] In 2018, Xi Jinping was honored by some Tibetans as "a living Buddhist deity."[14]

In the lower right corner of *Alternative Fiction*, a performance of the Thousand-Armed Avalokitesvara dance from the famous Chinese dance repertoire *Rain of Flowers Along the Silk Road* (*Si lu hua yu*) is taking place. *Rain of Flowers Along the Silk Road* was originally composed and choreographed in 1979 for the National Day of the PRC, based on material from the Mogao Caves, and it was part of the gala performance for international guests at the Dunhuang expo. In *Alternative Fiction*, however, the sinuous Thousand-Armed Avalokitesvara dance pose appears sinister, as the dancers' arms look grotesque and ghostly. The lead dancer is stationed in a greenish glass cup, a carryover from *Message in Art*.

Although the formal changes distinguishing *Alternative Fiction* from *Message in Art* seem minor, the frame of reference has shifted enormously. The Buddha is now unmistakably depicted as Xi. Instead of an altar, spectators see an emperor and empress granting an audience,

11 On this painting, see also Qinna Shen, "The New Silk Road and EU-China Relations through Jiny Lan's Visual Art," *The Newsletter of the Global Studies Center* 2 (March 2021), <https://www.gust.edu.kw/gsc/newsletter/issue-2/new-silk-road-and-eu-china-relations>.

12 André Laliberté, "The Two Tracks of Xi Jinping's Religious Policy," Berkeley Center for Religion, Peace & World Affairs, March 16, 2020, <https://berkleycenter.georgetown.edu/responses/the-two-tracks-of-xi-jinping-s-religious-policy>.

13 净空法师称习近平是菩萨化身 [Venerable Abbot Jing Kong Calls Xi Jinping a Bodhisattva Incarnate], *rfi*, November 4, 2016, <https://www.rfi.fr/cn/中国/20160411-净空法师称习近平是菩萨化身>.

14 "Xi Jiping's Latest Tag: Living Buddhist Deity, Chinese Officials Says," *Reuters*, March 8, 2018, <https://www.reuters.com/article/us-china-parliament-xi-boddhisatva/xi-jinpings-latest-tag-living-buddhist-deity-chinese-official-says-idUSKCN1GK0V6/>; Victor Mair, "Xi Jinping As A Living Bodhisattva," *Language Log*, March 9, 2018, <https://languagelog.ldc.upenn.edu/nll/?p=37158>.

evoking the heyday of Chinese dynastic history, when foreign guests from tributary nations came to China and were greeted with an extravagant reception, as depicted in the imaginary scenes painted during the Qing dynasty on giant scrolls titled *All Nations Coming to Court* (*Wan guo lai chao*).[15] Lan's painting is modeled on a contemporary painting by Wang Yongqiang that features the motif, also entitled *All Nations Coming to Court* (*Wan guo lai chao*, 2000).[16]

According to Li Xia'en, the grandiose spectacles arranged for foreign visitors were self-congratulatory and boastful masquerades designed to validate the Qing dynasty by claiming that it enjoys the esteem of all nations. Li underlines that "the Qing Empire was willing to pay a huge price and invest endless time, energy, wealth, and lives to perpetuate this myth and make it 'true.' This is, however, a gigantic vanity project that runs through Chinese history."[17] The spectacles were extremely costly for the Chinese court. Tribute envoys were treated as honored guests and received with great pomp. The value of the rewards and gifts bestowed on visitors was many times greater than the tribute received, because any sign of stinginess would make the emperor lose face. According to Lan, "Whereas the Tang dynasty [618–907 CE] could actually take pride in its prosperity and reputation among nations, the Qing dynasty only put on a façade of greatness, but this did not stop it from propagating images of how other vassals and foreign envoys still come to pay tribute." Lan's pastiche of the contemporary version of *All Nations Coming to Court* criticizes the BRI as a similar vanity project while emphasizing the courtly trappings of Xi's foreign policy.

Lan titled the painting "Alternative Fiction" as a nod to the phrase "alternative facts," first uttered by Kellyanne Conway, senior counselor to President Donald Trump, in a dispute over the size of the crowd that attended Trump's first-term inauguration ceremony. "Alternative facts" are widely understood to be falsehoods, contrary to Conway's attempt to redefine the term as "additional facts and alternative information."[18]

15 万国来朝图 [All Nations Coming to Court], Shuge.org, July 17, 2019, <https://new.shuge.org/view/wan_guo_lai_chao_tu/>; Wang Junfu, *All Nations Coming to Court*, The British Museum, <https://www.bmimages.com/preview.asp?image=00711806001>.

16 王永强 Wang Yongqiang, 万国来朝图 [All Nations Coming to Court], <https://auction.artron.net/paimai-art58890214/>.

17 Li Xia'en, 万国来朝大戏: 各朝皇帝面子工程 [The Spectacle of All Nations Coming to Court: A Vanity Project of [Chinese] Emperors of All Dynasties], 新周刊 [Newsweek] 421, October 15, 2015.

18 Brooke Seipel, "Conway Seeks to Define 'Alternative Facts,'" *The Hill*, March 18, 2017, <https://thehill.com/blogs/blog-briefing-room/news/324621-conway-defines-alternative-facts-additional-facts-and/>; also see Charlie May, "Kellyanne Conway: The American People 'Have Their Own

Thus, the title takes a swipe at the Trump administration, drawing an analogy between Trump's and Xi's vanity and disinterest in facts.

The BRI is Xi's signature foreign policy initiative and reveals China's ambition to increase its global influence. As historian Peter Frankopan has pointedly written: "These days, all roads lead to Beijing."[19] The Xi administration has touted the BRI as a win-win project.[20] Developing countries, in particular, cannot undertake infrastructure improvement without foreign aid. For this reason, some have compared the BRI to the Marshall Plan. However, in 2016, McKinsey reported that the projected capital expenditure of the BRI was twelve times greater than that of the Marshall Plan.[21] China had already spent an estimated $200 billion on the BRI by 2020.[22]

The German government has supported the BRI.[23] Hans von Helldorff, spokesman for the Board of the Federal Association of the German Silk Road Initiative (BVDSI), said in an interview with Xinhua that the BRI has created opportunities and new markets for German enterprises: "The future markets and the new markets, for example, are in Asia, Africa, as well as Eastern and Southern Europe. They are not so well-connected. China has been providing the connections; thus it

---

Facts,'" *Salon*, February 1, 2018, <https://www.salon.com/2018/02/01/kellyanne-conway-the-american-people-have-their-own-set-of-facts/>.

19 Peter Frankopan, "These Days, All Roads Lead to Beijing," *Huffpost*, July 28, 2017, <https://www.huffpost.com/entry/china-silk-road_b_5978d667e4b0a8a40e84cec7>; see also Frankopan, *The New Silk Roads: The Present and Future of the World* (London: Bloomsbury 2018).

20 China Power Team, "How Will the Belt and Road Initiative Advance China's Interests?," China Power, May 8, 2017, updated October 11, 2024, <https://chinapower.csis.org/china-belt-and-road-initiative/>; Anthony Morse, *China's New Silk Road*, consisting of 8 episodes and produced by CNA, a Singaporean public broadcast service, 2016; Andrew Chatzky and James McBride, "China's Massive Belt and Road Initiative," Council on Foreign Relations, last updated February 2, 2023, <https://www.cfr.org/backgrounder/chinas-massive-belt-and-road-initiative>; Thomas Zimmerman, "The New Silk Roads: China, the U.S., and the Future of Central Asia," Center on International Cooperation, October 2015, <https://cic.nyu.edu/wp-content/uploads/1662/65/zimmerman_new_silk_road_final_2.pdf>.

21 "China's One Belt, One Road: Will It Reshape Global Trade?" McKinsey Podcast, July 2016, <https://www.mckinsey.com/featured-insights/china/chinas-one-belt-one-road-will-it-reshape-global-trade>.

22 Chatzky and McBride, "China's Massive Belt and Road Initiative."

23 "Where the Rubber Meets the 'Belt and Road' – German Ambassador Answers the Big Questions," *South China Morning Post*, May 13, 2017, <https://www.scmp.com/news/china/diplomacy-defence/article/2093707/german-ambassador-answers-belt-and-road-questions>.

will generate great opportunities."[24] One of the BRI's rail lines stretches from China to Western Europe, ending in the German city of Duisburg. Located in the Ruhr region, Duisburg suffered economic decline in the 1980s and 1990s, but it is the world's largest inland port and one of Europe's biggest transportation and logistics hubs. Everyone in China heard about Duisburg when Xi went to the city in 2014 to welcome the first train from Chongqing. Erich Staake, head of Duisburg Port AG, commented: "It takes 45 days to ship goods by sea from Chongqing to Duisburg, and only about 13 days by rail."[25] BRI rail is faster than sea and cheaper than air.

While the BRI promises to distribute the benefits that accrue from increased connectivity, the project has faced strong criticism from inside and outside of China.[26] International critics have focused on the lack of transparency, potential debt traps, Chinese authoritarianism and corruption, environmental damage, and reliance on Chinese labor instead of local construction workers, among other perceived problems.[27] On platforms such as Voice of America, Chinese commentators abroad criticize the BRI as money squandered on vanity projects rather than remitted to China's impoverished population. Whereas other countries accuse the Chinese government of creating debt traps, Chinese critics fear that astronomical loans to countries in Asia, Latin America, and Africa, such as Venezuela, will not be repaid due to economic and political instability in those regions. One of Xi's critics, Ren Zhiqiang, a real estate tycoon in China, called Xi a "clown" in his essay "A Clown Who Stripped Himself and Insisted on Becoming an Emperor."[28] In 2020, Ren was sentenced to

24 "China's BRI Creates Opportunities for German Companies: Business Association Speaker," *China Daily*, June 18, 2019, <https://www.chinadaily.com.cn/a/201906/18/WS5d08a7b2a3103dbf14328ee8.html>.

25 Guy Chazan, "The Unlikely End to China's New Silk Road is in Germany's Rust Belt," *OZY*, April 10, 2019, <https://anti-empire.com/the-unlikely-end-to-chinas-new-silk-road-is-in-germanys-rust-belt/>.

26 dpa, "Germany Criticized Italy on Decision to Join China's Belt and Road Initiative," *Daily Sabah*, March 24, 2019, <https://www.dailysabah.com/europe/2019/03/24/germany-criticizes-italy-on-decision-to-join-chinas-belt-and-road-initiative>.

27 David Dollar, "Understanding China's Belt and Road Infrastructure Projects in Africa," Brookings, September 2019, <https://www.brookings.edu/articles/understanding-chinas-belt-and-road-infrastructure-projects-in-africa/>.

28 "Ren Zhiqiang – Who Called Chinese President a 'Clown' – Jailed for 18 Years," *The Guardian*, September 22, 2020, <https://www.theguardian.com/world/2020/sep/22/ren-zhiqiang-who-called-chinese-president-a-clown-jailed-for-18-years>; 任志強「被貪污」遭重判18年， 高瑜:「罪證」你就一點都別信 [Ren Zhiqiang Was Sentenced to Eighteen Years for "Corruption." Gao Yu: Don't Believe Any of the "Incriminating Evidence"], *rfa*, September 22, 2020, <https://www.rfa.org/cantonese/news/ren-09222020092558.html>.

eighteen years in prison on corruption charges—a move widely seen as an act of political revenge by Xi. The Hawaii-based émigré cartoonist Cheng Tao has also repeatedly mocked Xi as an emperor without clothes.[29]

China's vigorous attempt to sell the BRI to the international community is reminiscent of Qing-era strategies to control how the nation is perceived by the world. In 2017, the first BRI Forum for International Cooperation brought heads of state from 29 countries and representatives from over 130 countries to Beijing to discuss infrastructure development plans; in 2019, top leaders from over 30 countries and representatives from 150 countries participated in the second summit in Beijing. These BRI summits were designed to conjure up the glory of past Chinese dynasties, as expressed in the "all nations coming to court" tradition. At the same time, these summits were also intended to appease China's own population, over 600 million of whom had a monthly income of only $140 in 2020.[30] Li Xia'en wrote: "This spectacle of 'all nations coming to court' was performed for the subjects of the empire. It clearly told the people that it is a great honor and happiness to live in a country that is admired by all nations."[31] Tetsushi Takahashi, head of Nikkei's China headquarters, pointed out that even if the BRI fails, it will still have the effect of inflating Xi's status and power within the Party.[32] The elevation of Xi as a Buddha-like figure in *Alternative Fiction* is a reminder of the utility of the cult of personality as a tactic for winning power struggles within the CCP. Ordinary Chinese people seem to be persuaded by the Party's celebration of its own power and influence. Lan explained that she added two children at the front of the painting "to represent the younger generation in China, which is more patriotic than my own generation."

29 "The Emperor's New Clothes," Tao Comics 成涛漫画, March 9, 2018, <https://club.6parkbbs.com/bolun/index.php?app=forum&act=threadview&tid=15665457>.

30 K. J. M. Varma, "China Has Over 600 Million Poor with USD 140 Monthly Income: Premier Li," *The Times of India*, May 28, 2020, <https://timesofindia.indiatimes.com/china-has-over-600-million-poor-with-usd-140-monthly-income-premier-li/articleshow/76074863.cms>; Wan Haiyuan and Meng Fanqiang, "Opinion: China Has 600 Million People With Monthly Income less Than $141. Is That True?" *Caixin Global*, June 6, 2020, <https://www.caixinglobal.com/2020-06-06/opinion-china-has-600-million-people-with-monthly-income-less-than-141-is-that-true-101564071.html>.

31 Li Xia'en, "The Spectacle of All Nations Coming to Court."

32 Tetsushi Takahashi, "Belt and Road Conference Is Xi's Time to Shine: Power Play within Chinese Party Is Key Even If Investment Falls through," *Nikkei Asia*, May 16, 2017, <https://asia.nikkei.com/Economy/Belt-and-Road-conference-is-Xi-s-time-to-shine>.

Europe in Crisis and Participatory Art: *Left, Right* (2014–18) and *New Fellowship* (2018)

Whereas Chinese authoritarianism under Xi was increasingly embroiled in a return to Mao-style radical leftism, European democracy was rife with ideological tensions between left and right. In 2014, Lan painted *Left, Right* (Fig. 8.4b), a sub-version of *Value-Added Movement 4A* (2013, Fig. 8.4a), as a warning against simplistic labeling. *Left, Right* shows a crowd of naked men running toward the viewer through water. In the background are traces of the dome of the shopping mall in Milan and a coastal landscape. When Lan was a child, it was precisely a "class enemy" labeled as a "rightist" or a "capitalist element" who remembered to pick her up and carry her to safety during an earthquake (chapter 1). In the many waves of political purges that Mao carried out, from the Yan'an Rectification Movement (1942–45) to the Cultural Revolution, Mao persecuted rivals using anti-liberal ideology to consolidate or recertify his power within the party. It should be noted, however, that the "leftism" of the Chinese Communist Party and its namesake in the pluralist and democratic West cannot be simply equated, as they entail drastically different beliefs and values.

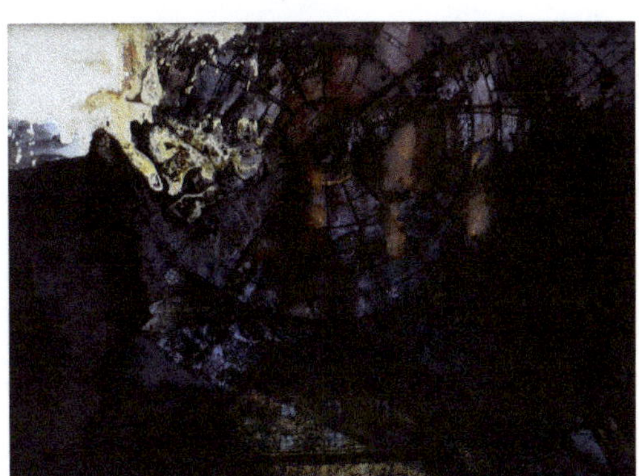

Fig. 8.4a. *Value-Added Movement 4A* (2013, 140 × 200 cm).

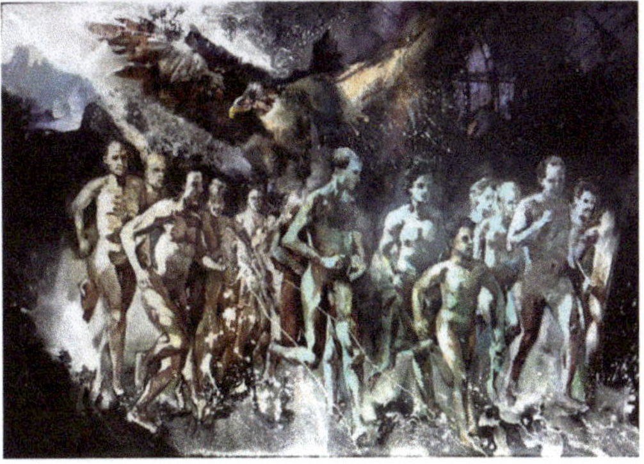

Fig. 8.4b. *Left, Right* (2014–18, 140 × 200 cm).

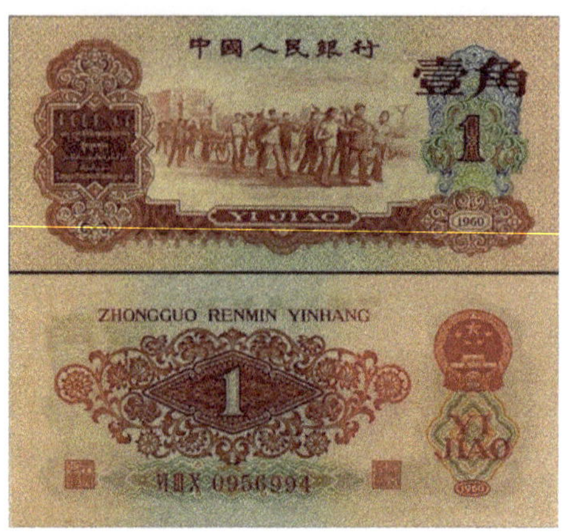

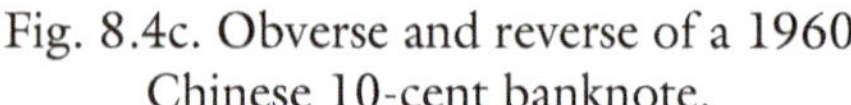

Fig. 8.4c. Obverse and reverse of a 1960 Chinese 10-cent banknote.

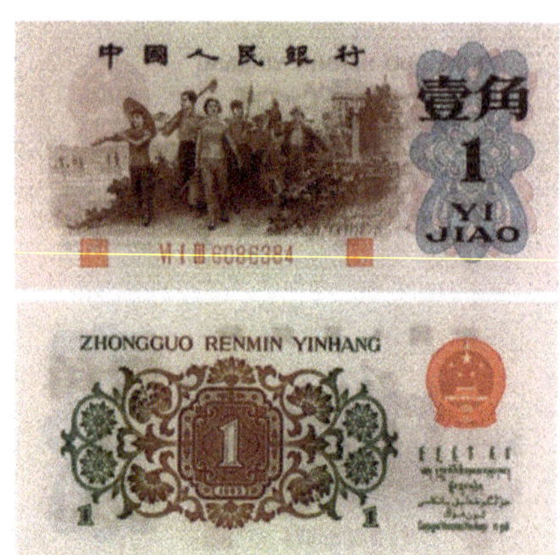

Fig. 8.4d. Obverse and reverse of a 1962 Chinese 10-cent banknote.

Left, Right was inspired by a ten-cent (*yi jiao*) RMB banknote from 1960 that was withdrawn just two years after its issue (Fig. 8.4c). Due to its scarcity it skyrocketed in value and was worth 4,900 RMB (approximately €642 or USD $690) as of January 2020.[33] The obverse of the banknote shows a number of people carrying agricultural implements marching along a roadway in the direction of the viewer. They will pass to the right of the viewer. As stated in Xinhua News: "According to legend among collectors, the problem with the note was that it showed some workers 'walking to the right' in the illustration on the back. Political ideology was a very serious issue in China at the time, and such a 'rightist deviation error' led the 'evil' note to total destruction."[34] But from their own perspective, the workers are actually heading left. The problem posed by the banknote is absurd, but it is indicative of a dictatorial regime in which people were afraid to speak out. On the replacement note issued in 1962, the group of peasants and workers are shown passing to the left of the viewer (Fig. 8.4d). In 2018, Lan added an enormous vulture with spread wings to the painting making the image even more ominous. She explained: "From the vulture's point of view, it makes no difference whether people run to the right or the left: the one who drops dead first will serve as dinner."

33 1960年的一角的价格多少 [How much are 1960's 10 cents worth today], July 1, 2020, <http://www.mdybk.com/art-44094-pro.htm>; 第三套人民币1962年1角价格表 [The Third Set of RMB 1962 10 Cents Price List], December 26, 2024, <http://www.58ybk.com/sc/4513.html>.

34 "China Exclusive: A Brief History of 'the people's money' of China," Xinhua, November 12, 2015, <http://www.china.org.cn/china/Off_the_Wire/2015-11/12/content_37045652.htm>.

As a Eurasian artist, Lan brings her own perspective to depictions of the political upheavals and crises that plague the EU. In 2018, she took part in the group exhibition *Confluentes III. Breaking through Boundaries*, held at the Ludwig Museum in Koblenz from July 29 to August 12.[35] She contributed seven paintings, including *Cool Guys Don't Look Back at Explosions* (2018), *New Fellowship* (2018), and *Volkswagnis* (Folk Audacity, 2018). Lan deliberately left all the paintings unfinished in the studio, with the intention of completing them during the exhibition. She also staged a performance, *Rent a Thirdhand Experience* (2018), in which she selected visitors by lottery and painted them into the paintings. Whereas "firsthand" refers to one's personal experience and "secondhand" to the indirect experience of others, "thirdhand" refers to an experience that the artist has conceptualized for museum visitors by allowing them to participate in the co-creation of the artwork. This is a typical performance that Lan does to draw spectators, in both sense of the phrase. Her ability to swiftly create portraits comes from her rigorous training in China and years of street painting abroad. Participatory art reflects Brechtian and Fluxus conceptions that involve the public in the making of art, turning "the viewer from observer to performer."[36] Practicing Beuys's concept that "everyone is an artist," Lan invites the audience to engage with her work and with the political and aesthetic messages she wishes to convey.

New Fellowship (Fig. 8.5c) is an allegorical painting about the EU in crisis. Its dominant blue hue is similar to the background of the ancestral painting *Value-Added Movement 6A* (2013, Fig. 8.5a). *New Fellowship* places three naked men on a seacoast amidst breaking waves as they struggle to right a listing model of a large ship. They represent the French president Emmanuel Macron, who took office in May 2017; Sebastian Kurz, chancellor of Austria; and Italian prime minister Giuseppe Conte. The boat stands for the EU, but the actions of these politicians seem indecisive and uncoordinated. Their discombobulated appearance makes the viewer wonder whether they take the political emergency seriously and can steer the boat safely through the waves. If one looks closely, another vague human contour is visible in the gap between the politicians. Lan said that she originally included Angela Merkel in the crew but then erased her when she announced in October 2018 that she would step

35 "Confluentes III. Breaking through Boundaries," July 29, 2018 – August 12, 2018, <https://ludwigmuseum.org/en/ausstellungen/confluentes-iii-breaking-through-boundaries/>; "Festival Confluentes: Wenn der Kaiser zum Kunstobjekt wird," *Rhein-Zeitung*, July 25, 2018, <https://www.rhein-zeitung.de/lokales/koblenz-region/festival-confluentes-wenn-der-kaiser-zum-kunstobjekt-wird_arid-1847080.html>.

36 "Fluxus," *The Art Story*, <https://www.theartstory.org/movement/fluxus/>.

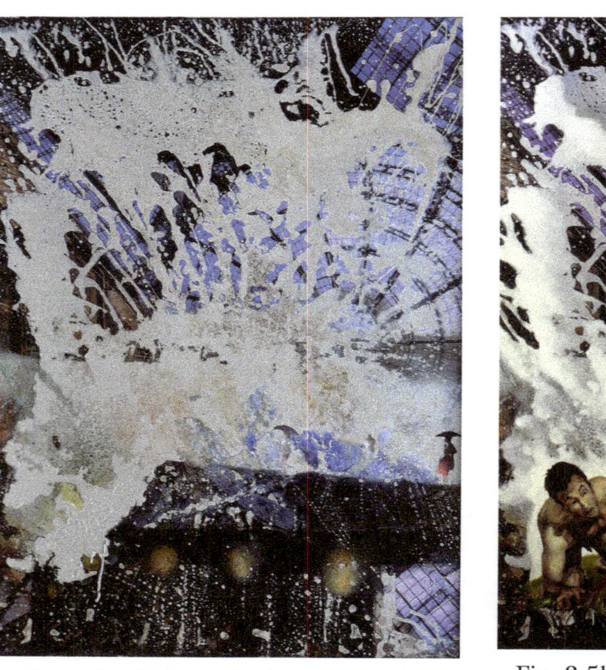

Fig. 8.5a. *Value-Added Movement 6A* (2013, 200 × 140 cm).

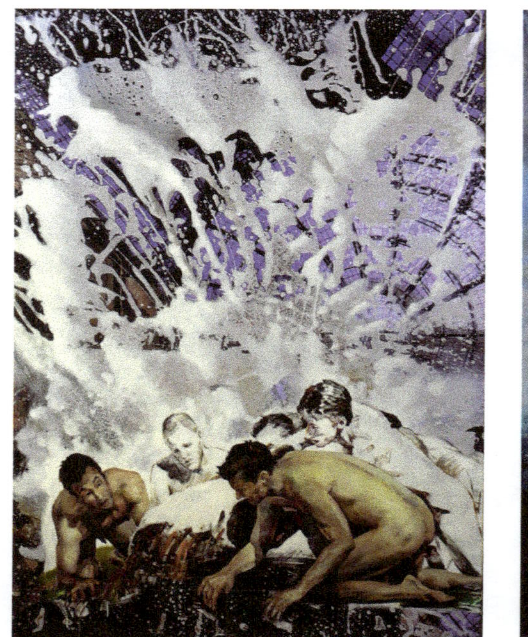

Fig. 8.5b. *The Wiseman Is Fond of Water and the Merciful Man Is Fond of Mountains* (2013, 200 × 140 cm).

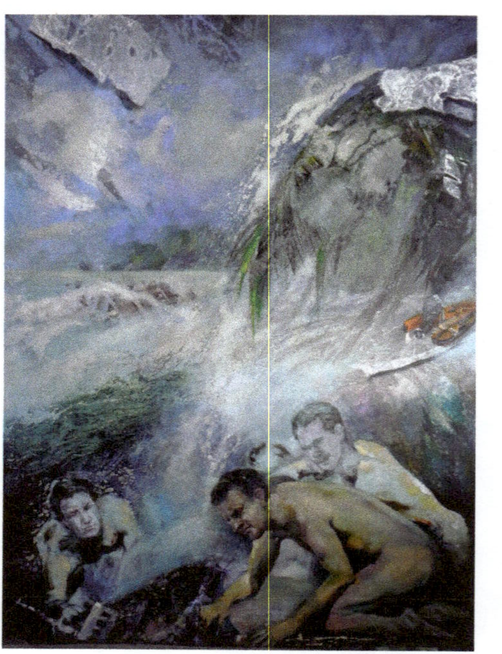

Fig. 8.5c. *New Fellowship* (2018, 200 × 140 cm).

down as CDU party leader after completing her term. Lan left the spot open, inviting viewers to put themselves in Merkel's shoes and ask themselves what policies they would pursue if they were in a "new fellowship" with the other three European politicians. In this way, *New Fellowship* became an interesting thought experiment and an example of the active, democratic art of inclusion.

The poses of the politicians are derived from an earlier diorama-like painting in the versioning to which *New Fellowship* belongs, *The Wiseman Is Fond of Water and the Merciful Man Is Fond of Mountains* (2013, Fig. 8.5b). The title is a literal translation of an aphorism from Confucius's *Analects*, "The virtuous love mountains and the wise love waters" (*Renzhe yao shan*, *zhizhe yao shui*). Instead of relishing serene scenes of mountains and rivers, several naked male figures at the bottom crawl about looking for something. A flood is about to overtake them. This painting warns mankind of the ecological consequences of focusing on one's own interests. But it offers an ironic reading of Confucius's saying, because these men are neither wise nor virtuous but short-sighted. This 2013 painting prefigures the environmental theme that Lan would return to in 2018, for example, in *Folk Audacity* (2018) and *Rauchverbot* (The Smoking Ban, 2019). She often draws on ancient Chinese proverbs to shed light on contemporary concerns.

Tauriform Destiny: Pandemic Art on Authoritarianism and the Future of Europe

China's public image hit rock bottom in 2020, in the midst of the pandemic. The Chinese government's initial handling of the coronavirus outbreak in Wuhan led to an international outcry against the CCP's authoritarianism and lack of freedom of press and speech.[37] During the Covid-19 lockdown in Germany in late 2020, Lan created *Tauriform Destiny* (Fig. 8.6, 2020), a colorful but unsettling abstract painting with thickly applied paint and some figurative elements. This painting explores the fate of Europe as well as Sino-European relations in the wake of the pandemic. It was the titular work in Lan's exhibition in Riegel am Kaiserstuhl, held from August 30 to October 14, 2020.[38] Its chaotic composition reflects the artist's raw emotions about the pandemic that broke out in her native country and later engulfed the world. Lan explained:

> The root of the pandemic is the totalitarian regime that silenced doctors, banned the media from reporting the truth, and only belatedly

37 See Fang, *Wuhan Diary*.

38 "Mal humorvoll, mal provokant, immer kritisch"; Haberer, "Angedeutete Klarheit."

> allowed international experts to investigate the lab a year later; if the outbreak had started in a democratic country, that government would have immediately opened the lab and cooperated with the investigation. The pandemic won't be the end. In the future, the AI developed by a totalitarian regime may endanger the world again.

In the upper left corner of *Tauriform Destiny*, a man is mounted on a creature that wears the beaked mask used by Venetian plague doctors during the Black Death to protect themselves from airborne diseases. This rider calls to mind the Four Horsemen of the Apocalypse from the Bible. The first of the biblical riders is associated with pestilence and plague, an allusion that befits a painting about the Covid-19 pandemic. The placement of this rider in the upper left corner indicates how the pandemic dominated the whole world at the time.

In the upper right quadrant, the ominous image of the bald old man with a bull on his head, his eyes shut and his mouth open, can be interpreted as another allegorical figure representing the pandemic. He is a ghostly giant, a terrifying figure out of Goya's imagination, like the giant in *The Colossus* (ca. 1808–12) or Saturn in *Saturn Devouring His Son* (1819–23). He could also embody the Chinese authoritarian regime. Lan identified the profile below the giant as that of George Washington on Mount Rushmore. The giant towers over Washington, yet at the same time he seems to be in agony, opening his mouth to gasp for air, as if a victim of the coronavirus. Ambiguous symbolism is a hallmark of Lan's work.

Atop the bald giant stands a black bull carrying a naked woman – a reenactment of the Greek myth of the abduction of the beautiful maiden Europa by Zeus, disguised as a white bull, as depicted by Titian in *The Rape of Europa* (ca. 1560–62). The bull – Taurus in the classical Western zodiac – indicates that *Tauriform Destiny* addresses the future of Europe, or the EU, as underscored by the EU Parliament building at the left edge of the painting. The abduction scene is mirrored in the center of the painting, where a brown bull carries a woman off in the opposite direction. In Lan's world, a brown bull is a Chinese bull, typically seen in the Chinese countryside, and in fact the painting was created near the beginning of 2021, the year of the bull in the Chinese zodiac. The woman riding the Chinese bull has black hair and looks Chinese. Thus, *Tauriform Destiny* concerns not only the future of the EU, but also the future of China and Sino-European relations.

According to Lan, the woman on the giant's bulging chest is the Russian empress Catherine the Great, and she is stabbing him with a knife while he screams in pain. Details such as this are difficult to discern without help from the artist herself. This frustrates her critics and viewers. But once these features are revealed, new meanings emerge. Catherine the

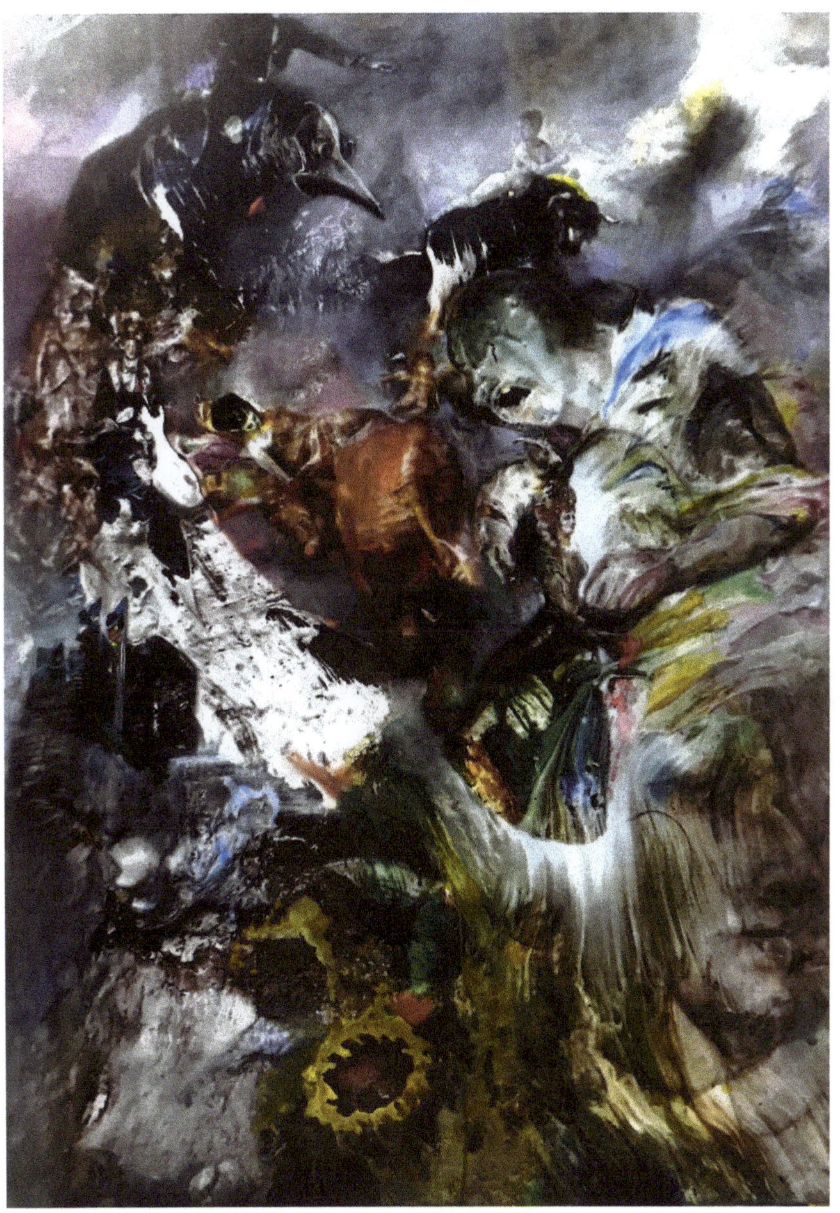

Fig. 8.6. *Tauriform Destiny* (2020, 140 × 100 cm).

Great overthrew her husband Peter III and became the ruler of Russia. Compared to the Empress Dowager Cixi, who is obscurely depicted underneath the rider, Catherine the Great was receptive to Enlightenment ideals. Raised as a princess in Germany, she began to westernize Russia after she became empress. Perhaps Lan whimsically equipped her with a knife to jab at anti-Enlightenment and anti-Western forces, represented by the bald old man. Next to Catherine the Great, Lan depicted a goat, which she associates with the Jewish Russian-French artist Marc Chagall, who featured goats in his art. In 1923, Chagall turned his back on Communist Russia and left for Paris; during the Second World War, he fled occupied France for New York. Thus, Lan's pastiche of Chagall is charged with personal associations and parallels: rejecting Communism and National Socialism, living in exile, and finding a *Heimat* in art.

Tauriform Destiny started with a photo of leftover paint on a palette, which was then printed on canvas. The shapeless and uneven palette bequeathed to the canvas an amorphous background with anarchic colors. Sunflowers represent the Chinese people in Cultural Revolution posters, yet the lone sunflower at the bottom of the painting is bent and withering. The reduction of a field of blooming flowerheads to a single ailing survivor turns a symbol of mass submission to the will of the leader in Chinese political iconography into an emblem of passive resistance. Lan's collage style and use of recondite symbolism enabled her to compose a painting filled with miscellaneous figures and objects that appear to be unrelated. When examined closely, however, *Tauriform Destiny* is a critical artistic representation of the Covid-19 pandemic from the unique point of view of a Chinese German artist.

The Scream (2021): Deterritorialized

The pale and anguished screamer in *Tauriform Destiny* reappears prominently in another painting about Sino-EU relations, *Der Schrei* (The Scream, Fig. 8.7), which Lan created in March 2021 during a three-month artist residency at the Künstlerhaus on Schwanenwerder.[39] At the time, a diplomatic crisis was unfolding over China's treatment of the Uyghur Muslim minority in Xinjiang, shortly after the signing of the long-awaited EU-China Comprehensive Agreement on Investment (CAI) on December 30, 2020.[40] On March 22, 2021, the EU agreed

39 The stipend (February to April 2021) was granted by the Cordts Art Foundation; see <http://www.women-artists-in-residence.berlin/en/women_artists.htm>.

40 Philip Blenkinsop, "EU Agrees Investment Deal with China to Rebalance Ties," *Reuters*, December 30, 2020, <https://www.reuters.com/world/china/eu-agrees-investment-deal-with-china-rebalance-ties-2020-12-30/>.

to sanction a list of Chinese officials in Xinjiang, as well as the Xinjiang Production and Construction Corps Public Security Bureau, for human rights abuses. These sanctions were highly symbolic, as they were the first to be imposed by the EU on China since the military crackdown on the pro-democracy movement at Tiananmen in 1989.[41] This was a tough decision for the EU to make because China is the EU's largest trading partner. China immediately countered with sanctions against EU entities and personnel.[42] Finally, on May 20, 2021, the EU Parliament voted to freeze the ratification of the China-EU trade agreement.

At first glance, the dark, abstract, cluttered painting overwhelms and confuses the viewer. But a handful of clearly discernible icons, such as Ursula von der Leyen on the right edge and the yellow umbrellas on the left edge, signal the political dimension of the artwork. Von der Leyen, the CDU politician and president of the European Commission, is portrayed sitting on a brown bull, which, as in *Tauriform Destiny*, represents China. The horns of a beast represent its power and strength, but this bull has only one horn, suggesting that it has lost some of its potency. Von der Leyen holds a laptop computer, in German a *Rechner*. Lan always likes to play with words, and here she capitalizes on the double meaning of *rechnen* as numerical computation and strategic calculation. In the intricate and complex relationship between the EU and China, von der Leyen must weigh multiple factors to balance universal values and economic interests.

China is not conspicuously represented in this painting by a symbol like Tiananmen. Nevertheless, a closer look reveals numerous references to the nation. Near the center is a camera labeled with four tiny Chinese characters that mean "Made in China." The camera could stand for China's ubiquitous surveillance operations and heavy-handed political control. Systemic difference is the political hurdle the EU faces in its relations with China. London's Tower Bridge and the Hong Kong World Trade Center, positioned above and below the camera, are two signature structures that hint at the historical and contemporary connections between Hong Kong and Great Britain. In 1997, China agreed to the Sino-British Joint Declaration, which ended British colonial rule over Hong Kong and returned sovereignty back to China. Hong Kong's status as a special administrative region was established for fifty years. However,

41 Sabine Siebold, "We Will not Back Down under Sanctions, China Warns EU," *Reuters,* March 16, 2021, <https://www.reuters.com/article/world/we-will-not-back-down-under-sanctions-china-warns-eu-idUSKBN2B8117/>.

42 "Foreign Ministry Spokesperson Announces Sanctions on Relevant EU Entities and Personnel," Ministry of Foreign Affairs of People's Republic of China, March 22, 2021, <https://www.mfa.gov.cn/eng/xw/fyrbt/fyrbt/202405/t20240530_11349690.html>.

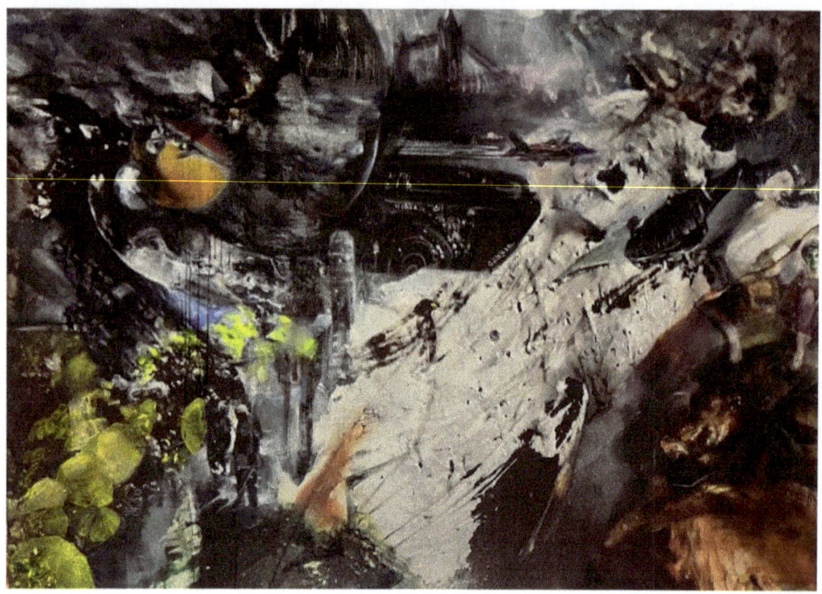

Fig. 8.7. *The Scream* (2021, 100 × 140 cm).

the new National Security Law has undermined the principle of "one country, two systems" that was used to articulate Hong Kong's relationship to Mainland China.

The title of Lan's composition nods to Edvard Munch's famous painting *The Scream* (1893). At the center is an all-white figure, lying back and gasping. Lan's screamer seems to convey the widespread anxiety and distress caused by the pandemic, as well as frustration with China's authoritarianism. "The Scream" is also the literal translation of *Call to Arms* (*Na han*, 1922), the title of a collection of short stories by Lu Xun, known as China's Gorky. His short stories deal with feudalism in Old China, social conflicts, fears for the survival of the Chinese nation, and a strong hope for social change. Lu Xun began his literary career after a life-changing experience. When he was a medical student in Japan, he saw a Japanese propaganda film that showed a Chinese man who was about to be beheaded by the Japanese because he was suspected of spying for the Russians during the Russo-Japanese War (1904–5). The apathy of the Chinese onlookers in the film deeply affected Lu Xun and instilled in him the urgency to awaken the national spirit through *Call to Arms.*[43] Lan's painting was included in her 2021 exhibition *Found in Translation.*

43 Lu Xun, "Preface to *Call to Arms*," in *Selected Stories of Lu Hsun* (Peking: Foreign Languages Press, 1960, 1972), <https://www.marxists.org/archive/lu-xun/1922/12/03.htm>.

However, her scream, being deterritorialized, largely falls on deaf ears, since the audience she needs to reach, that is, Chinese viewers, cannot see her painting.

Coda: Most Western Countries are Absent from the Xi Court

Using art to enter the discourse of fraught Sino-EU relations comes naturally to Lan. As a politically aware artist who relocated from China to Germany, she uses Eurasian symbols such as the Silk Road and Buddhalisa to highlight the cultural hybridity that characterizes her artistic identity. The revival of the ancient trope of the Silk Road through Xi's BRI project elicited several responses from Lan. Her participation in the first BRI Cultural Expo in Dunhuang inspired *The Empty City Strategy*, *Message in Art*, *Jinyology – Silk Road*, and *Alternative Fiction*. In retrospect, the BRI's success has been limited. Journalist Philipp Mattheis goes so far as to describe the New Silk Road as a "lose-lose situation."[44] Wang Yiwei, professor of diplomacy at the People's University in Beijing, stated: "China no longer has that much money, the domestic growth is slowing down, local governments are heavily indebted, so the focus of the New Silk Road at the moment is not on large-scale construction projects to build infrastructure."[45] A study by the Institute for World Economy in Kiel shows that 60 percent of all Chinese foreign loans are at risk of default.[46]

Together with events in Xinjiang and Hong Kong, the pandemic has further tarnished the positive image that the Chinese government has been trying to rebuild since 1989. The decline of China's soft power is the greatest dilemma facing China and EU-China relations. With the BRI, the Xi regime seeks to connect the country with the world by constructing a network where "all roads lead to Beijing," reviving the past dynamic of "all nations coming to court." Since the pandemic, however, the political discourse around China in Europe and the US has shifted to "de-risking" or even "decoupling." When Xi hosted the third BRI summit in 2023, ten years after it was first promoted, over 130 countries sent representatives to the two-day meeting, but the only EU leader who

44 Philipp Mattheis, *Die dreckige Seidenstraße: Wie Chinas Wirtschaftspolitik weltweit Staaten und Demokratien untergräbt* (Munich: Goldmann Verlag, 2023), 12.

45 Cited from Elisabeth Pongratz, Eva Lamby-Schmitt, and Jennifer Johnston, "Zehn Jahre Neue Seidenstraße: Verblasst der Mythos?," *Deutschlandfunk*, September 14, 2023, <https://www.deutschlandfunk.de/neue-seidenstrasse-verblasst-mythos-100.html>.

46 Pongratz, "Zehn Jahre Neue Seidenstraße: Verblasst der Mythos?"

came was the Hungarian populist leader Viktor Orbán. The majority of Western nations declined to pay their respects to the Xi court. Since the bull in Lan's work refers not only to Europe but also to China, "tauriform destiny" can be read as the future for Europe and for Sino-European relations. What is the tauriform destiny? We wait for the future to tell us.

Coda: Deterritorialized and Reterritorialized Messaging: Émigré and Immigrant Art

As a "self-glorifying" visual and conceptual artist of Chinese background, Jiny Lan is unique on the German art scene. 2012, the year of the first Bald Girls exhibit in China, marked a significant milestone in her career, but also a point of departure. The paintings she prepared for the exhibit played on Maoist visual tropes in the tradition of Chinese Pop art, but one of her paintings – in which she boldly inserted herself in the place of Mao – was censored. In the following year, to publicize her *One-Persons-Chorus* exhibit in Düsseldorf, she mounted a vigorous advertising campaign that featured the censored painting, but German viewers did not react to its political content as she had hoped. In the wake of this disappointment, Lan abandoned the Pop idiom and adopted not only a new visual style but also a new mode of production based on the reproduction and overpainting of her own paintings.

Lan named this mode of production after herself – Jinyology – and she has framed it as a response to Confucian patriarchy and its exclusion of women from genealogical lines of descent. In the Pictures Republic of Jiny, Lan is the creator of several lines of daughter paintings that are all descended from an original pair of progenitors, paintings that Lan christened *Adam* and *Eve*. These canvas forebearers are modeled on the transparent roof of the Milan Galleria, and its iron and glass latticework peeks through the overpainted surfaces of many of the daughter paintings. Although the ideological seed of Jinyology came from China, due to the Western nature of the Adam/Eve paintings, every Jinyology painting is painted, so to speak, on a European substrate.

Thus, there is a fundamental geographic and cultural hybridity that undergirds Lan's visual art. It is apparent in Lan's choice of the orange – the "Chinese apple" (*Apfelsine*) – as a symbol of feminism, in her cloaking of Markus Lüpertz in a Chinese costume, in her portrait of Angela Merkel as a counterpart of the Empress Dowager Cixi, and in her invention of Buddhalisa. Lan's visual art can be characterized as Chinese-German, which is meant to include both her China-facing art and Germany-facing art, as well as her Eurasian art, with its fluid borderline between Europe and Asia. This identitarian frame invites some comparisons, especially regarding China versus Germany. Comparing Lan's feminist art on Chinese themes versus German themes shows a stark difference: the Chinese-oriented feminist work discussed in this book mainly addresses her personal traumatic past and the nation's reproductive policy, whereas the German-oriented feminist work mainly concerns individual authority and sexism in the art world. Comparing Lan's political art on China versus Germany likewise shows clear differences: her critical political art targets China as a patriarchal and authoritarian state but valorizes German democracy and freedom of expression, singling out individual politicians for praise or censure. Her criticism of German policy seems to be limited to questions surrounding migration.

Oftentimes, Lan's own perception of her hybrid identity informs her art. In *Portrait with a Bat* (2010, Fig. 3.5a), she included a bat – a flying mammal – as a figure she identified with because as an immigrant she found herself in a liminal category. As befitting a naturalized Chinese-German artist, her artworks show a distinct East-West transcultural hybridity. The language and culture of China have inspired and enriched her creations. Some paintings are adorned with random Chinese texts she copied from a Chinese almanac, and some literally illustrate Chinese idioms and proverbs, such as "rooster's head and phoenix's tail" (*ji tou feng wei*, Fig. 5.1a), echoing the tradition of Renaissance proverb painting elaborated in Pieter Bruegel the Elder's *Netherlandish Proverbs* (1559).[1] Her use of ideogrammatic characters to ornament or structure paintings allows her to maintain a linguistic, cultural, and affective tie to her native tongue. To Western viewers, the Chinese elements may appear ornamental or self-exoticizing or self-orientalizing. But once deciphered, they contribute to the narrative and messaging of the painting.

Because of Lan's status as an émigré and immigrant, her work opens up possibilities for discussing modern Chinese history, contemporary Chinese and German society and politics, Chinese avant-garde art and Political Pop, modern art in the West, the Chinese diasporic community in Germany, and artistic influences and exchanges between China and the West. But to what extent her criticism of China is subversive or effective must remain an open question, given her location in Germany. The lack of interest of German viewers in the "subversive" *One-Persons-Chorus* advertising campaign is a case in point. The obstacle faced by Lan is the severe censorship in China. This book has discussed three of her projects that have been censored and has mentioned many other cases of censorship, such as the Tian Mingjian Incident, the cases of Mu Zimei and Ai Weiwei, the book *Nation of Giant Infants*, and posts about Covid and the chained woman. If Lan were in China, the political art she passionately

1 For an in-depth study of this tradition, see Walter S. Gibson, *Figures of Speech: Picturing Proverbs in Renaissance Netherlands* (Berkeley: University of California Press, 2010).

pursues would not be possible. Nevertheless, as a diasporic artist, she has the opportunity to change the minds of Chinese outside the Mainland. The political and ideological positionalities of Chinese in the West are diverse, and Lan's demand for democracy, the rule of law, and human rights in China is not universally shared among the diaspora.

When thinking of Lan's status as a Chinese émigré artist it is useful to compare her to her fellow Bald Girl Li Xinmo. Li is the only member of the collective operating in China. Her performances thematize women's victimization and involve strong emotion and affect, but they refrain from articulating the social and political roots of negative emotions. Li's art is symptomatic of contemporary Chinese art within China: artists may at best describe or indicate problems but cannot name their causes, let alone challenge the status quo. Lan's China-facing "hand" paintings (Figs. 1.5; 8.2b) resemble the native Chinese art that deals with negative emotions and painful personal experiences without articulating their political and structural roots. The *Red Sun, Black Moon* project and the Tiananmen paintings were her political coming-out, something out of reach for artists embedded within China. Thus, after a decade, the Bald Girls redefined themselves as Bald Girls 2.0, recognizing that the problem women (artists) in China face is not necessarily the lack of female subjectivity, but the lack of political subjectivity or agency.

The Bald Girls appropriated the term "timelag" to highlight the different temporalities of women's rights and human rights in the West and in China (chapter 3). The notion, commonplace in the West, that gender is a social construct is not a keystone of their platform. Rather, their China-facing feminist critique focuses on national reproductive policies, sexist conventions, and sexual violence. Although the violation of women's human rights is a global issue, the Bald Girls showed how that issue manifests itself differently in China than in the West. The captivity of the chained woman is a case in point. Her exploitation became a national scandal before the government could suppress her story, but the majority of similar cases go unnoticed and unreported due to censorship by the state.

The collective projects of the Bald Girls are mainly comprised of performances and installations. Performances and installations are public-facing participatory art aligned with the Fluxus movement and Beuys's concept of social sculpture and seemingly offer a more direct and more comprehensible way to convey messages. Yet the majority of Lan's solo artwork takes the form of painting, an old trade she is skilled in. Painting obtains additional significance as a consciously feminist, anti-authoritarian practice for Lan, who challenges Baselitz's claim that "Women do not paint so well." Below I will summarize some important aspects of Lan's painting while mapping out some questions for potential further inquiries, especially by placing her art in relation to space, power, corporality, and sex.

A reoccurring feature in her paintings is the configuration of space, which shows the artist's fascination with architecture, particularly in the West. Her architectural subjects are drawn from a wide range of geographical spaces, from New York to Hong Kong and from Dunhuang to Milan. The roof of the Milan Galleria is the germ of Jinyology. Subway stations and transit lines in New York figure in her early nomadic art as concrete symbols of mobility, a role played in her later Eurasian art by the Silk Road. Her citation of iconic political monuments such as Tiananmen aligns her with other Chinese avant-garde and Political Pop artists who use potent symbols of oppressive forces to target "a totalized society with its tradition and ideology."[2] She also juxtaposes Tiananmen with the Bundestag to contrast political opaqueness and transparency. Church buildings from Italy, Spain, Switzerland, and France are works of art in their own right but also represent conservative moral institutions that pass judgment on sexuality that does not serve reproductive purposes.

Portraiture is a major genre in Lan's figurative painting. Since a young age, she has been drawing or painting human subjects, including Lei Feng, Marx, Engels, and Mao, as well as strangers on the street. As a professional artist, she gradually specialized in painting *portraits of power*. She has depicted many public figures, such as Pope Francis, Xi Jinping, Sebastian Kurz, Donald Trump, Vladimir Putin, Liu Xiaobo, Uli Sigg, and Bruno Latour. Figural and architectural representations sometimes merge, as when Xi's magnified body fills the Sagrada Família Basilica. The subjects of her work mostly involve well-established, influential, authoritative, or newsworthy figures, be they politicians, male artists, art critics, or celebrities. The anonymous figures she paints tend to be "pretty women." Her portraits of establishment figures are clever self-promotion tactics and have contributed to her establishment as a successful artist in Germany. In 2022 she was invited to join the German feminist initiative Frauen100,[3] and in the following year she, along with twelve other prominent Düsseldorfers, was included in Kiki Kausch's photographic pastiche of da Vinci's *Last Supper*.[4]

Another prominent aspect of her portraits and self-portraits is nudity. Although depicting nudity was no longer a taboo in China during her

2 Gao, *Total Modernity*, 138.

3 "Frauen100: Moderner Feminismus," Frauen100, <https://www.frauen100.com/>.

4 "Inszenierung mit Prominenten: Kiki Kausch zeigt Düsseldorfer Abendmahl," *Rheinische Post*, June 21, 2023, <https://rp-online.de/nrw/staedte/duesseldorf/kultur/ausstellung-kiki-kausch-zeigt-duesseldorfer-abendmahl_aid-92519135>.

time, the representation of male nudity by a female artist is still a provocative gesture. It is part of her feminist program to counteract the predominance of female nudity in the history of art. Lan quipped: "If I paint figures naked, I do not have to worry about what clothes they wear"; but when politicians like Xi, Macron, Schröder, Kurz, or male artists like Beuys, Baselitz, Polke, and Kiefer appear unclothed in her paintings, they are often feminized and sometimes placed in humiliating poses. Nudity intensifies sexual dynamics and enhances the anti-authoritarian bent of Lan's work. Yet it may also communicate equality, as in the anti-racist performance she did with the Fluxus artist Benjamin Patterson, which ended with both artists shedding their paint-spattered raincoats to show their common humanity.

Although appropriation and pastiche are common practices in modern art, they constitute another important dimension of Lan's work, an inheritance from Narrative Figuration and Chinese Pop art. A most recent example is her reversal of Beuys's dictum "Kunst = Kapital" (Art = Capital, 1984), printed on a poster soliciting donations for the Jiny Lan Art foundation. For Beuys, the creative potential of a person is their capital: "Everyone is an artist," he claimed. Resisting the idea that capital was essentially monetary, Beuys redefined it as human creativity and potential. But Lan performed a verbal inversion, turning Beuys's catchphrase into the slogan "Kapital ist auch Kunst" (Capital = Art, 2025). As a deterritorialized artist, she has been able to reterritorialize and achieve institutional recognition in Germany. The fact that the city of Düsseldorf now administers an art foundation in her name is one measure of her success.

Appendix: Hanzi Equivalents for Words and Phrases Given in Pinyin

(Pinyin terms are listed first unless they have been omitted in the main text because of length; in such cases not pinyin but English is given first here.)

Titles of Lan's Works

(Not a complete list: only the Chinese titles that the author is aware of are included, and not all of Lan's works have Chinese titles.)

A, ti si ta 啊, 踢死他: *Ah, kick him to death* (2011)
Behind the Mountain There Is Another Mountain, Behind the Heaven There Is Another Heaven: 山外有山, 天外有天 (2013)
Tutou genü 秃头戈女: *Bald Girls*
Cainü youyan 才女油盐: *Bald Girls – Talented Girls in Oil and Salt* (2014)
Chen 尘: *Dirt* (2011)
Collective Efforts – Red Sun, Black Moon: 集体作业 – 红太阳 / 黑月亮 (2012)
Di qi jie 第七戒: *The Seventh Commandment* (2015)
Hongse niepan 红色涅槃: *Red Nirvana* (2016)
Hongwei lantu 宏伟蓝图: *Grand Blueprint* (2021)
Hua guo shan 花果山: *Kingdom of Flowers and Fruits* (2014)
Jiang shan huo shui 江山祸水: *River- and Mountain Destroyer* (2018)
Kong cheng ji 空城计 [记]: *The Empty City Strategy* (2016)
Pi fu zhi jian 匹妇之谏: *A Modest Proposal* (2014)
Puxijin feng bao 普希金风暴: *Pushkin Storm* (2022)
Qian nian qian xun 千年谦逊: *A Thousand Years of Humility* (2020)
Qixi zhi qi 七夕之凄: *The Tragedy of the Qixi Festival* (2014)
Renzhe yao shan, zhizhe yao shui 仁者乐山, 智者乐水: *The Virtuous Love Mountains and the Wise Love Waters* (2013)
sheng 圣: *Emperor* (2023)
Shi zhe sheng cun 适者生存: *Survival of the Fittest* (2014)
Sui bo liu shi 随波流逝: *Gone with the Wave* (2017)
Tian wen 天问: *Question Heaven* (2023)
Wu yue di guo 五月媂国: *Fempire de Mai / The May Female-Empire* (2016)
Xuexi Leifeng hao bangyang 学习雷锋好榜样: *Learning from Lei Feng's Good Example*
Xun 殉: *Martyr* (2011)
Zhi 旨: *Decree* (2023)

Other Titles

Chairman Mao Is the Red Sun in the Hearts of the People of the World: 毛主席是世界人民心中的红太阳 (1967)

Chairman Mao Is the Reddest, the Reddest, Red Sun in Our Heart: 毛主席是我们心中最红最红的红太阳 (1967)

Dahai hangxing kao duoshou 大海航行靠舵手: "Sailing the Seas Depends on the Helmsman" (1964)

Hongweibing zhandou chengji zhanlan, 红卫兵战斗成绩展览: *The Exhibition of the Accomplishments of the Red Guard's Military Struggles* (1967)

Hua Shang Bao 華商報: *Chinese Trade Newspaper*

Jie Tangwan sanzi: man man man 借唐婉三字: 瞞, 瞞, 瞞: "To Borrow Tang Wan's Three Words: Cover-up, Cover-up, Cover-up" (2020)

Ju ying guo 巨婴国: *Nation of Giant Infants* (2016)

Muqing a muqing 母亲啊母亲: "Mother, oh, Mother" (February 5, 2022)

Na han 呐喊: *Call to Arms* (1922)

Na'nian natu naxie shi'er 那年那兔那些事儿: *Year Hare Affair* (2011)

Ou hua dao bao 欧华导报: *Chinese-European Post*

Respectfully Wish Chairman Mao Eternal Life: 敬祝毛主席万寿无疆 (1968)

Si lu hua yu 丝路花雨: *Rain of Flowers Along the Silk Road* (1979)

Tuidao zhedu qiang 推倒这堵墙: *Tear Down This Wall* (2022)

Wan guo lai chao 万国来朝: *All Nations Coming to Court*

Wu mei niang chuan qi 武媚娘传奇: *The Empress of China* (2014)

Xiao tuzi kuang kuang 小兔子哐哐: *Kuang Kuang the Little Rabbit* (2011)

Yi qing shu 遗情书: *Remains of Love* (2003)

Personal Names

Ai Weiwei 艾未未
Bi Fujian 毕福剑
Chang Daichien 张大千
Chang Tsong-zung 张颂仁
Chen Lingyang 陈羚羊
Cui Xiuwen 崔岫闻
Dong Xiwen 董希文
Dong Yaoqiong 董瑶琼
Fang Lijun 方力钧
Gao Minglu 高名潞
Gao Qiang 高强
Gao Zhen 高兟
Geng Jianyi 耿建翌
He Chengyao 何成瑶
Ho Oscar Hing-Kay 何慶基
Huang Rui 黄锐
Jiang Qing 江青
Lan Jing 蓝镜
Lan Liu'er 蓝六耳
Lei Feng 雷锋
Li Maizi 李麦子
Li Shan 李鳝
Li Xianting 栗宪庭
Li Xinmo 李心沫
Liao Tianqi 廖天琪
Lin Chao 林超
Liu Hung 刘虹
Liu Renjie 刘仁杰
Liu Xiaobo 刘晓波
Liu Yang 刘洋
Lu Decheng 鲁德成
Lu Xun 鲁迅
Luo Weibing 罗卫兵
Luo Weidong 罗卫东
Luo Weiguo 罗卫国
Mu Zimei 木子美
Pan Yuliang 潘玉良
Peng Lifa 彭立发
Qi Zhilong 祁志龙
Qian Yuejun 钱跃君
Qu Yuan 屈原
Shang Yang 尚扬
Song Dong 宋冬
Sun Zixi 孙滋溪
Tian Mingjian 田明建
Wang Bo 王波
Wang Guangyi 王广义
Wang Huangsheng 王璜生
Wang Jinsong 王劲松
Wang Keping 王克平
Wang Xingwei 王兴伟
Wang Yaping 王亚平
Wang Youshen 王友身
Wang Ziwei 王子卫
Wu Zhihong 武志红
Xiang Jing 向京
Xiang Jingyu 向警予
Xiao Feng 肖峰
Xiao Lu 肖鲁
Xiu Haitao 修海涛
Xu Juan 徐娟
Xu Yihui 徐一晖
Yan Geling 严歌苓
Yan Yinhong 严隐鸿
Yang Yiping 杨益平
Yi Ying 易瑛
Yin Zhaoyang 尹朝阳
Yu Dongyue 喻东岳
Yu Hong 喻红
Yu Xingze 于幸泽
Yu Youhan 余友涵
Yu Zhijian 余志坚
Zhang Daqian 张大千
Zhang Xiaogang 张晓刚
Zhang Yi'ne 张逸讷
Zhao Bandi 赵半狄
Zheng Hao 郑好
Zhou Tiehai 周铁海
Zhu Qingsheng 朱青生

Idioms and Proverbs

Bu xiao you san, wu hou wei da 不孝有三, 无后为大: There are three things that make a man not filial, and not having an heir would make him the most unfilial
chaimi youyan 柴米油盐: firewood, rice, oil, and salt
Fubei daxia de jiangshan 父辈打下的江山: the rivers and mountains that our fathers conquered
fengchen nüzi 风尘女子: prostitutes or women of easy virtue
hongyan huoshui 红颜祸水: rouged face, treacherous waters
ji tou feng wie 鸡头凤尾: rooster's head and phoenix's tail
man shan bian ye 漫山遍野: over all the hills and fields
xin xi zuguo 心系祖国: literally, a string binds one's heart to one's country
yishou zhetian 一手遮天: to cover up the sky with one hand

Miscellaneous Other Terms and Phrases

85 *yishu xinchao* 85 艺术新潮: '85 Art New Wave
bai weibing 白卫兵: white guards
Cao ni ma, dang zhongyang 草泥马, 挡中央: Grass-mud horse covering the middle
cao ni ma 草泥马: an animal similar to an alpaca
chongji yishu 冲击艺术: Shock Art
chou gang 臭港: stinky harbor
da bai 大白: big white pandemic workers
Dandong 丹东: a city in Liaoning province
Deguo zhizao, zhongguo pinzhi 德国制造, 中国品质: Made in Germany, Quality of China
er'nai 二奶: mistress
erbatou 二把头: two handfuls of hair
guan erdai 官二代: princeling
guan nian 观念艺术: conceptual art
guohua 国画: Chinese traditional ink paintings
hei jiu lei 黑九类: Nine Black Categories
hei wu lei 黑五类: Five Black Categories
hong wu lei 红五类: Five Red Categories
hongse bopu 红色波普: red pop
jiang shan 江山: country
lingxiu 领袖: literally "collar and sleeves" and metonymically "the supreme leader"
Mao zhuxi wansui 毛主席万岁: Long Live Chairman Mao
Meige tuzi douyou yige daguo meng 每个兔子都有一个大国梦: Every hare has a dream of China becoming a powerful country
mo hei 抹黑: to blacken or black out something

pidou hui 批斗会: struggle session
po mo 破墨: broken-ink
pocai 泼彩: splashing colors
qiao 桥: bridge
qu le 取乐: to taunt
quan guocheng minzhu 全过程民主: whole-process people's democracy
taikong 太空: outer space
tang ping 躺平: lying flat
Tielian nü 铁链女: the "chained woman"
wang shi 王氏: surname Wang
Wen cangmang dadi, shei zhu chenfu 问苍茫大地, 谁主沉浮?: I ask the huge greenblue earth, / Who is master of nature?
xia zhong nong 下中农: slightly wealthier peasants
Xiang gang 香港: Hong Kong
xingwei yishu 行为艺术: Performing Art
xin xi zuguo 心系祖国: literally, a string binds one's heart to one's country
xiuke yishu 休克艺术: Shock Art
Xiuyan Manchu Autonomous County: 岫岩满族自治县
zi zhong 自重: self-respect
zu pu 族谱: family genealogy book

Selected Bibliography

(All sources are cited in the footnotes.)

Ai Weiwei. "Ai Weiwei's 81-Day Detention." In *Ai Weiwei: Disposition*, edited by Maurizio Bortolotti and Ossian Ward, 98–109. London: Koenig Books, 2014.

Ameline, Jean-Paul. "Figures and Fictions: The Contribution of Narrative Figuration to the Figurative Revival of the 1960s in Europe." In *The Narrative Figuration*, ed. Ameline, 10–21.

———, ed. *The Narrative Figuration*. Milan: 5 Continents Editions, 2017.

Andrews, Julia Frances. *Painters and Politics in the People's Republic of China, 1949–1979*. Berkeley: University of California Press, 1994.

Arasse, Daniel. *Anselm Kiefer*. New York: Harry N. Abrams, 2001.

Audretsch, Francesca Romana. "Künstlerin Jiny Lan: Spiegelbilder für selbstherrliche Malerfürsten." *Monopol: Magazin für Kunst und Leben*. June 14, 2019.

Beckmann, Lukas. "The Causes in the Future." Translated by S. Linberg and R. Brenner. In *Joseph Beuys: Mapping the Legacy*, ed. Ray, 91–111.

Beyer, Susanne, and Ulrike Knöfel. "Meine Bilder sind Schlachten." *Der Spiegel* 4/2013. January 20, 2013.

Boczar, Amber. "The Power of Creativity: How Web-Based Parody Encourages Chinese Civil Participation." *International ResearchScape Journal* 3 (2015), Article 1.

Buchhart, Dieter, Elsy Lahner, and Klaus Albrecht Schröder. *Ai Weiwei: In Search of Humanity*. Munich: Hirmer Verlag, 2022.

Buchloh, Benjamin. "Beuys: The Twilight of the Idol." In *Joseph Beuys: The Reader*, ed. Mesch and Michely, 109–26.

Bürger, Peter. *Theory of the Avant-Garde*. Minneapolis: University of Minnesota Press, 1984.

Büsing, Nicole, and Heiko Klaas. "Jiny Lan." In *Portfolio – Genealogies*, 28–31.

Butcher, Megan. "Fluxus: The Significant Role of Female Artists." Honors diss., Pace University, 2018.

Calvocoressi, Richard. "A Source for the Inverted Imagery in Georg Baselitz's Painting." *The Burlington Magazine* 127, no. 993 (1985): 894–9.

Chang, Felix K. "Legacy of Ostpolitik: Germany's Russia Policy and Energy Security." Foreign Policy Research Institute E-Notes. May 8, 2014.

Chang, Jung. *The Concubine Who Launched Modern China: Empress Dowager Cixi*. New York: Alfred A. Knopf, 2013.

Chang, Tsong-zung, ed. *China's New Art Post-1989: with a Retrospective from 1979–1989*. Hong Kong: Hanart T Z Gallery, 1993.

———. "Into the Nineties." In *China's New Art Post-1989*, ed. Chang, i–vii.

Christopher, Rachel. "The 4 Japanese Female Artists Who Changed the Game." *Japan Nakama*, February 13, 2014.

Conrad, Maximilian. "From the Eurozone Debt Crisis to the Alternative for Germany." *Frontiers in Political Science* 2, no. 4 (2020).

Cowart, Jack. "Expressions." In *Expressions: New Art from Germany: Georg Baselitz, Jörg Immendorff, Anselm Kiefer, Markus Lüpertz, A. R. Penck*, edited by Jack Cowart and Siegfried Gohr, 9–25. Munich: Prestel-Verlag in association with the Saint Louis Art Museum, 1983.

Cui, Shuqin. *Gendered Bodies: Toward a Women's Visual Art in Contemporary China*. Honolulu: University of Hawai'i Press, 2015.

Danto, Arthur C. *Andy Warhol*. New Haven, CT: Yale University Press, 2009.

Degler, Eva, and Thomas Liebig, "Finding their Way: Labour Market Integration of Refugees in Germany," OECD (Organization for Economic Co-operation and Development). March 2017.

Dollar, David. "Understanding China's Belt and Road Infrastructure Projects in Africa." Brookings, September 2019.

Eberhard, Wolfram. *Typen chinesischer Volksmärchen*. Helsinki: Academia Scientiarum Fennica, 1937.

Echols, Alice. *Daring to be BAD: Radical Feminism in America, 1967–1975*. Minneapolis: University of Minnesota Press, 1989.

El, Eugen. "Und ob Frauen malen können." *Schirn Magazin*. June 9, 2016.

Faison, Seth. "The Changing Role of the Media." In *Chinese People's Movement*, ed. Saich, 145–63.

Fang, Fang. *Wuhan Diary: Dispatches from a Quarantined City*. Translated by Michael Berry. New York: HarperVia, 2020.

Farnsworth, Beatrice. *Aleksandra Kollontai: Socialism, Feminism, and the Bolshevik Revolution* Stanford, CA: Stanford University Press, 1980.

Frank, Patrick. *Painting in a State of Exception: New Figuration in Argentina, 1960–1965*. Gainesville: University of Florida Press, 2016.

Frevert, Ute. *Women in German History: From Bourgeois Emancipation to Sexual Liberation*. Oxford: Berg, 1989.

Gao, Minglu. *Total Modernity and the Avant-Garde in Twentieth-Century Chinese Art*. Cambridge, MA: MIT Press, 2011.

Gardner, Belinda Grace. "Multidimensionale Um- und Neudeutungen von Jiny Lan: 'Jinyology.'" *ARTMAPP* 28 (Winter 2021/22): 28–30.

Gauthier, Michel. "The Ambivalence of Images: Notes on Pop Figuration." In *The Narrative Figuration*, ed. Ameline, 24–31.

Gehrig, Sebastian, Barbara Mittler, and Felix Wemheuer, eds. *Kulturrevolution als Vorbild?: Maoismen im deutschsprachigen Raum*. Frankfurt am Main: Peter Lang, 2008.

Gerding, Volker. "'Freiheit' als zentraler Begriff ihrer Kunst: Wenn schon das Malen von 'Pu der Bär' gefährlich ist / Die chinesische Künstlerin Jiny Lan zu Gast im Rosenhang Museum." *Mittelhessen*, August 10, 2023.

Graber, Lauren, and Daniel Spaulding. "The Red Flag: The Art and Politics of West German Maoism." In *Art, Global Maoism and the Chinese Cultural Revolution*, edited by Jacopo Galimberti et al., 109–27. Manchester: Manchester University Press, 2019.

Greenhalgh, Susan. "The Biopolitics of the Three-Child Policy." *Made in China Journal* 9, no. 1 (2024).

Guest, Luise. "'Space Invaders': Discourses of Gender in Contemporary Chinese Art." In *Stepping Out!*, ed. Ohlsen and Sadowsky, 27–31.

Guo, Ariana. "Introduction to the Beginning of Contemporary Chinese Art: 1979–1989." Hua Gallery, August 3, 2019.

Ho, Oscar Hing-Kay. "1989 and New Art Post-1989." In *China's New Art Post-1989*, ed. Chang, viii–ix.

Huyssen, Andreas. "Anselm Kiefer: The Terror of History, the Temptation of Myth." *October* 48 (1989): 25–45.

Jiang, Jin, and Qin Zhou. *June Four: A Chronicle of the Chinese Democratic Uprising*. Fayetteville: University of Arkansas Press, 1989.

Jiny Lan: The World is Sometimes Flat, Sometimes Round. Exhibition catalog. Berlin: Schultz Contemporary, 2018.

Kellein, Thomas. *Fluxus*. London: Thames and Hudson, 1995.

———. "Zum Fluxus-Begriff von Joseph Beuys." In *Joseph Beuys-Tagung: Basel 1.–4. Mai 1991*, edited by Volker Harlan, Dieter Koepplin, and Rudolf Velhagen, 137–42. Basel: Wiese, 1991.

Kiefer, Anselm. "Occupations 1969." *Interfunktionen* 12 (1975): 133–44.

Kleinsteuber, Mette, and Werner Tammen, eds. *Jiny Lan: Found in Translation*. Exhibition catalog. Berlin: Katalogdruck, 2021.

Kristeva, Julia. *About Chinese Women*. Translated by Anita Barrows. New York: Urizen Books, 1977.

Kühlem, Max Florian. "Tragödie oder Farce – neue Meisterwerke von Jiny Lan." In *Portfolio – Genealogies*, 80–1.

Kuhrig, Herta. *Die Gleichberechtigung der Frauen in der Deutschen Demokratischen Republik*. Berlin: DDR-Komitee für Menschenrechte, 1973.

Kurbjuweit, Dirk. *Alternativlos: Merkel, die Deutschen und das Ende der Politik*. Munich: Carl Hanser Verlag, 2014.

Kuspit, Donald B. "New German Painting: The Discovery of Expression." In *New Figuration: Contemporary Art from Germany: Work by Georg Baselitz*. Exhibition catalog, 1–10. Los Angeles: The Gallery, 1983.

Lan, Jiny. "Lob der alten weißen Männer." *Cicero: Magazin für politische Kultur*. December 2, 2020.

Leung, Mei-yin. *The Chinese Women's Calligraphy and Painting Society: The First Women's Art Society in Modern China*. Hong Kong: University of Hong Kong Press, 2005.

Li, Xia'en. 万国来朝大戏: 各朝皇帝面子工程 [The Spectacle of All Nations Coming to Court: A Vanity Project of [Chinese] Emperors of All Dynasties]. 新周刊 [Newsweek] 421. October 15, 2015.

Li, Xianting. "Major Trends in the Development of Contemporary Chinese Art." In *China's New Art Post-1989*, ed. Chang, x–xxii.

———. "About the Stars Exhibition." In *Stars 79–80*, ed. Li and Huang, 252–5.

———. "The Stars: Explorers of Chinese Contemporary Art." In *Stars 79–80*, ed. Li and Huang, 20–5.

———. "The Stars: The Flag-Bearers of Chinese Modern Art." Translated by Philip Tinari. In *Stars 79–80*, ed. Li and Huang, 258–9.

Li, Xianting, and Rui Huang, ed. *Stars 79–80.* Hong Kong: The Chinese University of Hong Kong Press, 2019.

Li, Xinmo. 中国女权运动与女性主义艺术发展历程. In *Bald Girls*, ed. Xu, 152–3; English translation: "History of Feminism and Feminist Art in China." In *Bald Girls*, ed. Xu, 154–5.

"Li Xinmo." In *Stepping Out!*, ed. Ohlsen and Sadowsky, 98–101.

Liepe, Lena Eva. "Introduction." In *The Locus of Meaning in Medieval Art: Iconography, Iconology, and Interpreting the Visual Imagery of the Middle Ages*, ed. Lena Eva Liepe, 1–10. Kalamazoo, MI: Medieval Institute Publications, 2019.

Lindner, Christian. "Vorwort." In *Jiny Lan: 天问 / Himmelsfragen*. Exhibition catalog. Weilburg: Rosenhang Museum, 2023.

Lippard, Lucy R., ed. *Six Years: The Dematerialization of the Art Object from 1966 to 1972.* Berkeley: University of California Press, 1973.

Lorde, Audre. "The Master's Tools Will Never Dismantle the Master's House." In *Feminist Postcolonial Theory: A Reader*, edited by Reina Lewis and Sara Mills, 25–8. New York: Routledge, 2003.

Mao, Zedong. "Changsha." In *The Poems of Mao Zedong*, translated by Willis Barnstone, 31. Berkeley: University of California Press, 2008.

Maurer, Simon. "Das Kombinationstier." In *Jiny Lan: The World is Sometimes Flat, Sometimes Round*, 15–17. English translation: "Combination Animals." In *Jiny Lan: The World is Sometimes Flat, Sometimes Round*, 19–21.

Meerapfel, Jeanine. "Jiny Lans poetisch-provokative Kunstwelt." In *Jiny Lan: The World Is Sometimes Flat, Sometimes Round*, 3. English translation: "Jiny Lan's Poetic-Provocative Art World." In *Jiny Lan: The World Is Sometimes Flat, Sometimes Round*, 5.

Merkel, Angela. *Freiheit: Erinnerungen 1954–2021.* Cologne: Kiepenheuer & Witsch, 2024.

Merlin, Monica. "Mapping Women Artists in Chinese Contemporary Art." In *Stepping Out!*, ed. Ohlsen and Sadowsky, 20–6.

Mesch, Claudia. "Institutionalizing Social Sculpture: Beuys's Office for Direct Democracy through Referendum Installation (1972)." In *Joseph Beuys: The Reader*, ed. Mesch and Michely, 198–217.

Mesch, Claudia, and Viola Michely, eds. *Joseph Beuys: The Reader*. With a foreword by Arthur C. Danto. Additional translation by Nickolas Decarlo, Kayvan Rouhani, and Heidi Zimmerman. Cambridge, MA: MIT Press, 2007.

Michael Sontheimer, "Gründung der Grünen vor 40 Jahren. Pfarrer, Grafen und Bauern mit (Sonnen-)Blume." *Der Spiegel*. March 15, 2019.

Mu, Zimei. *Journal sexuel d'une jeune Chinoise sur le net*. Paris: Albin Michel, 2005.

———. *Mein intimes Tagebuch*. Berlin: Aufbau Taschenbuch Verlag, 2007.

———. *Popioly milosci*. Warsaw: Albatros, 2007.

Müller, Herta. "Das chinesische Glasauge." In *Bald Girls*, ed. Xu, 140–5.

Niming, Frank. "Learning How to Protest." In *The Chinese People's Movement*, ed. Saich 83–105.

Nisbet, Peter. "Remarks on a Beuys Story." In *Joseph Beuys: Mapping the Legacy*, ed. Ray, 5–18.

Ohlsen, Nils, and Thorsten Sadowsky, eds. *Stepping Out!: Female Identities in Chinese Contemporary Art*. Berlin: Hatje Cantz, 2022.

Partl, Nora. "Jiny Lan: The Right to Speak via Art: Feminist Art and Activism." *Expanded Art*. March 6, 2023.

Penetsdorfer, Christina. "Walking on the Great Wall." *Stepping Out!*, ed. Ohlsen and Sadowsky, 36–9.

Perl, Jed. "Noble and Ignoble Ai Weiwei: Wonderful Dissident, Terrible Artist." *The New Republic*. February 1, 2013.

Perrigo, Billy. "Why a Blank Sheet of Paper Became a Protest Symbol in China." *Time*. December 1, 2022.

Perry, Elizabeth J. "Casting a Chinese 'Democracy' Movement." In *Popular Protest & Political Culture in Modern China: Learning from 1989*, ed. Jeffrey N. Wasserstrom and Elizabeth J. Perry, 74–92. Boulder, CO: Westview, 1994.

Phillips, Michael R., Xianyun Li, and Yanping Zhang. "Suicide Rates in China, 1995–99." *The Lancet* 359 (2002): 835–40.

Portfolio – Genealogies: Jiny Lan. Exhibition catalog. Venice: Biblioteca Nazionale Marciana, 2019.

Ray, Gene, ed. *Joseph Beuys: Mapping the Legacy*. New York: Distributed Art Publishers, 2001.

———. "Preface." In *Joseph Beuys: Mapping the Legacy*, ed. Ray, 1–4.

Reifenscheid, Beate. "Pedigree of Life – About Jiny Lan's Epic Painting." Translated by W. G. Müller. *Chinese-European Post*. November 12, 2017. Reprinted in German in *Jiny Lan: The World Is Sometimes Flat, Sometimes Round*, 7–9.

Reilly, Maura. "'Bad Girls' to the Rescue: An Exhibition of Feminist Art from the 1990s Has Much to Teach Us Today." *ARTnews*. May 16, 2018.

Röndigs, Uwe. "FDP-Lindner, das Geld und die chinesische Kunst." *Mittelhessen*. October 5, 2023.

Rupprecht, Caroline. *Asian Fusion: New Encounters in the Asian-German Avant-Garde*, Oxford: Peter Lang, 2020.

Saich, Tony, ed. *The Chinese People's Movement: Perspectives on Spring 1989.* Armonk, NY: M. E. Sharpe, 1990.

Saltzman, Lisa. *Anselm Kiefer and Art After Auschwitz.* Cambridge: Cambridge University Press, 1999.

Schwarzer, Alice, ed. *Der Schock: Die Silvesternacht von Köln.* Cologne: Kiepenheuer & Witsch, 2016.

Shen, Qinna. "The New Silk Road and EU-China Relations through Jiny Lan's Visual Art." *The Newsletter of the Global Studies Center* 2. March 2021.

Shiff, Richard. "Georg Baselitz Grounded." *Negotiating History: German Art and the Past* 8, no. 1 (2002): 52–65, 109–10.

Sigg, Uli. "Confusionism." In Ai Weiwei, *Ways Beyond Art*, edited by Elena Ochoa Foster and Hans Ulrich Obrist, 12–13. London: Ivorypress, 2009.

———. "How People Collect Contemporary Art: My Typology of Collecting Styles." In *China's Avant-Garde, 1978–2018*, ed. Daria Berg and Giorgio Strafella, 49–51. New York: Routledge, 2023.

Smith, Karen. *Nine Lives: The Birth of Avant-Garde Art in New China.* Zürich: Prestel, 2006.

Solomon, Tessa. "M+ Museum Pulls Three Politically Charged Works from Display, Spurring Speculation of Censorship." *ARTnews.* April 21, 2022.

Sontag, Susan. *"Against Interpretation" and Other Essays.* New York: Farrar, Straus and Giroux, 1966.

Sung, Doris. "Chinese Women Artists in the Early Twentieth Century." *AWARE (Archives of Women Artists Research & Exhibitions)*. October 12, 2021.

Tong, Yujie. "Li Xinmo: An Avant-Garde Critical Realist Artist in China." In *Bald Girls*, ed. Xu, 17–20.

Wakeman, Frederick, Jr. "Rebellion and Revolution: The Study of Popular Movements in Chinese History." *The Journal of Asian Studies* 36, no. 2 (1977): 201–37.

Walters, Victoria. "Joseph Beuys and EURASIA." *Tate Papers* 31 (2019).

Wang, Huangsheng. "Joseph Beuys and China." In *Social Sculpture: Beuys in China* 社会雕塑: 博伊斯在中国. Bilingual edition, edited by Wang Huangsheng, 18–20. Beijing: 中国青年出版社 China Youth Publishing House, 2013.

Wang, Keping. "Memories of the Stars Exhibition." In *Stars 79–80*, ed. Li and Huang, 160–75.

Wang, Yaqiu. "Silenced in China, Grassroots Activists Commemorate the White Paper Protests Abroad." *The Diplomat.* November 29, 2023.

Wangwright, Amanda. *The Golden Key: Modern Women Artists and Gender Negotiations in Republican China (1911–1949).* Leiden: Brill, 2021.

Watanabe, Shinya. "Searching for EUR-ASIA: Joseph Beuys and Nam June Paik' [sic] Life Long Collaboration." PhD diss., Universität der Künste Berlin, 2017.

Weikop, Christian. "'Occupations': A Difficult Reception." Tate, 2016.

Wiermer, Christian, and Gerhard Vogt. *Die Nacht, die Deutschland veränderte: Hintergründe, Fakten und Enthüllungen zu den dramatischen Übergriffen der Silvesternacht in Köln*. Munich: riva, 2017.

Wilson, Sarah. *The Visual World of French Theory: Figurations*. New Haven, CT: Yale University Press, 2010.

Wolin, Richard. *The Wind from the East: French Intellectuals, the Cultural Revolution, and the Legacy of the 1960s*. Princeton, NJ: Princeton University Press, 2010.

Wright, Robin. "Russia and China Unveil a Pact Against America and the West." *The New Yorker*. February 7, 2022.

Wu, Hung. *Contemporary Chinese Art: A History, 1970s–2000s*. London: Thames & Hudson, 2014.

———. *Remaking Beijing: Tiananmen Square and the Creation of a Political Space*. Chicago: University of Chicago Press, 2005.

———. *Transience: Chinese Experimental Art at the End of the Twentieth Century*. Chicago: The David and Alfred Smart Museum of Art and University of Chicago Press, 2005.

Xu, Juan. "Art Vision and Authenticity: Lan Jiny, Avant-Garde Jovial Feminist Artist." In *Bald Girls*, ed. Xu, 42–8.

———. 秃头戈女: 序 [Bald Girls: Preface]. In *Bald Girls*, ed. Xu, 2–6.

——— [under pen name Yong Xian], ed. 秃头戈女: 三个女性主义艺术家展 [Bald Girls: Three Feminist Artists' Exhibit]. Exhibition catalog. Tai Pei: 自由文化, 2012.

———. Interview with Bai Yilan 白一岚, 关于<秃头戈女>的一次访谈 [An Interview about the "Bald Girls"]. 画廊网 *Hua lang Wang*. April 21, 2014

Xu, Juan, and Jiny Lan. (庸现/蓝镜). 信息资本主义时代的博伊斯 – "社会雕塑"与"理性利己"的博弈 [Joseph Beuys in the Capitalistic Information Era – Struggle between "Social Sculpture" and "Rational Self-interest"]. In *Social Sculpture: Beuys in China* 社会雕塑: 博伊斯在中国, ed. Wang Huangsheng, 100–13. Beijing: 中国青年出版社 China Youth Publishing House, 2013.

Yan, Geling. "The Price of Free Expression: Geling Yan on Censorship." Lecture at Bryn Mawr College. November 19, 2024.

Zhang, Anya. "Ai Weiwei: Blurring the Lines between Artistry and Absurdity." *Harvard Political Review*. September 6, 2023.

Zhang, Faye Yan. "Portraits of Mao." *The Harvard Advocate* 149, no. 3 (2014).

Zhang, Ming, Chi Zhang, and Yuxin Liu. "From One-Child Policy to Three-Children Initiative: A Feminist Critique of the Population Planning Policies in China." *Communication, Culture and Critique* 17, no. 2 (2024): 103–11.

Zimmerman, Thomas. "The New Silk Roads: China, the U.S., and the Future of Central Asia," Center on International Cooperation, New York University. October 2015.

Index

www.ingramcontent.com/pod-product-compliance
Lightning Source LLC
LaVergne TN
LVHW052350100826
845147LV00013B/809
9781640142916